History and Ethnicity

ASA Monographs 27

History and Ethnicity

Edited by

Elizabeth Tonkin, Maryon McDonald, and Malcolm Chapman

ROUTLEDGE
London and New York

This volume includes papers delivered to the 1987 ASA Conference by Edwin Ardener (1927–87) and Edmund Leach (1910–89), both of whom have since died. Si monumentum requiris . . .

First published 1989
by Routledge
11 New Fetter Lane, London EC4P 4EE

Simultaneously published in the USA and Canada
by Routledge
a division of Routledge, Chapman and Hall, Inc.
29 West 35th Street, New York, NY 10001

© 1989 Association of Social Anthropologists

Typeset by Input Typesetting Ltd, London
Printed and bound in Great Britain by
Mackays of Chatham PLC, Chatham, Kent

British Library Cataloguing in Publication Data

History and ethnicity. – (ASA monograph; 27)
  1. Social identity
  I. Tonkin, Elizabeth   II. McDonald, Maryon
  III. Chapman, Malcolm   IV. Series
  302.1′2

Library of Congress Cataloging-in-Publication Data

History and ethnicity / edited by Elizabeth Tonkin, Maryon McDonald, and
  Malcolm Chapman.
    p.   cm. — (ASA monographs; 27) (Social science monographs)
  Based on the 1987 ASA Conference held at the University of East
Anglia.
    Includes bibliographies and indexes.
    1. Ethnohistory. 2. Ethnicity. 3. Historiography. I. Tonkin,
Elizabeth. II. McDonald Maryon, III. Chapman, Malcolm (Malcolm
Kenneth) IV. ASA Conference (1987: University of East Anglia)
V. Series. VI. Series: A.S.A. monographs; 27.
GN345.2.H58   1989
907′.2—dc19   88–32328
                                                                  CIP

ISBN 0–415–00056–4

Contents

List of Contributors   vii

Introduction – History and Social Anthropology   **1**
Malcolm Chapman, Maryon McDonald, and Elizabeth Tonkin

1. **The Construction of History: 'vestiges of creation'**   22
   Edwin Ardener

2. **Tribal Ethnography: past, present, future**   34
   Edmund Leach

3. **Fiction and Fact in Ethnography**   48
   Raymond Firth

4. **Wārībi and the White Men: history and myth in northwest Amazonia**   53
   Stephen Hugh-Jones

5. **Triumph of the Ethnos**   71
   Roger Just

6. **Investigating 'Social Memory' in a Greek Context**   89
   Anna Collard

7. **The Social Relations of the Production of History**   104
   John Davis

8. **Israel: Jewish identity and competition over 'tradition'**   121
   Robert Paine

9. **German Identity and the Problems of History**   137
   Diana Forsythe

Contents

10. **French Historians and their Cultural Identities**   157
    Peter Burke

11. **Mormon History, Identity, and Faith Community**   168
    Douglas Davies

12. **'We're Trying to Find Our Identity': uses of history among
    Ulster Protestants**   183
    Anthony Buckley

13. **The Cultural Work of Yoruba Ethnogenesis**   198
    J. D. Y. Peel

14. **Afrikaner Historiography and the Decline of Apartheid: ethnic
    self-reconstruction in times of crisis**   216
    Gerhard Schutte

15. **Ethnic Identities and Social Categories in Iran and Afghanistan**   232
    Richard Tapper

16. **Catalan National Identity: the dialectics of past and present**   247
    Josep Llobera

    Name Index   00
    Subject Index   00

List of Contributors

Edwin Ardener was University Lecturer in Social Anthropology and Fellow of St. John's College, Oxford.

Anthony Buckley is Assistant Keeper at the Department of Non-Material Culture, Ulster Folk and Transport Museum.

Peter Burke is Reader in Cultural History and Fellow of Emmanuel College, Cambridge.

Malcolm Chapman is completing a project for the Wenner-Gren Foundation for Anthropological Research.

Anna Collard is completing a D. Phil in Social Anthropology at the London School of Economics.

Douglas Davies is Lecturer in Theology, University of Nottingham.

John Davis is Professor of Sociology, University of Kent.

Raymond Firth is Emeritus Professor of Anthropology, University of London.

Diana Forsythe is Postdoctoral Scholar, Knowledge Systems Laboratory and Department of Anthropology, Stanford University.

Stephen Hugh-Jones is Lecturer in Social Anthropology, Fellow of King's College, Cambridge.

Roger Just is Lecturer in Greek, Department of Classical Studies, Melbourne University.

Edmund Leach was Emeritus Professor of Social Anthropology, Cambridge.

Josep Llobera is Principal Lecturer, Department of Sociology, Goldsmith's College, London.

Maryon McDonald is Lecturer in Social Anthropology, Brunel University.

Robert Paine is Lecturer in Social Anthropology, Memorial University of Newfoundland.

J. D. Y. Peel is Professor of Sociology, University of Liverpool.

Gerhard Schutte is Lecturer at the Department of Sociology and Anthropology, Loyola University of Chicago.

Richard Tapper is Reader in Anthropology, University of Liverpool.
Elizabeth Tonkin is Lecturer in Social Anthropology, Centre of West
   African Studies, University of Birmingham.

Editors' Acknowledgements

The editors would like to thank the local organizer of the 1987 ASA conference, Mark Holmstrom, for the many efforts he made to ensure the success of the conference. They would also like to thank the University of East Anglia for its hospitality in hosting the event.

Malcolm Chapman
Maryon McDonald
Elizabeth Tonkin

December 1988

Introduction
Malcolm Chapman, Maryon McDonald, and Elizabeth Tonkin

History and social anthropology

This volume is a selection of papers delivered to the twenty-seventh annual conference of the Association of Social Anthropologists of Britain and the Commonwealth (the ASA), held at the University of East Anglia, Easter 1987. The title of the conference was 'History and Ethnicity'. Two previous ASA conferences are obviously related to the theme of this volume – *History and Social Anthropology* (Lewis, 1968), and *Urban Ethnicity* (Cohen, 1973), and much that is presented in those works can be taken as background.

The conference was not convened with the intention that 'ethnicity', for example, be taken too seriously as an analytical concept, to be refined or promoted. This was just as well, for the term proves to be of interestingly limited value (see p. 11). Nevertheless, without worrying too much at this stage about definitions, the conference topic was comprehensible – social anthropologists knew what was meant. The collocation of history and ethnicity was intended to capture a rather broad range of growing anthropological interests, concerned with the definition and self-definition of human groups, and with the relationship of these definitions to history – not only how the past has led to the present, but also how history is used, experienced, remembered, or created. Two questions, so to speak, were set up against one another – 'How did the past lead to the present?', and 'How does the present create the past?' The conference was about the relationship between history, ethnicity, historiography, and historicity, with the awareness that every one of these terms is problematic in relation to the others.

The study of how an ethnic group or groups used and selected history in the process of self-definition was clearly suggested by the conference topic, and most of the papers are concerned to some extent with this problem. It was also hoped that we could discuss the larger question of what kinds of history and historiography, if any, different societies might have and require. This question was perhaps less thoroughly explored, although some valuable contributions are made by, for example, Davis, Collard, Davies, and Burke. The very term 'historiography' raises, of course, another range of relevant questions concerning writing and speech, written records and oral records, which are now part of the background to much social anthropological thought. They are touched on by most contributors, although one might cite particularly Ardener and Hugh-Jones.

The conference did not only reach out to 'history and ethnicity', but also, and characteristically of recent conferences, to a range of anthropological queries relating to classification, and to the problematic status of the anthropological object and of anthropological knowledge. As such, it has clear affinities to other recent ASA volumes (for example, to Parkin, 1982; Overing, 1985; Jackson, 1987). Problems such as these tend to override, quite legitimately, all attempts at thematization.

'Ethnicity' takes us straight into social and political problems of a most urgent nature, and many of the issues discussed in this volume can be taken as explanatory background for crises that are relentlessly paraded before us on the newscreens – Schutte on South Africa, Paine on Israel, Tapper on Afghanistan and Iran, Buckley on Northern Ireland, Davis on Libya. Other scenes of ethnic differentiation and conflict are none the less dramatic and potentially violent, of course, simply because the media are not, for the moment, greatly interested in them, as witness the contributions of Hugh-Jones, Peel, and Forsythe.

Ethnicity also, however, as already noted, takes us into issues of classification and cognition – into structure, symbol, myth, opposition, perception, and the rest. This is an area of thought in which social anthropology is particularly at home. The tranquillity and detachment of the debates within this area, however, may sometimes seem improper to analysis of worlds where (for example) bombs are being thrown. It is an urgent task, therefore, to show without ambiguity that issues of classification and cognition are tied into the very heart of the drama and conflict that we observe. This still needs saying. Ethnicity will not allow us to separate the tranquillity of thought from the upheavals of action, will not allow us to separate the dream world of mere ideas from the materiality of people and things. Or, if we allow ourselves still to keep these things apart, then our expression is at fault (see Ardener, 1982:11; Sahlins, 1985:155). Acts of naming, and the classificatory, cognitive, and symbolic niceties surrounding these, are immediately implicated in the most trenchant material and political realities.

The title 'History and ethnicity' had been used for a series of weekly seminars in Oxford organized by Edwin Ardener, which ran continuously from the late 1970s until his death in 1987. All three of the conveners of the 1987 conference had been his students, and two were long-standing participants in the Oxford seminars. The inspiration of the conference was, therefore, to a great degree owing to him, and it is entirely fitting that his last conference paper, given only a few months before his death, should be included here.

We must remember, as part of the background to this volume, the long estrangement in this century of social anthropology and history. Although this has by now been much discussed, and many remedies attempted, its consequences are still with us in many ways. A brief statement of the problem may be useful, therefore. Throughout the nineteenth century, scholarship in the humanities was overwhelmingly historicist. This historicism was greatly reinforced in the middle of the century by Darwin's *On the Origin of Species*, and the formalization of the notion of evolution, carried into the developing social sciences through the work of Herbert Spencer. The developments of species, cultures, languages, and peoples, were all interpreted within a historical and evolutionary framework. It is of immediate interest to the concerns of this volume that, during this period, race, language, and culture were often treated as virtually consubstantial phenomena, evolving together. The break with this structure of interpretation tends to be credited, in linguistics, to Saussure (1955), and in anthropology, to Malinowski and Radcliffe-Brown, with Durkheim in the background. Saussure brought about the possibility of a synchronic (or, rather, timeless) linguistics, which led to structural linguistics and, in part at least, to structural anthropology. Malinowski and Radcliffe-Brown repudiated what they called 'conjectural' history in evolutionary studies of society. Instead, they developed theories of the structure of (primitive) societies, which implied that such societies were inherently stable and changeless, and so timeless and history-less. Academic history, as a distinct and developing subject, was up to this time above all the history of nations, and demanded written documents. For Radcliffe-Brown, however: 'In the primitive societies that are studied by social anthropology there are no historical records' (Radcliffe-Brown, 1968:3).

This assurance of the absence of records, along with a theory of functional equilibrium, made history irrelevant, impossible, and unnecessary. Within the older shared historicism, the interests of history and anthropology were in many respects congruent. Henceforth, however, they were estranged (see the debate between Firth and Leach in their respective papers, and the argument offered by Hugh-Jones). The coming of structuralism did little to change this, for structuralism also had its background in an earlier repudiation of historicism. Structure and history seemed, in many of Lévi-Strauss's formulations, or at least in interpretations of them, to be inimical. There is not space here to go into the many confusions of method, theory, and observation that led to this divorce of history and anthropology, but we must remember that the position seemed at the time both compelling and coherent in its functional, structural–functional, and structuralist forms. And there was also a curious and temporary empirical self-fulfilment in the political and cultural stasis imposed by colonial rule.

When it became impossible to sustain the notion of equilibrium, as societies were manifestly changing, a series of compensatory theories were added on – theories of social change, urban life, 'Western contact', and the like. These incorporated change as an exogenous, urban, and modern phenomenon, and left the core of equilibrium theory untouched – a theory for primitive society in its pristine, native state (see Leach's paper, in this volume). This uneasy separation of unitary realities into two aspects – a theory for stability, a theory for change, is still implied in much anthropological thought.

As is well-known, Evans-Pritchard early contested the exclusion of history from social anthropology. He argued in 1950 that anthropology is 'a special kind of historiography', and that it was only as such that it could be 'really empirical and, in the true sense of the word, scientific' (Evans-Pritchard, 1962:26). Since then there have been many studies that could be called 'in all essentials the same as social history' (ibid.:24), by which he meant studies of 'a society developing in time' (ibid.). Evans-Pritchard also contested the notion that primitive societies were isolated, and existing in their own timeless time. Anthropologists, he argued, were:

> studying communities, which if still fairly simple in structure are enclosed in, and form part of, great historical societies . . . They can no longer ignore history, making a virtue out of necessity, but must explicitly reject it or admit its relevance.
>
> (Evans-Pritchard, 1962:21)

ASA Monograph 7, *History and Social Anthropology* (Lewis, 1968), showed amongst other things that anthropologists could, as it were, 'do' history. Since this time, the attempt to incorporate history in some way has become commonplace, and the 1987 conference, twenty years on, was not one of anthropologists who needed to be convinced of the importance of historical material to their subject. In the meantime, something rather like an historical anthropology has developed (for which, see, for example, Macfarlane, 1978; Hastrup, 1985). As the present volume shows, however, social anthropology and history, social theory and history, are still far from being entirely reconciled.

In the consideration of nations, ethnic groups, and identities, modern scholarship, drawing upon long-established genealogical traditions, has tended to take the modern condition as the object primarily requiring explanation, and to look to history to provide the explanation. Thus, the history of a group was traced to its origins, through its development, and to the modern state – how the past, so to speak, created the present. The great nineteenth-century successes in historiography and comparative philology were of this kind, and the habit of mind is still very strong in the humanities and social sciences. In the world of nations and groups with confident historiographical traditions, well-established histories, and professional historians, the dominant question, therefore, was something like 'How did the past create the present?'

Social anthropologists, however, have come to be rather interested in turning this formulation upside down, and asking the previously much less-often asked question, 'How did the present create the past?' In order to account for the present, to justify it, understand it, or criticize it, the past is used, selectively appropriated, remembered, forgotten, or invented (see McDonald 1986). The question has proved to be an interesting one, and it has proved also to be a question that social anthropologists are at least modestly good at asking. Long reflection upon the meeting of cultures has led social anthropology to some understanding of the great differences there can be between categories and classifications from one culture to another. Categories that, within one culture, have all the appearance of being part of the natural order, turn out, upon inspection, to be, so to speak, only 'creations' after all, and anthropologists have studied the means of this creation with some thoroughness. The 'deconstruction' of categories of thought, action, and understanding has been, as Ardener notes (p. 29), a social anthropological skill and practice for many years (since well before 'deconstruction', under this title, became modish in other spheres). Historians are aware, of course, that another time is like another culture, which requires an effort of imagination before it can be understood. Social anthropological fieldwork, however, requires this effort as a matter of everyday experience, in matters both mundane and subtle. Within historical research, however profound, the problem must tend to remain a library exercise, which can be put down, or closed with a book. It will perhaps not be too contentious, therefore, to suggest that anthropologists are more *prepared*, at least, to put into question the validity of categories of historical understanding, than are historians. At the same time, it must be noticed that historians are, in general, very much better prepared empirically than anthropologists in their approach to historical problems, and that all acts of conceptual and categorical finesse in the interpretation of the past depend, in one way or another, upon the grasp of empirical material.

The question 'How did the present create the past?' has provoked some interesting responses. We are shown, by many examples, how social, moral, and political considerations can render people selective in their treatment of the past, and surprisingly indifferent or hostile to alternative accounts. Peel, in this volume, argues that the form of the question is evidence of 'the blocking presentism to which anthropologists are so prone' (p. 200), but the evidence of the other papers in this volume is hardly that of anthropologists who are blocked. Nor is this book evidence of anthropologists who are, as Peel seems to imply, indifferent to the past

(p. 198). The present might be, as Peel notes, no more than the hinge between the past and the future. This is already saying rather a lot, however, since the hinge is the one part of the formulation that exists. One forgets too easily that the past is no more, and the future not yet born. Certainly, as Peel notes, the present might look like the result of a coherent project from the past, and so the future like a project from the present, but then any future is made up of a myriad such projects. It is up to a future present to look back and judge whether or not, or how, any such project was successful, and to chart meaningful direction through time. The historiographies of all self-realizing modern entities are historiographies of successful or partially successful projects, but this is no more than tautology. Most of the failures are, in retrospect, completely invisible. It is, in this context, perhaps worth remembering T.S. Eliot's formulation, from the *Four Quartets*, that the present is 'where past and future are gathered'. The *Four Quartets* represent a thorough and explicit attempt to work through some problems in the conceptual relationship of past, present, and future, and echo familiar problems for anyone who has tried to think about the historiography of a modern social entity, and about the constitution of apparent historical fulfilment, in both the long and the short term. Minor citation in this case cannot do full justice to the poetic context, but one might mention, in relation to the problem that Peel poses:

And what you thought you came for
Is only a shell, a husk of meaning
From which the purpose breaks only when it is fulfilled
If at all. Either you had no purpose
Or the purpose is beyond the end you figured
And is altered in fulfilment

(Little Gidding, 1)

We should indeed expect history to be replete with examples of impressive acts of creation and foresight. As is shown, however, it is also rich in examples of failure, and of the wilful blindness, forgetting, and imaginative restructuring that can turn failure into success, and success into failure (see Collard and Just on Greece at both local and national levels; Hugh-Jones on Amerindian mythology, and many other examples). Past, present, and future are tied into one another in the human imagination far too tightly for it to be worth our while arguing about the relative importance of one or the other. And the tying in is perhaps even more tight than suggested by the 'dialectics of past and present' of which Llobera speaks (p. 247). There is, as Ardener puts it, 'an infinite sequence of rememorizations', of *bricolage* and *debricolage* (p. 25). Speaking of the processes involved in the generation and memorization of events, Ardener says:

There are . . . plenty of grounds for saying that the 'memory' of history begins when it is registered. It is encoded 'structurally' as it occurs. The structuring . . . is actually part of the 'registration' of events. Then we can say that since not all events do survive, but only 'memorable' or 'significant' events, the structural processes are not necessarily retrospectively imposed, but are synchronic – all part of the very nature of event-registration.

(p. 25)

At all levels, from individual concerns through to the histories of nations, these remarks have their relevance. At the most intimate level of personal action and understanding, in daily circumstance, decisions are made about the significance of the present – the simultaneity of action and definition is played, an event is realized – and a whole range of potential histories is simply defined out of existence. The structure within which they could be remembered is not created, and they pass away as if they had never been. Only a small fraction of 'what happened' is embodied in experience, and so tied to the present by intelligible and memorable structures. All human reality is made up of events of this order, with multiple and mute closures – unintelligible, undecipherable – all around. This is difficult to express, and it is an enduring problem that the phenomenon in question should be at once so banal and so difficult of expression; it must be the task of anthropology to find a language with which to explore this.

At the level of the histories of nations, analogous processes take place on a much greater scale, in society, space, and time. A nation draws history behind it, like the wake of a great ship. Useless or irrelevant events either do not happen, or are ignored, or are conceptually stillborn. The process is one with centuries of history, with the efforts of generations of people, literate and non-literate, intellectual or otherwise. It is small wonder that a nation with a long history looks to have its destiny carved out for it in advance, as if everything before were a preparation for something still to come – the logic by which the present appropriates the future, and by which the present understands the past, are contained in microcosm in the registration and memorization of meaningful events at the individual level, many times repeated. Many aspects of this are merely repetitive, but some are creative (or 'prophetic', in Ardener's sense; see Ardener, 1975 and forthcoming), leading to some novelty, which then picks up behind it a new trajectory to replace or modify the old. This process is familiar enough in the restructuring of genealogical material in non-literate societies (as Davis shows, p. 108; see Chadwick, 1912; 1949, for some early European examples). The appearance of writing, and the structure of its distribution and use, do of course bring about changes, but the process does not stop for that.

The capacity of a successful self-defining entity like a nation to define and create its relevant history, both as it happens and in retrospect, has the corollary that minority, subnational entities within it simply cannot compete on the same scale. They are, in important senses, history less and event-less by comparison. Thompson has argued that 'the very power structure worked as a great recording machine shaping the past in its own image' (Thompson, 1988:3). But we should not take this to mean, necessarily, that the history of minority or underprivileged groups is 'really' there, waiting to be rediscovered and expressed. This is true to some extent, of course, but for a minority or underprivileged group in a modern nation–state, independent history is in important senses missing. Indeed, this formulation itself borders on tautology. This is not *only* to say that the history was unrecorded or ignored, but also that, to an important degree, it did not happen; and to note, also, that the temporal grain of action and interpretation is not one that can be readily inspected for histories other than that sanctioned by majority perception.

Many of the papers in this volume refer to the legitimacy that history (and preferably long, prestigious, and verifiable history), gives to modern groupings in their self-understanding. Some remarkable examples are given in this volume, by, for example, Buckley, Davies, and Schutte. As a corollary, we find frequent resentment of the practice, of which this book is a sustained example, of showing how the past is malleable and ambiguous in its message. We might characterize this as a tension between, on the one hand, the apparently irreverent and nihilistic scribblings of deconstruction, and on the other, the destinies of nineteenth-century historicism at their most grandiose. Certainly, those who live within a particular historically defined identity are liable to take serious exception to neoanthropological analysis, which appears to take their history away, to render it contingent, arbitrary, or fictitious. Any such attempt will appear as an attempt to illegitimize the modern identity, and will be resented accordingly. Nor is this surprising. In any situation of ethnic conflict, or of competitive assertion, the ability to render history malleable is a potent one. Schutte gives us a dramatic example of the eruption into violence of this tension (p. 217), and Just (p. 86) and Ardener (p. 24) both show that resentment can be easily stirred when true historicity is denied or queried. And even in the torpor of the seminar room, the issue can take fire. As Richard Fardon later noted, discussion at the ASA conference was characteristically disengaged, until someone or other began to suspect that they themselves were being deconstructed on the other side of the room, upon which the debate assumed an altogether more real-life character (see Fardon, 1987:16).

As we have seen, functionalism denied history, and structuralism in popularly received forms seemed to confirm this denial. Society and social thought were depicted in fine detail – the social machine was, so to speak, fully functional, beautifully structured. But it was also, or so it seemed, motionless – like Frankenstein's monster without the lightning. Many supposed theoretical innovations have been attempts to grapple with this problem – theories of social change, transactionalism, forms of structural Marxism, and so forth. It is from within this problematic, also, that we hear variations on the theme 'ethnicity is not a structure, or an entity, it is a process' (this point was variously made during the conference, and see Peel, p. 200). If ethnicity is defined by oppositions, then it is in a structure. But ethnicities are manifestly involved in change, and so they must be rescued from structure, by process. We might feel, however, that the phrase 'ethnicity is a process' is only another form of expression of the problem presented on p. 3 – that structure and history, structure and change, seem, in many expressions, to preclude one another. We can escape from the entire problem, however, and still keep the enormous potential of the classificatory approach, if we follow Ardener's formulation, that we are dealing with 'simultaneities' of action and definition (Ardener, 1982:6). Time, and events in time, are part of the subject matter on which the classificatory imagination is brought to bear, and 'action and definition' come in the same breath. We are permitted, in potential at least, to keep a conceptual grip upon procedures of classification, without denying time and change in any way. This whole volume, in a sense, is about the interpenetration of the classification of time and of people.

Fact or fiction?

It is perhaps not surprising that a conference that invited discussion of 'how the present creates the past', should find itself exercised over questions concerning fact and fiction. During conference discussion, a paper-giver suggested that one analysis of a historical and ethnic situation, held by certain members of the society in question, was unequivocally wrong (see Tapper, p. 239). The question was then asked: was it an anthropologist's business to tell people under study that they were 'wrong'? Surely, it was queried, as far as a modern social anthropologist was concerned, if people believed a thing to be true, then it *was* true. Some then countered with the assertion that things had come to a pretty pass when an anthropologist could no longer permit himself to distinguish between the true and the false. And then, in the final session, Leach and Firth joined issue over Leach's assertion (p. 34) that 'all ethnography is fiction'.

As already noted, the ability of ethnic histories to be reconstructed does suggest their 'fictional' quality, and several contributors to this volume employ various dualities that anthropologists have long used to discuss this problem. Hugh-Jones differentiates between 'myth' and 'history', using these terms to describe two genres of narrative as differentiated by the Barasana themselves (p. 55). Davies speaks clearly of 'the practical distinction between history and myth' (p. 171). Tapper says that genealogies are not true history, but rather are 'mythical', 'not a pure line of

9

descent . . . but a disputed and changing ideological charter' (p. 237). Collard, citing E.P. Thompson, refers to ' "experience 1 – lived experience" and "experience 2 – perceived experience" ' (p. 91). Schutte contrasts 'outsider definitions' with 'folk history' (p. 216 ff).

And there are other possibilities. The same contributors are, however, engaged in demonstrating extremes of creativity in the use of the past, and of the consequent contingency of empirical material. We may begin to feel, therefore, for this and other reasons, that the dualities listed previously are reaching the end of their analytical usefulness. Reference has already been made to the interventions of the human imagination in the understanding and generation of events at the most micro-temporal level, and to the analogous large-scale defining powers of nations (and all points in between). We are increasingly aware of the structuring properties of discourse, through which all anthropological experience has to be represented. There has been considerable recent work on the reflexivity of the social anthropological enterprise, and on the necessary partiality of any single account (provided by ethnographer or native, native as ethnographer, ethnographer as native, and so on; see Jackson, 1987). Our attention is drawn also to the possibilities of dramatic collapse of what once seemed the most empirically secure of pasts, the most authoritative historiographical structures (and see Forsythe, in this volume). Given all these, it is reasonable to hope that we can try to go beyond the aforementioned dualities.

How can we find a productive approach that will not generate sterile argument? We might observe, at least, that the aptitude and willingness to treat what people believe to be true as if it were, indeed, true, is in many respects a hard-won anthropological privilege. It has been won against a powerful combination of positivism, scientific rationality, assumptions concerning the suspect rationality of other peoples, and observer prejudice (or, to put these another way, against the ethnocentrism of the modern western intellect). It is a privilege constantly at risk from overindulgence, and subsequent reaction. The observations that other people's truths are contained in their own classifications and understanding, and that our own culture offers no self-evidently privileged standard of verity, have been perhaps social anthropology's major intellectual contribution in the twentieth century. Philosophers and anthropologists have, of course, joined issue over the question of whether there is any true context-free truth left at the end of the exercise. Whatever one might think ultimately about this, and wherever ultimately might be, most anthropologists would probably feel little doubt that the habit of according to other peoples their own truths, and their own right to these, is, as a working practice, one of great power and usefulness, multiply attested in ethnographic analysis in this century (and see Tonkin, forthcoming).

The opposition between fact and fiction is of course deeply embedded in literary and scientific practice and understanding. The virtues of the one are the vices of the other, and any amount of debate can be conducted across the divide. Because the discourse in which fact and fiction are opposed is so well-established, it is difficult to escape from it – difficult to find a position that is not, in some way or another, an espousal of conventional oppositions. We can perhaps take the assertion that 'all ethnography is fiction', and the debate around it, as a warning against, on the one hand, a too complacent empiricism, and on the other, extremities of idealism and conceptual nihilism. In dealing with the problems raised by the creation, interpretation, and memorization of events, however, many of the dualities that we have traditionally employed (fact/fiction; history/myth; reality/symbol; action/meaning; reality/perceived reality, and so on) are coming to the end of their term.

Ethnicity

Ethnicity permits us as anthropologists to come close to home, as it is both cheap and fashionable to do. It also allows us, however, having come close to home, to retain that grip on significant difference from ourselves (whoever *we* might be), that has been the moral and intellectual motor of the anthropological enterprise from the very first (cf. Just, 1978). It also takes us quickly into many politically contentious areas, where intellectual interests can find themselves readily congruent with media and political concerns.

Ethnicity, however, is a term still obscure to the great majority of ordinary native speakers of English, and either justification or apology for its use is therefore suggested. It is also a term that invites endless and fruitless definitional argument among those professional intellectuals who think that they know, or ought to know, what it means. No attempt will be made here to provide the *right* definition, for such would be far from the spirit of this volume. Nevertheless, some consideration of the term may be useful.

As a term, ethnicity is a product of a long-standing feature of English sociolinguistics – the tendency to look to Greek, Latin, French, or more generally, Romance models, when a new word is needed to fancify a plain idea or expression. It comes from the Greek term *ethnos*, and survives as a fairly common intellectual's word in modern French, *ethnie*, with the associated adjective *ethnique*. The possible noun expressing what it is you have to have to be *ethnique*, *ethnicité*, is still not common in modern French. The adjective exists in modern English as 'ethnic' (cf. ethnic group, ethnic clothing), with a suffix added to give *ethnicity*. Neither the adjective nor the suffixation are particularly self-evident in vernacular English, and the result is an arguable and murky intellectual term. One

11

of the problems for English speakers is that the concrete noun from which it is derived does not exist in our language. We have no *ethnos*, no *ethnie*.

It is worth looking at the etymology of this term, not for any essential meaning, but because it provides an interesting commentary on the fate of any term that tries to delimit human groups. In the earliest recorded uses, as *ethnos* in Homer, it was not a word used for familiar groups of people sharing a culture, an origin, or a language. It was used, rather, to describe large, undifferentiated groups of either animals or warriors. Frequently, *ethnos* is used for an animal multitude (bees, birds, or flies), which is then used as a simile for a like multitude of warriors, where great size, amorphous structure, and threatening mobility are the qualities to which attention is being drawn (e.g. *Iliad* 2.87 and 2.91; 4.59–69; 12.330). We might gloss it as 'throng' or 'swarm', both of which terms have ambiguously animal and human possibilities. Aeschylus uses *ethnos* to describe the Furies (*Eumenides* 366), and also the Persians (*Persai* 43, 56; see also *Herodotus* 1.101). Sophocles uses it for wild animals (*Philoctetes* 1147; *Antigone* 344). Pindar, again in very early recorded use, employs the term to describe groups of like people, but again people whose location or conduct put them in some way outside the sphere of Greek social normality (the husband-killing women of Lemnos, for example; Pythian Odes 4.448). Aristotle uses it for foreign or barbarous nations, as opposed to 'Hellenes' (*Politics*, 1324.b.10). When Herodotus describes the Greeks in his famous passage (8.144; see Just, p. 73), *ethnos* is not a term he employs. Romans, writing in Greek under the Empire, use the term to describe a province, or the provinces in general – areas that were, that is, *not* Rome (see *Appian Bella Civilia* 2.13; *Herodianus* 1.2.1; *Dion Chrysostom* 4.3.11).

We might perhaps compare early Greek use of *ethnos* to modern English 'tribe' – a term still used by many educated people to describe all political units that are not of the familiar nation and nation–state kind. Aspects of naturality, of non-legitimate social organization, of disorganization, and of animality, are strong in *ethnos*, and we might well remember 'the tribesmen swarming like ants over the rocks' in an account of some British Imperial campaign. It is characteristic of this area of vocabulary, perhaps in all languages, that any term for 'people' in a general sense, has the potential for being taken up into a duality of 'us' and 'them', and from early use this has been the fate of *ethnos*. The term co-existed with *genos*, more commonly used by Greeks of Greeks themselves, in a more-or-less restricted kinship sense. In later uses, in New Testament Greek, *ethnos* comes to be used, as we might expect, to mean non-Christian and non-Jewish, in an attempt to render the Hebrew *goyim*. The derived adjective *ethnikos*, at this stage, is very nearly synonymous with *barbaros*, with all its moral, social, and linguistic content – the barbarians were those who spoke unintelligible languages, and wanted for civilization, who were beyond the bounds of meaning, order and decency.

The term *ethnos*, of course, took its meaning in a vocabulary of related terms, most of which have come down to us in some form or another – *genos* (Gr.), *gens* and *genus* (L.); *populus* (L.); *tribus* (L.); *natio* (L.); *polis* (Gr.); *barbaros* (Gr.) and *barbarus* (L.); *civis* and *civitas* (L.), and so on (to cite only a few of many possibilities). There is no space for a thorough study of these, but it is important to notice that the legacy of these words in the modern Romance languages, and in English, is a rich and complex moral vocabulary, laid out along dimensions of inclusion and exclusion, dignity and disdain, familiarity and strangeness – gentle, Gentile; popular; tribe; nation, national; polite; barbarous; civil, civilized; and so on (see Autenrieth, 1876; Liddell and Scott, 1890 and 1958; Cunliffe, 1924; Balsdon, 1979; Rankin, 1987).

The immediate successor to terms related to *ethnos* was, in an important sense, *gentile*, which, as *gentilis*, was how the Greek term was rendered in the Vulgate version of the Bible (see Elcock, 1960:37). It was Church Latin that dominated literacy in Europe throughout the middle ages, and terms related to *ethnos* had no place in this. After the Reformation, and the English vernacular rendering of the Bible, it was as 'gentile', not 'ethnic', that the term appeared.

Just shows, in his discussion of the use of *ethnos* in modern Greek, that the term can now be used within a discussion of what is essentially Greek. This is a rather remarkable change from classical usage, and merits comment. Just comments upon the use of *ethnos* for 'non-structured', 'tribal', peripheral peoples in classical Greek, but remarks that the term has, in some sense at least, been 'transmitted unchanged (except phonetically) from classical antiquity' into Modern Greek (p. 72). An inversion of meaning has clearly occurred, however, and we are grateful to Dr Just for the subsequent (tentative) suggestion that this probably occurred during the Ottoman period. In the Byzantine and Mediaeval period, the term continued to be used for the 'gentiles' – a grouping of religious 'otherness'. Within the Ottoman empire, however, the Orthodox Christians themselves were the most prominent religious 'other', defined as such by the majority Muslim definition of the Empire. The various religious communities of the empire were termed 'millets', and it seems probable that *ethnos* was the term used to translate the Turkish term *millet*, as it applied to Orthodox Christians. The already existing sense of 'ethnos', a term suggesting both a religious grouping and 'otherness', would have made such a solution plausible. The Greeks may, then, have been referring to themselves as the *ethnos* (that is, the Orthodox millet) from the fifteenth century onwards. When Greece became a kind of experimental laboratory for modern nationalism, in the early nineteenth century (see Just, p. 83), the Greek *ethnos*, in both semantic and political opposition to the crumbling Ottoman Empire, came to be seen as a quintessentially self-realizing, self-defining entity; as such, the idea would have been generalized throughout classically educated intellectual Europe.

The term 'ethnic', along with various derived forms, has long been used in English in its Greek New Testament sense, as an unusual intellectual synonym for 'gentile', denoting 'pagan' or 'non-Christian', and it retained this sense until well into the nineteenth century (see the *Oxford English Dictionary*, 1971). From about the mid-nineteenth century, however, scholarship has made of *ethnos* a word meaning something like 'group of people of shared characteristics'. The term *ethnos* itself has not passed into common Anglophone intellectual discourse, but a variety of compound and derived terms have been formed, which are now in common academic use – ethnology, ethnography, ethnocentric, ethnic, ethnicity, and others. The term *ethnos* itself was not needed, in a sense, since all these terms relate to the discourse built around the idea of 'race', for which 'ethnos' would have been no more than a redundant synonym. Ethnology was 'the study of races'.

This is not a book about 'race', but the discourse of race is an essential background to any concern with ethnicity today. We now tend to regard 'race' as a concept primarily concerned with biology, but in nineteenth-century usage this biological component was only a part of a complex use. The term was frequently used to express commonalities of various kinds, and although the echo of biology was always there, many uses of the term could have been substituted by, for example, 'nation', 'society', 'culture', 'language', or 'tribe'. The interweaving of biology, culture, and language in the concept had itself a very simple basis in experience – in many societies, then as now, social and linguistic recruitment were often entirely congruent with biological recruitment. A child was born into the society of which it was to become a part, whose language and manners it would learn. In such a context, a concept which did not distinguish very clearly between social, cultural, linguistic, and biological classifications of people, and which tended to make a unity of all these, was very much at home.

Just says, in the context of discussion of ethnicity and ethnic identity, that 'there is, however, a Joker in the pack (and it seems to be a Joker studiously avoided by the academic proponents of ethnicity): namely, "race" ' (p. 76). There can be little doubt that the reason for this studious avoidance is a sense of revulsion and shame at the events that racial doctrines, and specifically Nazi racial doctrines, brought about in Europe in the 1930s and 1940s. It was in the post-war period that the term 'ethnic' came into widespread employment in its modern sense. As Just observes, 'ethnic group' is very like 'race' without the biology (and with the biological implications always tending to creep back in; compare Wallman, 1986:228–9). In Africa it has come to replace 'tribe', which latter has come to be considered pejorative (and as will, perhaps, 'ethnic group' in its turn). The extent to which 'race', as a concept tying linguistic, cultural, and biological descent into the same thread, is still popularly accepted, is shown by a variety of the papers in this volume, and what Just says for the Greek case could be generalized for many other examples: 'Outside of a (growing) intellectual minority, one is Greek because one has . . . "Greek blood"' (p. 77; see also Tapper; Schutte; Buckley; Hugh-Jones; and others).

'Ethnicity', as an abstract noun meaning what it is you have if you are an 'ethnic group', followed on behind the adjective 'ethnic'. The *Oxford English Dictionary* gives a first recorded usage in 1953, and an early compilation discussing the concept begins 'Ethnicity seems to be a new term' (Glazer and Moynihan, 1975:1). A variety of dictionary citations follows, dating from the 1960s and 1970s. What is immediately interesting is that the terms seem to have rediscovered, even without intention, the 'us and them' duality that related terms have had through most of recorded history. 'Race' as a term did not, so to speak, discriminate. Within the discourse of race, everybody had one, everybody belonged to one. In actual use, however, not everybody belongs to an 'ethnic group', or has an 'ethnicity'. In their common employment, the terms have a strong and familiar bias towards 'difference' and 'otherness'. It is, incidentally, not surprising that social anthropology should have found 'ethnicity' consonant with its ambitions and wishes, since an appetite for significant difference has always been present in the anthropological project, even when this has been disavowed.

The adjective 'ethnic', in common usage within say, England, has no obvious point of application within the indigenous patterns of social structure, or of geographical subordination and superordination, inclusion and exclusion. The adjective, however, is readily applied to groups of relatively recent immigrants who are perceived to be sufficiently different, and indeed one measure of perceived difference would be the ease with which the adjective 'ethnic' could be employed. These reflections relate, it must be stressed, to how the terms are used in practice, and not to how they ought to be used, supposing anybody to be competent to judge the matter. It might well be felt that 'ethnicity' is something that inheres in every group that is self-identifying – or at least that it ought to be considered as such. It was very much in this spirit that the conference topic that led to this volume was conceived, since we explicitly invited contributions dealing with 'majority' as well as 'minority' experience. Modern social anthropology, in dealing with 'ethnic' or 'race' relations, or with popular classification of populations, would recognize without difficulty that minimal significance required some kind of dyadic situation. In some situation in which two distinct groups meet, where it is generally accepted that 'ethnic group' might be a suitable description of one and not of the other, it is clear that the definition of the populations involves them both, in some kind of conceptual and practical collusion – the 'opposition' involves them both. New and acute problems of understanding and self-understanding are posed to both parties, in a manner that is in many respects reciprocal. It would seem appropriate, therefore, that the term we use for the kind of grouping created by such a situation should be readily applicable to all groups involved. 'Ethnicity', however, has so far refused to be socially neutral in this way. The problem is neatly presented, albeit inadvertently, by an article in the journal *Ethnicity*, in which the author begins by making fun of those who:

> somehow regard all newcomers to our country as ethnics but, simultaneously, in some vague way, regard themselves as non-ethnic. A false premise if there ever was one. Everett C. Hughes is entirely correct when he declares that 'we are all ethnic'.
> (Schermerhorn, 1974:1, citing Hughes and Hughes, 1952)

By the time, however, that we have been given a definition of ethnicity (Schermerhorn, 1974:1, citing 1970:12), and been given a few examples ('Japanese Americans, the French in Canada, the Flemish in Belgium'), we have been talked into a blunt denial of the first formulation: 'In nearly all cases, however, ethnic groups are a minority of the population' (Schermerhorn, 1974:2).

Ethnicity, and ethnic group, like so many less scholarly terms of human identification, occupy one side of a duality, tacit or otherwise, of familiarity and strangeness. It is, therefore, unsurprising that their appropriate application would vary very much from one context to another. Even given an agreement about the meaning of the adjective (which is not to be taken for granted), those groupings that look 'ethnic' from south-east England are not those that look 'ethnic' from California, Moscow, or Peking.

'Ethnicity', then, is an abstract noun, derived by non-vernacular morphological processes from a substantive that does not exist. 'Ethnic group' is a collocation often used in covert synonymy for another term, 'race', which has been morally and politically disallowed in many areas. 'Ethnicity' is a term that only makes sense in a context of relativities, of processes of identification, and that nevertheless aspires to concrete and positive status both as an attribute and as an analytical 'concept'. It is a term that half-heartedly aspires to describe phenomena that involve everybody, and that nevertheless has settled in the vocabulary as a marker of strangeness and unfamiliarity. No surprise, then, that the question 'What is ethnicity?' might often be asked, and that the answers should be less than lucid. Given this, it is easy to agree with Just's contention that it is 'a somewhat retrograde step that "ethnicity" should ever have entered into the *analytic* vocabulary of the social sciences' (p. 76).

Is the term 'identity' any better? It is certainly in common use, in senses that often overlap with those pertaining to ethnicity. It has been argued that difficulties arising from the term 'ethnicity' are not properly specific to the term, or to its etymology, but rather are the result of systematic features of human naming, and of attempts to delineate types of human group. If this is so, then no terminological innovation is going to solve these problems, which we might expect 'identity' to share.

We can, perhaps, contrast two notions of the term 'identity': one more-or-less essentialist notion, with identity as something (an attribute, entity, thing, whatever) which an individual or a group has in and of itself, an 'identity' that is subject to growth and decline, to health and sickness; and another much like that of ethnicity as already discussed – a notion only existing in a context of oppositions and relativities. This latter is no radically novel idea, but it is far from being well understood outside social anthropology, and it coexists uneasily with the discourse of identity as an essential and unitary entity. Social anthropologists have discussed in some detail what we might call, in this context, and in the search of neutral terminology, the 'classification of peoples', and some of this work is now quite old (see, for example, Leach, 1954; Barth, 1969; Southall, 1970; Ardener, 1972; 1974; Lévi-Strauss *et al.*, 1977; Epstein, 1978). Within this discussion, a group or an individual has no *one* identity, but a variety (a potentially very large variety) of possibilities, that only incompletely or partially overlap in social time and social space.

The appropriate object of study

We have seen that the discourse concerning ethnicity tends to concern itself with subnational units, or minorities of some kind or another. The prevalence of the nation–state in the world can, of course, lend the appearance of similarity to subnational, substate entities that might arise in contradistinction or opposition to it, and so give some substance to the notion that 'ethnicity' (say) was an empirically and theoretically coherent phenomenon. It is, however, notorious that attempts to define the nation, and to fit realities to the definition, are fruitless, with counter-examples suggesting themselves at every turn. There is no reason, therefore, to expect that *sub*national phenomena will form a coherent class. And indeed, there is no reason to regard 'ethnicity' and 'identity' as different in kind from all other acts of classification and identification. It is, perhaps, best to regard those things that, for the moment, look like 'ethnicities' and 'identities', as phenomena to be subsumed under the general study of the classification of people (by themselves and by others). And then to regard the 'classification of people' as subsumed by classification in general – an area of expertise that anthropology has made its own.

We have come to recognize that groups 'identify' other groups, as a logical means of asserting or constructing 'self'-identity (for whatever moral, economic, cognitive, or political purpose). Majority groups use the minorities around them in this way, attributing identities to the minorities (not always desirable ones). The minorities are therefore relentlessly involved in a discourse that expects them to have 'an identity'. It is notorious that minority groups are seen both to have particularly coherent identities, and to find that their real identities are nevertheless curiously threatened and elusive. These are both different sides of the same coin, however, for it seems that the assumption of a true identity, the search for it, and the discovery that it is difficult to find, are all consequences of competitive pressure. It is surely in relation to this that we can understand the sometimes eery silence that is found at the heart of majority self-presentation. The discourse of identity does not require the majority to ask itself the question, 'Who then are we, *really*?' (cf. Ardener, 1987:44), and it is thus that identity (like ethnicity) seems characteristically to be something that is found, and found problematic, in minority areas. This silence on the subject of majority identity is often, in fact, taken by intellectuals at face value, and regarded as evidence of pathological loss of identity in the majority (alienation, and so on) – a condition perhaps best summed up by the common contention that 'the English have no national dress'. And when a majority is posed the question, either by circumstance or by the curious ethnographer, then the answers are far from unambiguous, as Forsythe demonstrates on p. 137.

Just as both 'ethnicity' and 'identity', in different ways, tend to lead towards 'minority' groups, so it is clear, from anthropological practice in Europe at least, that the bent of the social anthropological imagination leads away from the majority experience, and towards the interest and difference that the fringe represents (see Chapman, 1982; McDonald, 1982; 1987; Jackson, 1987). The invitation to anthropology to 'come home' is still only a recent one, and not all anthropologists have accepted it, or have known how to do so. Anthropological study of the nation, or of the nation–state, is not, therefore, obviously suggested. If we are to study ethnic groups, however, we are necessarily involved in taxonomies that include nations, and can only continue to ignore them by acts of studied blindness. At an onomastic level, and it is this primary level that organizes much scholarship, it is clear that 'ethnic groups' and 'nations' are of the same stock. From this point of view, it is no more than a tautology to say that nations have ethnic origins (a tautology, however, that is thoroughly and interestingly explored by Smith, 1986). It is also true, of course, that the ethnic map of Europe at any time in its history is littered with the names of ethnicities that have disappeared virtually without trace, and that, as Gellner notes, only a very few have 'survived' to give a language and a name to a modern nation–state (see Gellner, 1983).

We might feel, therefore, that the study of nations was implied and required by the study of ethnic groups. It remains true, however, that anthropologists have tended to be happy to study ethnic groups, and have been much less happy studying nations, as if the latter were defined out of their vision and capacities. There are, of course, long-standing and constitutive features of the anthropological imagination that bring this about.

The 1987 ASA conference, in order to try to overcome this self-imposed incapacity, explicitly invited contributions concerning 'majority' as well as 'minority' experience. The terms 'majority' and 'minority' are, of course, far from satisfactory, but they made a readily comprehensible point – we wanted, so to speak, papers not only about the Basques, the Bretons, the Catalonians, and the Welsh, but also papers about the Spanish, the French, the Germans, and the English. And we got some (see, for example, Forsythe, and Burke, below).

It is clear from several of the papers that many societies around the world are still shaking from events that had their origin in Europe. The events of the 1939–45 war particularly, and the discourse of political morality and racial identity that accompanied them, echo still in the lives of many people – not only in the lives of those that have ethnographies written about them, but also in the lives of those who do the writing. Reaction and counter-reaction to ideas and events of this period are strongly evident in the papers given by Llobera and Collard; they are a background, in different ways, to the work of Paine, Schutte, and Burke. It is all the more strange, therefore, that study of the society (or its modern counterpart) that was at the centre of these events – Germany – should not be unequivocally welcomed.

It was clear from the reception given to Forsythe's paper, however, that some still regarded the study of so large and untypical an anthropological object as a major Western European nation, as undesirable and inappropriate. This dissatisfaction expressed itself for some as a question of scale – a nation like Germany was too big, as it were, for participant observation. Its truth could only be seized statistically, by other and less intimate forms of study. It is of interest here, however, that the question of scale is itself a relative one. Llobera's study of Catalonia caused none of these problems, and it seems likely that this is because Catalonia, for all the millions of people that inhabit it, is a minority (morally, politically, demographically). Minority status seems to induce, *ipso facto*, an illusion of smallness and intimacy, sufficient to permit of anthropological work, however huge and faceless the true social context might be. The dissatisfaction with studying Germany also expressed itself in a series of questions about length of fieldwork, linguistic capacities of the fieldworker, and so on, which would have been considered frankly bad form if asked of a fieldworker engaged in a more traditional study (and the answers to which, incidentally, would have been found entirely satisfactory in the same traditional context). It seemed as if the boundary separating the small face-to-face community appropriate to anthropology and participant observation, and the large-scale society appropriate to political science, sociology, and the questionnaire, could be put somewhere between Catalonia (with its five million people), and Germany (with its fifty million).

It is clear, perhaps, that there is little logic in this, and that there is no longer any need to consider any area of collective representation, European or otherwise, as outside the bounds of anthropological interest. The specific limitations to which anthropology has so far acceded are, however, themselves revealing evidence of the nature of the categories with which we deal.

References

Ardener, E. (1972) 'Language, ethnicity and population', *Journal of the Anthropological Society of Oxford* III (3); reprinted in R. Moss and R. Rathbone (eds) (1975) *The Population Factor in Tropical Africa*, London: University of London Press.

Ardener, E. (1974) 'Social anthropology and population', in H. Parry (ed.) *Population and its Problems*, Oxford: Clarendon Press.

Ardener, E. (1975) 'The voice of prophecy – further problems in the analysis of events', The Munro Lecture, Edinburgh University, in E. Ardener (forthcoming) *The Voice of Prophecy – Collected Essays of Edwin Ardener*, Oxford: Blackwell.

Ardener, E. (1982) 'Social anthropology, language and reality', in D. Parkin (ed.) *Semantic Anthropology*, ASA 22, London: Academic Press.

Ardener, E. (1987) 'Remote areas – some theoretical considerations', in A. Jackson (ed.) *Anthropology at Home*, ASA 25, London: Tavistock.

Ardener, E. (forthcoming) *The Voice of Prophecy – Collected Essays of Edwin Ardener*, Oxford: Blackwell (ed. and intro. by M. Chapman).

Autenrieth, G. (1876) *A Homeric Dictionary*, translated by R. Keep, revised by I. Flagg, for 1958 edition, Norman: University of Oklahoma Press.

Balsdon, J.P. (1979) *Romans and Aliens*, London: Duckworth.

Barth, F. (ed.) (1969) *Ethnic Groups and Boundaries: The Social Organization of Culture Difference*, London: George Allen and Unwin.

Chadwick, H. (1912) *The Heroic Age*, Cambridge: Cambridge University Press.

Chadwick, H. (1949) *Early Scotland*, Cambridge: Cambridge University Press.

Chapman, M. (1982) 'Semantics and the Celt', in D. Parkin (ed.) *Semantic Anthropology*, ASA 22, London: Academic Press.

Cohen, A. (ed.) (1973) *Urban Ethnicity*, ASA 12, London: Tavistock.

Cunliffe, R. (1924) *A Lexicon of the Homeric Dialect*, London: Blackie and Sons Ltd.

Darwin, C. (1859) *On the Origin of Species*, London: J. Murray.

Elcock, W.D. (1960) *The Romance Languages*, London: Faber and Faber.

Epstein, A. (1978) *Ethos and Identity: Three Studies in Ethnicity*, London: Tavistock.

Evans-Pritchard, E. (1962) 'Social anthropology: past and present – The 1950 Marett Lecture', in *Essays in Social Anthropology*, London: Faber and Faber.

Fardon, R. (1987) 'History, ethnicity and pageantry – The 1987 ASA Conference', *Anthropology Today* 3 (3): 15–17.

Gellner, E. (1983) *Nations and Nationalism*, Oxford: Blackwell.

Glazer, N. and Moynihan, D.P. (1975) *Ethnicity – Theory and Experience*, Cambridge, Mass.: Harvard University Press.

Hastrup, K. (1985) *Culture and History in Medieval Iceland*, Oxford: Oxford University Press.

Hughes, Everett C. and Hughes, H. MacGill (1952) *Where Peoples Meet: Racial and Ethnic Frontiers*, Glencoe, Ill.: The Free Press.

Jackson, A. (ed.) (1987) *Anthropology at Home*, ASA 25, London: Tavistock.

Just, R. (1978) 'Some problems for Mediterranean anthropology', *Journal of the Anthropological Society of Oxford* 6 (3).

Leach, E. (1954) *Political Systems of Highland Burma*, London: Athlone Press.

Lévi-Strauss, C. *et al.* (1977) *L'Identité* (Seminaire interdisciplinaire dirigé par Claude Lévi-Strauss – 1974–5), Paris: Presses Universitaires de France, Editions Grasset et Fasquelle.

Lewis, I.M. (ed.) (1968) *History and Social Anthropology*, ASA 7, London: Tavistock.

Liddell, H.G. and Scott, R. (1890, 1958) *A Greek–English Lexicon*, Oxford: Clarendon Press.

McDonald, M. (1982) 'Social aspects of language and education in Brittany', unpublished D. Phil thesis, Oxford University.

McDonald, M. (1986) 'Celtic ethnic kinship and the problem of being English' in *Current Anthropology*, vol 27, no.4.

McDonald, M. (1987) 'The politics of fieldwork in Brittany', in A. Jackson (ed.) *Anthropology at Home*, ASA 25, London: Tavistock.

McDonald, M. (1990) *We are not French! Language, Culture, and Identity in Britain*, London: Routledge.

Macfarlane, A. (1978) *The Origins of English Individualism*, Blackwell: Oxford.

Overing, J. (ed.) (1985) *Reason and Morality*, ASA 24, London: Tavistock.

Parkin, D. (ed.) (1982) *Semantic Anthropology*, ASA 22, London: Academic Press.

Radcliffe-Brown, A. (1968) *Structure and Function in Primitive Society*, Oxford: Oxford University Press.

Rankin, H.D. (1987) *Celts and the Classical World*, London: Croom Helm.

Sahlins, M. (1985) *Islands of History*, Chicago: Chicago University Press (in paperback 1987, London: Tavistock).

Saussure, F. de (1955) *Cours de Linguistique Generale* (5th edn), Paris: Payot (eds C. Bally and A. Sechehaye) (1st edn, 1915).

Schermerhorn, R. (1970) *Comparative Ethnic Relations – A Framework for Theory and Research*, New York: Random House.

Schermerhorn, R. (1974) 'Ethnicity in the perspective of the sociology of knowledge', *Ethnicity* 1: 1–14.

Smith, A. (1986) *The Ethnic Origins of Nations*, Oxford: Blackwell.

Southall, A. (1970) 'The illusion of tribe', in P. Gutkind (ed.) *The Passing of Tribal Man in Africa*, Leiden: Brill (reprint of *Journal of Asian and African Studies* 5 (1–2), special issue).

Thompson, P. (1988) (1978) *The Voice of the Past*, Oxford: Oxford University Press.

Tonkin, E. (forthcoming) 'History and the myth of realism', in P. Thompson and R. Samuel (eds) *The Myths We Live By*, London: Routledge.

Wallman, S. (1986) 'Ethnicity and the boundary process in context', in J. Rex and D. Mason (eds) *Theories of Race and Ethnic Relations*, Cambridge: Cambridge University Press.

Chapter one

The Construction of History: 'vestiges of creation'

Edwin Ardener

A theory of history has long eluded social anthropology. Even Evans-Pritchard seemed to see it, at one level, as a series of synchronic sections (1950; 1961), at least when discussing practical fieldwork method. At another level, he clearly saw history as a matter of retrospective interpretation (as in his own reinterpretation of the history of social anthropology). Lévi-Strauss (1958; trans., 1963) saw it as the uncovering of unconscious processes (*Structural Anthropology*). It is not, therefore, entirely an objective matter. Yet the absence of a sound theoretical protection against the dangers of total arbitrariness is evident. In 1971 I drew attention to the problem of the chess puzzle. Some chess problems show a state of the chessboard that has as a 'history' previous real states of a game that has really been played. Others are 'constructed' states that might have been reached in a game, but were not. These constructed states are passages in games that have never been played. Yet we cannot tell the difference.

Phillip Gosse, the father of Edmund Gosse, and a natural historian, was a committed nineteenth-century creationist. He was unable to bring himself to reject the Biblical chronology of Archbishop Ussher in the light of the tremendous geological and palaeological advances of his period. Darwin's great work was a considerable shock and challenge to him. He argued that Adam's body had been itself created bearing the evidences of a non-existent biological growth and development. It was not enough to posit that he must have lacked a navel (a common creationist argument!): the problem was more fundamental than that. In the same way, he argued, the earth was created *together with* its fossil history of millions of years. The fossils were for Gosse (1907) likewise mere 'Vestiges of Creation', which itself took place only a few thousand years ago (Ardener, 1971b:227). Thus this anti-evolutionist Plymouth Brother stumbled on a real question, lost although it was in the preposterousness of its particular polemical application. For, in a sense, all baselines of history are conceptually in this situation: real histories are, in the absence of total documentation (what would total documentation be like?), rearranged by changes in the infinite sequence of successive presents, producing, as with the chess puzzle, histories that did not happen.

If we could artificially start the game, somewhere, we might trace the shape of the changing historical space. Partial approximations are possible. Hastrup's account of the trajectory of the internal categories of the Icelandic Free State, from its foundation in about 800 (by settlement) to its total redefinition in the eleventh century (by absorption into the Norwegian state), is the most advanced we have in social anthropology (Hastrup, 1985). It incorporates a model of catastrophic rearrangement over time, that takes into account the continuity of the human rearrangers (Ardener, 1975). Yet no historical space is truly independent. The Free State was part of the wider Atlantic space of its own period, and now forms part also of our own historical (or historiographical) space, while Hastrup's own study is itself part of our social anthropological space. It is thus not a matter of spaces nesting in hierarchical sequence, relatively tidily. On the contrary, we may argue, all such spaces englobe each other anti-, or better, a-hierarchically. The ordering feature is the frame. Perceptually and cognitively the framing 'rules' (fluctuating and ambiguously evidenced as they frequently are) are the source of the very concept of the space. We may say the frame and the space are just the internal and external aspects of the same concept.

Where is the real world among these possible worlds? Is it worth asking this question? Some have seemed happy enough to do without it – hence the extreme idealist tendencies of many approaches that have otherwise been ready to undertake the specification of the cognitive aspects of human social life. The approaches loosely seen as structuralist were ultimately subject to this criticism. In their strong form they are totally nihilistic in their contemplation of the question of reality. Nevertheless, in a 'post-structuralist' world we can attempt to unpack this anomaly in structural analysis, for its nihilism is technically most evident in the matter of history. In the structuralist frame, history is subject to the same structuring as other narrative, and is ultimately reducible to text. This achievement (which was anticipated and paralleled outside social anthropology) is a genuine one. The study of mythology is now seen to encompass at one level all history, or at least all historiography. It seems, then, that structuralism is 'Gossian' in its view of the past. Any 'historical' elements (in the older, securer sense) in a narrative are mere 'vestiges of creation'. Although likely to be hotly rejected, even by structuralists in their heyday, this is a strong position (as I have already argued) and not something to be ashamed of. Nevertheless, this 'flatness of vision' in structuralism is a result of its essential 'textuality', the demonstration of which I will not repeat here (Ardener, 1985).

Edmund Leach was early involved in this controversy through his analysis of Old Testament sources (Leach, 1969). This is a field in which the documents are seen as both text and truth by many experts. I recall that, in a public lecture, he extended his analysis to the New Testament, and showed Christ and John the Baptist to be structural transformations of each other. A theologian rose and said: 'To some of us present these were real people'. That is: the text was indeed history. I do not intend to go into all the possible discussion. With Biblical data all neoanthropological analyses produce versions of this reaction. For example, Mary Douglas's analysis of Leviticus (1966) produced parallel objectivist discussions. The Biblical objections merely raise in relatively explicit doctrinal form the question of whether the very possibility of structuralism denies the possibility of history, save perhaps by a version of Piaget's inadvertently appropriate remark (cited in a previous discussion) that 'God is a structuralist' (Piaget, 1971; cited in Ardener, 1985:53).

Nevertheless, the answer to the implicit question, like what songs the sirens sang, 'is not beyond all conjecture'. It is interesting to compare two classes of text with this question in mind. Leach (1969:81) cites various memorable features of the rulers of the Tudor Dynasty of England. Henry VIII and Elizabeth I appear as structural transformations of each other (broadly as male/overuxorious: female/underuxorious). They and other royal figures associated with the dynasty also appear in structural opposition to each other. Although intended lightheartedly (but no less revealingly), this sort of thing (or rather, the very possibility of this sort of thing) inevitably raises questions about Lévi-Strauss, just as the 'proof' that Max Müller was a Sun-deity did concerning that other great mythologist.

Let us suppose that such analyses *are* possible on 'historical' narrative, and there is plenty of evidence that they are, how could they come about?

(1) For oral history, 'traditional' history, or the like, we may simply argue that the memory of events has been totally restructured. They have been turned into narrative, and obey the structuring processes of narrative. In effect this is the position taken about the majority of texts that tell a story about the past – before the advent of 'professional' history, or alongside it. It is the uncomplicated structuralist position. In cases like the Tudors, however, the documented accounts of the period itself have strong narrative features, which give it a certain 'epic' quality. If these derive from retrospective restructuring, does it occur particularly in particular periods? Is it possible that certain historical conjunctures are prone to crystallize historiographically in such ways? 'Happy the country whose history is boring', the saying goes. Why, if history is simply (unconsciously) restructured as narrative, is *any* history boring? We may have been able to conceive such a question since the 'objective' recording of poorly structured times and places has become possible (Ardener, 1987). In oral

history there are, indeed, actual blanks, which suggest the failure of the structuring process.

(2) A second approach would be to admit the aforementioned, but to propose instead that sometimes events arrange themselves, and individuals fall into relationships that have resemblances to the structure of more mythological narrative. This solves the problem of embarrassingly 'fictional'-looking stretches of history and keeps such questions as the historicity of Jesus and John the Baptist (as well as of Henry VIII and Elizabeth I!) satisfactorily open. This is essentially a concession to the existence of professional history, and it is not without value as accounting for the greater narrative richness of certain stretches of even conventional narrative. This is, however, only another way of conceding in advance that structuralist patterns are coincidences in 'real' history – which does not help the structuralist analysis of any text, which someone, somewhere, is prepared to declare historical. Furthermore, when we are dealing with oral or traditional statements we *still* cannot separate, by inspection, any fortuitous stretches of structuralized *history* from the hypothesized total restructuring or 'mythologizing' that is expected to mark a piece of traditional text in any case, and which was after all the original point of structural analysis.

(3) So we would be better placed to argue alternatively that structural oppositions are built into history as it happens. There are, indeed, plenty of grounds for saying that the 'memory' of history begins when it is registered. It is encoded 'structurally' as it occurs. The structuring, by this view, is actually part of the 'registration' of events (Ardener, 1978). Then we can say that since not all events do survive, but only 'memorable' or 'significant' events (Ardener, 1987), the structural processes are not necessarily retrospectively imposed, but are synchronic – all part of the very nature of event-registration (with or without any specific physical recording). It is what I have referred to as the 'slaughter of the event', the creation of the 'dead stretches' of the registering process. Such a conclusion is uncontroversial enough nowadays. Retrospective restructuring simply continues the process, since each restructured event is freshly objectivized and there could be an infinite sequence of rememorizations.

(4) Finally, we may go further and say that the relations between persons, and their mutual definitions, actually embody 'structuralist' processes. The relations between parent and child, between lineages, between affines, are self-defining relations of symmetry and opposition. Not only does this recognition properly embody the structuralism of *Les Structures Elémentaires* and its successors into the historical process (which Lévi-Strauss never did), it also recalls the Freudian processes of identity construction in the family. Henry VIII (uxorious, male) and Elizabeth (non-uxorious, female) then ceases to be a structuralist whimsy, and becomes part of an intergenerational psycho-analytic drama. Freudianism and struc-

turalism are metaphysics of a similar order, as I have argued before (1971a). Nevertheless, we begin at this point to part with structuralism as such, although we are near the world of Lacan and revisionist Marxist-structuralism. The important point is that event-specification begins in one important aspect, in the structuring of relations between persons.

So far in the language of 'structure' I have elicited four levels, and a fifth by implication, which I will summarize not in the order of unpacking but in reverse order.

(a) **Structures** *of* personal relations, or structures inherent in the mutual self-definition of persons.

(b) Structures by which relationships are registered or perceived ('events').

(c) Structures through which registered events are remembered.

(d) Structures 'imposed' on events, retrospectively (restructuring).

(e) Structures of text. This is, for our historical purposes, the implicit fifth level, which is critical for our discussion; for narratives can be structured *de novo* in the absence of all the preceding levels. Mythologies, pseudo-histories, are precisely the core materials which originally lent themselves to structural analysis and which are notionally without history at all.

This summary unpacks further the implications of a fully structuralist discussion of history as fairly as possible, although it has never been previously articulated. It is, as a result, no longer structuralist at all, since it has been possible to articulate it only by revising structuralism in the light of history itself. And, even so, we still cannot dissolve the problem with which we started; for if we have no historical documentation, only a narrative, the levels are obliterated and structuralist analysis cannot 'recover' them. All resemble level (e).

Restatement

Memory has been an evident theme in the preceding discussion. Sperber (1975) has been responsible for emphasizing this theme, although Leach had early on linked structure to memorability. The structures of structuralism, with their pluses and minuses, work at such a relatively unconscious level, that the apparently banal observation that myths (for example) are structured as they are for their memorability is an explanation of honourable simplicity. Sperber cites Bartlett's pre-war experiments, whereby messages are modified in transmission in the direction of deterioration modified by reconstruction. We may recall the comic case, immortalized by the late Will Hay, in which the message: 'Am going to advance: send reinforcements', ultimately became 'Am going to a dance: send three and fourpence'. The most stable thing about the message is the structural pattern. What, however, is memory when moved from the individual to the social, from its organic context to a collective simulacrum of itself? It seems that it is mainly a way of labelling that stability of pattern. Once more, the term has moved up a level: the 'story' behaves like a memory: but it is the story that is now memorized, not the events it purportedly embodies; and, it must be repeated, we still cannot on structural grounds tell the difference. This is the material basis of the movement of 'life into text' (Ardener, 1985), which eventually accounts for the perennial existence of the problem of the actual confusion of life and text.

When regarding the aforementioned summary of levels, we see that they clearly partake of what I call a 'simultaneity'. The movement from (a) to (b) is a movement from individual experience to social experience; the passage through (b) and (c) and (d) is a passage through the social space. The distinction between (b) and (c): whether historical structuring is laid down as the events occur, or is 'adventitiously' perceived retrospectively, is not a difference in principle. Restructuring is a continuous revision of previous states. Again, the distinction between (c) and (d): the perceiving of structural coincidences in past events, or the complete reconstruction of the past, is similarly ambiguous. We can speak of (d), complete reconstruction, only in the absence of knowledge about a continuous series of intermediate stages. What then about (e) or mere myth or story, complete un-history? How do we know that it actually occurs?

By now it seems clear that we have here a total analogue of the theoretical problem presented by sets of unit categories; on the surface they picture a totally relativistic universe. At the level of the social space itself they produce a historically relativistic universe. It is my argument that as materiality is perceived through the concept of 'semantic density' in the linguistic aspect, and of variable 'event-density' in the synchronic aspect of the social space, so are its effects revealed as an underlying feature of the space as a whole, in the form of 'historical density'. The problem of the 'flatness' of the Gossian world – the inability to decide how much of it was created yesterday – is the macrocosmic aspect of the 'flatness' of category sets. 'Historical density' is the trace left by previous reconstructions of the space, each of which forms in some sense a barrier to perceiving the realities of their predecessors by wiping out the 'structures' that expressed them. Charles Kingsley, in his response to Gosse, exclaimed that he could not believe that God (the Structuralist?) had written 'an enormous lie upon the rocks'. We may ourselves ask how the shadow of the 'vestiges of creation' would appear to us in the search for real past states.

Some cases

In Northern stories to be discovered in Scandinavian, Old English, and German sources appear the names of peoples and persons who are documented on the Continent between the years 360 and 500. During those years Gothic dominance expanded from the Baltic to the Black Sea under Ermenaric, only to be shattered by the Huns. The Western Roman Empire succumbed under the resulting pressures and was replaced by successor German states including that of Theodoric the Great. A minor event was the destruction of the Burgundian settlements on the Rhine, casually swept aside by Attila, now leader of the Huns, and a mass of subject forces, on their great push into Gaul to eventual stalemate and defeat on the Catalaunian Fields. The destruction of the Burgundians led to the death of their king Gundahar (Gunthaharius, Gunnar, Guthhere, Gunther) in 437. He, together with Ermenaric (Jormunrekr, Eormenric, Ermenrich) who died in about 370, Attila (Atli, Aetla, Etzel) who died in 453, and Theodoric (Thjodrekr, Theodric, Dietrich von Bern) who died in 526, all appear as contemporaries in the common stock of tales.

What picture do we receive? There is no trace of the Roman Empire. The scene is set in a world of royal or chiefly lineages, in which Attila and the Huns are indistinguishable from the Germans. The marital problems of Gunnar dominate the action. Two queens, Gunnar's wife Gudrun (Kriemhild) and Brynhildr, the wife of his friend or vassal Sigurdr, quarrel over precedence when bathing. Gudrun blurts out a statement that leads to the unravelling of a skein of relations by alliance or contract, and to the death of all concerned. The beneficiary, and the cause, is Atli, who marries the widowed Gudrun/Kriemhild, who eventually is the cause of his death. At this point we may note that the 'real' Attila died, according to Roman sources, after spending the night with a Germanic slave girl Ildico (Hildiko, little Hildr), who it seems was absolved from blame.

The stories are enriched and expanded in numerous recensions, but most of these were transmitted *not* in the Rhenish area of history, but in some Norwegian world that never participated in the original events, finally being preserved and elaborated in a mass of material (the Poetic *Eddas* and related prose sagas) redacted in the North Atlantic, in Iceland. Meanwhile, in mediaeval Germany, the tale was differently restructured in romantic ways as the *Nibelungenlied*. The *Volsungasaga* and the *Nibelungelied* belong now in different social spaces. Hardly an event can be identified as 'historical', yet the Norse recensions are perceived as patriotic records. Rising German nationalism in the late nineteenth century utilized the stories for new purposes. The Wagnerian recension belongs to no tradition; it is a new recension, a restructuring in its own right.

We meet here some remarkable continuities in names and genealogical relationships, among the debris of an historical period. Every level of structuring treated earlier appears in it. Every conventional analysis, thematic or textual, leads deeper and deeper into certain cruces: the central constellation of characters swing round the peculiar quarrel between the two queens, leading to the death of one and involving the other in the collapse of the alliance with Attila. To regard the Northern Tales as mythology is perfectly justified. We find almost every feature of fifth-century reality completely removed. Motivations for the characters are contradictory and obscure. They are never 'artistically' resolved. The basic political themes have dissolved. Other themes have been pressed into service. Not even its status as a Burgundian epic survives. Its time and place have evaporated. Yet certain personal configurations and an anomalous unresolved conflict have everywhere been transmitted.

If names and relationships are in some way 'real', but the events have vanished, or have been transformed or recontextualized, can history in some way have survived? I am reminded of a letter by L. Sprague de Camp in *Astounding Magazine* (February, 1939: 154–5), which raises this question in relation to the historicity of King Arthur:

> Consider this hypothetical case: I'm writing a story of the super-titanic-colossal type, involving a war between the galaxies, with the fighters shooting planets at each other for missiles . . . I want a name for my hero, so I look on the obituary page of the New York *Times*, and discover the obit of a certain Platypus McDandruff, who was a corporation lawyer specializing in railroad legislation. I like the name, so my hero becomes Platypus McDandruff. Would a future historian, comparing my story with the obit of the real Platypus, be justified in saying that [my hero] and the lawyer were 'the same'?

Nevertheless (*pace Astounding Magazine*) we know, by the still unoverturned theory of *bricolage*, that all structures are put together from 'events' of some kind (the fashionable, but old process of deconstruction, in which we are now involved is thus *debricolage*). It is a hypothesis that existing structural relationships of a strong kind are not lightly abandoned. These are the flotsam and jetsam of real life. In the Burgundian case, it is a possibility that unresolved anomalies, always located in the same area in the various surface texts, evidence the core of the traumatic event in Western Europe as seen, not by the Romans, but by those upon whom the effects were like an extraordinary explosion and expansion of reality: the Germans of the period. It would be as if we were looking at the scattered remains of a supernova.

I argue that the fragmented remains of the transforming event are still perceivable, preserved in the ambiguous relations at the heart of the story. The destruction of that family and the Attilan events were closely related, and were seen as a collapse in the internal relations of contract, service, and alliance. A small domestic scandal unravelled their world at a critical moment, and so many worlds were similarly overwhelmed together that this one, with its ambiguous but clearly familial causation, became the model for them all. We should not be surprised that that ultimate deluge was drawn into the Norse prediction of *Ragnarokr*: the collapse of the cosmological order; or that the fateful scandal should be tied to even greater mythological precursors, involving gold and dragons, and divine interventions. In the case of Brynhildr, she is the centre of some sort of rebellious, headstrong claim. She has status but is under no consistent family control, save that of her husband Gunnar. She claims her sister-in-law's husband. She is in some dependent relationship to Atli. Gudrun/ Kriemhild is, in structural contrast, locked into family relations at all turns. It is, again, not a surprise that the separate story of the valkyrie Sigrdrifa and her fire should be tacked on to account for the disruptive Brynhildr's ill-omened autonomy – at least in the North. In the *Nibelungenlied* she is an heiress addicted to athletic sports!

The case of Maelbetha, a Scottish king of the pre-Norman period of Britain, exemplifies a similar situation in some ways. All early Scottish historical record is perceived through layers of political restructuring, and a passage through a linguistic redefinition, from Gaelic to English. In the course of the latter, his name was twisted into the form 'Macbeth', which passed through several Scottish sources into Shakespeare's play. The earliest record, which survives significantly in a genealogical tract, shows his story to be motivated by the destruction of the regular rotation of royal succession between two collateral lineages. 'Young' king Duncan is the beneficiary who inherits out of turn, succeeding his grandfather Malcolm directly. The claims of the disinherited line survive in the female line, in the persons of the lady Gruoch and her son Lulach. She marries Maelbetha. He himself has weaker claims through female links, as well as representing even more ancient Northern claims of Moray to the crown.

For Shakespeare, following centuries of restructuring by Scottish historians, we have a tale of usurpation by Macbeth based on fantasies of legitimacy (a version before Shakespeare's has only a vision of the three witches) personified as evil. Yet somehow Lady Macbeth is to blame. Gruoch's bloodstained claim emerges anomalously in the sanitized Stewart tale. She 'has given suck' she states, but where is the infant with those 'toothless gums' to which Shakespeare makes her allude? Where is Lulach, her son, who succeeded her husband briefly after his seventeen years of apparently fairly harmonious rule? In 1603 Macbeth must be childless: that is the point. His line and his claim *must* have died out. Macbeth belongs to a world before the Stewarts. The restructuring is orderly, however: young upstart Duncan (minus) killed in fair fight (plus), now transformed into good old Duncan (double plus) treacherously killed in bed by his host (double minus!). The lady Gruoch's relationship, stripped of its legal context, remains an 'anomaly' in the heart of the story.

The deficiencies of structuralism include a too 'cognitive' view of narrative. Gruoch is, at the level of the flat surface of the later redactions, a peculiarly marked element in the narrative. The principle of 'density', which reshaped our view of categorical sets by shadowing realities underlying the arbitrariness of classification, elicits, when applied to the structure of the Macbeth narrative, an area of relative structural silence round Lady Macbeth, which is semantically dense, and potentially event-rich (Ardener, 1987). The excellent principle of 'the dog that did not bark in the night'.

I have been able only to sketch lightly a few implications of these two examples – themselves only two out of a range of available examples. My basic conclusion is that certain 'event-related' structures do not restructure easily. It is my hypothesis that a certain clustering of anomalous features will show the trace of the survival of a structure from 'life'. Pure text were it to exist, would, in contrast, present almost no barriers to quite arbitrary restructuring. This would be excellently exemplified, indeed, by Sprague de Camp's fantastic case.

Finally, it was not my purpose to carry as a subtext to this paper a further demonstration of the theory of muting. If the strangely unarticulated characters of Gruoch, Brynhildr, and Gudrun/Kriemhild are all women, we should not be surprised by that. They are not the only centres of event-richness in their mythological domains – not by far (Atli for example and his absent Huns). Nevertheless, it is as well to remember that the tradition is, in both cases, a male one, in that the dominant restructuring has gone through males. However, if these texts also suggest that deeply structured areas in the traditions involve areas at the heart of key familial relations, then we shall obviously expect the 'evidences of creation' to lie, in part, in the history of women.

Editorial note to E.W. Ardener: The Construction of History

This paper is published here in the same form as presented to the ASA conference, Easter 1988. Mr Ardener died on 4 July of the same year, and the paper was unrevised at the time of his death. He would certainly have wished to add to this paper, to amplify some of the argument, and to include discussion of points raised during the conference. The paper, however, stands without this.

The conference paper was distributed with one final note: 'the notes and references to this paper will be available later'. Unfortunately, nothing has been found in Mr Ardener's papers to suggest that the notes and references existed even in partial form at the time of his death. The conference text included various author/date references, which are filled out below (and it is reasonably clear in all instances to which works he was referring). The section relating to old Germanic sources is unreferenced, and the original contained the sentence, 'The details of this case will appear in the fuller version of this paper'. No attempt has been made to add this detail, but some probable bibliographical suggestions can be made. It seems possible that Mr Ardener relied to some extent upon the work of H.M. Chadwick (see particularly 1912; also 1940), who provides detailed discussion of appropriate sources, events, characters, and historiographical traditions. For the *Nibelungenlied*, see Mowatt, 1962, and Andersson, 1987. For the *Edda* and the *Volsungasaga*, see, for example, Dronke, 1984. For the early sources of the Macbeth legend, see A.O. Anderson, 1922, and M.O. Anderson, 1973. Shakespeare's main sources were probably Hector Boece's early-sixteenth-century Latin reconstruction of Scottish History, *Scotorum Historiae*, disseminated in the Scots translation of 1531 by John Bellenden, *The Chronicles of Scotland*, and passing through later recensions at the hands of George Buchanan and Raphael Holinshed.

All the papers by Mr Ardener, which are cited below, are to be found in a volume of his collected papers, *The Voice of Prophecy* (Oxford: Blackwell, 1989). Mr Ardener was working on the preparation of this volume at the time of his death, and it has since been completed.

Mr Ardener suggested, during the conference, that he was probably the first person to cite *Astounding Magazine* in an ASA conference paper. This seems probable. Out of respect for the historiographical imponderable presented by the case of Platypus McDandruff, no attempt has been made to check this source.

MKC, May 1988

References (including editorial additions)

Anderson, A.O. (1922) *Early Sources of Scottish History*, Edinburgh: Edinburgh University Press.

Anderson, M.O. (1973) *Kings and Kingship in Early Scotland*, Edinburgh: Scottish Academic Press.

Andersson, T.M. (1987) *A Preface to the Nibelungenlied*, California: Stanford University Press.

Ardener, E.W. (1971a) 'The new anthropology and its critics', *Man* (ns) VI:3.

Ardener, E.W. (1971b) 'Social anthropology and the historicity of historical linguistics', in E.W. Ardener (ed.) *Social Anthropology and Language*, London: Tavistock.

Ardener, E.W. (1975) 'The voice of prophecy – further problems in the analysis of events', The Munro Lecture, Edinburgh University, in E. W. Ardener (forthcoming) *The Voice of Prophecy – Collected Essays of Edwin Ardener*, Oxford: Blackwell.

Ardener, E.W. (1978) 'Some outstanding problems in the analysis of events' (conference paper first delivered in 1973), in E. Schwimmer (ed.) *The Yearbook of Symbolic Anthropology*, London: Hurst. Reprinted in M. Foster and S. Brandes (eds) (1980) *Symbol as Sense*, New York: Academic Press.

Ardener, E.W. (1985) 'Social anthropology and the decline of modernism', in J. Overing (ed.) *Reason and Morality*, London: Tavistock.

Ardener, E.W. (1987) 'Remote areas: some theoretical considerations', in A. Jackson (ed.) *Anthropology at Home*, London: Tavistock.

Boece, H. (1536) *The Chronicles of Scotland*, translated into Scots by John

Bellenden (1531) from *Scotorum Historiae*, Paris, 1527. (Republished 1941, for the Scottish Texts Society, Edinburgh: Blackwood, E.C. Batho and H. Winifred Husbands (eds).)
Chadwick, H.M. (1912) *The Heroic Age*, Cambridge: Cambridge University Press.
Chadwick, H.M. and Chadwick, N.K. (1940) *The Growth of Literature*, Cambridge: Cambridge University Press (reprinted 1986).
Douglas, M. (1966) *Purity and Danger*, London: Routledge and Kegan Paul.
Dronke, U. (ed., intro., and trans.) (1984) *The Poetic Edda*, Oxford: Oxford University Press.
Evans-Pritchard, E.E. (1950) 'Social anthropology: past and present', The Marett Lecture, *Man* 50: 118–24.
Evans-Pritchard, E.E. (1961) *Anthropology and History*, Manchester: Manchester University Press.
Gosse, E. (1907) *Father and Son*, London: Heinemann; Harmondsworth: Penguin (1949).
Hastrup, K. (1985) *Culture and History in Medieval Iceland*, Oxford: Clarendon Press.
Leach, E. (1969) *Genesis as Myth, and Other Essays*, Cambridge: Cambridge University Press.
Lévi-Strauss, C. (1949) *Les Structures Elémentaires de la Parenté*, Paris: Presses Universitaires de France.
Lévi-Strauss, C. (1958) (trans. 1963) *Structural Anthropology*, London: Penguin.
Mowatt, D. (ed. and trans.) (1962) *The Nibelungenlied*, London: Dent, Everyman.
Piaget, J. (1971) *Structuralism*, London: Routledge and Kegan Paul.
Sperber, D. (1975) *Rethinking Symbolism*, Cambridge: Cambridge University Press.

© 1989 Edwin Ardener

Chapter two

Tribal Ethnography: past, present, future
Edmund Leach

I do not claim any originality for what I am saying. Roger Keesing's glossy-paper undergraduate textbook *Cultural Anthropology: A Contemporary Perspective* (1981) devotes three pages of his first chapter to the problems of objectivity in fieldwork with which I am largely concerned. But Keesing does not go on from there to reach my radical conclusion that all ethnography is fiction. I argue that any ethnographic monograph has much more in common with an historical novel than with a treatise in natural science and also that the still widespread belief that the pre-literate societies of classical ethnography were static and outside history is wholly unjustified.

The words tribe and tribal are now seldom used by British social anthropologists but this is a recent development. Hose and McDougall's *The Pagan Tribes of Borneo* (1912) may seem pretty old hat, and even Radcliffe-Brown's *Social Organisation of Australian Tribes* (1931); but Fortes' two-volume classic is still widely read; it calls the Tallensi a 'Trans-Volta Tribe'. Gluckman wrote about 'tribes' in the mid-1960s.[1] Keesing's aforesaid 1981 textbook is about 'The Tribal World'. And so on.

Nevertheless the word tribe, like the word native, has now come to seem derogatory. This is because the expressions primitive tribe/savage tribe were formerly used to denote people who were presumed to be low down in an imaginary hierarchy of social evolution. The difference was believed to be physical as well as mental. Radcliffe-Brown was still writing about the Australian Aborigines as prototypical representatives of 'the lower races' as late as 1945.[2]

As a consequence, all kinds of euphemistic circumlocutions are now used in place of the simple term 'tribe'. The most common are 'people' and 'traditional society'. 'People' seems to me too vague; 'traditional society', with its suggestion of stasis, is the target of my attack. Hence 'tribal ethnography'. Generally speaking tribal ethnographers concentrate their attention on communities in which the level of literacy among the older members of the adult population is very low and in which there is a very marked gap between the technological sophistication and resources of the ethnographers themselves and those whom they are studying.

34

In the past, tribal ethnographers have been primarily interested in the contrast between European culture and non-European culture. By the time the ethnographer came on the scene the empirical contrast had usually become blurred. In order to bring things into sharper focus, palpably European elements in the ethnographer's notes were omitted from the published record or else treated as an alien contamination grafted onto whatever was there before.

Among the evidence that is thus omitted are nearly all references to the cultural background of the ethnographer him(her)self. Yet there are many situations, both in the distant and recent past, in which the ethnographer's personal 'cargo' must have had drastic repercussions. As anthropologists we need to pay closer attention to such distortions.

It is now becoming fashionable to say that the field worker should 'give an historical dimension to the ethnography'. But what should this imply? History is about change; one thing happens after another, but the things that happen are different things. History does not repeat itself. By contrast, ethnography is about cultural differences that are ordinarily presumed to be stable over long periods of time; the manners and customs of primitive tribes are endlessly repeated; year after year, lifetime after lifetime. Or so it is said.

In a celebrated radio interview given in 1961,[3] which he has never repudiated, Lévi-Strauss made this issue definitional. Anthropologists study 'cold' societies that run on and on like clockwork; historians study 'hot', hierarchical societies that work like steam engines and in which change is self-generating through internal contradiction. I do not agree. But the presumed relationship between history and ethnography itself has a history that deserves attention.

For the ancient Greeks ethnographic description was a part of geography rather than history. Maps were vague but the diverse peoples of the world could be distinguished by their customs. Accounts of such alien customs often derived from the principle that the barbarian others must always behave in a manner that is the obverse of that of the civilized Greeks. The female society of warlike Amazons who reduced their male partners to slavery and then killed off all their male children is a case in point.

Ethnography became more closely linked with (fictitious) history after Columbus' discovery of the Americas. How had the American Indians got there? The diverse and often bizarre answers to this question (e.g. they were survivors from a separate pre-Adamite creation, their ancestors had walked across Asia from Mount Ararat, and so on) are important in the history of anthropology because they set people thinking about how the tribal peoples of the world had come to be the way they are, and about the criteria that might be used for applying the distinction savage/civilized.

These pseudo-historical theories of social development fell into two broad classes. During most of the eighteenth century and again during the latter half of the nineteenth century, evolutionism was in fashion. The customs of Primeval Man had evolved over time like the species in a Darwinian tree. Europeans with their high technology, superior forms of government and true religion were at the top of the tree. Other peoples with other customs had got side-tracked onto minor branches and had been left behind on the general ladder of progress. This type of theory fitted very well with the age of European colonial expansion since the non-White local inhabitants of the colonial territories could be rated as inferior by nature. All the ethnographic facts reported of these inferior peoples were then treated as markers of their inferiority.

The other broad class of theory that is still favoured by the archaeologists and was fashionable among the anthropologists from about 1890 onwards was diffusionism. It was assumed that the customs observed by ethnographers had always come from somewhere else. If the evidence recorded in locality 'A' appeared to be similar to that recorded in locality 'B' then this proved that parts of the two populations had migrated to where they are now from a common original homeland. Most British social anthropologists now shy away from such arguments but their predecessors at the beginning of this century called themselves ethnologists; they claimed to be pre-historians who studied the past movements of peoples and of cultural traits.

These two types of theory, the evolutionist and the diffusionist, had one major feature in common. Both assumed that mankind was originally made up of large numbers of races that are distinguishable in much the same way as species of birds and mammals. They are of different genetic origin; they speak different languages; they have different manners and customs: they do not mix. Or if they do mix this is an aberration brought about by the impact of colonialism and the diffusion of individual traits. A very late example of this racialist doctrine, which amounts to an unintended self-caricature, is provided by Hutton (1965).[4]

But fashions change. During the early years of this century the general style of British ethnography had been set by W.H.R. Rivers who had ended up as an ardent diffusionist disciple of Elliot Smith. But by 1924 Rivers was dead and Malinowski had launched his functionalist seminar at the LSE. The reconstruction of pre-history was no longer seen as the anthropologist's prime objective. The new purpose was to gain understanding of how tribal societies had worked before the coming of the Europeans.

Even to start on such an enterprise the ethnographer had to assume that it is possible to know about what had been the case in the past by observing a different state of affairs in the present. Despite the obvious flaw in such a premiss the specious guarantee of stability provided by colonial rule at first gave this new, sociological style of enquiry an appearance of scientific objectivity that diffusionist guesswork had lacked. But the Second World War broke up the hegemony of the European colonial powers and in the aftermath of that historical cataclysm the functionalists' rejection of 'conjectural history' has come to seem sterile. History and social change have once again become central to the anthropologist's enquiries.

But how should we *now* distinguish history and ethnography? Perhaps we should not distinguish the two categories at all. But in common parlance the distinction certainly exists.

History is about the past and the sequences of events that it records are supposed to have actually happened. History is thereby distinguished from legend or myth. Such history necessarily depends on the existence of written records or datable artifacts or stratified archaeological remains.

By contrast, ethnography records what has been directly observed by the ethnographer; it refers to the present. This opposition is easy to understand but it does not fit easily with the empirical data. For example, a datable historical document may contain observations that appear to match up with modern ethnographic records, thus suggesting long-term cultural stability. Raymond Firth claims that records of early European contacts with Tikopia have this quality.

But much more relevant for my present purposes is the belief that ethnographic records, made by direct observation during the present century, can, with suitable editing, be treated as referring to a 'traditional culture' that was free of European influence and had existed from time immemorial.

The details of what the ethnographer reports as survivals from the 'traditional past' may be derived from many different sources but the story is always phrased as if it were an objective description of known facts, rather than the author's personal interpretation of ambiguous history. If European traders, Christian missionaries, and colonial administrators are discussed at all, they are perceived as having a destructive impact on the tribal society that was there before. They are the prime cause of 'detribalization'. Indian and Chinese traders or Buddhist and Islamic missionaries or the ethnographer him(her)self are not usually accorded this privileged disruptive status.

These characteristics can be illustrated from the classics of British social anthropology to which I shall now refer but they are also typical of much more recent work.

I consider that my teacher Raymond Firth, now aged 86, is by a wide margin the greatest living ethnographer. Although I am arguing that, with the passage of time, Firth's assumptions about the nature of ethnographic reality have become open to question, I am not suggesting that they are naive. On the contrary, Firth's treatment of his materials is the finest of its kind.

Two of Firth's key assumptions are (1) that 'traditional' Tikopia society had objective reality and (2) that it was more or less impervious to historical change. My contrary assumption is that all the traditional societies of the ethnographic map are products of the ethnographer's imagination. In *this* respect a monograph in social anthropology is no different from a monograph in history.

Tikopia is a tiny Pacific island roughly 3 square miles in total area. In 1928, when Firth first arrived, it had a population of around 1200. The inhabitants spoke a Polynesian language quite closely related to that of the New Zealand Maori, which Firth already knew. Firth has now been describing the 'traditional culture' of Tikopia in the most meticulous detail for almost 60 years. His first Tikopia publication dates from 1930;[5] his latest, a full-scale dictionary of the 'traditional' Tikopia language, appeared in 1985.[6] In this dictionary 'loan words', which Firth does not consider to be authentic Polynesian, are put in an Appendix. In between there have been eight major monographs and scores of shorter pieces. Firth reports that in 1928 about half the population of Tikopia were baptized Christians but in his earlier Tikopia monographs he pays little attention to this fact. Even in *Social Change in Tikopia* (1959), which is explicitly intended to point up the key differences between Tikopia society in 1929 and Tikopia society in 1952, (when 100 per cent of the population was nominally Christian), Firth continues to write as if he believed that if it hadn't been for the missionaries and the administration, no changes would have occurred at all.

Firth's belief that he can present to his readers an account of an intrinsically stable, but fast-disappearing, social system that he was privileged to observe 57 years ago was shared by nearly all the ethnographers of his time. What is unusual in Firth's case is that he has been back to Tikopia on two subsequent occasions and has discussed his view of the 'traditional society' with various Tikopia notables living both in Tikopia and elsewhere. He does not disguise the fact that when the behaviour of contemporary Tikopia corresponds to his own ethnographic record, the individuals concerned may be play acting. They may be self-consciously seeking to preserve what *they* believe to be traditional custom. But Firth seems to assume that these Tikopian ideas about their own past must have originated in local, and very ancient, tradition. This is the obvious presumption but there are other possibilities.

Here is a trivial example of what I have in mind. The symposium volume edited by Maurice Bloch, entitled *Political Language and Oratory in Traditional Society* (1975), (note the title and the date), includes a paper by Firth on 'Speech making and authority in Tikopia'. It is mainly concerned with a secular institution known as the *fono*, a word which, in the Samoan dictionary of 1852, is glossed as 'legislative assembly'. Firth makes it clear that his own ethnography in this case dates from 1952 and 1966 and *not* from 1928–9. The only *fono* he observed on his first visit to Tikopia was part of the annual religious cycle 'The Work of the Gods'.[7]

Firth is meticulous in distinguishing hearsay from what he actually observed and he himself remarks that: 'I think it significant that whereas no (secular) *fono* were held in Tikopia during my first stay there in 1928–9, there were many during the famine period in 1952–3, and several even in my short stay in 1966'. So he evidently assumes that if there *had* been (secular) *fono* to observe in 1928–9, they would have been ethnographically identical to what he observed in 1952 and 1966.

Firth explains the absence of secular *fono* from his first set of notebooks by arguing that the pre-1928 *fono* (which he did not witness), was a 'traditional' cultural device for meeting crisis situations: 'With new problems, involving more intensive relations with the outside society . . . public meetings and public speeches became more necessary than in the times when the traditional problems and institutions operated in a very local environment'. Well perhaps that is so, but it *might* be that, far from being a part of 'traditional' Tikopia culture, the *fono* that Firth witnessed during his later visits were an innovative response to colonialism and perhaps even to ideas that Firth, with his wide knowledge of comparative Polynesian ethnography, had himself introduced into the thinking of high-ranking Tikopia individuals! Firth would say that this is ridiculous and it is certainly true that the word *fono* was part of the Tikopia lexicon in 1928, but did it then have any kind of secular meaning?

Despite the triviality, the principle seems to me important. Until very recently it would not have occurred to even the most experienced ethnographers, even when working in a tiny area of the map such as Tikopia, that they might be 'contaminating' their own evidence simply by being there at all. But what I am in effect arguing is that it is impossible for any ethnographer ever to record 'uncontaminated' evidence. 'Traditional culture' in the sense used by Firth is simply not available for inspection and it never has been. The observer is *always* a key part of the *changing* scene that he/she observes, and this is especially the case when the number of persons involved is very small and the economic resources of the observees technically impoverished.

Most professional field research is a co-operative effort between the anthropological observer and the 'tribal' observee. The observer learns from the observee and vice versa. But, that being so, how many of the 'objective' observations of earlier ethnographers should be rated as a reflexive feedback of what the observer has unintentionally suggested in the first place? Here is another trivial example, this time from my own records.

The Christian missionaries (Catholic and Baptist), and also the earliest British administrators, who worked among the Kachins of North Burma at the end of the nineteenth century all reported that the Kachin name for the Supreme Being is Karai Kasang and it was duly so recorded in the dictionary of the Jingphaw (Kachin) language published in 1906.[8] The French Catholic missionary, Father Gilhodes, devoted a whole chapter of his ethnographic monograph[9] to the subject largely because he had been given special instructions by the German-Catholic anthropologist Pater Schmidt to look out for evidence of an original autochthonous belief in a High God. But no cult or mythology of Karai Kasang was recorded by any of the early ethnographers and Gilhodes notes that Karai Kasang is quite unlike any analogous term in neighbouring languages. It seems to me almost (though not quite!) certain that the name Karai Kasang is a corruption of some version of Christian/*Chrétien*. But should the author of the Kachin dictionary have treated it as a 'loan word'? Certainly not! Modern Kachin Christians are distinguished from non-Christians by the fact that they worship Karai Kasang.

As I have indicated, the belief that observer and observed belong to totally different social worlds is a hangover from the idea that ethnographic enquiry is an 'objective' science on a par with zoology. I find it surprising that ethnographers of the present century could have been so confident that this was the kind of enterprise on which they were engaged. But it was so. An interesting example is provided by Ian Hogbin's *Experiments in Civilisation: the Effects of European Culture on a Native Community in the Solomon Islands* (1939). Hogbin, like Firth, was a pupil of Malinowski. His study of Malaita is divided into three sections: The Past, The Present, The Future. The Future is simply an optimistic thirty-page eulogy of the social benefits of indirect rule within a system of colonialism. The Present, which is all about exploitation by traders, plantation owners, administrators, and missionaries, describes what Hogbin actually observed. The Past is a reconstruction. Hogbin assures his readers that:

> We now know what native life was like in Malaita before the coming of the white man . . . In most areas, however, Western civilisation had made profound changes, and my aim now is to examine how the aboriginal culture has been modified in consequence.

So The Past is an invention of the author; yet it is The Past that provides Hogbin with his images of social reality; he writes about it in the present tense.

If this kind of ethnography is to seem credible, the content of 'traditional custom' has to be selected with care so as to fit in with the ethnographer's prejudices. As we have seen, Firth, who is a committed atheist, has consistently belittled the possibility that the presence of Christians on Tikopia could have influenced his own observations.

In a similar way, Malinowski, who was from the start committed to a belief in his own originality, manages to ignore the fact that in 1916 there had been Christian missionaries in the Trobriand Islands for over twenty years and European traders for even longer.

In contrast to the atheist Firth, Evans-Pritchard was an ardent Roman Catholic convert. The main texts of his original accounts of the Nuer make hardly any reference to the dense population of Roman Catholic missionaries to whom the author elsewhere expresses his debt. The same is true of Godfrey Lienhardt's account of the Dinka who are immediate neighbours of the Nuer. Lienhardt was another Catholic convert. But various 'traditional' Nuer and Dinka religions that these authors describe[10] appear to have a number of strikingly Jesuitical characteristics. And then there is visual imagery. Malinowski and 'the ethnographer's tent' occasionally appear in his Trobriand photographs (most of which were taken by the trader Billy Hancock) but no other item of European origin does so except Malinowski's typewriter. Firth's early photographs of Tikopia never reveal a European artifact. Evans-Pritchard's Nuer are nearly all naked. But we know from the writings of Francis Mading Deng,[11] who holds a PhD in social anthropology and is the son of the former Dinka Paramount Chief, that the first motor car arrived in Dinkaland before Evans-Pritchard began his Nuer researches and that at Wau, the Catholic missionary headquarters, there was a full-scale, brick-built romanesque cathedral. All the individuals in Dr Deng's photographs are fully clothed.

Incidentally, in Hogbin's account of Malaita the photographs that illustrate The Present are packed with images that are of blatantly European origin but fourteen out of the fifteen pictures illustrating The Past also contain at least one European object. It is plain that when Hogbin's (1939) text uses the present tense to describe the imaginary past he has to cheat!

This is not intended as hostile criticism. This was the task we were set: describe the institutions of the local 'traditional tribal society'. To this end the ethnographer was entitled to ignore all 'obviously recent' European influences. Only in one respect do I claim any superiority over most of my anthropological contemporaries. When I came to study the Kachin, it quickly became obvious that although the existing ethnographic literature was full of references to tribes there were in fact no tribes and no tribal boundaries. A central theme in my published study (*Political Systems of Highland Burma*, 1954) was that an individual might start life as a Kachin and fetch up as a Shan, or vice versa. In the concluding pages, I expressed considerable scepticism concerning the ethnographic validity of the various monographs by J.H. Hutton, J.P. Mills, and others about the tribal peoples of Assam.[12] But at that time I still accepted the conventional view that my task was to discuss an indigenous social system of which I myself was not a part. Thus the missionaries and the colonial administrators and the British military recruiting officers were not really part of my story. I see now that this was a mistake.

And this is a view that is now becoming very general, especially in the area of visual ethnography and material culture. The capacity of ethnographic film makers to reinvent tribal societies that have long ago ceased to exist has made it much more obvious than before that most ethnographic monographs are fiction even if the author intended otherwise. Furthermore, wider familiarity with nineteenth-century photographic archives has shown how impossible it is to draw a sharp demarcation line between the 'detribalised' present and the 'tribal' past.

In the autumn of 1986 the Museum of Mankind (which is the Department of Ethnography of the British Museum) had three special exhibitions that were directly relevant to this theme.

The first was entitled 'Treasures of the Museum of Mankind'. Rare ethnographic objects were displayed in isolation with the minimum of contextual explanation. The objects in question were all entirely 'uncontaminated' by European influence. There were no photographs. Until a few years ago nearly all exhibitions of ethnographic artifacts were displayed in this way. They were treated like works of art, the value of which lay in the authenticity of their provenance.

The second exhibition had been set up with the collaboration of the artist Eduardo Paolozzi. It was a mixture of constructions by Paolozzi himself; old photographs from the colonial era in which Europeans as well as 'natives' were very prominent; material objects from the 'tribal' world almost all heavily contaminated by European influence. Detailed comment is impossible but the White colonial administrators in their preposterous white solar topees were certainly quite as interesting as ethnographic images as the Nigerian chiefs with their ebony walking sticks and European-style suitings.

The third exhibition was of Kalabari funerary screens from the delta area of Nigeria. They date from the eighteenth and nineteenth centuries when the Kalabari were flourishing middlemen in the slave trade. The imagery of the screens is a wonderful combination of African and European elements. The historical background of the Kalabari from the sixteenth century until independence is well documented by the log books of European sea captains. At the exhibition, this history is summarized in a single-sheet hand-out. Between 1500 and 1960 nothing had remained stable for more than a few years at a time. At no time during the last 450 years has there existed a 'traditional' Kalabari society.

The point that I am trying to make is that Malcolm McLeod, the Keeper of the Museum of Mankind, is as keen as ever to demonstrate to his visitors the enormous variety of material objects that are in his charge, but he is clearly no longer interested in showing that the people who made these objects were outside history.

We now understand much better than formerly just how culturally destructive was the Third World's experience of the colonial expansion of Europe but, precisely because of this destruction, the polarization of traditional/post-traditional, tribal/detribalized has often seemed sharper than before.

Many ethnographers continue to write their monographs and journal articles as if they believed that the original pre-colonial tribal society still existed inside a carapace of colonial and post-colonial bureaucracy and western technology. Chip the colonial shell away and you will get back to the traditional core.

The methodological problem here is very fundamental. The functionalists of the Malinowski/Firth era wanted to demonstrate that the culture they were studying (Trobriands, Tikopia, etc.) had an organic unity; everything fitted together like the gear wheels of a mechanical watch. But this could only be shown, even approximately, if the time depth of the data was very shallow. If long-term diachronic sequences were to be taken into account then traditional culture had to be static or else the doctrine of functional interdependence had to be reformulated as structural transformation after the manner of Michel Foucault. Diachronic historical studies cannot be accommodated to synchronic functionalist studies; the functionalists were obliged by their acceptance of Durkheim's thesis of the organic unity of society to ignore historical change.

A later generation of anthropologists have indeed substituted the algebra of structural transformation for the missing sequences of recorded history. But either way the past becomes a fiction invented by the ethnographer.

But why should anthropologists, or at any rate *some* anthropologists, want to believe that pre-colonial social systems had been stable over time? In the modern world, wherever there is any evidence in the form of literature or archaeological residues, the record of the past is a record of rapid change. Why should it have been any different in pre-literate societies?

Nineteenth-century ethnographers felt a commitment to social stability because they equated the variety of 'cultures' with a postulated variety of 'races'. The races of man were thus very numerous and were talked about as if they were virtually equivalent to zoological species; they could not mix, they had hard edges like billiard balls. In the circumstances of colonialism, European culture bumped into non-European culture without merging. Even in the late 1930s respected anthropologists still wrote about 'the study of culture contact' as if 'cultures' were separate unit entities.[13]

Furthermore, it was assumed that the primitive societies studied by European ethnographers in remote corners of the map could somehow be regarded as survivals from an earlier epoch. While 'we' had moved on to greater technical, economic, and political mastery over the environment, these 'other' people had somehow stood still, awaiting detribalization and incorporation into the cheap-labour market required by colonial capitalism.

Colonial governments usually encouraged the various agents of detribalization; this was the path of progress. In this they have been imitated by their post-colonial Marxist successors. But the anthropologists have usually (but not always) adopted a conservationist approach. Just as in a zoo, rare species of mammal are preserved out of curiosity or for the entertainment of the visitor, so also specimens of antique 'cultures' could be preserved on native reservations under the supervision of white-skinned jailors. And even if it was too late to do anything about preserving the past you could write books about what the past had been like, or at any rate about what you imagined it had been like.

This is all familiar country but it is easy to forget that something like 95 per cent of what passes for the ethnography of 'traditional' American Indian cultures derives from research carried out on native reservations and that, in most other parts of the world, ethnographers of high repute have been much less than frank about the thinness of their data and the extent to which their cultural descriptions have depended upon imaginative reconstruction. Radcliffe-Brown is said to have interviewed many of his Andamanese informants in a prison; some of his Australian kinship data was collected in a hospital for venereal diseases.[14] Well why not? But I would like to have been told.

Admirers of the work of Claude Lévi-Strauss very rightly draw attention to his marvellous ethnographic erudition but few of them consider the level of fiction that is entailed when, in the pages of *Mythologiques*, the author cites, in French, a one-paragraph summary of an Amazonian Indian myth that is a translation of a similar summary made by a Portuguese Catholic missionary many years previously, before tape recorders were invented. We know from comparable materials in recent ethnography that the 'original' vernacular version of these brief 'summaries' would probably have taken several hours to recite and that they would have contained a vast variety of detail that the Portuguese missionaries never recorded at all.

But my basic complaint against Lévi-Strauss is not the fictional nature of his materials. After all, I hold that *all* ethnography is fictional. What I object to is Lévi-Strauss's opposition between 'cold' static, primitive societies, which 'tend to remain indefinitely in their initial state' and 'hot' modern societies, which are constantly evolving because of Marxist-type internal contradictions resulting from 'different forms of social hierarchy'.[15]

On the contrary, I insist that primitive societies, however defined, are, like modern societies, caught up in history. Everything is always changing. History only begins with literacy because without a written (or archaeological) record there can be no historical evidence. But we cannot assume that just because we have no evidence of social change therefore there was in fact no social change. A changeless cultural system would be a complete anomaly.

To return to my title. There can be no future for tribal ethnography of a purportedly objective kind. Ethnographers must admit the reflexivity of their activities; they must become autobiographical. But with this changed orientation, ethnographers should be able to contribute to the better understanding of historical ethnography.

A case in point, about which much has been written during the past few years, is the Hawaiian reaction to the arrival of Captain Cook in 1778. The event and its consequences were recorded in great detail by a variety of Europeans who assumed that what they were observing was the 'traditional custom' of Ancient Hawaii. Marshall Sahlins, the principal contemporary commentator on these matters also makes this assumption.[16] He argues that what was a dramatic and tragic novelty for the Europeans was only an annually repeated ritual for the Hawaiians. But that is impossible. In objective fact nothing like this had ever happened before. What the Europeans observed was an Hawaiian improvisation. The Hawaiians declared that Cook was an incarnation of the God Lono who was graciously participating in the annual 'Easter' festival that was then in progress. This worked all right as long as Cook, by accident, fulfilled correctly his assigned role; but then, still ignorant of what he was doing (in Hawaiian eyes), he transgressed the rules and was sacrificed as an offering to himself (as Lono).

Other religions, for example, Judaism, Christianity – allow, in theory, for the appearance of the Messiah or of God incarnate, but only in theory. Even in Polynesia (and despite anything J.G. Frazer and Sahlins may have said) God does not ordinarily appear in flesh and blood form in a huge ship of a type that no-one has ever seen. Cook had drastically altered Hawaiian mytho/history even before he went ashore.

This special case exemplifies a very general situation. Myth is not just badly remembered history. But we have no grounds for supposing that mythology is unchanging or that it incorporates no history at all. Stephen Hugh-Jones assures me that in the past all sorts of 'White' undesirables – slave hunters, rubber extractors, rogue traders – have become assimilated into Barasana 'tradition'. As like as not Stephen and his wife Christine have by now themselves achieved this semi-divine status.

Historical ethnography is not just a matter of recognizing that the way 'we', the ethnographers, see 'them', the people about whom we write our books, changes over time; there is also the question of how they see us. We need to look again at the mythology and traditions of 'tribal peoples' to see what they can tell us about their *changing* evaluations of the others (i.e. the foreigners, especially the Europeans).

Notes

1. Fortes (1945), (1949); Gluckman (1965) Chapter 1.
2. Radcliffe-Brown (1945) p. 41.
3. Lévi-Strauss (1961) Chapter 3.
4. Hutton (1965).
5. Firth (1930).
6. Firth (1985).
7. Firth (1975).
8. Hanson (1906).
9. Gilhodes (1922).
10. Evans-Pritchard (1956); Lienhardt (1961).
11. Deng (1972).
12. Most of the monographs in question are listed in the bibliography to Hutton (1965).
13. *Africa* (1938).
14. Untraced assertion by Lidio Cipriani; Daisy Bates' unpublished journal.
15. Quotes from English version of Lévi-Strauss (1961).

References

Africa (1938) 'Methods of study of culture contact in Africa' (IIALC Memorandum XV reprinted from articles in *Africa* vols. VII, VIII, IX).
Deng, F.M. (1972) *The Dinka of the Sudan*, New York: Holt, Rinehart & Winston.
Evans-Pritchard, E.E. (1956) *Nuer Religion*, Oxford: Clarendon Press.
Firth, R. (1930) 'Report on research in Tikopia' *Oceania* vol. 1.
Firth, R. (1959) *Social Change in Tikopia*, London: George Allen & Unwin.
Firth, R. (1975) 'Speech making and authority in Tikopia', in M. Bloch (ed.) *Political Language and Oratory in Traditional Society*.
Firth, R. (1985) *Tikopia–English Dictionary*, Aukland: Aukland University Press.
Fortes, M. (1945) *The Dynamic of Clanship among the Tallensi*, Oxford: Oxford University Press.
Fortes, M. (1949) *The Web of Kinship among the Tallensi*, Oxford: Oxford University Press.
Gilhodes, C. (1922) *The Kachins: Religion and Customs*, Calcutta: Catholic Orphan Press (translated from several articles in French which appeared in *Anthropos* from 1904 onwards).
Gluckman, M. (1965) *The Ideas in Barotse Jurisprudence*, New Haven: Yale University Press.
Hanson, O. (1906) *A Dictionary of the Kachin Language*, Rangoon: American Baptist Mission Press.
Hogbin, H.I. (1939) *Experiments in Civilisation: The Effects of European Culture on a Native Community in the Solomon Islands*, London: George Routledge & Sons.
Hose, C. and McDougall, W. (1912) *The Pagan Tribes of Borneo*, 2 vols, London: Macmillan.
Hutton, J.H. (1965) 'The mixed culture of the Naga tribes', *Journal of the Royal Anthropological Institute* vol. 95: 15–39.
Keesing, R.M. (1981) *Cultural Anthropology: A Contemporary Perspective*, 2nd edn, New York: Holt, Rinehart & Winston.
Leach, E.R. (1954) *Political Systems of Highland Burma*, London: Bell.
Lévi-Strauss, C. (1961) *Entretiens avec Claude Lévi-Strauss*, G. Charbonnier (ed.),

Paris: Plon. (English version *Conversations with Claude Lévi-Strauss* (1969), London: Jonathan Cape).

Lienhardt, G. (1961) *Divinity and Experience: The Religion of the Dinka*, Oxford: Clarendon Press.

Radcliffe-Brown, A.R. (1931) *The Social Organisation of Australian Tribes* (Oceania Monographs no.1).

Radcliffe-Brown, A.R. (1945) 'Religion and society', *Journal of the Royal Anthropological Institute* 75.

Sahlins, M. (1985) *Islands of History*, Chicago: University of Chicago Press.

47

Chapter three

Fiction and Fact in Ethnography
Raymond Firth

The interest of modern social anthropologists in ethnography is complex. A systematic record, based upon observation of the institutions, behaviour patterns, and concepts of the people of a society or community is looked upon in a sophisticated way, not given any particular authority but seen as a reflection or illustration of the ethnographer's personal interpretation of the situations observed. It has long been realized that any ethnographical text is a *crafted* job. To turn observation of – or participation in – a turbulent field of social action into a written account that can only be a summary demands much selection, with possible bias. The ethnographical text is constructed by elaborate processes of winnowing, imaginative inference, identification of the abstract in the concrete, recognition of pattern in event. However faithful be the intent, the text clearly cannot be just a 'representation' of the society. Some critics would go further, and stress an ethnography as an ideological product, a kind of mask for concealing notions of power or the moral ideas of allegory. Edmund Leach's idea of ethnography as 'fiction' seems to embody some elements of all these approaches.

'Fiction' has various shades of meaning, but those commonly accepted from the seventeenth century onwards include 'statements proceeding from mere invention' or those 'feigning an imaginary existence'. Such gross glosses are not relevant here. The Trobriands are not Laputa, Tikopia is not Lilliput. In a more subtle sense, however, the Leachian proposition might be defended. In a legal sense a fiction is a supposition known to be at variance with fact but accepted by convention, presumably for convenience. In this sense it may be argued, as Leach has done, that much of the older ethnography has presented descriptions of exotic societies that by a kind of tacit consensus have been defective in important respects – too holistic, too static, ignoring external influences and internal changes. In particular, Leach sees the concept of 'traditional society' as an ethnographic fiction (see p. 37). Many of us may admit the occasional lapse of such kind in our attempts to offer a coherent brief picture. But a gap or an inadequacy is not necessarily fictional.

In his zeal to make his case, Leach sometimes gets the facts wrong. For instance, after a most generous tribute to my own ethnographical writing he states that 'with the passage of time, Firth's assumptions about the nature of ethnographic reality have become open to question' (see p. 37). This is delicately put, and I would go along with it to the point of saying that I like to think all my assumptions have always been open to question. And those about ethnographic reality have become less assured, though I hope more sophisticated, as time has gone on. But Leach has selected two 'key' assumptions that he thinks have been incorrect. The first lies in the use of the term 'traditional'. This is a convenient but admittedly slippery term. In its ordinary dictionary meaning, tradition refers to a statement, belief, or practice transmitted (especially orally) from generation to generation. Leach seems to imply that as used by me the term traditional means also unchanging or unchanged, and that as such, the Tikopia society I have described, so far from being an objective reality, is a product of my imagination. But in using the term I have applied it rather carefully to those social features that, by information given to me in detail, appeared to have been in vogue in past generations for a considerable time – from house forms and fishing practices to modes of burial and sacred songs. When one is taking part in solemn dances, in religious ritual, or in ceremonial exchanges that one is assured have been part of Tikopia usage 'from olden times', it seems merely eccentric to argue that all this, or the society of which they have been characteristic, is merely 'a product of the ethnographer's imagination'. But to state that these customs have been transmitted from past generations is not to assert that they have never changed.

The second 'key assumption' attributed by Leach to my description of 'traditional' Tikopia society is that it was 'more or less impervious to change' (see p. 38). I find this an odd view. In *History and Traditions of Tikopia* (Firth, 1961) I discussed internal upheavals – struggles by different groups for land and power, with consequent changes of control, on the basis of Tikopia narratives that, plausible or not (and many seemed quite plausible) at least pointed to the feasibility of historical change. And in various early publications I examined the effects of population growth, ecological disaster, labour recruitment abroad, and Christian-missionary influence. In 1940, in *Work of the Gods in Tikopia*, after considering the effects of the defection of one chief who became a Christian upon the structure of the pagan ritual cycle, I put forward a general view about Polynesian history:

It may be put forward as a proposition for the study of Polynesian cultures that these have been much more flexible in the past than has often been assumed, and that what we have to consider in any single island group is not merely a mixture or fusion of elements from other groups but a very high degree of local variation, arising in part from consciously motivated individual change, and in part from the establishment of errors and defections from traditional practice as recognised cultural forms . . . Polynesian cultures must be regarded not as static arrangements resting upon an original fusion of diverse elements, but as a dynamic arrangement with a tendency to variation perceptible in each generation, and with a selective process by which some at least of these variations are built into the cultural system.

(Firth 1940:13)

So much for the assumption of imperviousness to historical change.[1]

I am not much impressed by blanket pronouncements such as 'all ethnography is fiction'. One might say equally 'all ethnography is autobiography', or 'all ethnography is self-advertisement'. Each contains an element of truth, but the baby has been thrown out with the bathwater. Such all-embracing pronouncements belong to a much wider trend of opinion that is perceptible most obviously in literary criticism and in reflection upon history. In such work, attention now is focused on the persona of the author as revealed by the record, or as contributing to its interpretation. Hence a view that all biography smacks of autobiography. The issue goes much deeper. It is part of a broad anti-positivism, a rejection of empiricism, and what has been termed the 'documentary model of knowledge'. Sometimes it goes further, to a questioning of notions of reality itself. My own position here is still that of a modified empiricist. The world may be an illusion – I know of no means of proving it is not. But it is expedient to behave *as if* there be a substantial reality that can be encountered, with chartable effect and some possibility of prediction.

Anthropologically, one implication of explorations of this sceptical kind is that they have lessened our assurance about the nature of our propositions. In my own case, I have always seen my generalizations about Tikopia society as tentative, subject to methodological qualification. But in recent years I have come to see them as even more problematic than I used to envisage. I had not been unaware of alternative ways of looking at the phenomena, but had tended perhaps to dismiss them too easily.

The significance of personal elements in interpretation has emerged, as I see it, particularly with the growth of interest in 'cognitive anthropology'. When anthropologists were busy charting the still relatively unknown structures of lineage systems, kinship networks, exchange relations, or even describing the qualities of a novel range of putative spirits, such personal elements did not seem to the fore in interpretation. But when they came to examine concepts of space and time, of superiority and inferiority, of identity and discrimination, of good and evil, then the personal stance of the enquirer became more significant. When in 1969 David Eyde and I disagreed about the way in which Tikopia organize space (Eyde, 1969) it became clear to me that we were arguing not about facts but about the differential emphasis to be placed upon facts, and the figurative forms that could be assigned to their relationships. I wrote then:

> Anthropological theory, like any other, is built upon imaginative insight, the perception of relationships and of pattern in relationships not previously recognised, which therefore stimulates further enquiry. But the line between insight, which is controlled and susceptible of validation, and speculation, which is not, is very thin, and opinions can differ about the validity of the evidence.
>
> (Firth, 1969:65–6)

In estimating how a personal stance may affect the interpretation of an ethnography, early social or religious conditioning and later professional training may well be important. But to me that mysterious elusive element called temperament seems often to be crucial. And here is the crunch of the problem.

To say that ethnography is fiction, or allegory, or autobiography, is not enough. How is it to be distinguished from other forms of fiction, allegory, or autobiography? If it be admitted that there is any substratum of actuality in the ethnographic account, how is this to be identified? If the concept of a 'traditional society' is vitiated by a failure to stress the elements of western culture that have intruded, does this mean the written ethnography is just a bogus record? An estimate of the degree of penetration achieved by western elements is itself a personal matter, perhaps a reflection of temperamental convictions about the historical necessity of change! The issues are confused, not clarified by the 'fiction' concepts, unless some criteria for sorting out the 'fictional' elements are demonstrated. The issue may be phrased another way. In all ethnographic record the representation of *alter* is mingled with that of *ego*, that is, with conscious and unconscious representations of the self of the author. But are *alter* and *ego* inextricably mixed? They are certainly hard to separate. But I would argue that they are conceptually and to a considerable degree empirically separable – that there are observable events, some of which can be participated in, and can be described with a high degree of objectivity, not completely, but in significant detail. This description requires abstraction, i.e. a personal input of imaginative perception of pattern. But if observation and record have been careful, according to well-known systematic procedures, another interpreter can separate off much of the personal element and arrive at a different set of conclusions. If all were 'fiction', this would not be possible.

Note

1. Leach has certainly misread the record at one point. He states (p. 38) that in
   1952 100 per cent of the Tikopia population was nominally Christian. In fact
   there were then still over 200 pagans (Firth, 1970:343), including three chiefs,
   and the annual cycle of pagan rites was still carried on, attended by Spillius
   and myself. I have given elaborate documentation of the changes in Tikopia
   institutions due to Christianity, including a study in modifications in ritual
   between 1929 and 1952 (Firth and Spillius, 1963).

References

Eyde, D.B. (1969) 'On Tikopia social space', *Bijdragen* 125:40–63.

Firth, R. (1940) *The Work of the Gods in Tikopia*, LSE monographs in social
anthropology, nos 1 and 2, London: Lund Humphries, 2nd edn 1967, Athlone.

Firth, R. (1961) *History and Traditions of Tikopia*, Wellington: Polynesian Society.

Firth, R. (1969) 'Tikopia social space. A commentary', *Bijdragen* 125:64–70.

Firth, R. (1970) *Rank and Religion in Tikopia*, London: Allen & Unwin.

Firth, R. and Spillius, J. (1963) 'A study in ritual modification: the work of the
gods in Tikopia in 1929 and 1952', Occasional paper no. 14, RAI, London.

Chapter four

Wãrĩbi and the White Men: history and myth in northwest Amazonia
Stephen Hugh-Jones

If contact between cultures is as old as society itself, that which took place between Europe and the Americas after 1492 was none the less unique. For the first and last time two whole populations, living in separate physical and mental worlds and previously unaware of the other's existence, met face to face. Reports from the New World gave rise to intense intellectual debates in Europe. At issue was how new human beings could be accommodated within an established cosmology and theory of man, and the answers to this question transformed the anthropology of the time and laid the foundations of the anthropology of today.

The discovery of America was the result of European mercantile expansion and, in his book *Europe and the Peoples Without History*, Eric Wolf examines the impact of this expansion on the world's tribal peoples. He aims to give back history to those who have been denied it, but the history he provides is doubly our own: not only is it dominated by our European world but it is also seen through our western eyes. This is clear when he states that 'the global processes set in motion by European expansion constitute *their* history as well. There are thus no "contemporary ancestors", no people without history, no peoples – to use Lévi-Strauss' phrase – "whose histories have remained cold" ' (Wolf, 1982:385).

Alongside one global history of tribal peoples, there is room for another kind of ethnohistory: the many tribal peoples' histories of their worlds. To recognize and return to this other kind of ethnohistory is also a step in the direction of demythologizing our own view of tribal peoples, and a recognition that construction of the world and action within it are inseparable. Tribal peoples did not only suffer history, they also made it and continue to do so.

Wolf's reference to Lévi-Strauss is perhaps misplaced for Lévi-Strauss makes clear that it is not history that is supposed to remain 'cold'. Rather, 'hot' and 'cold' have to do with the opposed orientations and practices of different societies with respect to history; they thus refer to the realm of culture and not to the kind of history that Wolf has in mind. Yet Wolf's hint of criticism may still be justified in another way for although Lévi-

Strauss recognizes that 'cold' societies are subject to historical change, he pays little attention to the impact of such change on the cultural systems that he analyses and makes no allowance for an historical consciousness within them. Although White people are often present in Amerindian myth and thought, they are largely absent from the pages of *Mythologiques*.

However, Lévi-Strauss is not alone in this respect for it can be said more generally that, in their efforts to understand the 'other', anthropologists have as yet shown a remarkable lack of interest in documenting and analysing how that 'other' makes sense of the alien world of which anthropology itself is both a part and a symptom.[1] When Boon writes that 'anthropologists from any culture (and they exist in every culture) engage in translating and interpreting the rumours of other cultures' (1982:x), it has to be said that we have so far paid precious little attention to our non-western colleagues at least as regards their anthropology of ourselves.

In this paper I shall examine some ways in which White people, their activities, possessions, and beliefs have been incorporated into the mythology of the Barasana and other Tukanoan Indians of the Vaupés region of the Colombian northwest Amazon.[2] Despite being the essence of timeless tradition, myth is still subject to a constant process of change, which allows it to keep pace with reality. I am interested in the mechanisms of this change, in how novelty is incorporated into myth, in why this incorporation takes the form it does, and in what the content of such myths can tell us about more general ideas and attitudes that the Indians hold towards White people.

Lack of space precludes a proper discussion of historical narrative, ritual speech and oratory, or daily conversation, but I want to begin by stressing that an excessive focus on myth, in isolation from other narrative and verbal genres, is liable to lead to a very distorted impression of how small-scale tribal societies view historical events, whether these have to do with internal relations, relations with other tribal groups, or contact with foreigners. Whilst there is no doubt that myths do play an important role in their views of the past and present, to pretend that such societies have no consciousness of history and that they have only one mode of thought ('mythic thought'), displayed in a specific mode of discourse (myth) and which marks them as being a particular kind of society ('cold') is unwarranted.

Ideally, I would begin with an outsider's account of the history of the Vaupés region as it is both the counterpart to and background of the material I shall discuss. Instead I shall say only that the Vaupés Indians have been in contact with White society since around the mid-eighteenth century, first with Portuguese slavers and their Indian allies and then with missionaries, traders, and rubber tappers. Economic relations took the form of debt-peonage through which manufactured goods were exchanged for Indian products and labour. Exploitation through this system, together with missionary pressure on Indian society, led to a series of messianic revolts in the second half of the last century.

Three points are worth stressing about this all-too-brief historical sketch. First, contact with outsiders has been most intense and long-lasting along the main rivers and both more recent and less intense in the Pirá-Paraná region where the Barasana live. Second, Indians with a longer history and experience of contact have often acted as middlemen between White society and the more isolated Indian groups. Contact has never been that sudden, traumatic event that forms part of the mythology of travel literature but rather a sporadic, drawn-out affair involving both foreign White people and their more familiar Indian allies from downriver. Third, this contact has caused an increasing dependency on manufactured goods, which forces the Indians to seek and maintain relations with outsiders.

How then does this history of contact figure in Barasana mythology? The short answer is that, in a direct way, it hardly figures at all. Personal experiences of contact with foreigners and traditions of the arrival and activities of different White people – slavers, traders, missionaries, and travellers – handed down from parents and grandparents, form part of a quite different narrative genre. When telling such stories, the speaker will use different verb endings and other cues to distinguish personal experience from hearsay and use kinship or well-known events as reference points to locate them in a time frame relative to the present. But these 'histories' are clearly distinguished from myths – stories of animals, spirits, heroes, and ancestors before and beyond the experience of any normal human being. Nevertheless, as a significant component of reality, White people do also figure in Tukanoan myth but in a way that transforms contemporary experience and past memories so that they are mythologized along with everything else.

The domains of myth and history have different contextual relevance. When asked about specific White people – their identity, time of arrival, activities, and motives – the Barasana will reply in the form of narratives that are not unlike those of local White people when describing the same events. But when asked about White people in general – their origins, existence, and characteristics – they will either speculate like anyone else confronted with the unknown or they will resort to the transcendent certitude of myth.

Before discussing this mythological treatment of White people I should briefly elaborate on the distinction between the categories of 'myth' and 'history' as I have used them in this paper. One term, *bikirā keti* – stories of the old people – may be used in a general sense to cover all narratives and traditions of past events that lie beyond the speaker's own experience. But the term has a more specific reference to myths as distinct from stories about the more recent past, which are specified by reference to their principle actors (*Barea gawa keti* – stories of slave raids by Baré Indians from the Rio Negro, *ri bõari bãsa keti* – stories of rubber gatherers, *Godowa keti* – the story of Cordoba, a Tatuyo leader killed by White people, etc.).

Temporal succession applies to the episodes of individual myths and to the whole mythological corpus, which consists of mythic cycles ordered in a chronological sequence. The myths describe a cosmogonic process that culminates in the transformation of true human beings from animal and supernatural ancestors. This process, called the 'awakening of the people' (*bãsa yuhi*), depends on the establishment of an antithesis between life and death, and it marks the separation of people from animals, culture from nature, and the mundane from the mythic.

The time of 'history', the more recent, follows but is divided from the remote past of myth, which now persists in the present as an extra dimension of reality. This division between macro- and micro-time is also a division of space for whilst the events of myth take place within a universe compared to a single house, those of history take place within the world of normal experience. Furthermore, nothing happens in historical narrative that could not also happen today, whilst myths are full of impossible happenings that pertain to a level of reality only accessible through dreams, shamanism, and ritual.

Mythical and historical narratives are never confused and Indians would clearly recognize the differences mentioned previously. Further differences relate to the style and content of the two genres and to their different relevance to the contemporary world. For myths there is a correct version of the story to which all are expected to conform, whilst historical narratives are more prone to idiosyncratic variation and correctness applies more to the truth of the details rather than to the telling of the story.

In myths about White people, complexity is reduced, real events disappear, and named individuals are replaced by unitary categories – White men with stereotyped and generalized attributes opposed to equally stereotyped and generalized Indians. In historical narrative and daily talk it is the details and complexities of individuals and events that are the focus of elaboration. As collective representations, myths reduce the chaos of real experience to manageable order. Finally, although myths may be used to validate or legitimate political claims (to territory, status, etc.) they are not used in the way that historical narratives are used in order to provide models or precedents for contemporary action.

My first point then is that for the Vaupés Indians, and presumably for many other tribal societies too, myth and 'history' are not mutually incompatible but coexist as two separate and complementary modes of representing the past, each with its own appropriate narrative style and each with its own context of relevance. This point, obvious enough in itself, would hardly be worth making if it were not for the fact that it is often minimized, ignored, or denied. Often it is assumed that in 'totemic' societies with a 'cyclical' view of time, history is dominated by and subsumed under a mythic mode of thought, or comes into existence only after the trauma of contact with western society.[3]

This argument, based on precisely those modes of symbolic discourse – myths and totemic classifications – which do indeed appear to negate history, is circular and has probably diverted attention away from the recording and analysis of oral history in such 'cold' societies, thus reinforcing the impression of the dominance of myth. Mythic thought or structure does not engulf history but distils from events and individuals, memories and experiences, an ordered set of categories – but it does not obliterate its sources from consciousness.

The traditions that follow mythological beginnings deal first and in a very general way with the slave raids mentioned on p. 54. Stories of the more recent past give precise and detailed accounts of the activities of rubber tappers, missionaries, and travellers. Some of the stories tell of atrocities committed against Indian men and women and describe a life of fear and hiding, but they also celebrate acts of bravery and resistance that are in marked contrast to the pervasive fatalism of the myths about White people.

An immediately striking feature of the occurrence of White people in Barasana myth is that virtually all reference to them is confined to a single mythic cycle.[4] The cycle concerns a culture hero called *Wārībi* (He who went away) or *Sie* (Bitter) who is often identified with Christ and the Christian God. Here is a brief summary of his story.[5]

Wārībi was the child of an incestuous union between the Moon and his sister *Bēderiyo*. As a punishment, the girl's father *Bēdi Kūbu*, sent her up into the sky. Later she returned to earth, by now very pregnant, and arrived at the house of the jaguars, her father's affines. The jaguars' mother tried to hide and protect her granddaughter but she insisted on joining in with their dancing and they killed her. Their mother took her body to the river where she allowed *Wārībi* to escape from his mother's womb into the water.

Wārībi swam to his grandfather *Bēdi Kūbu*'s house where he played with the children swimming in the river. He caught butterflies and painted patterns on their wings, the origin of the White people's writing. To catch him, the children buried a young girl in the sand, urinated on the spot above her crotch to attract the butterflies and then went and hid. As *Wārībi* played with the butterflies the girl caught him between her legs and, though previously a bodyless spirit, he was now born as a real baby.

Wārībi grew supernaturally fast and later accompanied his grandfather on a visit to his affines, the jaguars. The jaguars were playing football with *Bēderiyo*'s head, the origin of the White people's game, and *Wārībi* joined in their game, kicking the head across a river. He made a bridge of snakes disguised as logs and vines and sent the jaguars to fetch the ball. At *Wārībi*'s command, the bridge came undone sending the jaguars into the river where they were eaten by piranhas.

Although he lost a leg, one jaguar managed to get to the other bank and became the ancestor of White people and foreign Indians. His name was Steel Tapir or One Leg and it is through him that White people acquired steel and he explains why there are so many amputees in their towns. *Wārībi* made One Leg's descendants strong and fierce and gave them the power to make all kinds of manufactured goods but he sent them far to the east where they would not cause trouble. As one informant put it: '*Wārībi* left us Indians with nothing. To him we were like animals living amongst the trees and eating wild fruit.'

Later, *Wārībi* obtained loads of manufactured goods from the spirits of White people in the sky. As his grandfather was angry with him for killing his affines, he did not visit him but instead took the goods in a large canoe downstream to the White people living in the east. After many further adventures in which he' stole curare poison, invented the gun and blow-pipe, and killed a man-eating eagle, *Wārībi* finally created true human beings.

This is a condensed summary of a small fragment of what is in fact a very long myth but even the full version reveals little that can be readily identified with the people and events of the history of the region discoverable either from documentary sources or from the traditions of the Indians themselves. The fact that the jaguars live at Yauareté (Jaguar Rapid) on the Vaupés river suggests a link with the Tariana Indians who live there today and who once sold individuals from more isolated groups to White people as slaves. *Wārībi*'s killing of the jaguars might then be taken as the expression of an actual or desired revenge against the Tariana but although the Barasana emphasize that the jaguars are soldiers and policemen, the agents of foreign oppression, they do not accept this specific interpretation. However, the more general identification of White people with jaguars is consistent with the Indian experience of them as powerful, murderous, and predatory and as being outside the bounds of civilized society, themes that are also expressed in traditions of the more recent past.[6]

Wārībi is the ancestor of all White people but, as the prototype shaman, he is above all identified with God and Christ and, through them, with the religious component of White society. Although the jaguars are the ancestors of White people, they are most closely identified with soldiers and policemen. *Wārībi*'s hostility to the jaguars might thus reflect the historical antagonism between the religious and secular elements of White society, for the missionaries have traditionally defended the Indians against the abuses of traders, soldiers, and policemen. But apart from possible instances such as these, the myth has only a very general relation to the specific individuals and events of history.

The story of the creation of true human beings follows the section of the myth summarized previously and it repeats and amplifies some of its themes. Variants of this part of the myth are known from a number of different Vaupés groups, and what follows is a composite version designed to bring out specific points.[7]

When he had finished preparing the world, *Wārībi* created the first people. They came from the east in the belly of an anaconda and when it reached the Vaupés region, they emerged from the water as true people, the ancestors of the different exogamous language groups of the area. Last to be born was the ancestor of the White people but when the culture hero ordered the people to bathe, it was he who plunged into the water first and came out clean and white. He was followed by the ancestor of the Blacks who acquired his colour from the now dirty water. The Indian was frightened of the water and did not bathe at all and so became inferior to White people.

The culture hero then offered the people a gun, a bow, and some ritual ornaments. Given first choice, the Indian chose the bow and ornaments leaving the White Man with the gun. Because they came from the same ancestral body, the people all spoke one language but, when given salt to lick, each began to speak in his own tongue. In a Barasana version of the story, they were offered beeswax mixed with coca, a key symbol of contemporary ritual.[8] The Indians refused to eat but women, snakes, spiders, and White people all ate the wax, which is why women menstruate, snakes shed their skins, and White people wear clothing. Their common ability to shed their skins explains why snakes never die, why women live longer than men, and why White people are so numerous, healthy, and long-lived. The Barasana liken the burning of beeswax to the Catholic use of incense in the Mass, and the Indians' refusal to eat the wax and their refusal to bathe are both seen as a refusal to accept Christianity.

The ancestor of the Whites then began to threaten the others with his gun. To keep the peace, the culture hero sent him far away to the East and declared that war would be the White peoples' equivalent of Indian ritual and that through war they would obtain the wealth of other people.

This story of the differentiation from a common ancestor may be told either to account for the origin of all the groups in the Vaupés or to account for the origin of the different, ranked clans that make up each one. In the former case, although the ancestors of each group are brothers ranked according to the order of their emergence or birth from the ancestral anaconda, the acquisition of different languages converts them into affines of equal status according to the principles of linguistic exogamy that apply in the area. In the latter case, no differences of language are introduced and the clans remain ranked according to the birth order of their respective ancestors.

Mention of White people is often omitted altogether, but when they are introduced into the story, they are treated initially as if they should have had equal status to any other Vaupés group, each of which is traditionally associated with a different language and with the manufacture of a particular material object (stool, canoe, basketry, etc.). They are thus treated as if they were to have been equal partners in the system of marital and ritual exchanges that regulates Indian society.

The myth sets up an initial distinction between an animal-like anaconda ancestor and true people or *bāsa*, a category that applies equally to Whites and Indians and is subdivided by linguistic and cultural markers. This initial situation is then transformed into an opposition between Whites and Indians as generic and ethnic categories between whom exchange is no longer possible. White people are banished from the social space of the Vaupés Indians and turned from potential affines into real enemies. They are now excluded from the category *bāsa* in its restricted sense of 'true people' or 'people like us' (i.e. Vaupés Indians) and put into the category *gawa*, which also applies to foreign Indians such as the Baré and Carijona who were once the allies of White people.

This transformation from affine to enemy and the denial of exchange is prefigured in the earlier part of the myth. Whereas *Bēdi Kūbu* has the jaguars as affines with whom he exchanges women and basketry, his son, the moon, prefers incest with his sister over marriage to these affines, and his grandson *Wārībi* kills all but one of them and banishes the survivor to the East, a separation also marked by a piranha-filled river.

Wārībi is the prototype shaman who sent all White people away to the East and it was from the East that the first White people, the Portuguese slavers, and Brazilian traders, and missionaries, entered the Vaupés region. If westerners saw, and still often see Indians in temporal terms as representing an earlier stage in the development of humanity, the Indians see these differences more in spatial terms and not as a matter of relative progress. In Indian myths White people share an equal creation, but one that is followed by an original separation and moral decline. However, the progressive incursion of White people into Indian territory, an incursion described in historical narratives, is seen in temporal terms as a cumulative change that results from the failure of later shamans to keep foreigners at bay.

The establishment of an opposition between Whites and Indians and the denial of the possibility of exchange and affinity between groups who are, in principle, equal but different, also introduces the question of their relative status. As a brother who was last to emerge, the ancestor of White people is logically younger and inferior to his Indian counterpart, but his acquisition of the gun allows him to usurp his elder brother's status and to become dominant over him. This theme of a fateful choice between two brothers who swap status through one's cunning or the other's stupidity is common to many South American myths about the origin of White people, and it is usually represented as a choice between the gun and the bow. I want now to examine this theme in more detail.

The contrast between Whites and Indians is characterized by an ambiguity that is also evident in contexts other than that of myth. Although in reality it is the more powerful White people who have largely determined the Indians present situation, and although it was they who imposed the category 'Indian', which the Indians themselves now use, the myth suggests otherwise. By failing to choose the gun and by refusing to accept baptism and incense, the symbols of Christianity, the Indians are presented as being responsible for their own status and present situation. In the same way, because it was *Bēdi Kūbu*, the Indian, who was angry with *Wārībi* for having killed his jaguar affines, *Wārībi* went off and gave his merchandise to the White people instead. This same theme of responsibility for one's own fate also occurs in a number of other Barasana myths in which, through their own doing, different animals either miss the opportunity to become human or lose their original human status.

The goods chosen by the Whites and Indians stand for whole differences in economy, life style, and values, which define each group socially and which determine the relations between them. The choice of the bow implies a forest-based economy and condemns the Indians to be powerless against White men armed with guns. Their refusal to bathe reinforces the Indians' weakness by giving them a lower status and a declining population. To quote the culture hero of a Tukano version of the myth:

> After the arrival of the Colombians and Brazilians in your land, you shall have only one wife and she shall have only one or two sons; your brother's wife will have no sons and that is how the Tukano will die out . . . They will humiliate you and have you as their slaves.
>
> (Fulop, 1954:132)

The Indians' choice of ritual ornaments also represents a system in which goods are obtained through ritualized exchange rather than through warfare, theft, and coerced labour backed by the gun.

The myths reveal a fatalism that is also manifest in the ordinary talk of many of the elder Barasana who are aware of themselves as the last, rapidly disappearing representatives of a culture that was once common to the whole area and whose last shreds are now being abandoned by a mission-educated youth. Such myths concern the recognition, interpretation, and acceptance of White domination, and by placing it at the beginning of time, they present it as something inevitable and beyond human influence. They cannot serve as the basis of political action, and they stand in marked contrast to the more aggressive political rhetoric of the younger Indian leaders.

The myths show also that, in their thinking about the place of White people in their cosmology, the Indians have been influenced by the negative values and inferior position assigned to them in the cosmology of the Whites. This influence is clear in the following passage from a Tukano myth in which the culture hero declares:

> The Indians of the Vaupés are like animals. One day I shall send you chickens, dogs and pigs so that you can compare yourselves with them. I am cursing you. Look at the Colombians and Brazilians. They are really fine people.

> (Fulop, 1956:367)

But if Indians seem to invert the values of the White people so also do White people invert the values of Indians. Alongside the self-blame and self-denigration of the myths, there also runs a countercurrent, which suggests the Indians' moral superiority. For the Vaupés Indians, the idea of language embraces notions of character, essence, behaviour, and temperament. It was their greedy, uncontrolled, and thoughtless character, received by White people along with their language, that made it inevitable that they should bathe without fear, grab the gun, and not share their possessions.

Whilst recognizing the power of their knowledge, Indians frequently stress the poor memories, unsharing habits, and uncontrolled aggression of White people. The myths draw an explicit contrast between these negatively evaluated qualities and the reflective, controlled, and ritualized character of Indians, epitomized in the person of the shaman. It was this character that lay behind their refusal to bathe and grab the gun. If the Indians chose to be Indians, it was because they chose as Indians who rejected the values of the Whites' lifestyle. The bow implies powerlessness but it also represents an adaptation to the forest in which White people are so inept. The ritual possessions stand for a ritual ordering and mastery of the human and natural worlds by the shaman–priest or *kūbu*. The Indians' shamanic powers are seen as the counterpart of the religious powers that lie behind the technology and life style of the Whites. As the creator of the gun and the Bible, the sources of power of the Whites, and the creator of Indian material culture and shamanic power, *Wārībi* is both God and shaman, and personifies ambiguity.

Thus far I have been discussing the content of one particular mythic cycle that accounts for the origin of White people. I want now to look at this myth as a whole in relation to other Barasana myths in order to try to provide some insight into why it should be the only myth in which White people figure and to which all new experience of them is referred.

I have shown on p. 59 that the myth represents Whites and Indians as two brothers who swap relative status. This same motif occurs in a number of other Barasana myths and, in each case, the two brothers can be directly or indirectly linked with the sun and moon. Both are called *būhihu* and, in myth, today's sun was once the moon and today's moon once the sun.[9]

Wārībi, the son of the moon, has a pair in the person of *Yeba*, the son of the sun and the hero of another mythic cycle about the origins of Barasana culture.[10] Not only does the fuzzy logic of mythological kinship suggest that *Wārībi* and *Yeba* are brothers, but in practice they are often confused with each other. Like the sun and moon, these two also share features of both identity and opposition. Although he is the creator of all peoples, *Wārībi* is the ancestor of White people in particular, whilst *Yeba* is the ancestor of the Indians. *Yeba*'s counterpart in the *Wārībi* myth is *Bēdi Kūbu* who is also known as *Yeba Bēdi*, anaconda and, like the Indians that he represents, he too is left without manufactured goods.[11]

The opposition between *Wārībi* and *Yeba* applies also to their respective myths. *Yeba* is a normal Indian, the ancestor of the Barasana, who begins life as a jaguar and is socialized and made human by his affines, the Fish People or Bará, and it is from them that he obtains cultivated plants. The myth of *Yeba* stresses the value of agriculture and it concerns the internal order of society in which peaceful relations with other groups are mediated by marriage and ceremonial exchange. By contrast, *Wārībi* is a shaman and his myth is about the negation of exchange and alliance with a group of jaguar affines, which leads to the creation of White people and their possessions, which Indians cannot obtain through normal exchange. It is a myth about shamanic powers, warfare, relations with outsiders, and it concerns the invention of the hunting technology that *Wārībi* gave to *Yeba*. In this myth, women and goods are obtained through violence and theft, which imply relations of asymmetry and dominance.

The contrast between White people and Indians, established within the myth of *Wārībi*, is thus replicated at a higher level in the contrast between *Wārībi* and *Yeba* and between their respective myths. Through this latter contrast, analogous to that between the sun and the moon, White people are structurally integrated into the heart of Barasana myth and cosmology. Although the lack of written records make an archaeology of myth impossible, there thus seems to be no reason to suppose that the appearance of White people would call for the invention of totally new myths. More probably they would have been slotted into a pre-existing schema provided by the corpus of myth and one that would already account for various kinds of foreigners and outsiders. That White people are identified with jaguars, and categorized along with foreign Indians might lend support to such a view. The fact that much of the myth of *Wārībi* is taken up with topics having nothing to do with White people and that it is a variant of a myth found throughout Amazonia also suggests that the myth was not created specifically to account for White people.[12]

Through the opposition between *Yeba* and *Wārībi*, the myth of *Wārībi* becomes *the* myth about White people, opposed to the myth of *Yeba*, which concerns the foundation of Indian society. Given this pattern, it then makes sense that the Barasana should continue to restrict their integration of newly acquired elements of knowledge of White society to this myth alone and this is precisely what they do. It is as if by doing this, they are able to contain White people and to exert some measure of control over their impact on the total system of myths.

Whenever the Barasana tell the eternal myths of the past they do so with reference to some contemporary pretext that exerts an influence on what is said. The myth must be made relevant to the pretext and the teller must use his judgement as to what to elaborate upon or omit. The myth of *Wārībi* is often told with almost no reference at all to White people, but when it is told to me, as one of them, my informants will usually make sure to lace the myth with as many such references as they can muster. Some of these references, such as the invention of writing and football, function almost as an obligato accompaniment; others are less well known and are rarely mentioned, and yet others are clearly invented on the spur of the moment. Here is an example of one such invention.

I once told a shaman, who had never heard of them before, about submarines – big underwater canoes full of people and firing great arrows from their bows. Later, I heard him tell a friend the episode of the myth of *Wārībi* in which the hero is swallowed by an anaconda, takes two of its ribs, makes a pair of scissors, cuts a hole in the side, and fires out an arrow. 'And that', he added nonchalantly with me as his other audience, 'that is how White people have those things they call submarines. That's what my grandfather told me.'

Examples such as these are common for this same creative analogical matching between myth and life is constantly employed to make any myth relevant to new experience and daily issues. Apart from his superior knowledge, one of the defining characteristics of the Barasana shaman is his skill and authority in making just such creative use of myths.

All Barasana myths are used in this way, and there is normally no particular reason why one is chosen over another. When it comes to things associated with White people, however, reference is made exclusively to the myth of *Wārībi*, thus effectively limiting their impact on the system as a whole. But this specific use is part of a more general process whereby myths are made to keep pace with an ever-changing present in such a way as to convey the impression that nothing changes at all. Just as White people already had a virtual existence in the belly of the anaconda, an existence made actual by the acquisition of their language and the gun, so also are all new things treated as if they had a potential existence somewhere in myth that experience merely makes manifest and actual. It is as if submarines had been there all along, lurking under the surface of the myth and waiting to be discovered by some chance remark.

This view is consistent with the statement by a Barasana shaman that nothing can exist that is not already known for, given the fact that everything came into being at the beginning of time, anything new would be a lie. It is a view that sees human memory in a constant battle with entropy and one entirely at odds with our own ideas of progress. In the case of White people and their creations, it is a manifestation of the fact that myth must account for everything if it is to account for anything at all, and also an assertion of the continued relevance of a system of knowledge under increasing threat from the competing modes of explanation taught by White people. By analogically matching the new with the old, the unknown with the known, the shaman exerts a symbolic power over new phenomena. Simultaneously he asserts the extent of his knowledge, puts new things in their place, and domesticates them by reducing them to the familiar and mundane – the power of writing brought down to the marks on a butterfly's wing.

Apart from their existence, their habits, and the things that they make, another attribute of White people is the myths they tell. Through persistent rumours, missionized neighbours, itinerant priests, and resident missionaries, the Barasana have been exposed to Bible stories and Christian teaching for a considerable period of time. In their attitudes to Christianity they display an ambivalence that is consistent with their own relativism on the one hand and with their awareness of the compulsory nature of the message contained in Christian myths on the other.[13] As the Indian myths make clear, White people's culture, like that of any Indian group, is part of the heritage that they received at the beginning of time. As such it forms part of an ordered system of difference that makes society possible and, for this reason, it would not make sense to suggest to White people or to one's affines that they should adopt one's own language or attributes, for to do so would be to invite chaos. But the same myths make clear that the Indians have assimilated the White peoples' stereotypes and negative views of Indian culture and now apply them to themselves. As the Tukano culture hero gloomily predicts: '(the Indians) will learn to read and write and after that (their) *malokas* (longhouses) will be finished' (Fulop, 1954:131).

One Indian reaction to Christian myth is to say simply that it is what Whites believe, that it is true for them, and that it is what makes them what they are. Another is to apply to it the same analogical matching that is applied to other aspects of White peoples' culture and which, by implication, suggests that their myths too were known all along. In this way, *Wārībi* comes to be identified with God and Christ, his father the moon with the holy spirit, while he himself is the son of two virgin mothers. Similar treatment is given to elements of Christian ritual so that shamans are priests, dance songs are hymns, chants are prayers, ritual beeswax is incense, and hallucinogenic *yagé* is communion wine.

Such elements of Christianity are not incorporated as elements of doctrine or dogma. Rather it is as if in Christianity the Barasana find echoes of their own ideas and it is these that determine which elements are selected, organized, and interpreted according to a pre-existing model that lends them its own specific values. Thus the fact that *Wārībi* is identified with Christ in no way affects the fact that in other parts of the myth he engages in both rape and murder.

Coming from a system of acknowledged power and forming an integral part of White peoples' domination over the Indians, these elements of Christianity lend their power and prestige to the indigenous elements with which they are paired. But at the same time, the Barasana are keenly aware of their relative lack of power, declining numbers, low prestige, and lack of manufactured goods, a predicament that the myths portray as being due to their ancestors' rejection of Christianity and to *Wārībi*'s own desertion of the Indians in favour of the Whites. The shamans also state that the White people took the best ritual beeswax gourd, the source of their wealth and power, and left the Indians with a second-best substitute.

The myth of *Wārībi* makes clear that the knowledge and power of White people is conceived as a transformation and concentration of the shamanic power and knowledge by which Indian society was created and which ensures its reproduction today. This leaves open the possibility that contemporary shamans might re-establish contact with *Wārībi* and so redress the imbalance between Indians and Whites.

From 1850 to around 1880, a series of messianic cults spread throughout the Vaupés region. These cults were led by shaman–prophets who claimed identity and direct contact with God and Christ and who took on many of the functions and attributes of the missionary priests. They carried out baptisms and weddings and led their followers in rituals that brought together Christian symbols and more traditional ritual elements. The shaman–prophets visited ancestral heroes and powerful shamans in the world of the dead and returned to use their powers to heal the sick. They also promised their followers relief from exploitation by White people and came into conflict with both traders and missionaries who sent troops and police against them.

Although they happened long ago, memories of these cults, their leaders, the songs, and the dances are still fresh in the minds of the Indians. Barasana stories of the cult they call *Sie basa*, the dance of Bitter or *Wārībi*, are a blend of myth and history. With the myth of *Wārībi* as a prologue, these accounts then tell how *Wārībi* returned to the Vaupés region to offer the Indians a second chance to live long and to acquire material wealth. With these mythological beginnings, the stories then go on to describe the cult activities and to recount the activities of the famous shaman–prophets who led them.

By merging mythical and historical time and merging the distinction between the living and the dead, themes that are repeatedly stressed in the stories, it is as if these cults sought to undo, replay, and reinvent the mythical history that places the inequality between Indians and Whites immutably at the beginning of time.

Much more could be said about these cults but the point I wish to make should already be clear. *Wārībi* is the prototype shaman and his story forms the basis of all shamanism today. Modern-day shamans are identified with him and in their activities they re-enact aspects of his myth. If shamans are identified with *Wārībi* as his representatives on earth and if priests are the representatives of Christ, then if *Wārībi* is the analogue of Christ, it makes sense that shamans should take on the role of priests. This is precisely what we find in the cults where the shamans imitated the Mass and claimed to have been sent by God and Christ.

Here then, we have an example in which elements of myth are not only identified with aspects of Christian belief, but are also transformed so as to take on new values and to give rise to new forms of action. In this way myth not only serves to represent the contact between Whites and Indians but also influences its outcome by forming the basis of Indian resistance to White oppression. Although my example concerns events that happened some time ago, they still have contemporary relevance. Like the stories of fights with rubber gatherers, those about cult activities are not simply memories of the past. They provide a store of alternative ideas, interpretations, and courses of action with potential application to the present.

The cults belong to the past but modern shamans continue to assert that they and their rituals are equivalent to their Christian counterparts. These claims have a political aspect as part of the rivalry between shamans and the missionaries over politico-religious leadership and control over the younger generation, a rivalry that also relates to the fact that the shamans' traditional role as mediators between Indians and White people is now increasingly taken over by the mission-educated youth and by the missionaries themselves. Rather than directly questioning what the missionaries teach, by implication the shamans come to question the missionaries' exclusive right to educate the young for, if God is *Wārībi*, who needs missionaries anyhow?

I have shown how White people are integrated into myth at levels that range from off-the-cuff parallels drawn between new phenomena and elements of myth, through to higher-level contrasts and oppositions between whole myths that emphasize the differences between Whites and Indians and systematize the relations between them. The unknown is constantly matched with the known and brought into myth though analogies of much the same kind as those that led the conquistadors to see tigers in jaguars and fir cones in pineapples. I have suggested that this same kind of thinking probably allowed the historical integration of White people into myth for even they had a precedent in the form of mythological jaguars and very real stranger Indians with whom the Whites were often allied.

However, I have also suggested that this process of classification and matching must be set against real differences in power, wealth, and prestige of which the Indians are fully aware. White people are not simply the equivalent of another Indian group, the Bible is not just another myth, guns are not merely the alternatives to bows, and writing is much more than the patterns on the wings of a butterfly. For this reason, each time the system of myth is applied to new experience it is transformed and the values of its elements are changed so that, in the end, the whole system is called into question by other forms of explanation that exist alongside it.

Through looking at the way White people are treated in myth, we can gain insight into both the workings of myth itself and into the way in which Indians view outsiders, a view that is a reflex of their image of themselves. In addition, because the different representations of the contact situation, held by both sides, are an integral part of the way in which that situation evolves, a proper history of contact between native and western society must take such representations into account. But in this context, as in any other, it should not be assumed that native representations will only and always take the form of myth.

Notes

1. For exceptions to this generalization see Burridge (1960), Sahlins (1981; 1985), Harbsmeier (1985), Blackburn (1979), Görög (1976), and Lips (1937).
2. Fieldwork amongst the Barasana (1968–70; 1979; 1981; 1984) was variously supported by the Social Science Research Council, King's College, Cambridge, the Museum of Mankind, and Central Television. This support is gratefully acknowledged.
3. See, for example, da Matta's (1971) analysis of a Timbira myth concerning the origin of White people where he asserts that the myth 'introduces historical awareness into tribal consciousness' (p. 288) and that such consciousness begins with the contact of a tribal society with the outside world (p. 272). On the evidence he provides there seem to be few grounds for claiming either that the myth has to do with historical consciousness or that such consciousness was absent prior to the invention of the myth or to the arrival of White people.
4. The tendency to restrict reference to White people to only one or two myths is common throughout the Vaupés region and, judging from the compilations published by Wilbert (1978) and by Wilbert and Simoneau (1982; 1983), appears to be true of lowland South America more generally.
5. For fuller versions of this myth see S. Hugh-Jones (1979:274–83) and Bidou (n.d.).
6. The animal-like status of White people is expressed not only in the very fact

that they are identified with jaguars but also by the fact that although their second creation occurs simultaneously with that of the Indians, their first creation (as jaguars) precedes the creation of true human beings.

By the logic of Barasana myth, this would imply that White people are on a par with the spirits of the dead, an inference supported by Barasana accounts of the exploits of the shaman–prophet leaders of last-century millenial cults. These men are said to have made regular visits to the world of the dead, a world described as being identical to the towns of White people.

7. For other versions see Alemán (1979), Bidou (1976:33–4), Buchillet (1983:26–9), Espinoza-Torres (1976:16); Fulop (1954:112ff), Kumu and Kenhíri (1980:73–4), Morales (1976:218–19); and Santa-Cruz (1977:7).
8. See S. Hugh-Jones (1979:163–92).
9. See S. Hugh-Jones (1979:227–33) for a discussion of this theme.
10. See S. Hugh-Jones (1979:295–301).
11. In an analysis (1986) of a Tatuyo version of the *Wãrĩbi* myth. Dr Patrice Bidou has shown that *Bẽdi Kũbu* and *Wãrĩbi* also swap positions of relative power. Both are in a canoe with *Bẽdi Kũbu* in the prow and *Wãrĩbi* at the stern. When *Bẽdi Kũbu* paddles and *Wãrĩbi* steers, the former is dominant over the latter but then *Wãrĩbi* creates an outboard motor from his paddle thus inverting their positions of relative power.
12. Roberto da Matta (1971) shows convincingly that the Timbira myth of *Auke*, the story of the origin of Brazilians, is a systematic inversion of the structure of the principle myth of origin of Gê society and culture and, on the basis of this analysis, describes the *Auke* myth as an 'anti-myth'.

The myth of *Wãrĩbi*, which leads to the creation of White people, is similarly a structural inversion of a key myth of origin of Barasana society and culture, but I would hesitate to call it an anti-myth as I am not happy with the unstated but implied idea that such myths are created specifically to account for the origin of White people.

There is, however, an intriguing similarity both in the characters of *Auke* and *Wãrĩbi* and in the details of their respective myths.
13. C. Lévi-Strauss writes:

> We have changed our table manners and adopted others, the norm of which at least has been generalized throughout the Western world, where different ways of chewing no longer denote national or local traditions; they are merely good or bad. In other words, and contrary to what we have observed in exotic societies, eating habits, for Westerners, no longer constitute a *free code*: we opt for some habits and prohibit others, and we conform to the first in order to transmit a *compulsory message*.
>
> (Lévi-Strauss, 1979:499)

The same distinction between free code and compulsory message can be usefully applied to the contrasting attitude of Tukanoan Indians and White missionaries to each others' mythologies: for the Indians the Bible stories are merely different from their own, whilst for many of the missionaries the Indians' myths are simply wrong.

References

Alemán, E. (1979) 'Origen de la communidad Desana', *Almas* XLII (408):6–8.
Bidou, P. (1976) *Les Fils de L'Anaconda Céleste (Les Tatuyo). Étude de la Structure Socio-Politique*, Thèse de 3e cycle, Paris: Université de Paris IV.

Bidou, P. (1986) 'Histoire de Hungue Walimi', unpublished ms.

Bidou, P. (1986) 'Le mythe: une machine à traiter l'histoire', *L'Homme* no. 100, XXVI (4).65–89.

Blackburn, J. (1979) *The White Man*, London: Orbis.

Boon, J. (1982) *Other Tribes, Other Scribes*, Cambridge: Cambridge University Press.

Buchillet, D. (1983) *Maladie et Mémoire des Origins Chez les Desana du Vaupés (Brésil)*, Thèse de 3e Cycle, Paris: Université de Paris X.

Burridge, K. (1960) *Mambu*, London: Methuen.

Da Matta, R. (1971) 'Myth and anti-myth among the Timbira', in F. Maranda and P. Maranda (eds) *The Structural Analysis of Oral Tradition*, Philadelphia: University of Pennsylvania Press.

Espinoza-Torres, P. (1976) *La Presencia Misionera como Factor de Deculturación Indígena dentro la Comisaría del Vaupés*, Tesis de Grado: Universidad de los Andes.

Fulop, M. (1954) 'Aspectos de la cultura Tukana: cosmogónia', *Revista Colombiana de Antropología* 3:97–137.

Fulop, M. (1956) 'Aspectos de la cultura Tukana: mitologia', *Revista Colombiana de Antropología* 5:335–73.

Gorog, V. (1976) *Noirs et Blancs: Leur Image dans la Littérature Orale Africaine*, Paris: SELAF ('Langues et Civilisations, a Tradition Orale', 23.)

Harbsmeier, M. (1985) 'On travel accounts and cosmological strategies', *Ethnos* 50:273–312.

Hugh-Jones, C. (1979) *From the Milk River*, Cambridge: Cambridge University Press.

Hugh-Jones, S. (1979) *The Palm and the Pleiades*, Cambridge: Cambridge University Press.

Kumu, V.P. and Kenhiri, T. (1980) *Antes o Mundo Não Existia*, São Paulo: Livraria Cultura.

Lévi-Strauss, C. (1966) *The Savage Mind*, London: Weidenfeld & Nicholson.

Lévi-Strauss, C. (1969) *The Raw and the Cooked*, London: Jonathan Cape.

Lévi-Strauss, C. (1973) *From Honey to Ashes*, London: Jonathan Cape.

Lévi-Strauss, C. (1978) *The Origin of Table Manners*, London: Jonathan Cape.

Lévi-Strauss, C. (1981) *The Naked Man*, London: Jonathan Cape.

Lips, J. (1937) *The Savage Hits Back*, London: Lovat Dickinson.

Morales, L.A. (1977) *Integración Economica y Transfiguración Economica en el Vaupés, II*, Tesis de Grado, Bogotá: Universidad de los Andes.

Sahlins, M. (1981) *Historical Metaphors and Mythic Realities*, Ann Arbor: University of Michigan Press.

Sahlins, M. (1985) *Islands of History*, Chicago: University of Chicago Press.

Santa Cruz, J. (1977) 'Creación del hombre y origen de las tribus segun la historia de los Guananos (Vaupés)', *Almas* XLII, (398):2–7, (399):6–7, 25.

Wilbert, J. (ed.) (1978) *Folk Literature of the Gë Indians*, Los Angeles: University of California Press.

Wilbert, J. and Simoneau, K. (eds) (1982) *Folk Literature of the Toba Indians*, Los Angeles: University of California Press.

Wilbert, J. and Simonean, K. (1983) *Folk Literature of the Bororo Indians*, Los Angeles: University of California Press.

Wolf, E. (1982) *Europe and the Peoples Without History*, Berkeley: University of California Press.

Chapter five

Triumph of the Ethnos
Roger Just

With some few exceptions foreign anthropologists of Greece have not dwelt on the question of ethnicity.[1] From one point of view this is scarcely surprising. Greece does not consider itself a multiethnic or multicultural society. Within its borders there appear to be no minority groups struggling for recognition or for independence under the banner of a different history, a different language, a different religion, a different culture – or at least none that commands public sympathy or support within Greece. The 'Macedonian Question' – that is to say the ethnic status of the slavophone population of northern Greece and the argument over to whom 'Macedonia' (both the name and the region) rightfully 'belongs' – still simmers; but it is a propaganda battle fought across established national boundaries rather than within them, or else amongst expatriate groups (notably in Australia).[2] With the exceptions of the Turkish-speaking muslims of Thrace, some gypsies,[3] and that clearly recognizable band of aliens – expatriates and foreign spouses – the population of Greece considers itself uniformly Greek. Indeed, Greek identity not only in a political sense but with all the connotations of unbroken continuity with the classical past (and beyond) is an almost universally claimed possession.[4] Little wonder, then, that field workers have not confronted the problem of ethnicity; within their local settings there was seldom a 'problem' to confront. But once focus shifts from small-scale communities and the ethnographic present to matters of historical and national significance, Greek ethnicity assumes an immediate centrality; for the Greek *ethnos* – whence our neologism 'ethnicity' – is one of the most frequently invoked and at the same time one of the most problematic concepts of Hellenic discourse.

In this connection it is instructive to note that ethnicity does make its appearance in the classic ethnography of rural Greece – J.K. Campbell's *Honour, Family and Patronage* – but in the historical and geographical introduction, not the body of the work, for in the introduction Campbell was obliged to take account of an established controversy: were the Sarakatsan shepherds whom he studied 'Greek'? (1964:3–6). Nationalist historians and foreign friends were pleased to argue their descent from pre-classical nomadic tribesmen (thus making them more Greek than the Greeks); Rumanian scholars had asserted them to be 'hellenized' Koutsovlachs – erstwhile romance-speakers and hence 'Rumanians'. After summarizing the state of the question, Campbell wisely moved on. As he states, the problems of origin are not his concern. Indeed, nothing could have been served by prolonging a debate that, for want of evidence, could not be resolved. More to the point, nothing could have been served by prolonging a debate on which, for the purposes of his ethnography, nothing depended. The Sarakatsani were as they were and as Campbell brilliantly described them – and for them that was indubitably Greek.

But if for a study of the institutions and moral values of the Sarakatsani the question of their historical ethnicity is an irrelevance, the existence of the controversy points to the importance given by nationalist writers and scholars to the defence of the Greek *ethnos*' integrity and perhaps raises other questions: why was (and is) the issue so sensitive a one, and in what terms and under what conditions has the notion of the *ethnos* been formed? The Sarakatsan debate is but an example. Much of the history of Greece has been written in terms of the *ethnos*. Much of its politics has been informed by a notion of the *ethnos*. And, were the concept itself deemed problematic (rather than simply the evidence upon which its integrity is asserted or denied), much of the history of Greece could be rewritten in terms of the *ethnos*. I shall be attempting no such grandiose task; but in what follows I should like to indicate for those unfamiliar with modern Greek history the role that the concept of the *ethnos* has played and to suggest how and why on a number of levels it is both so important and so problematic.

At first glance the term *ethnos* seems an innocent one – or no more suspect than the term 'nation' by which it is conventionally translated and which in many contexts renders it and its adjectival forms convincingly: e.g. *Ethniki Trapeza tis Elladas* (National Bank of Greece), *Ethniko Kentro Kinonikon Erevnon* (National Centre of Social [Science] Research). It has, however, one important difference from the modern understanding of the English word nation, for though *ethnos* may mean nation, it does not mean nation–state and it cannot mean state (for which the English word nation has become a near synonym). On the contrary, in many contexts it contrasts with the word for state, that is with *kratos*, which specifically refers to a political entity and to the apparatus of the state (as well as being a general term for power/rule).

One could argue that this is merely a matter of language. The word *ethnos* has been transmitted unchanged (except phonetically) from classical antiquity, and there again it did not refer to a political structure – or if it did it was to label a sort of non-structure, that of the loose-knit, tribal (?) peoples mainly of north-western Greece (indeed the putative ancestors of the Sarakatsani) whose 'primitive' social organization contrasted with that of the *polis*, the centralized city–state, which political theorists of the classical period took as their starting point (Austin and Vidal-Naquet, 1977:78–81). The word *ethnos*, then, has always referred to some form of unity other than the strictly political. It has referred to a nation in the sense of a people, not a state. The separation of *kratos* (state) and *ethnos* (people) is thus in some ways intrinsic to the history of the Greek language. But on philological grounds what can be argued for *ethnos* can also be argued for nation. The Latin *natio* did not refer to a form of political organization, but rather to a breed, a stock, a kind, a race, a tribe, a people. Indeed, the anglophone assimilation of 'nation' and 'state', whether effected by the academic's hyphen or the unrefinement of popular speech, is itself quite recent. It might therefore be more profitable to look for social and historical factors that have gone towards maintaining the distinction between nation/state (*kratos*) and nation/people (*ethnos*) and which, by the same token, have promoted the importance of the latter. They are not difficult to find.

As every historical primer reminds us, the Greeks have been around for a long time. Perhaps they are outdone by the Egyptians or the peoples of Mesopotamia, but in Europe their civilization is the beginning of civilization-as-we-have-learned-it; nor is it my intention to dispute either their antiquity or their achievements. But both the antiquity and the pre-eminence of Greek civilization serve to obscure another fact (not least in Greece itself): namely, that prior to the Greek War of Independence (1821–30), there never was a single cohesive political entity that went by the name of Greece (or rather, Hellas) or that construed its unity in terms of being Greek.[5] In short, before the middle of the nineteenth century there was no nation–state of Greece. In a much quoted passage from Herodotos the Athenians, faced with the Persian invasion, assert Hellenic unity in terms of a commonality of language, religion, customs, and consanguinity;[6] moreover, a reading of almost any classical Greek author (and especially of Aristotle) is enough to convince one of the fundamental distinction made between Greeks and non-Greeks, between Hellenes and barbarians. But while the Greeks certainly recognized themselves as Greek and condemned the rest of the world to barbarity, the members of the club were mutually antagonistic. The dominant political formation of the *polis* meant that one was a citizen of Athens, Sparta, Thebes, Corinth, Corcyra, etc., not of 'Greece'. What followed (to cut a long story short) was domination by the Macedonians and Philip's empire, the intricacies of Hellenistic internecine strife, and eventual incorporation into the Roman Empire as a province. But then, it might be said, there was Byzantium. But although Byzantium, Constantinople, the New Rome, the capital of the Eastern Empire was Greek-speaking, and although we owe to its scribes and scholars the survival of the greater part of extant classical

Greek literature (Browning, 1964), the Byzantine Empire did not see itself as a specifically Hellenic state.[7] Like the Roman Empire before it, it incorporated within its bounds a diversity of languages, of cultures, of peoples, while 'Greece' (as now geographically defined) declined to a relatively obscure province of the Empire, a large part of it to be lost after the Fourth Crusade to the Franks (themselves anything from Rhinelanders to Normans). The Empire's cohesion lay in its Christianity, not its ethnicity, and in military contexts at least the Byzantines continued to call themselves *Romaioi* (Romans) – the pretensions of Charlemagne and his successors notwithstanding.

Then, on Tuesday 29 May 1453, Constantinople fell to the Ottoman Turks, and thus began, as every Greek schoolchild knows, 'Greece's four hundred years of slavery'. It was not exactly four hundred years for many regions: Crete, for example (a Venetian possession) held out until 1669. Nor was it exactly slavery for a considerable section of the Christian population. The more inaccessible parts of mainland Greece and the Peloponnese and some of the islands enjoyed various degrees of recognized local autonomy (Dakin, 1972:9–16). Moreover, however oppressed the peasantry of peninsular Greece, in Constantinople (now Istanbul – *Istin-poli*, Greek for 'in-the-City') Greeks held amongst the highest positions within the Ottoman administration including, of course, that of the Patriarch, now given secular as well as religious authority over all the Empire's Orthodox subjects, the *Millet-i Rum* or 'Roman Millet' (Clogg, 1986:19), while as traders, merchants, businessmen, and professionals the Greeks emerged as an economic (and intellectual) elite throughout the Empire by the end of the eighteenth century (Clogg:1981). But one thing is undeniable. Under Ottoman rule – an increasingly corrupt and arbitrary rule – there was no free and independent Greek state. Nor, of course, had there ever been; but by the eighteenth century, the period coinciding with the Greeks' economic ascendency, new ideas of nationalism based on the congruency of territorial sovereignty and ethnic unity were making their appearance throughout Europe. And though there might have been no Greek *kratos*, no-one could doubt that there were Greeks and hence a Greek *ethnos*. The problem of modern Greek history has been to create the former and to extend it to embrace the latter. But how was, and is, that *ethnos* defined?

Let me make two preliminary remarks. First, I take Edwin Ardener's (1976) proposition that 'social entities are self-defining systems' as axiomatic. Thus if (a) someone considers him- or herself to be a member of the Greek *ethnos* and (b) all other persons who consider themselves to be members of the Greek *ethnos* consider that person to be a member of the Greek *ethnos*, then that person is a member of the Greek *ethnos*. Second, whatever the problems that may be encountered in the establishment of

Greek ethnicity, in principle they are no more problematic than those involved in the establishment of any other ethnic identity. But unfortunately, the matter cannot so lightly be dismissed. Though my definition of the criteria for membership of the Greek *ethnos* is, I trust, formally sound, it is also essentially empty. In practice, empirical criteria are appealed to: and however vague, fuzzy-edged, inconsistent, historically misleading, or scientifically invalid those criteria may be, they are what give *substance* to a claim to ethnic identity. And though defining a Greek is no more impossible (or possible) than defining an Englishman, a Frenchman, or a Spaniard, with reference to those empirical criteria, particular problems have arisen.

It is somewhat rash to attempt to specify in the abstract what the sorts of 'empirical' criteria are that the concept of ethnicity invokes (after all, for some 'peoples' there might, happily, be none), but within a European context I suspect the following are commonplace. They are not all of the same order; they do not all work in the same way; some must function in combination; others overlap or subsume each other. For these reasons I do not present them in rank order, but roughly they amount to:

1. *Political incorporation into/membership of a sovereign state*. This assumes the identity of 'nation' and 'state' (of *ethnos* and *kratos*) to the extent that the specific question of ethnicity may become irrelevant or redundant. One is French because one is a citizen of France – and, for the majority at least, there may be no need to look further. A legally and politically valid civic status coincides with self-conceptions of self-identity. No further concept of ethnicity is required for it is subsumed by what legally one already has. To question Frenchness under such circumstances is absurd; to assert it unnecessary.

2. *Geographical circumscription/location*. This goes hand in hand with the aforementioned since the existence of a state presupposes the existence of its territory. Importantly, however, it can also work against the state, challenging its authority and asserting the rights of regional autonomy or even secession. But in either case an identity is asserted between 'people' and 'place'. Politically and polemically it is usually the people who lay claim to their territory; but the relationship is reversible and a metaphysic of locality sets in. A people is what it is because it is 'of' its land.

3. *Historical continuity*. Neither political incorporation nor present location are in themselves enough. 'Origins' and the sanctity of history must also be invoked. It is not sufficient merely to live in a place or to be granted citizenship of it in order to claim the ethnic status associated with it. There must also be roots. One must be able to claim some historical rights to it as a place of origin; in short, one must be able to

claim 'its' history as part of one's 'own' history so that the individual claimant is somehow the product of some collective past.

4. *Culture*. This, as history's 'present witness', comes quickly into play. Tradition is the banner of the ethnic nationalist; and certainly as an anthropologist one would not want to deny the reality of 'culture' (even if it is notoriously difficult to define). But culture is an uncertain ally. If social history has any meaning, then it means that societies change, and with them culture. Within those changes continuities, traditions, may certainly be traceable. Language is a paradigm case, its history often demonstrable, its possession seen as the guarantor of ethnic legitimacy. But languages not only change – they may be suppressed, lost, or even 'stolen' (for, after all, others are always capable of learning them). The same applies *a fortiori* to other cultural possessions. Religion (central in the Greek case) is open to both conversion and apostasy. As for material culture and those 'customs and habits' so beloved of the folklorist, they of all things have been acquired, shed, transformed, and reinterpreted over time; yet together with language and judiciously selected customs they are always presented as part of a cultural tradition, which proves their guardians to be of the ethnic origin they espouse.

If the aforementioned are even an approximate summary of what is commonly appealed to by the notion of ethnicity, it must also be immediately apparent that they are incapable of generating or revealing any distinct status for the notion of ethnicity (and I take it as a somewhat retrograde step that ethnicity should ever have entered into the *analytic* vocabulary of the social sciences). Moreover, for the ethnic nationalist, such a deconstruction of the concept reveals it as altogether too arbitrary, altogether too historically contingent. In practice political incorporation, geographical location, historical continuity, language, and culture are appealed to not as a *definition of* ethnicity, but merely as *evidence for* membership of a particular ethnic group.

Ethnicity itself, ethnic identity, is left to have some independent existence, some essential definition, even if that definition remains wisely unarticulated. It is left to inhere in the very existence of those who collectively make their claim to particular ethnic identity. There is, however, a Joker in the pack (and it seems to be a Joker studiously avoided by the academic proponents of ethnicity): namely, race!

Lest I be gravely misunderstood, let me clearly state that I hold no brief for the notion of race. Its definition, too, is utterly elusive, its scientific status a nonsense (and there should be no need to argue that here). But in fact the notion of race has acted (and, regrettably, continues to act) as a biological substitute for – indeed, as an earlier formulation of – ethnicity. Moreover, as a biological substitute for the notion of ethnicity, race has, ideologically, a singular advantage, for not only can it act as an alternative encapsulation for the empirical contents of ethnicity – at the same time it is also capable of overriding and ignoring any absences in their array. Historical origins, historical location, the transmission of language and culture are interpreted and linked in terms of a notion of physical 'descent'; but should such origins, locations, and cultural possessions be difficult to prove or to demonstrate, that is of no fundamental consequence, for they are, after all, only *evidence for* what is conceived of as an independent reality whose persuasiveness is actually inherent in the common understanding of a people, an *ethnos* – that it biologically reproduces itself. The arbitrariness of social definition is avoided, the contingencies of history bypassed, the uncertainties of cultural manifestations removed, and a satisfying bedrock arrived at. One is actually, really, truly, and all the vagaries of society, history, and culture notwithstanding, what one claims to be. This, I suspect, is still one of the common, though nowadays increasingly unspoken, axioms of ethnicity. In the Greek case, however, it is still relatively explicit. Outside of a (growing) intellectual minority, one is Greek because one has *elleniko ema* – Greek blood; and even if the notion of blood is perhaps increasingly seen as metaphorical (or metonymic), the notion of descent is not.

In fact, as I have implied, I do not think the Greek case to be exceptional. But at this stage I would hazard a sociological and historical generalization (it can be taken, at least, as an hypothesis): that it is in those cases where the commonplace contents of ethnicity – political incorporation, geographical location, historical continuity, language, and culture – are most problematic that the essence of ethnicity in terms of race and physical descent (indeed the very notion of ethnicity itself as distinct from any or all of the aforementioned) is most likely to be asserted. This does not mean that questions of politics, geography, history, and culture are abandoned. Far from it. They, too, must be argued and with the utmost force. But ontological priorities are reversed. They are not argued in order to justify the notion of a particular ethnic identity. Rather, ethnic identity is already a given, and arguments about politics, geography, history, and culture are adduced not as elements creative of a sense of ethnic identity, but as manifestations of it.

With these general comments in mind, let us return to the particulars of the Greek case.

The historical absence of a specifically 'Greek' *kratos* (state) prior to the War of Independence has already been noted. What runs parallel to this is the geographical dispersal of the *ethnos* – or rather, the geographical dispersal certainly of a population, but more importantly of those cultural elements upon which later claims to ethnic identity could be based.

The spreading-out of Greek-speaking peoples starts as early as the archaic or pre-classical period (and even that dating is somewhat arbitrary). Marseilles, Southern Italy, Sicily, as well as almost the entire littoral of the eastern Mediterranean and the Black Sea were hellenized. Alexander's empire extended a Greek presence even further east, while under Roman rule, Greek (rather than Latin) remained the lingua franca of the eastern Mediterranean. But such expansion is only a prelude. It is the split between east and west, the growth of a separate eastern Empire with its capital in Constantinople, which adumbrates the problem of Greek ethnicity. On the one hand, the centre of Greek-speaking culture moves east (to Byzantium); on the other, Greek culture (or rather Byzantine culture with Greek as the language of prestige and rule and Christianity as its basis) spreads throughout an empire that consolidated itself over most of the Balkans and the entirety of Anatolia until relentlessly compressed by Islam. The political demise of Byzantium did not, however, entail the disappearance of Greek-speaking Christian culture. By the end of the eighteenth century Greek-speaking Christians constituted perhaps one-third of the entire population of the Ottoman Empire and again, as already noted, Greek merchants were a major presence (sometimes *the* major presence) in every city within its bounds – not just in such traditional Hellenic centres as Constantinople and Smyrna (Izmir) but, for example, throughout the Danubian provinces of Moldavia and Wallachia (ruled on behalf of the Ottoman authorities by Greek *hospadars* – in effect, hereditary princes). At the same time the very definition of a Greek ethnos becomes consolidated and given new precision as a result of Ottoman rule, for within its theocratic (but pluralist) structure, divisions of its population were made on the grounds of religion. The *millet-i Rum*, the 'Roman Millet', all the Empire's Orthodox Christian subjects are given corporate identity and placed under the jurisdiction of the Greek Patriarch in Constantinople as *millet-bashi* or 'ethnarch'. The Orthodox Christians now constitute a separate nation within the Empire, and although not all of them were Greek-speakers, with their leadership officially devolved on the Greek-speaking Patriarch (and the small group of Byzantine aristocrats who vied for that high office), a new equation between Hellenism and Christianity was forged (Campbell and Sherrard, 1968:189ff).

The Ottoman period also saw, however, a further dispersal of the ethnos, and Orthodox Greek-speaking communities flourished well beyond the bounds of the Empire, notably in Italy, Russia, Hungary, and Transylvania, but also in every major commercial and financial centre of western and central Europe: Paris, Amsterdam, Vienna, Liepzig, etc. To take a random fact: by the end of the eighteenth century it was estimated that there were 80,000 Greek families within the Hapsburg domains alone (Clogg, 1986:34ff; 1981:93ff). These Greeks of the Diaspora were to play a major part (ideologically, at least) in the formation of a new national consciousness, for on the one hand they were exposed to the political radicalism of late-eighteenth and early nineteenth-century Europe (and especially of the French Revolution); on the other hand (and in contrast with the inhabitants of geographical Greece), they became acutely aware of the all-pervasive prestige of classical Greece throughout the west (Clogg, 1986:36–7).

On the eve of the Greek War of Independence, then, Constantinople was the spiritual centre of the Greek world, but it could be argued that Bucharest and Jassy were its intellectual capitals (Mackridge, 1981), while its economic strength was dispersed throughout the Greek merchant houses of both the Ottoman Empire and western Europe. The success of the Greek War of Independence resulted in the establishment of a specifically Greek *kratos*, the Kingdom of Greece (complete with Bavarian monarch); but by the same token, the problem of the disjunction of *kratos* and *ethnos* is immediately created, for the new Kingdom of Greece comprised only the Peloponnese, the southern half of Peninsular Greece, and some of the Aegean islands. This was, admittedly, the area in which Greek-speaking Christians formed a clear majority of the total population (Dakin, 1972:1). It was also, not unimportantly with regard to international support, the area that contained most of the celebrated sites of classical antiquity. Nevertheless, the total population of this new sovereign state was a mere 750,000 while well over two million Greek-speaking Christians remained scattered throughout the Ottoman Empire (Clogg, 1986:70).

The subsequent political (and military) history of Greece, at least up to 1922 and the 'Asia Minor Catastrophe', can be read as an attempt to rectify this situation: to expand the *kratos* to encompass the *ethnos*, to 'redeem' the Greeks of the Ottoman Emprie and to 'regain' Greek lands. This 'Great Idea', the Megali Idea, received what is perhaps its best-known expression in the words of John Kolettis at the opening of the Greek parliament (*vouli*) in 1844:

> The Kingdom of Greece is not Greece. [Greece] constitutes only one part, the smallest and the poorest. A Greek is not only a man who lives within this kingdom but also one who lives in Jannina, in Salonica, in Serres, in Adrianople, in Constantinople, in Smyrna, in Trebizond, in Crete, in Samos and *in any land associated with Greek history or the Greek race* . . . There are two main centres of Hellenism: Athens, the capital of the Greek Kingdom, [and] 'The City' [Constantinople], the dream and hope of all Greeks.
>
> (trans. R. Clogg, 1986:76; my emphasis)

And Greece did indeed expand, gaining the Ionian Islands in 1864, Thessaly and Arta in 1881, a substantial part of Macedonia, Crete, and the north-eastern Aegean islands in 1913 (thus arriving at what are approximately her present-day borders), and then, briefly, eastern Thrace and Smyrna on the Anatolian coast in the wake of Turkey's defeat in the First

World War and before Greece's ill-fated attempt to march on Ankara led to the Asia Minor Catastrophe, the destruction of Smyrna, and the expulsion of the Greeks from Anatolia after a presence of nearly two and a half thousand years (as well as from Bulgaria and Russia).

Whatever the successes and failures of the Megali Idea, however, it can be seen to raise two aspects of the problem of ethnicity: which were those lands 'associated with Greek history or the Greek race', and who was to be counted a member of 'the Greek race'? The two questions have inevitably fused in the claims and counterclaims of ethnic nationalism. Kolettis' answer to the former question is clear enough in that it is enumerative: a man who lives in Jannina, Salonica, Serres, Adrianople, Constantinople, etc., 'or in any land associated with Greek history or the Greek race'. But the very spread of the Greeks over their two and half thousand years of recorded history – or, since this is in some ways to beg a rather large question, the spread of Hellenic cultural elements, notably language and Orthodox Christianity – meant that the net that such a phrase as 'any land associated with Greek history or the Greek race' cast was geographically a very large one indeed. Inevitably it brought the expanding (and expansionist) Greek state into conflict not only with the crumbling Ottoman Empire, but also with other peoples whom the Ottoman Empire had kept in harness alongside the Greeks and who equally were striving to assert their ethnic independence and to regain their national lands: 'Albanians', 'Bulgarians', 'Serbians', 'Rumanians' (ethnic nationalists of whatever persuasion must forgive my inverted commas). For Greece this problem climaxed in the 'Macedonian Struggle' and from the 1890s onwards Greece was involved in a continual campaign to 'redeem' Macedonia – a campaign that involved both the use of irregular volunteer forces beyond her borders and also a 'cultural' campaign to hellenize (or re-hellenize) its inhabitants. At one stage Macedonia was simultaneously being contested by Greek guerrillas, Bulgarian guerrillas, Serbian guerrillas and even 'Macedonian' guerrillas (not to mention the Ottoman authorities themselves) (Dakin, 1972:159–70).

The outcome of the Balkan Wars (1912; 1913) effectively settled the question of Greece's northern borders, with Macedonia being divided between Greece and Serbia and a smaller section falling to Bulgaria; but the issue still rankles, especially in recent years with the emergence (resurgence?) of an officially tolerated and specifically 'Macedonian' ethnic nationalism within Yugoslavia (and particularly amongst overseas emigrant groups) claiming Macedonian ethnic identity not only for the inhabitants of Yugoslav Macedonia, but also for the slavophone (though usually bilingual) minority of Greek Macedonia. For the Greek state this is anathema. Though it is willing to recognize the existence of Slav-speakers in Greece, it cannot tolerate the notion of Macedonian ethnicity, nor the use of the term Macedonian to designate any ethnic identity separate from

Greek, since, from the Greek point of view, the terms Macedonia and Macedonian are intrinsically Greek – see, after all, the role of Macedonia, Philip, and Alexander the Great in 'The History of Greece'. Slavs there may be – but they are latecomers, 'invaders', and certainly not 'Macedonians', since by definition to be a Macedonian is to be a Greek.[8]

The argument from historical continuity thus comes quickly into play. Macedonia (and other areas) are Greek because 'the Greeks' were there first, and historical headcounts, ethnographic maps of the past, and the linguistic analysis of place names and personal names all become part of the armoury of Greek nationalism. When Salonika, now Greece's second city, was liberated by the Greek army in 1913, the largest section of the city's population in fact consisted of Spanish-speaking sephardic Jews, followed by the Turks (muslims), and then Orthodox Greek-speaking Christians with the slavophones last. But the actual distribution of populations is an irrelevance in the face of history's careful justifications. Macedonia is Greek because Philip, Alexander, and the Macedonian Empire were Greek. Constantinople, Smyrna, the coast of Asia Minor, too, are Greek – they have merely been lost.

The question of Greece's historical lands and who-was-there-first-and-how-many merges almost imperceptibly, however, with an equally vexing one: who do you count? the question, that is, of the actual historical identification of 'the Greeks' and thus (so the argument would have it) of their present descendants. In 1923 in the aftermath of the Asia Minor Catastrophe, that question had to be faced in quite clear-cut and pragmatic terms, for a population exchange was arranged between Greece and Turkey to put an end to the cause of hostilities. In short, the Megali Idea went into reverse: instead of the *kratos* expanding to encapsulate the *ethnos*, the *ethnos* was to 'return' to the *kratos*. The exigencies of the situation demanded the immediate recognition of ethnicity, and it was recognized on one criterion alone: religion. If you were Orthodox Christian you were 'Greek'; if you were muslim you were 'Turk' (Llewellyn Smith, 1973:335–6).[9]

In fact this very pragmatic decision was probably a perfectly sound one – or at least the soundest that could be made. Throughout the Ottoman period it was precisely Orthodox Christianity that had given the Greeks their sense of ethnic identity, their self-definition. *Christiani* had been their own term of self-reference just as it had been the Ottoman administration's classification for them. Moreover, after four hundred years of co-existence the distinction between 'Greek' and 'Turk' could not clearly be made on other cultural grounds, except possibly language. Admittedly, there were anomalies and oddities. Many of the 'Turks' exiled from Crete were the descendants of those who had apostasized to Islam during the seventeenth century and they arrived in Anatolia speaking only Greek. Conversely, Greece received the Karamanli, Orthodox Christians to be sure, but turkophones and in most other cultural respects Turkish (Clogg, 1986:120–1). But on the whole the politicians probably got it right. In terms of self-perceptions, in terms of self-identification, in terms of the *social construction* of ethnicity, the 'self-definition of a social entity', religion, Orthodox Christianity *versus* Islam did constitute the cornerstone of the distinction between 'Greek' and 'Turk'. The irony is that it was only under such extreme circumstances and in the face of having to make a clear-cut and practical decision that what might now be seen as a 'theoretically correct' position was adopted. Ideologically I doubt that it was a satisfying one – or rather, I doubt that religion was seen as the crux of 'ethnicity as *self-identification'*. Rather, along with other cultural phenomena (again, notably language) it was seen as *evidence for* something more 'essential'. Kazantzakis' novel *The Life and Politics of Alexis Zorba* (1961) is revealing. Following the Asia Minor Catastrophe it was not only from Turkey that the Greeks had to flee (Clogg, 1986:120), and the author's 'friend' writes back from Russia:

> Half a million Greeks are in danger in the south of Russia and the Caucasus. Many of them speak only Turkish or Russian, but their hearts speak Greek fanatically. They are of our race. Just to look at them – the way their eyes flash, rapacious, ferrety, the cunning and sensuality of their lips when they smile, the way they have managed to become bosses and have moujiks working for them in this immense territory of Russia – it's quite enough to convince you that they are the descendants of your beloved Odysseus.
>
> (trans. Clogg, 1986:145)

'Culture', language, give way to the intuitive perception of something less mutable, of something more fundamental, of something eternal: race.

What I have been trying to suggest, in a ridiculously compressed fashion, is that the normal criteria for ethnicity, or rather the normal criteria for a *sense* of ethnic identity – political unity, geographical unity, cultural unity, all within the embrace of a unified historical tradition – have been harder to maintain within the Greek context than in some other European contexts. The paradoxical (but not unexpected) effect has actually been to promote the notion of the *ethnos* in defiance of these and to promote it in the one form that would seem to afford it a 'natural' unity: physical continuity and descent. But in fact two other specific considerations must be taken into account, which have promoted both the concept of ethnicity itself and the particular form that ethnicity assumes in Greece: namely, the prestige of classical Greece and the challenge that the German scholar Fallmerayer made to the modern Greek state's claims to it.

In 1821 Prince Alexander Ipsilandis, a 'Phanariot' Greek aristocrat from one of the great families of Constantinople and one-time aide-de-camp to the Tsar of Russia proclaimed in Jassy (Roumania) the liberation of 'the classical land of Greece' and, with an army that included a 'Sacred Battalion' of 700 university students (in imitation of ancient Thebes) prepared to march south to liberate Greece. They were wiped out (Clogg, 1986:50–2).

The War of Liberation was, however, fought and won by a somewhat unlikely combination of highly educated, idealistic, aristocratic, and westernized Greeks (such as Ipsilandis' brother, Dimitrios); the tough, uneducated mountain brigands of Greece itself (the *klephts*); and finally the military and diplomatic intervention of the Great Powers (not to mention the less-effective intervention of a peculiar crew of university students, soldiers-of-fortune, charlatans, and genuine Philhellenes of whom Lord Byron is merely the best known).[10]

Differences between the categories of participants in the war were many, but one concerned their vision (or lack of vision) about Greece itself. The westernized, educated Greeks who came to liberate Greece came, as Ipsilandis pronounced, to liberate its *classical* lands. They came invoking Miltiades, Themistocles, Leonidas, and all the rest to restore Greece to her former glory[11] – to a glory that was frankly unknown and of no concern to the inhabitants of mainland Greece itself whose ambitions were both more pragmatic and more limited: to kill their muslim masters and take their property. Greeks they may well have been, but classical Greece meant little to them, not even its name. They were Christians and (like the Byzantines before them) they tended to call themselves 'Romii' (though with no knowledge of the Romans) and the language they spoke 'Romaika' (in fact demotic Greek). The great hero of the war, Kolokotronis, did address his men as 'Hellenes', but he thought the title referred to some mythical race of supermen. It was only later in the company of scholars that he discovered his historical ethnicity (Dakin, 1972:8 n. 3).

But if it was the muscle and the muskets of such men as Kolokotronis that won the war on the ground, ideologically it was the views of the externally educated Greeks – the Greeks of the Diaspora and the aristocratic Greeks of Constantinople – that prevailed, for the Liberation of Greece became the *cause célèbre* of liberal Europe, and popular support was based almost on a single notion: the resuscitation of Ancient Greece (St Clair, 1972:51ff). Indeed the war was reported in the western press as a virtual replay of the Battle of Marathon and the Persian Wars. Brought up on a diet of romanticized classicism the west offered to the Greeks a version of their ethnic identity that they were simply in no position to refuse.

The problem was that on direct acquaintance the Greeks of Greece did not much resemble the classical Greeks of the west's imagination. Nor is that surprising. It was rather as if Victorian England had been asked to paint itself blue and drive around in knife-wheeled chariots to prove its cultural legitimacy. Nevertheless, in the Greek case the attempt was made. In fact that project had been embarked on before the War of Liberation. Financed by the Diaspora Greeks and wealthy Greek merchants, hundreds of books extolling Greece's classical past were printed in Europe to be distributed at Greek schools whose purpose was to 're-educate' the Greeks in the glories of their ancestors and to promote classical Greek (or a version of it) to replace the degenerate and 'unworthy' tongue of demotic Greek.[12] With their kilts and their coffee, their moustaches and their worry-beads, the inhabitants of mainland Greece and the Peloponnese might not seem very 'classical', and certainly they were not well acquainted with their past – but what *had* to be proved was that they were the very descendants of Pericles – and this for a remarkably diverse population whose villages were as likely to speak Albanian or Vlach as they were to speak demotic Greek. What now was on every nationalist's lips was not only the liberation of Greece but also the 'regeneration' of the Greeks. The patina of 'four hundred years of slavery' was to be removed; only then would Greece's true metal shine.

From its inception the Greek educational system played a vital role in this enterprise; so, as Michael Herzfeld (1982) has shown, did the study of Greek folklore (*laographia*), an enterprise that was to be both archaeological and patriotic.[13] The search for cultural continuities became an obsession to the point of absurdity. Thus, for example:

> It is known that in Homeric antiquity . . . the basic food was, according to Homer, baked barley flour. Corresponding (sic) today, the basic food of the Greek people is bread, which, although usually made of wheat flour, is frequently made from ground corn . . .
>
> (Kyriakides, 1968:77)

And where a very judicious selection of material culture and of the 'customs and habits' of the Greeks, *ta ithi ke ethima* as the stock phrase goes, begins to flag, then the argument can always be shifted to the metaphysical plane where the various achievements of the Greek-speaking peoples (and some who forgot their Greek) can nevertheless be attributed to the manifold expression of a constant 'genius', of, indeed, the *elliniko pnevma*, the 'Greek spirit'.

Such a concern with cultural continuity was not (and is not) a concern to demonstrate the historical transmission of culture itself; rather it is a concern to demonstrate the literal continuity of a race, a people, an *ethnos* who are the natural *bearers* of that culture despite their historical dispersion, and despite what might seem to the uninitiated (or the malevolent) their present cultural diversity and their present departures from the stereotype of classical Hellenism. And it was the very success of classical Hellenism, the prestige of ancient Greece, which from the inception of the modern Greek state made this a necessity; for it was only by asserting a direct and physical link with the classical past that the Greeks could reclaim as their particular and unique possession a cultural inheritance that had been systematically appropriated (in various forms) by the entirety of the western world for nearly two thousand years and throughout a period during which its manifestations within the Greek world itself were meagre to say the least. Edinburgh might be 'the Athens of the north', but it was understandably important to remind the world that it was built in imitation of a genius still present and alive in the south (even if Athens' own neoclassical architecture had been largely designed by foreigners) (Fletcher, 1977:160).

But what, perhaps more than anything else, galvanized the Greeks into their assertion of direct lineal descent from the Greeks of the classical period and into the parallel assertion of the racial integrity and unity of the *ethnos* were the publications in 1830 and 1836 of a two-volume work by the German scholar Fallmerayer whose thesis was that the Slavs who entered Greece in the sixth and seventh centuries (in fact the seventh and eighth centuries) so overran the country that not a drop of pure Hellenic blood was left. In short, the Greeks were not 'Greeks'. If the west in its admiration for the classical past gave the new Greek state a compelling need to proclaim its unique heritage, it also forced it to defend its claims and, indeed, set the terms in which that claim had to be defended (Herzfeld, 1982:75ff). From the start it was not just the unity of the far-flung *ethnos* from Odessa to Alexandria, from Jassy to Cyprus that had to be maintained, but also the integrity of the population of mainland Greece itself, which, from village to village, might be found speaking Albanian, Slavic, or Vlach (romance) as well as or instead of Greek and whose customs and habits might seem to bear as much if not more relation to those of the other peoples of the Balkans and indeed of Anatolia as they did to what were fondly imagined to be those of Periclean Athens. Fallmerayer's thesis is now universally rejected (though it was revived by the Third Reich)[14] and largely on the grounds of the survival of the Greek language itself. But it has left an indelible mark on the Greek consciousness. For all that cultural continuity has been the obsession of Greek scholarship, culture itself turned out to be a double-edged weapon. An essentialist definition of ethnicity had to be maintained: the Greeks of Greece and the *ethnos* as a whole, whatever their language, whatever their customs, whatever their location, and whatever their citizenship, are Greek because they have 'Greek blood'. And if I have called this paper 'Triumph of the Ethnos', it is because, in popular understanding, it is this concept of 'the' *ethnos* that has prevailed. In Greece there are no Vlachs claiming separate status (though their grandparents spoke Vlach); there are no Albanians claiming separate status (though their fathers spoke Albanian); even in northern Greece, and despite the arguments of Macedonians both in Yugoslavia and overseas, there appears to be little demand from Greece's slav-speakers for separate recognition. Indeed, it has been one of the remarkable achievements of Greece to forge within a little over one hundred and fifty years a nation–state of which Greek ethnicity is the cornerstone. In Greece itself there is no 'ethnic problem': only for the historian a problem of 'the *ethnos*'.

Notes

1. In this context Michael Herzfeld is an honourable exception. *Ours Once More: Folklore, Ideology and the Making of Modern Greece* (1982) deals precisely with the concept of Greek ethnicity as it manifested itself in the works of the early Greek folklorists, and his subsequent ethnographic volume, *The Poetics of Manhood: Contest and Identity in a Cretan Mountain Village* (1985) again touches perceptively on local notions of 'what it is to be Greek'. Amongst scholars in Greece itself, the question of Greek identity and ethnicity now appears to be receiving serious sociological attention. See, for example, *Ellinismos, Ellinikotita (Hellenism, Greekness)*, D.G. Tsaousis (ed.), 1983.

2. Melbourne was the scene of the First International Congress on Macedonian Studies in February of 1988. Its organizers, AIMS (Australian Institute of Macedonian Studies) is representative only of Greek Macedonians, and since the papers delivered were almost exclusively concerned with Greek culture and included such topics as 'The Falsification of the History of Macedonia', and since, moreover, invited guests included the Hon. Stelios Papathemelis, Minister for Northern Greece, it was seen by Melbourne's Slavic Macedonian community as a direct challenge to their own claims to Macedonian ethnicity and occasioned public demonstrations by the Slavic Macedonian community. More recently it has been reported that the Minister for Northern Greece requested the Prime Minister of Australia (Robert Hawke) to change a chapter concerning Australian Macedonians in the forthcoming Australian Bicentenary encyclopaedia *The Australian People*. The request was refused. (Slavic) Macedonian groups have also approached various Australian politicians requesting changes to the contents of the encyclopaedia and had asked the Yugoslav government to intervene. Similar problems occurred with the publication in 1980 of the Harvard University Press encyclopedia of the American peoples over the inclusion of a chapter on 'Macedonians' with the current Democratic presidential nominee, Michael Dukakis, being a vocal opponent (The Melbourne *AGE*, Monday 2 May, 1988).

3. Neither the Turkish-speakers of Thrace (who are officially a religious minority but not an 'ethnic' minority) nor Greece's gypsies appear particularly well-studied. Peter Loizos has prepared an unpublished memorandum on the position of Thracian Turkish-speaking Muslims in Greece (1981) but I know of no published anthropological report. Meraklis (1984:84) claims that Greece's total gypsy population is approximately 50,000. A brief article on their dialect appeared by Messing (1986).

4. The words of Constantine Tsatsos, then President of Greece, which appeared in an official publication (in English), *Greece: a Portrait* (1979) are not unrepresentative of the prevailing attitude:

   For thousands of years this race has pursued its course, full of event (sic) and striving, and it has often mapped out brilliant and luminous paths in the history of mankind.

A living reality still is the Greece of Homer, of Aristotle, of Praxiteles, of Photios, of Pletho.
A living reality also is present-day Greece . . . Thermopylae, Mesolonghi, the Albanian front, the Battle of Crete are all of a piece, one, and indivisible.

(Tsatsos, 1979)

5. When, for example, such statements are made as 'Greece invented democracy' (as they often are by both Greek journalists and politicians), there is, of course a 'telescoping' of the modern Greek state with the city–state of Athens – otherwise it would also have to be admitted that Greece also invented tyranny, oligarchy, and most other institutionalized forms of rule.
6. Herodotos 8:144.
7. The degree to which there was a specifically Greek 'ethnic' consciousness *within* the Byzantine Empire is, however, a matter of some debate. See, for example, Vryonis (1978).
8. I am greatly indebted to George Hadzikosmidis, 'The Macedonian Question', unpublished fourth-year honours dissertation, Monash University, for much of my understanding of the present state of the Macedonian Question.
9. Exception was made for the Christian inhabitants of Constantinople and the Muslim inhabitants of Western Thrace who were allowed to remain *in situ* (Llewellyn Smith, 1973:335).
10. For a full account of the activities of the Philhellenes, see St Clair, 1972.
11. For a translation of Ipsilandis' speech, see Clogg, 1976:201.
12. For the dissemination of classical learning in Greece, see Clogg, 1983.
13. Orlandos, 1969, cited in Herzfeld, 1982:11.
14. See Kyriakidis, 1968:47.

References

Ardener, E. (1976) ' "Social fitness" and the idea of "survival" ', *JASO* vii (2):99–102.
Austin, M.M. and Vidal-Naquet, P. (1977) *Economic and Social History of Ancient Greece*, London: Batesford Academic and Educational Ltd. (Orig. French edition 1972.)
Browning, P. (1964) 'Byzantine scholarship', *Past and Present* 28:3–20.
Campbell, J.K. (1964) *Honour, Family and Patronage*, Oxford: Oxford University Press.
Campbell, J.K. and Sherrard, P. (1968) *Modern Greece*, London: Ernest Benn.
Clogg, R. (1976) (ed. and trans.) *The Movement for Greek Independence 1770–1821, a Collection of Documents*, London: Macmillan.
Clogg, R. (1981) 'The Greek mercantile bourgeoisie: "progressive" or "reactionary" ' in R. Clogg (ed.) *Balkan Society in the Age of Greek Independence*, Totowa, New Jersey: Barnes & Noble, 85–110.
Clogg, R. (1983) 'Sense of the past in pre-independence Greece', in R. Sussex and J.C. Eade (eds) *Culture and Nationalism in Nineteenth-Century Eastern Europe*, Columbus, Ohio: Slavica Publishers Inc. & Humanities Research Centre, Australian National University, 7–30.
Clogg, R. (1986) *A Short History of Modern Greece*, 2nd edn, Cambridge: Cambridge University Press.
Dakin, D. (1972) *The Unification of Greece 1770–1923*, London: Ernest Benn.
Fletcher, R. (1977) 'Cultural and intellectual developments 1821–1911' in J.T.A. Koumoulids (ed.) *Greece in Transition*, London: Zeno, 153–72.

(1979) *Greece: a Portrait*, Athens: Research and Publicity Center, KEDE Ltd.

Hadzikosmidis, G. (1988) 'The Macedonian question', unpublished 4th-year honours dissertation, Monash University.

Herzfeld, M. (1982) *Ours Once More: Folklore, Ideology and the Making of Modern Greece*, Austin, Texas: University of Texas Press.

Herzfeld, M. (1985) *The Poetics of Manhood: Contest and Identity in a Cretan Mountain Village*, Princeton: Princeton University Press.

Kyriakides, S.P. (1968) *Two Studies on Modern Greek Folklore*, Thessalonika: Institute for Balkan Studies (trans. R.A. Georges and A.A. Katranides).

Llewellyn Smith, M. (1973) *Ionian Vision: Greece in Asia Minor 1919–1922*, London: Allen Lane.

Loizos, P. (1981) Unpublished memorandum on the Turkish-speaking Muslims of Western Thrace.

Mackridge, P. (1981) 'The Greek intelligensia 1780–1830', in R. Clogg (ed.) *Balkan Society in the Age of Greek Independence*, Totowa, New Jersey: Barnes & Noble.

Meraklis, M.G. (1984) *Elliniki Laographia* (Greek Folklore), Athens: Odysseas.

Messing, (1986) 'A Greek gypsy dialect in historical perspective', *Journal of Modern Greek Studies* 4(2):121–8.

St Clair, W. (1972) *That Greece Might Still Be Free*, Oxford: Oxford University Press.

Tsaousis, D.G. (1983) (ed.) *Ellinismos, Ellinikotita* (Hellenism, Greekness), Athens: Estia.

Vryonis, S. (1978) 'Recent scholarship on continuity and discontinuity of culture; classical Greeks, Byzantines, modern Greeks', in S. Vryonis (ed.) *Byzantina kai Metabyzantina, the 'Past' in Medieval and Modern Greek Culture*, Malibu: Undena Publications, 237–56.

Chapter six

Investigating 'Social Memory' in a Greek Context[1]

Anna Collard

In this paper I explore some of the ways in which a particular history is experienced, conceptualized, and used in the present. By doing so I hope to show how the identity of a modern Greek village is in part created. My fieldwork took place among a group of six mountain villages in the province of Evritania, Central Greece.[2] I lived in a 'head' village, Agios Vissarios, and the data on which the following is based relate mainly to that village.

The particular history to which I refer covers three main periods.[3] The first is a generalized Ottoman period, which in fact refers to the late-eighteenth and early nineteenth centuries in the villages concerned.[4] The villagers today vividly 'remember' this period despite the obvious fact that they did not live through it. The second historical period covers the 1930s and the early 1940s. During the latter years, Greece entered the Second World War and was subsequently occupied by the Germans (1941–4). In the 1930s and throughout the occupation period, these villages found themselves, in one way or another, in opposition to the State and practised forms of 'self-government'.[5] The final historical period covers the civil war of 1946–9, a time of considerable political and social upheaval in the course of which these villages were forcibly evacuated to neighbouring urban centres for a period of three years (1947–50). Obviously, there is another sense in which the particular history of these villages might cover a continuous period from their settlement to the present day. And the present, 'now' (1950–79), is seen as another distinct historical period of conceptual importance to the villagers. The reasons for pinpointing these three periods, however, has precisely to do with 'social memory'.[6]

My concern is to investigate why the villagers have chosen to remember certain historical periods or events, the first and third outlined previously. Indeed, it was a puzzle to me why these periods alone should be selected for memory when others – the second period, for example, remain understated though they appear as equally eventful and formative, and how this type of memory bears on contemporary aspects of social life or of social relations.

My point is that social memory provides certain historical data – interesting in the absence of other written sources but not a substitute for them[7] – for the reconstruction of an 'effective' past. At the same time, it illustrates just how 'history' is actually experienced, reconstituted, and finally used in the present. My interest here lies in exploring how the wider forces of history – changes in objective conditions brought about, for example, by such events as war or civil war, and generated outside the community – are brought to bear on that community and how they are defined by its inhabitants. As such, memories of the past may supply some of the terms for understanding the historical process itself; a process involved in structuring the social conditions and practices being investigated. Through this, social memory can also be seen to bear on the identity of the village in a particular way.

I have used the term social memory to cut across other types of memory but also to mark it off as a particular type of discourse. It is, for example, individual and 'privatized'; that is, biography, but biography in a context that masquerades as historical fact. It is also collective memory in that it is shared by a group of people who share a history and over which there is some consensus. It is popular in that it does not necessarily accord with dominant, public, or official historical representations but is nevertheless in relationship with, and influenced by these. Nor has it a chronology; there are omissions, and different time scales are juxtaposed. An Ottoman past immediately precedes the present day, for instance, related in what might be called a dichotomy of time.

Finally, it is social because it derives from a social milieu, not in this case one derived from genealogy, the life cycle, or 'the history of the village' (with its particular seasons, festivals, and so on[8]) but from the social effects of history itself.

Theoretical underpinnings of social memory

My point of departure for the term social memory is twofold. It lies partly in my attempts to look at change in general among these villages; that is, change brought about by historical events. Partly it lies in certain anomalies I faced in my specific fieldwork situation. Namely, why do certain, seemingly crucial historical events, or 'moments', appear to be forgotten or ignored, while others assume a greater importance than might at first appear warranted?

I shall state the first argument at its simplest. As has been debated for some time, especially among Marxist historians and aided by the findings of anthropology, it is clear that historical change is not a simple process. It is not just a structural feature nor something that can be superimposed on a 'normal', static view of social life in the community. Nor does change eventuate because a given 'infrastructure' gives rise to a corresponding 'superstructure'. In the words of E.P. Thompson, changes also 'are experienced in social and cultural life, refracted in men's ideas and their values, argued through in their actions, choices and beliefs' (Thompson, 1978). As, for instance, a mode of production changes or relations of power or of ownership change, as a result perhaps of certain conflicts into which the community is drawn, or between the community and the dominant social order, so does the *experience* of men and women. And to cite Thompson (1978) this can be understood in a variety of ways: in 'the cognitive organisation of social life', in new ways of thinking, as well as in kinship, gender, and class ways and in 'a variety of different actions of consensus, resignation or resistance'.

For Thompson, the category 'experience' becomes crucial for understanding the part played by conscious human choice, beliefs, and particular actions in history. It is for him:

a category which however imperfect it may be, is indispensable to the historian, since it comprises the mental and emotional response, whether of an individual or of a social group, to many inter-related events or to many repetitions of the same event.

(Thompson, 1978)

He later refines the category by dividing it into 'experience I – lived experience' and 'experience II – perceived experience' (Thompson, 1981). Thompson's argument, of course, relates to a whole body of knowledge and profound theoretical and philosophical issues concerning, among other things, the relationship between 'social being' and 'social consciousness'.

The point for me is simply how 'history' can be said to work through experience. Lived experience here includes war, death, resistance – fighting, civil war, economic crisis. This type of experience forces people to think in new ways, to reconsider, for example, the balance of power, the law, the economy, and even kinship. The changes resulting from the lived conditions and the new thinking give rise to changed 'experience', that is, to different lived experiences and new perceptions.

It seems to me that access to this kind of experience is in part provided by considering social memory. As a type of discourse on both past and present it can assist in identifying the *meanings* people give to their conditions and social relations, reflecting the ways in which these are actually lived by the community with its norms, expectations, and the 'popular mentalities' it reveals more generally. Social memory as such may also help in outlining the conflicts that arise within a community or between it and the 'outer', dominant society.

The initial ethnographic question, the early 1940s

What I initially set out to investigate were aspects of the decade of war, 1940–50 and in particular the self-governing[9] institutions of the occupation period (1941–4).

The period of national resistance (1941–4) left many communities in Greece without formal government. As a result popular institutions known as local 'self-government' and 'people's justice' emerged. What became crucial in the investigation were the ways in which people are seen to interpret and use their particular history in the present.

To begin with I focused on two issues. The first arose from my interest in the nature and legacy of the institutions of self-government; the extent to which these institutions represented a radical departure from the past and whether they had changed the form of certain social relations or assisted in transforming them in such a way as to give the area a distinctive development today. Second, I was interested in the specific development of Evritania, and of Agios Vissarios in particular today. This issue was to provide a wider context for the first and to deal with aspects of local government as well as the relationship between village and the State.

Alternative local questions

It comes as no surprise that the whole of the war period had profound effects on the local inhabitants and consequences that, in specific ways, are still fresh in people's minds.

Most significantly, the later Civil War has meant that nearly every family today has lost at least one member who was either killed, or went missing, or fled to Eastern Europe or emigrated elsewhere as a direct result. The devastation of fields, crops, fruit trees, and livestock changed the topography of the area and meant, among other things, that production had to change after 1950. Political repression consequent to the Civil War also changed the forms of local political representation and the general power structure. There are many reminders of this past.

I was struck by the fact that I came up against a lack of suitable data in trying to reconstruct the period of occupation and by the unwillingness to discuss the institutions of self-government in any detail despite a general, tacit agreement that they had indeed occurred in the village and many of those living in the village today had, in one way or another, been involved with them. I concluded that this lack of information went beyond the mere sensitivity of these subjects; first, because there was not a uniform conspiracy of silence surrounding them; second, because they were not condemned outright in the way that most other things pertaining to the resistance movement in general, or suggesting 'communism' or the Left tended to be vociferously attacked; last, because the whole manner in which the institutions were obliquely referred to seemed to suggest something more than this.

In brief, major events of the war period were mentioned but mostly in terms of the personal experiences they afforded or sometimes to pin down another kind of memory or make a general proverbial point. But the specific events of the early 1940s and especially the institutions of self-government, remained clouded in a shadowy silence.

In contrast to this silence, the period of the following Civil War was constantly referred to every day and in most conversations, whatever the subject. It is interesting in this context, but at first surprising, that the village under Ottoman rule also proved to be a very common referral point in everyday conversation.

This state of affairs, the lack of detailed information on the occupation years or indeed on the 1930s – which were loosely alluded to as a vague reflection of 'how things were' as many informants were growing up – the importance of the Civil War and the emphasis on an Ottoman past seemed to suggest other possibilities. In fact, the lack of local data (or the lack of consensus on certain historical events) and the selective use of history over which there was considerable village consensus, led me precisely to the question of social memory.

Social memory and the Civil War

Part of the centrality of the Civil War lies in the fact that during it, all the communities of Evritania were removed to neighbouring towns.[10] Among other things this meant that the physical continuity of the villages was actually broken for the first time since their settlement. Apart from the hardships the villagers underwent as refugees, their removal from the villages had a variety of other consequences. With the break-up of the village, the social community was dispersed and all forms of social reckoning – a whole body of knowledge – were, temporarily at least, rendered meaningless. For instance, property ownership, kin status, social values, and criteria for the judging of everyday events and social behaviour, were no longer appropriate when removed from the well-defined boundaries of the community of which they were a part. Social relationships in general assumed new, and often national, political significance in which, however unwittingly, few villagers remained neutral. In addition, conflicts between the village and the 'outer' society, that is, the whole articulation of the village with the State, acquired different dimensions redefining assumed boundaries and acts of both consensus and resistance.

It is reasonable to assume that the consequences of Civil War were such that however the preceding institutions of self-government were applied, and whatever their significance at the time in the life of the community, the Civil War coloured the assessment of the earlier events. Previously, self-government had taken place within the framework of daily community life and could be assessed in those known terms.

This may go some way in explaining why the villagers are today unwilling to discuss the events of the early 1940s. It is likely that combined with intense post-war, anti-resistance and anti-left wing reprisals and propaganda, the events of the Civil War – and especially evacuation – deprived the people concerned of a framework within which to discuss the institutions of self-government, and of a basis on which to judge them in the future. Under the circumstances it was perhaps easier to obscure them from memory and deprive them of any continued historical significance.

The 1930s

On the other hand, the lack of information could suggest that the self-governing institutions of the early 1940s only scratched the surface of village life. Historical and eyewitness accounts of the time suggest that this was not the case. Villagers in these mountain areas were actively involved in running their affairs and attempts were made by them to bring about radical reforms in existing rural–agricultural conditions.[11] Even the unsympathetic are agreed that this period (1941–4) saw wide-scale changes that fundamentally altered rural life.[12]

The silence surrounding the events of the self-governing institutions has possibly a third basis. Perhaps the institutions did not constitute a radical change in community life. It is possible, for example, that they were seen as a *continuation* of developments that had been gathering momentum at least throughout the 1930s and perhaps in earlier periods. That is, various attempts at improving local rural and agricultural conditions and in establishing certain legal and other politico-economic rights had long been on the agenda. There is evidence to support this view.[13]

My point is that these institutions have not been selected by memory as being important in the sense of being radical innovations. Instead, they are comprehended as part of a more general state of affairs that had certainly begun in the 1930s and had intermittently existed in earlier periods. Self-government of the early 1940s, then, took place within this framework. The real break came with the Civil War. For this reason social memory clearly divides the modern history of the village into (1) the prewar years up to 1946/7, (2) the Civil War, and (3) 'after', that is, 1950 to the present.

This local periodization redirected my own investigation. It became obvious that the self-governing institutions had to be appraised in a longer historical context and one that included a whole set of relationships, or perceived relationships, between the State and the village. Understanding this context might help explain the silence surrounding the early 1940s, the centrality of the Civil War as well as the reconstruction of an Ottoman past, and how the village today defined itself within such a framework.

The Ottoman period

A generalized Ottoman age is another major period selected for constant comment by the local inhabitants. The way in which this period is discussed suggests that it is part of a continuous present that was personally witnessed. It is common for villagers to describe in graphic detail the actual appearance of Ottoman Turks as 'they strolled round the village', what exactly they wore, and how they behaved. One informant even 'recalled' a 'Turkish woman sitting on a swing' under the plane tree that stands today in the village square, 'her eyes looking out from under her veil, the most beautiful woman in the world!' These statements are quite acceptable to the rest of the village who would never question their validity unless they wished to challenge an informant's authority in general.

Some of the events of the Ottoman period commonly referred to clearly have a basis in fact and have been passed down the generations, illustrating either the history of a particular family or of the village in general. Others may have been learnt about at school.

What is interesting is the apparent correspondence between, for example, the recalling of events and an informant's claims to wealth, dignity, or a certain social position either in the past or in the village today. In other words, there appears to be a relationship between the alleged biography of an informant and the way he/she might discuss the period.

Here, I cannot give the necessary quotations that illustrate these points in detail showing just how individual informants talk about their lives and express their 'experience' of Ottoman rule and their various claims. Instead, I shall make a few summary points. First, an individual's social memory about the Ottoman past is revealing for a number of different reasons, not least because it is contrary to existing documentation.[14] None of the documentation found for the area suggests any degree of hardship or servility to Turkish overlords as some of the informants vividly describe. Agios Vissarios is, in fact, singled out in these documents as being superior in its landholdings, cultivated areas, expanse of surrounding forests, number of springheads, and the 'general prosperity of its inhabitants'. The village was also the seat of both a flourishing Greek school and an important monastery, which became a known refuge for Greeks fleeing the Ottoman authorities (Vasiliou, 1979b). Of course, the lack of reference to any hardship may say more about the documentors themselves. At the same time, however, the notions of suffering under the Ottoman yoke were officially encouraged as Greece began to fight for its independence in the early nineteenth century as an emergent nation–state and are kept alive today for different political reasons.

Second, an individual's social memory of this past is closely related to his/her economic and political standing in the village today, biographical details, and family claims in both the present and past. Thus, for example, biographical details are presented as historical 'facts' about life under the Ottoman Turks and, indeed, the relationship between Turk and Greek becomes strikingly different according to whether a person considers him- or herself and is considered by others to be 'rich/powerful' or 'poor' today.

Third, the emphasis on an Ottoman past also suggests a general belief about when and how the village was first settled. It is something of an origin myth. There is no firm evidence confirming when this might have been, but it was well before the late-eighteenth century. All the present patronymic kin groups, however, trace their origins to this period and the early nineteenth century. Many insist on direct kinship with famous freedom fighters (*klephts*) of the War of Independence of 1821, and others to renowned brigands who had operated in the area free of 'the yoke of Turk and State'. There is some dispute as to how many Turkish families settled in the village and the nature of their relationship with the Greeks. Each informant represents this relationship differently as one of greater or less hardship.

Another revealing element in the villagers' views of the past has to do with their use of language or image. Several older informants described their early schooling in the village during the first two decades of the twentieth century in terms almost identical to those used by others to describe the 'secret Greek school' under the Ottoman Turks. Similar images and identical phrases are used to describe very different periods.

Apart from these examples, the Ottoman period is celebrated as a time of freedom fighters (and brigands), of national resistance, of patriotism and heroic deeds. Importantly, it was viewed as a time when a great degree of regional autonomy existed and 'government didn't sit on our heads', or 'no-one could reach us up here in *Agrafa*'. Local forms of government, elected councils of elders, and the fact that people took their own decisions are also referred to when discussing this period, or at least the years leading up to Independence.

This brings me to another reason why the Ottoman period should be singled out by social memory. It is possible that it also provides a means of talking about some aspects of the early 1940s. It may be that one historical 'story' has come to stand in for another which, for a variety of reasons, cannot be spoken of in any other way. The use of language in talking about the past and 'nowadays' – which are normally presented together – reveals a particular verbal style that indicates just how the past is conceptualized in relation to the present. To make this fully comprehensible would require a paper in its own right. Two points can be made about this. The one underlines the use of common images to describe very different periods or events suggesting that there is some kind of culturally

constituted format for certain types of historical thinking. The second has
to do with the vague terms used to describe historical time. 'Then', 'after',
'before', 'not like now' emphasize this point as does the common use of
'they' instead of spelling out exactly who is meant. The latter term is
particularly important in references to the Civil War where 'they' can refer
to just about anyone. Thus, for example, one old woman described her
experiences of the Civil War:

> It was July when we left. Our men were already in Karpenisi and had
> arranged with the Nomarch, who knows with whom else, to come and
> take us from our villages. And we went together women and children
> from place to place hiding from them . . . I took the two girls and two
> goats that's all. Not that we ate anything of the goats because they took
> our food from us in Karpenisi and whatever else they could find in the
> shops.

Repeated questioning revealed that 'our men' were the national army;
'hiding from them' meant hiding from different extreme right-wing bands
as well as guerrillas of the left; that 'they' who took the goats were actually
Red Cross officials helping to resettle these refugees and the 'they' taking
from shops, hearsay about guerrillas and/or members of the national
army. Of course, to a co-villager these terms might not be as vague as
they appear to an outsider, just as the terminology applied to the Civil
War itself ('intertribal war', 'bandit war', etc.) immediately indicates to
another Greek one's political beliefs. On the other hand, the use of a
more neutral 'they' for everyone does seem to be a way of minimizing the
implied conflicts as well as fitting into a whole spectrum of convictions as
to which was the 'correct' side.

In summary, the Ottoman period seems to provide a vehicle for a
continued, often critical, commentary on contemporary village life and
what is accepted, by and large, as the norm. Through it are expressed
(changing) local inequalities of wealth and/or power. Other types of
relations are also expressed in this way, for example, those of conflict or
of acceptance of a broader field of power or of the State. At the same
time, it affords a way of talking about a personal past – of poverty, of
hardship, even of wartime experiences – which, in this form, is less open
to challenge or criticism. The Ottoman period also takes on the guise of
an origin myth, suggesting the origins of the village but also those of
inequalities in wealth and power.

At one point, however, the Ottoman past links up with a national
culture of patriotism, Greek heroism, and ideas about a united Greek
nation. At the same time it can provide a type of discourse about a less
officially acceptable past. It may be that it is a way of talking about the
'forbidden' topic of self-government in the occupation period.

In contrast, the Civil War expresses very real and threatened disorder as well as the discontinuity of the past with the present. It also represents another set of social relationships. For instance, many current agrarian disputes are often couched in terms of the Civil War when, it emerges, they involve contemporary issues. Disagreements among kin also tend to be attributed to the Civil War when more recent causes are at stake.

The legacy of Civil War and the present

The way in which the local inhabitants remember their past led me to reformulate my historical periods. The war period (1940–50) is not seen as a single unit but becomes separable into two distinct parts. In this the institutions of self-government appear as part of a longer process and the Civil War emerges as crucial and determining. The Civil War brought about a radical transformation of village life within a few years and for most people marked the end of an old era and the beginning of widening horizons. This break in continuity manifested itself at every level, demographically, topographically, in agriculture, and in social relations. The human death toll, evacuation (many people never returned to their villages after it), and increased migration for direct political reasons, not to mention those imprisoned and in concentration camps, extensively depopulated the whole province.[15] The wide-scale destruction of houses, fields, forests, and livestock changed the villages physically. New houses, in different styles, were built on new sites, different village centres emerged; nearly all the fields beyond the immediate periphery of the village were abandoned. There were numerous direct effects on the economy and on kinship structures; on norms and expectations.

In Agios Vissarios, chestnut production was intensified as a cash crop and cereals that were grown before the war were no longer grown. The loss of working hands altered the productive unit and the recruitment of surplus labour gave kin categorization a new dimension. The loss of labour and the increased production of a single cash crop made the village less self-sufficient. There was an increased dependence on the State for subsidized grain and other foodstuffs, and on foreign remittances. The changes in production also meant the loss of various co-operative agricultural practices and customs.

The most notable change in political life was the prohibition of any left-wing or progressive party after the Civil War. The way in which the Civil War was subsequently interpreted by the dominant, right-wing status quo, influenced political thought as well as publicly instituted representations of the past.[16] In this sense, thinking about the village in both the present and the past had to change. History itself had to be reformulated. This was assisted by the official version of events and a particular terminology.[17] The rest had to find other means of expression.

In villages like Agios Vissarios there were corresponding changes in the power structure. The formation of the paramilitary civil guard, the TEA, with its locally appointed members played a role in this, thus constituting a permanent barrier to the penetration of any nonconformist or even mildly critical thinking, let alone leftist views, and of course, to the development of any alternative local power bases. To be counted as a 'communist' – which was very broadly defined – meant, among other things, the forfeiting of agricultural insurance and pension rights or of government loans; and that one could not obtain a 'certificate of national probity', which was required for State employment, access to university education, acquiring a passport, or even getting a hunting permit. The powers of the village president became pivotal in this. He was still locally elected but he had to conform to the State's strictures otherwise he would be prevented from carrying out his duties. At the same time, his election in the first place required some compromise with those who might be defined as 'mildly critical'. Any rights that had been acquired during the 1930s, or especially under the later system of self-government, were again lost.

In these ways the Civil War helped to put an end to the relative autonomy of these villages, but in another way to State indifference as well. Benefits came to the villages but with them came an increasing dependence as well as a greater emphasis on securing personal ties ('patrons') with people in acceptable positions of some authority in the workings of the State.

Attitudes to the State, which before the war had been largely those of antagonism, anger, and resistance, and which in the 1930s had led to wide-scale protests and the development of alternate administrative, economic, and legal systems, changed into ones of dependence, resignation, and fear. The village could no longer be thought of as a defensible and valid entity in itself. At the same time, a new awareness and different ambitions fostered by the Civil War and evacuation, came into play.

Interpretations: a double dichotomy

I mentioned at the beginning of this paper that social memory, which retains particular historical moments, keeping them alive through a continuous discourse in which past events (and relations) combine with the present, bears on the identity of the village in a specific way. It seems to me possible, that this identity is largely predicated on a type of double dichotomy.[18] In general, the historical past of the village is conceptualized through a dichotomy within space. That is, the village is defined through memory in its relation to society at large and in terms of 'them' and 'us'. This is summarized by such common sayings as 'No-one sits on our heads for long up here'; 'Here we are in *Agrafa*, that means unwritten, unknown'; but also, 'People don't come here, they have passed us by'; 'We are a million miles from civilization. . . .'

After the Civil War, however, the fact of this spatial opposition could no longer be maintained because the village and the State became in one sense, a single unit, and because the spatial boundaries of the village had been challenged, first by evacuation and then by wide-scale 'emigration'. Spatially 'them' now included all those who had left the village but who were still looked to as part of the community. In other words, the community itself was divided into 'us' here and 'them' abroad and looked 'outwards' in redefined ways. In the event, a time dichotomy of 'then' and 'now' assumed a new importance.

But this itself is not a simple conceptual juxtaposition. 'Then' is a static time, exemplified in particular by the Ottoman era but which is in one way outside time altogether, as it is outside lived memory. Simultaneously, the perception of this period is itself subject to changes and deals with transformations in village life and aspects of a more recent, unacceptable past.

Less obviously, 'then' is also the innovations of the 1930 period (and the institutions of the early 1940s) but seen against a backdrop of permanence. Such permanence, in fact, suggests the innovations are hardly worth 'remembering'. 'Then' is also, in everyday speech, the Civil War, which is in contrast the epitome of discontinuity, impermanence, and transformation.

In this the present – 'now' – becomes the contrast to the earlier, 'static' past as a time of rapid changes and into which the Civil War continually intrudes in daily life and discourse. At the same time, 'now' is a relatively ordered period in comparison to the Civil War. But it is a present that recognizes – through the Civil War as an idiom of dispute – the contradictions of village life and its vulnerabilities.

To maintain its continuity, and thereby an enduring identity, it seems that the village must stress this double dichotomy. A spatial dichotomy which, through memory separates it from the State. And a time dichotomy, which recreates its past to explain the present.

The Civil War represents one part in a complex of features that go towards making up the identity of the village, in both fact (it bears the scars), and conceptually. The relationship it establishes, however, between the past and the present is one of discontinuity. If the social memory of the Civil War does act in this way – representing disconnection, instability, and the refraction of historical time – it might help explain the obscuring of the period of relative 'spatial' stability and social continuity immediately preceeding it in the 1930s and early 1940s. For that period belongs to 'the past' and therefore cannot explain discontinuity in the present. Thinking in the present, the post-war village, is another part. Its permanence is held together by reference to an Ottoman period, which represents a type of ongoing (Greek) village life. This in turn encapsulates the memory of a life time.

I mean two things here. First, that despite subsequent events and especially the disintegrating effects of the 'recent' Civil War – despite history – the village exists and has an enduring past. Second, the personal history of an individual (or of a patronymic kin group) is thus mapped out. Experiences of the past and in the present are revealed through an informant's social memory.

In looking at the ways in which a particular history is experienced, thought about, and used in the present, it is clear that memory is profoundly influenced by discourses and experiences in the present. This makes it a very complicated construction as well as a very active process.[19] At the same time, as others have shown,[20] it can be seen in different ways in different societies springing from a wide variety of categories and mobilized for a variety of reasons. I have been concerned here with the memories springing from particular historical events that have shaped a whole nation and about which there are very varied memories and many different discourses, some violently opposed to each other.

Notes

1. This is a shortened version of a paper presented to the 1987 ASA conference. Mainly I have had to omit illustrative material and the last section, which raised questions about changes in and for social memory.
2. My fieldwork was undertaken between 1977 and 1979. The total population of these six communities was then approximately 1100. They depended on subsistence farming, cash crops (chestnuts, walnuts, or potatoes), and on foreign remittances for their existence.
3. I use the term 'particular history' to underline both the fact that it refers to a history peculiar to these villages – each village has its own experience of the war years, etc. It also refers to the way in which this history is mapped out and selected in certain ways by the inhabitants.
4. That is, not all the 400 years of Ottoman rule over what is now Greece. It is not known precisely when Turks settled in Agios Vissarios, but there were some families there in the mid-eighteenth century and it is known that they had all left the area by July 1821 (Vasiliou, 1978).
5. These villages were in fact never occupied by the Germans and consequently became a main centre of the resistance movement, which assisted the development of self-government. Unlike other parts of Greece, the Germans remained a relatively distant threat for the inhabitants.
6. A term coined by Daniel Nugent 'Anthropology, handmaiden of history?' (1985:71–86). I am indebted to his article as a whole as it provided an important focus for my thoughts on similar fieldwork experience.
7. See p. 00 for definition of social memory. Karpenisi, the provincial capital, was burnt during Ottoman rule and again during the German occupation. As a result, virtually no records, registries, notary deeds, and so on exist from before 1950. The wide-scale destruction of villages throughout the province during the Civil War also means that most community records were destroyed,

including personal records, letters, local newspapers, copies of court proceedings, etc. Available statistical information also tends to be scant, recent,
and often inaccurate. The local historian Panos Vasiliou found some papers
among the Church archives in Mount Athos pertaining to Agios Vissarios
under the Ottoman Turks and also a number of other church documents
scattered round the country.

8. Zonabend, 1984.

9. Self-government refers throughout to both the system of local administration
and 'people's justice'.

10. The National Greek Army forcibly removed whole villages in the province
mainly to Karpenisi and Lamia. The aim was to deprive the guerrillas of
manpower, information, and supplies.

11. Beikos, 1979. For example, attempts had been made, successfully in some
cases, to bring about land reforms.

12. For examples of eyewitness accounts of these events see Arseniou (1977)
Thessaly in the Resistance; Beikos (1979); Kastrinos (1963–4); Kotzioulas,
(1976); and Woodhouse *The Apple of Discord* (1948), for a revealing, unsympathetic view.

13. See, for example, Beikos (1979) and *I Foni tis Evritanias* (The Voice of
Evritania), a local newspaper published in Karpenisi during the 1930s.

14. Vasiliou, 1929–31; 1960; 1978a.

15. In 1940, for example, the total population of the province was 53,474 and in
1951, 39,678. Today it stands at approximately 20,000.

16. Tsoucalas, 1981:319–41.

17. In fact, there are several 'official' versions of events. First, the more-or-less
uniform one propagated by post-war governments in Greece that by and large
discredited the whole resistance movement, attributed the Civil War entirely
to a 'handful of fanatical, Russian-inspired thugs', and kept thousands of
patriotic, resistance fighters in prison until the mid 1960s. The version propounded by the group of British Establishment and academic figures, usually
involved themselves in undercover military missions in Greece during the
German occupation, constitutes another official version (see for example,
Woodhouse (1948) *The Apple of Discord* and *The Struggle for Greece*. Both
versions reflect in their way the beginnings of the pervasive Cold-War ideology
following World War Two. The first is more easily discredited for being both
crude and so fanatically anti-Communist, though a variety of Greek laws still
reflect this version. The second version is now being hotly debated as a
younger generation of historians and political scientists have access to a variety
of archival material being released according to the thirty-year rule, and with
the help of new insights from those who were involved at the time and those
now allowed back to Greece for the first time since the Civil War.

18. I am grateful to Brian Morris for first suggesting this idea in a seminar at
Goldsmiths College in February 1987 and to Annabelle Black for her interest,
ideas, and assistance with earlier drafts of this paper.

19. See 'Popular Memory: theory, politics, method', (Popular Memory Group,
1982).

20. See, for example, Zonabend, 1984.

References (selected)

Arseniou, L. (1977) *Thessaly in the Resistance*, vol. 2, Athens: P A Press.
Beikos, G. (1979) *H. Laiki Exousia stin Eleftheri Ellada*, Themelio vols 1 and 2, Athens.
Kastrinos, A. (1963–4) 'H Laiki Dikaiosini ke Autodikisi eis tin Eleftheri Ellada', in *Historiki Epitheorisi*, vols 1–3.
Kotzioulas, G. (1976) *Theatro sto Vouno*, Athens: Themelio.
Nugent, D. (1985) 'Anthropology, handmaiden of history?' *Critique of Anthropology* 15 (2), 71–86, September.
Popular Memory Group (1982) 'Popular memory: theory, politics, method', in *Making Histories – Studies in History-Making and Politics*, Centre for Contemporary Culture Studies, London: Hutchinson.
Thompson, E.P. (1978) *The Poverty of Theory*, London: Merlin Press.
Thompson, E.P. (1981) 'The politics of theory', in S. Raphael (ed.) *People's History and Socialist Theory*, History Workshop Series, London: Routledge & Kegan Paul, 396–409.
Tsoucalas, C. (1981) 'The ideological impact of the Civil War', in J.O. Iatrides (ed.) *Greece in the 1940s – a Nation in Crises*, New England: University Press of New England.
Vasiliou, P. (1929–31) Collection of articles, etc. in *Evritania*, Athens.
Vasiliou, P. (1960) *H Episkepi Litsas kai Agrafon epi Tourkokratia*, Athens.
Vasiliou, P. (1978a) 'O Laos tis Evritanias sto '21' in *Evritaniko Vima*, Karpenisi, 5.
Vasiliou, P. (1978b) *Ol Skoles ton Agrafon sta Chronia tis Tourkokratias*, Charlotte, North Carolina.
Woodhouse, C. (1948) *The Apple of Discord*, London: Hutchinson.
Woodhouse, C. (1976) *The Struggle for Greece*, London: Hart, Davis, & McGibbon.
Zonabend, F. (1984) *The Enduring Memory, Time and History in a French Village*, Manchester: Manchester University Press.

Chapter seven

The Social Relations of the Production of History
John Davis

When a radio announcer on some tooth-brushing chat show says 'Barnsley Council will make history today', he means that they are about to do something significant, unusual, and innovative. He does not mean they will give an historical account of something, create a historical text. And English speakers do generally hold the two senses of history (event and text) distinct. Making *a* history is different from making history, though the announcer's guess is that whatever it was that the council was about to do, will turn up in future history books. None the less the two senses are really connected. People give meaning to events,[1] and then decide on current actions partly in the light of their knowledge of the past, thus creating events that in turn are given meanings that . . ., and so on. Of course history is only one among many factors that contribute to decisions about current actions, and the whole area of decision-making is fraught with problems; but the argument is that the social relations of the people who make history determine in some part the meanings that they attach to events: the typical products (texts) of villagers and tribesmen are different in specifiable ways, and these produce different actions (events). 'The history of the common man' is the history produced and consumed in daily life by common men as well as that which members of hierarchically organized elite academies write about them; it has a determining role in shaping experience and events.

This argument derives from reflection on Lison-Tolosana's under-appreciated ethnography of Belmonte de los Caballeros, which includes perhaps the first ethnographic account anywhere of how people make history (Lison-Tolosana, 1966:170–210). But his work is resolutely specific, claims to deal only with one Aragonese town; and it seems interesting to try to apply Lisonian methods to different cases: to contemporary (1975–9) Libyan tribesmen, and to the official Libyan historians engaged in 'rewriting' history.

Lison-Tolosana's model

In Belmonte de los Caballeros in 1961, political power was concentrated in the hands of men aged between 39 and 54. They were what Lison-Tolosana calls the 'controlling generation'.[2] They had shared experiences, shared attitudes, and significantly similar responses to the opportunities that Spanish society offered them. They had been adolescents during the troubled period of the 1920s, and had been of military age during the Civil War. At that time political power had been in the hands of the generation born between 1893 and 1907: it was a generation ('declining' in 1961) that had been riven by conflict between Left and Right. The young soldiers of the Civil War seem to have learned two things: first, they gained experience of the wider Spain and brought back knowledge and a willingness to innovate in agriculture. Second, they came to perceive formal politics as essentially divisive and dangerous. As controllers, they determined never to repeat the mistakes of their predecessors; they concentrated on their families, on strengthening the domestic economic base through agricultural innovation; they withdrew from commitment to national affairs and politics and became family-centred. Their future successors – the emerging generation of 1961, born between 1922 and 1940 or so – were men formed in prosperity and peace and in the perhaps rather stifling family-centred apolitical world created by the controllers. They sought 'the enjoyment of greater freedom . . . greater independence of their parents . . . absolute independence . . . in sentimental problems' (ibid.:195). Lison-Tolosana characterizes them as 'unconcerned about politics' (ibid.:197), but they were concerned with freedom, resented censorship, and had experience of work in the cities and abroad. They will have become the controllers of 1976.

The driving force in Lison-Tolosana's account is the relations between generations: in 1961 the controllers had decided never to repeat the errors of their predecessors; the declining generation expressed contempt for the emerging one (ibid.:195); and the emerging generation – conditioned in the prosperity, familism, and political quietism of the period after the Civil War – wanted freedom and the enjoyment of wealth. The generations were in important respects in opposition to each other, perhaps partly because of their experiences as emergers under the control of their predecessors. And their reactiveness influenced their actions: they created new conditions, new environments to which in due course their successors would react in their turn. Lison-Tolosana compels assent with his account of how, in Belmonte, each new generation takes its inheritance from its predecessor, reacts against it and, in response to 'the historical situation', creates a new environment that again is the object of reaction. The dynamo of history, in Belmonte in the period 1900–61, was the reactive reinterpretation of events; and the social relations that produce the history (and further events) were primarily those of opposition or even hostility between generations. So he explains the history of Belmonte within a national context: growing prosperity, and changes in family structure, in the roles accepted by the different age grades could have been different, but were as they were because men interpreted the past in the way they did. Lison-Tolosana suggests that the structure of generations in Belmonte was relatively permanent. Power was reserved to men past their first youth, supplanted as their married sons reached maturity.[3] He does not produce much evidence about previous generations[4] and it is clear that the emerging generation of 1914–29 was itself riven by the division between Left and Right;[5] Belmonte was also, quite clearly, a stratified society. Nevertheless, he argues, 'the history of Belmonte' was primarily a product of the relation of generations.

In Belmonte in 1961 generations had specified social roles, and the horror of the Civil War had crystallized relations between them into hostility or opposition. But that was contingent, specific to Belmonte as Lison-Tolosana describes it. The essence is the insight and demonstration that history is a social, cultural product, consists of events *plus* the structure of relations among those who construe events. When we say in ordinary speech 'She learnt that at her mother's knee' we generally imply that it is something she has known for a long time (since she was knee-high to her mother). The essential point to be drawn from Lison-Tolosana's work is that it is not only the knee that is important, but the fact that it was Mummy's: the relationship of utterer and listener is crucial – and variable. So, what if it is not generations that are the chief relationship of production, but something else? Say, for instance, patrilineal descent groups?

Patrilineal descent groups provide a structure for a person's social world which is derived from a genealogy. Genealogies explain why everyone exists: they had fathers who begat them, who were in their turn begotten, and so on: that is *why* people are. And they also determine *who* people are, provide them with an identity: a person born to that father has those particular loyalties to other people, and those claims on them. The more patrilineal ancestors individuals share, the greater their claims on each other, although usually a person claiming support from others tries to measure the gradations in units greater than single degrees of cousinage. For reasons amply discussed by Professor Peters, the base unit (lineage) is generally about five or six generations deep, and the members claim undifferentiated loyalty from each other, while offering relative hostility to members of remoter groups, and expecting it from them (Peters, 1960).

A lineage in contemporary (1975–9) Libya is a group of living people who define their membership and loyalty by referring to past acts of procreation.[6] Like members of Lison-Tolosana's generations, they have their basis in the past. But unlike generations, the shared attitudes and expectations, the common response to opportunities shown by lineages is got from a paternal relationship: opposition and conflict arise from fraternity, arise between groups descended from coeval brothers.

Zuwaya historians and their history[7]

All Zuwaya men, and women too (though this is only hearsay), learned the basics of their history from an early age, and used them in conversation and argument from then on. The youngest person I heard reciting his genealogy was about ten years old, and two years later he was referring to an epic event in Zuwaya history in a discussion. Old men, it is true, both knew more and talked about it more often than younger ones; and poets also composed poems about the past, usually about the past of the Zuwaya as a whole.[8] But with these exceptions, talk about the past was not a specialism. Poets in any case were criticized and praised for the beauty, wit, and metre rather than for the truth and accuracy of their product. Most history-speaking was informal, fragmentary, and it was the concern of all men, each a repository of facts and details, which often differed slightly from the next man's.

A Zuwayi historian's sources were mostly oral. Some men had books that dealt with events in which Zuwaya played some part, and others had seen them.[9] Heads of families often kept personal archives,[10] but these were specific to a particular line of descent. Some people kept copies of public documents, but most papers were personal. And even the books were read as lineage histories: Hassanein Bey's report of his expedition to Kufra, on behalf of the Royal Geographical Society, was read eagerly for his encounters with particular Zuwaya and his remarks on their influence and importance; people also read aloud (but only in select company, for it was thought politically dangerous) his account of the envy of other tribes against the Zuwaya: they had the standing of most-favoured tribe with the Sanusi family (Hassanein Bey, 1925). Similarly, Graziani's history of his conquest of Eastern Libya was read and marked for what he had to say about Zuwaya and about particular Zuwaya, rather than for his assessment of the political and military events of his time.

But most sources were oral: they were what a man knew from his father or grandfather; and the phrase 'Our grandfather told me that his grandfather told him' was a fairly common marker of the beginning of historical talk. A span, then, of a century and a half or so, perhaps more, allowing for the imprecision of 'grandfather'. This history tended to be local to a lineage, at most including more general events to indicate changing contexts. 'The Turks wished to subdue us at that time, and our grandfather and his brothers' did whatever they did in response to that threat. The content of the history, what Barthes calls the *collection* (Barthes, 1981), was typically a series of homicides, marriages, and trading expeditions to Black Africa and Cairo, as well as battles against governments: against Ottoman tax patrols; against French encroachment in the Sahel and, most heroically, against the motorized and airborne troops of the Italian colonial armies. These events were structured by genealogy; narratives of feuds and peaces, of battles and defeats grew out of genealogical recitation. Or a man would enquire about the battle of Kawz and get his answer, which would in its course turn into a discussion of genealogy, of who fell and who was named after him.

Genealogies give an approximate date: 'That peace was made when my grandfather was alive'; and sometimes people would recount special circumstances that stretched or foreshortened time. So 'My father's brother died in Chad' (before 1900) 'and my father died at Hawaria' (in 1932) 'but my grandfather was a hundred years old when my father was born'. But I think discussion of the dates of events was chiefly stimulated by my questioning: I think it is true to say that not many Zuwaya were interested; or perhaps they all knew and had no need to question.[11] For the chief effect of genealogy was to eliminate time. Both the noted alternation of names between generations[12] and the use of the names of childless kinsmen for one's own children[13] relate individuals directly to the past: a man named after another is in some sense the man himself, with at least his procreative and political duties. In addition, a genealogy is characteristically related to the present.[14] It is now a truism that genealogies explain the contemporary allegiances and locations of people 'on the ground' (Evans-Pritchard, 1940:94–138). They do so in particular by producing a generative model: one that has a necessary sequence, but no essential time reference. In that sense at least, a genealogy is a set of rules for deriving the present state of political and matrimonial alliances. A genealogy collapses time.[15]

Just as sources were oral, so most history texts were spoken. As far as I know only one Zuwayi wrote history, keeping a notebook in which he listed important and curious events in chronological order, dated. He wrote of Kufra the place and of Zuwaya the tribe: his scope was wider than most. It was possible to discuss with Hamad Hasan al-Harash whether particular dates were accurate; whether the person noted as the first Christian to come to Kufra really was the first, and so on: the written text exciting exactly the kind of criticism and appraisal that (*pace* Parry) Goody has suggested it should: a concern not with the beauty or metre of a text, but with its consistency and plausibility (Goody and Watt, 1968; Parry, 1985). But Hamad was unique (although people rumoured that an engineer in Benghazi collected Zuwaya documents); and most history was spoken, and spoken to an audience that was involved by descent in the deeds and heroisms of the protagonists. The commonest linguistic sign that a man was about to begin speaking history (what Barthes calls a 'shifter') was the phrase 'We have always': always made war against

government, or made peace with our aggressors, or been willing to exchange brides with our enemies. The significance of the 'we', varied with
the audience. To an outsider, lineage history was made to stand for
Zuwaya history. After a meal, in a company consisting mainly of members
of the same lineage, 'we' meant a lineage, its ancestors, and living members. On such an occasion, too, a mature man might interrogate an older
one: 'Grandfather, tell us about', and ask for a recitation of a battle or a
peace, what had happened, who had participated. Or a father might
interrogate his son in front of the company:

'Who are you?'
'Muhammad.'
'Muhammad who?'
'Muhammad son of Abdulla.'
'Abdulla who?'
'Abdulla son of Muhammad.'
'Muhammad who?'
'Muhammad son of Bilal.'

and so on, until the boy had demonstrated how smart he was, by tracing
his ancestry back to Hasan bin Nib min Najd, 'the first Zuwayi'. And
sometimes this catechism would be contested. People would interrupt, the
boy's father had taught him wrong, someone had been missed out, it was
not like that at all. And to support their arguments people would say,
'Look, the Muhammad I'm talking about is the one who' did this or that,
and was the father also of the girl who married someone in Bu Shauq
lineage when we made peace with them. Such arguments were commoner
when men were present who were from some other close lineage, as might
happen at a funeral or wedding; or when a member of the same lineage
was present, who lived in another place, had a slightly different perspective
on the genealogy and the practical relations it represented. Another typical
discussion would begin with a question: 'Are the so-and-so true Zuwaya?',
or a statement that the behaviour of someone was only to be expected
because they were not true Zuwayi; or they had behaved well in spite of
the fact that they were not true Zuwaya. And this would stimulate a
discussion about whether the ancestors of that person were born Zuwaya
or had been acquired by other means, were *mukatibin*, 'written in'.

In all these cases the 'we' was inclusive, with the effect of telling the
audience who they were, what sort of people they were. In other cases
'we' was used to distinguish. A Zuwayi shopkeeper, irritated beyond the
bounds of self-control by a Zuwayi customer who criticized his goods and
prices, hissed a furious rebuke: 'We did not guide the Italians through the
desert'. The customer was from a lineage some of whose members had
indeed been employed by Italian colonial authorities. The phrase 'We
killed Pasha Naiz' (heard sometimes in Zuwaya conversations) usually
claimed responsibility for homicide with an inclusive *we*. But on one

occasion Zuwaya youths shouted it at Magharba. Pasha Naiz was a member of the Magharba tribe, given office by an Ottoman governor, and apparently assassinated by Zuwaya. His death evoked the purity of Zuwaya rejection of government, and the irremediable taint of all Magharba through their association with hierarchies of authority. In the circumstances of that occasion, it may also have carried the contemptuous challenge, that the Magharba should avenge the death of a quisling. In this usage, 'we' is contestatory, exclusive, and provocative; and the history is used in a segmentary way, to mark boundaries of hostility – just as, when it is inclusive, it reassures, creates a lineage character common to ancestors and the audience by collapsing time in a genealogy.

This kind of history, produced by lineages, is different from the history produced by the interaction of generations. On the one hand it is different as *text*. It emphasizes the identity of people of different ages and the continuity of their mutual loyalties, the consistency of their attitudes and actions.[16] Genealogy provides a structure in which life and loyalty are mutually determining, and are granted by members of one generation to members of the next. Generation provides a structure of reactive reinterpretation in which the emphasis, at any rate in Belmonte, is on discontinuity: the fathers of the controllers got involved in politics, sent their sons to war, and that shall never happen again. Of course it is possible to suggest that the nature of the events themselves affect the relation of individuals: civil war is different from colonial war, and it is easy to see why veterans of the one should decide to open a new page, and veterans of the other should glory in their solidarities. One problem with that argument, however, is that the surviving veterans from Belmonte had been on the winning side. They could (as controllers) have identified with the regime they helped establish, used their combatant status to gain privilege and authority. But in fact, very few of them were active in 'politics' at all.

The two manufacturing processes produce very different stereotypes of the past: the 'never again' of the controlling generation in Belmonte contrasts sharply with the 'always so' of the Zuwaya. Zuwaya idealized the past: they told of the rights men had, and how they had asserted them; of their duties, and how they had performed them. Their history was a tale of the working principles in an essentially timeless world. People did not say 'On that occasion we were on the verge of being annihilated, and so we sent a message to the nearest Turkish patrol and they helped us survive'. They said, rather, 'We fought boldly and nobly, and constrained our enemies to make peace'. But the admittedly slim evidence does suggest that on more than one occasion Zuwaya and other tribesmen called for government protection when faced with overwhelming forces. Perhaps they considered that they would rather survive tainted by government than die in a principled segmentary way.[17] With these compromising incidents omitted, their history had the character of a set of examples of the working of right principle, structured by genealogy rather than by duration or progress or a chain of cause and effect. The characteristic Zuwaya text was a narrative of generative acts (Abdulla begat Muhammad) to which Zuwaya attached tales of right and wrong, cases like Law Reports, partly determining future decisions but presenting no narrative linkage between them.

The characteristic text of a Belmonte controller is a reaction grounded in the apparently natural opposition of apparently natural groups. Lison-Tolosana argues that Belmonte texts to some extent explain the following events: making new history (events) is a reaction against the socially construed past. Do the different texts of the Zuwaya also produce different future histories?

Zuwaya history (text) was static, idealized, and confrontational. And the case I wish to make is that this produced decisions and actions that were intended to be replications of the past, were idealistic and dissident (or: backward-looking, unrealistic, and subversive). A tendency to replicate an idealized past was apparent for instance in Zuwaya formation of segmentary blocs in elections (Davis, 1982). So in Ajdabiya, Zuwaya opposed Magharba for seats on the popular committees that partly ran local affairs, while in Kufra, where Zuwaya hegemony was uncontested, Zuwaya sections opposed each other. In lamb-barrel politics the lines of distribution were lineages, and when disputes broke out about the allocation of (say) Agricultural Development funds, the shaikhs of the lineages concerned would travel to the scene and make a peace (*sulh*) that was self-consciously traditional in every aspect except the scale of compensation that had to be paid. In conversations about current events the past was a constant touchstone: when the radio reported that two students at Benghazi had been publicly hanged for their part in a dispute about elections to the students' union, a man, hearing the news, made the apparently mild remark: 'Wasn't that what we fought the Italians for?' In implication it evoked the twenty-one year struggle against the colonial state, the last Zuwaya military stand for statelessness, the cause of many deaths, the beginning of years in exile for many men still living: fighting the Italians was an emblem of Zuwaya rejection not just of the Christian or Fascist state, but of all states. And in pointing out the similarity of states, whether Libyan or Italian, it threatened more of the same. When Zuwaya youths shouted 'We killed Pasha Naiz' in 1979, at the height of a disputed election, Magharba reported Zuwaya to the authorities for dissidence, bringing (so Zuwaya claimed) instant reprisals from the government.

Zuwaya and their allies and enemies had an idealized image of the past that was essentially static, had little content of change or progress, and inspired men to confront their contemporaries rather than to oppose history. It should be said that the men who did this were not wild and ungovernable Bedouin: most were settled; they included bank managers and petroleum executives, policemen, teachers, chemical engineers, headmasters, shopkeepers, and electricians as well as herders and gardeners. In Kufra, two-thirds of all adult men were on the government payroll. So they were not benighted, ignorant natural savages, but in many cases sophisticated, educated people operating successfully in a recognizably modern world. They knew the state, and contested it.

Lison-Tolosana is possibly correct to say that in Franco's Spain, twenty-five years after the Civil War, a Spanish town could very well have one dominant mode of production of history; but in Libya in the 1970s, during a revolution, that was not so. The nexus of genealogy, lineage, and collapsed time is a selection, made by me, from a plethora of materials.[18] Zuwaya were in turmoil, with their social worlds become uncertain, full of dilemmas and unpredictabilities, and they had at least one other historical option open to them. One of the reasons Zuwaya chose as they did is that Qaddafi in fact used a very similar image of the past for guidance on how to abolish the state (or, as an anthropologist might say, 'how to make the Libyan nation stateless') and how to organize a society that should have no system of representation. Qaddafi's theory of the inviolability of personal sovereignty and his attempt to create a non-representative polity struck chords, drew responses from Libyans as steeped as he was in the social relations and history of tribe and lineage. Zuwaya and Magharba and Majabr, however, not only responded to the rhetoric of smashing the state; they used their version of the past to oppose Qaddafi's more statelike actions: executions and wars, taxation and socialist legislation.

The main difference between tribesmen's version of statelessness and Qaddafi's rhetoric, merely partly realized, was that tribesmen conceived of the tribe as the highest level of fusion of descent groups. Qaddafi, however, thinks that nations are descent groups, or ought to be so; and after nations, all mankind:

> A tribe is a family which has grown as a result of births. It follows that a tribe is a big family. Even the nation is a tribe which has grown demographically. So the nation is a big tribe. So the world is one nation which has branched into lesser nations. The world is therefore a big nation.
>
> (Mua'mmr al-Qaddafi, 1975–9: Chapter 3, 13)

He does not say much about the world; and he is uncertain about which nation (Libyan or Arab); but he knows that nations are really families writ large, organized on the same principles, demanding the same sacrifices. His ideological aim was to persuade Libyans that the principle they admitted for tribes applied equally to nations. He told them that nations, not states, are the motive force in human affairs, that polities created by immigrants (the USA and Israel) are artificial, unnatural, doomed because they have no focus of natural loyalty. This aim carried two intellectual problems with it. First, he had to convince Libyans that the war with colonial Italy had been a national one. For the really devastating major significant suffering of the Libyan past was the intermittent colonial war of 1911–32, and the period of *pax italica* that followed: if that was not the nation in action, then the claim that nationalism is the motive force in human affairs looks rather thin. Second, he had to minimize the part played in the struggle by the regime he supplanted. So to achieve this aim he had to 'rewrite' history, to dispossess the grandfathers and to replace their history with a national one.

Imagine the dusty, hot reception room of a Government Rest House in Ajdabiya in Eastern Libya. The date is August 1976, and a young history lecturer from the University of Benghazi has brought a class of a dozen or so students to interview one of the janitors. Everyone sits on hard upright chairs: the students in a semi-circle behind their teacher, who faces the informant almost eyeball to eyeball. The janitor has fetched the chairs, made tea, explained that there were no ashtrays, but not to worry because he will sweep up afterwards. He is an old man, aged about 75, deferential to the young scholar, bemused by his sudden arrival and his entourage of jeans-wearing, cigarette-smoking young men. The lecturer switches on his tape-recorder:

'Grandfather', he begins in the loud tone people use when they are not sure they will be understood, 'tell us how you participated in the national struggle of the Jihad'. At first indeed the older man does not understand; after some discussion he realizes that he is supposed to describe the Battle of Yellow Hill, and begins to tell his story with much animation and gesture and laughter. He had been 14 years old, or perhaps 15 or 13, and his uncle had spotted an Italian patrol on the road. They had rushed to attack it, and had lain in wait before opening fire. They had killed an Italian, and had suffered heavy losses, were almost wiped out. He, the janitor, had been wounded in the leg. He begins to pull down his trousers to show the scar. The scholar laughs 'No, no, Grandfather, it's not necessary, we all believe you', and he continues:

'How many of you died there at Yellow Hill?'

'Six or seven.'

'And how many of you were left?'

'Me and my brother, but he wasn't wounded, and he carried me back to our father.'

After an hour or so, when the cassette is full, the doctor thanks the old man, says it has been a privilege to speak with a hero and to record his words for posterity, that the Libyan people owe him and his kind a great debt. And the students, apparently bored by their fieldwork (for they all probably have grandfathers or great uncles with scars and stories), stub

113

out their cigarettes and move out to their government minibus to return to the city. The janitor begins to clean up; he was flattered by the interest, had told a good story that redounded to his credit, and he was pleased to have had the opportunity.

The historian had followed instructions that university education should be useful, relevant to the real problems of Libya; he had shown his students how to do oral history; he had added to his collection of tapes of stories of the struggle of the Libyan people. But in doing so he had, in my view, fundamentally distorted the experience of both the young boy who had fought and the old man who remembered. The boy who joined in the ambush with his uncle had become a retrospective nationalist in the ears of the oral-history team. The doctor had managed to insert the old man's party piece into a history of Libyan nationalism entirely by 'verballing': putting leading questions that could then be transcribed: 'I participated in the Libyan struggle at the Battle of Yellow Hill in 1914 . . .'. Never once did he ask the janitor what he had thought about the battle, why he had fought the Italians, what he had thought he might achieve.

The facts of the case are relatively clear. In the Libyan cities (Tripoli, Misurata, Benghazi) from the late-nineteenth century onward, people did form a rather large number of parties in which they discussed the future of Libya, or at any rate of Tripolitania, Cyrenaica, perhaps Fezzan. But the city dwellers were few; and they were conquered early in the colonial war. The desert and desert fringes were less easily invested, and they provided the battle grounds for a long-lasting resistance that was largely the affair of tribesmen. But the survivors of those battles did not give much emphasis, in 1979, to the Libyan nation. They had resented Christians; they had resented intruders, they had resented attempts to govern them. In the battlefields-become-cemeteries most graves are those of men who died on their lineage or tribal territory, and died in the company of members of their lineage or tribe. An Italian patrol came; it was ambushed by local men who were mown down with machine guns and by airplanes, and were buried where they fell. The Libyan hero Umar al-Mukhtar achieved some greater co-ordination than that: he organized and directed a guerrilla force that harried the Italians, inflicting losses and wounding Italian national pride until 1932, when he was captured and hanged. The intelligence, heroism, and sacrifice of that force is not in question; but it seems likely that the guerrillas fought for freedom from government rather than for national independence. The companies were tribal units recruited with their officers from particular groups, and named after them. That was strategically effective, allowing the men to become invisible again, after a strike. It also seems beyond doubt (from the evidence of survivors) that it corresponded to the temper and inspiration of the fighters themselves: they fought as tribesmen in temporary alliance with others against a common enemy, rather than as Libyan nationalists.[19]

Qaddafi clearly did lead a nation in 1979. Libyan tribesmen did have loyalty towards a larger entity than their tribes, larger – in many cases – than Cyrenaica, Tripolitania, or Fezzan. They shared in Libyan triumphs; they were humiliated by its internal and external failures, and then perhaps reasserted their separateness. But Qaddafi confronted a history of undoubted heroism and suffering that was ideologically awkward because it did not correspond to his need to show the ineluctable force of nationalism at work, culminating in himself. That led him to 'rewrite' history.

The issue is a morally complex one. In my view Qaddafi is telling the past as it never was, and encouraging others to do the same; but he is not in fact corrupting a text, cutting pages out of an encyclopedia, retouching photographs. In the first place, most of the history Libyans knew was oral; it was what grandfathers told to their grandchildren and had no pretensions to being a national history: rather, it was a sectional account of the activities of the ancestors of the group, which heard the stories and poems and genealogies that were the main kinds of historical knowledge. When recounted to foreigners, lineage history could stand for Libyan history; but the same stories also served to mark genealogical boundaries. Qaddafi's version of old events therefore did not replace or corrupt a truer history text. If anything, it filled a gap, since it is reasonable that people whom we all recognize to be Libyans should have a general account of their antecedents.

Just as 're-' causes some hesitation, so too '-writing' is problematic. For the main vehicle of this new account of the past was not primarily a written text. Rather than school books and learned journals, Qaddafi's government produced television programmes and speeches, and financed one spectacular movie.[20] They did not violate a scholarly critical tradition dedicated to the pursuit of truth, but insinuated through political argument and entertainment. It is true that schoolbooks reproduced an official version of history; but they seem to have replaced a series of texts that gave very little space to Libya at all. The Institute for the study of the Jihad, in Tripoli, was one of the main instruments of historical policy. It was created *ex novo* with a small group of historians, employed to make a bibliographic base for the study of Libyan history, and to issue specialist publications. The Jihad was precisely the war against Italian colonialism, and undoubtedly the viewpoint expressed was often anachronistically nationalist. But it is hard to imagine that the Institute received orders to rewrite the colonial war, to de-emphasize the Sanusi element, to over-emphasize the Tripolitanian mistrust of the Order. It is more likely, that the people employed there shared the preconceptions of the government, and needed no instruction.

Libyan national history confronts, moulds, and distorts flourishing grandfathers' histories, which are sectional, partial, and (from the government's point of view) polemical. Our belief that it is wrong for the state to nationalize a free academic enterprise is beside the point, therefore, since what is expropriated is grandfathers' history rather than that of the academy. Moreover, we are generally happy when professional historians, working in a free academy, rewrite history; and we praise them for having given new meanings to known facts. We know that the relations of production of professional historians (their rivalry, their easy acceptance of vitriol in the ink) give an edge to their critical faculties, which in some sense establishes their work, allows us to call it at any rate provisionally true. It is the relations of production of professional history that guarantee the product. We can also accept as genuine cultural products those different homebrews made by different sorts of common men, even though they are just moonshine by professional standards. But official Libyan history is nationalized in two senses: it is a government enterprise served by people who have a government career to make; and they make a national history, serving the interest of a man who (if he were more approved of) would be called a nation-builder. The power of the state is closely involved in this history, and it does not guarantee even a provisional truth.

'Social relations of production' directs attention not only to different types of history, but also to power relations, to control of resources; and this is another area that attracts moral judgements: statements about tradition, about how 'we' have always done things, are produced with authority by old men, and serve (as Bloch has elaborated) as devices of control in rhetoric, reinforcers of power (Bloch, 1975). In Belmonte, although no doubt people tried to influence the interpretation their sons would put on their actions, opposition between generations seems to have minimized control: each generation, Lison-Tolosana suggests, had substantial autonomy to remake its history. In Libya the keepers of tradition perpetuated a relatively timeless image of a free past, and came into conflict with history-makers commanding some part of the resources of a state: they each served rather different interests, and easily arouse moral sensibility.

What *are* kinds of history? Perhaps historians would list ancient and medieval and modern and their subdivisions, cross-cut by local, diplomatic, ecclesiastical and of-the-common-man. This qualification is cross-cut again by qualifiers from the range between true and false – a range that some, but by no means all, would recognize as separate from the categories French, American, and English. I have distinguished histories by how they are made, what the relations of their production are, and have tried to identify three kinds: Belmonte (generational), Zuwaya (genealogical), and Libyan (nationalized), which are characterized by three different kinds of text. And I have argued that these histories play some part in producing different futures: the connection between text and event is a real one. If I am right there is another item to add to the list of essentially moral issues: it is not only the relations of production, and the control of history resources, but the future histories they may produce that excite moral judgement.

Notes

1. The distinction between 'events' and 'events clothed with meaning' is a difficult one: undressed events are not describable since it is impossible to isolate them one from another, and then because they cannot be described without giving them meaning. To invent a notation for these theoretically necessary but ineffable things serves to make the point, though it is tiresome for readers: as it might be *(events), for example, *(the opening of the Suez canal). If you imagine a great heap of all *(events), clearly only some of them are known; the distribution of knowledge of them is uneven, and the various histories that include them give them different meanings. Nevertheless it is reasonable to assert that a peasant in the Nile Delta, the biographer of Disraeli, and a French historian all refer to the same *(event). I am concerned with significant dressed events, although it is interesting that some *(events) may be unknown, but still may be important causes. A *(decision to cultivate wild grains) has had far-reaching consequences, even though its existence can only be deduced.
2. 'A generation . . . comprises an age-group of men and women who share a common mode of existence or concept of life, who assess the significance of what happens to them at a given moment in terms of a common fund of conventions and aspirations' (Lison-Tolosana, 1966:180).
3. Men married at *aet.* 28 or so; women at about 25 (ibid.:180).
4. Were they always three generations? Were they always fifteen or sixteen years wide? Was the middle generation always in control? Were they always in opposition to each other?
5. Though he argues that they had the shared expectation that social and other problems could be resolved through ideologically-based political action.
6. I realize that speaking about lineages in any modern society, and perhaps even more so in Libya, runs counter to expectation. For a full account see Davis, 1987. Briefly, the tribes of southwest Cyrenaica maintain genealogies that define groups whose members sustain each other with welfare payments when needed, and make peace with the members of other like units. In the smaller settlements, and in some of the intermediate ones, they maintain residential segregation. They appoint shaikhs, claim common ownership of some property, build mosques, make collective representations to the government, and contest elections as tribal groups. They are *not* property-owning groups, though they sometimes speak as if they were; they do not undertake collective pilgrimages; they are part of a modern socialist revolutionary society.
7. Fieldwork with the Zuwaya was funded by the SSRC (now ESRC) and the University of Kent at Canterbury, with important aid from the Gemeente Universiteit van Amsterdam and the CNRS: I am grateful to them. The Zuwaya, who aided, protected, and comforted me during twenty-two months of research in the period 1975–9, numbered about 18,000 men, women, and children, and lived chiefly in Ajdabiya, Kufra, Tazarbu, and Ajkharra in eastern Libya.
8. Poets spoke to a wider audience than most Zuwaya historians. I have not done a content analysis of their works, but my strong impression is that they

addressed the history of the tribe; and that when they sang of events with genealogical reference, they were concerned with the higher reaches of genealogy: they spoke of origins, and the matrimonial and political events in the life of the founder of Zuwaya and his sons. And such agreement as there was among Zuwaya about these relationships was derived from the consensus of poets. Most historians were concerned with the more recent generations.

9. The commonest was an Arabic version of Field Marshal Graziani's account of his campaigns and government in eastern Libya (Graziani, 1932). People read it and commented on his interpretation of events, and many people were familiar with his version of the battles of Kawz and Hawaria. One household certainly had Hassanein Bey's book about his travels in Libya, from Siwa to Ajdabiya and Kufra, and some other people said they knew of it. It is available in Arabic. Like Agostini's survey of Cyrenaican tribes (Agostini, 1922–3) it speaks of Zuwaya and their connections with the Sanusi, and people considered it unwise to advertise ownership. Agostini indeed surfaced only once during fieldwork, in the form of a photocopy of the map of tribes and their landholdings in the Ajdabiya region.

10. Many heads of households kept small archives of letters, contracts, old permits and licences, and photographs. Some people had copies of public documents that they had inherited or had copied for their own use and enjoyment. For instance, several people had copies of an agreement made by fifty-six shaikhs in 1946, in which they promised to live at peace within the borders of their territory. In 1979 the document was read for its reminders of who the old men had been in 1946, as well as for its proof of Zuwaya hegemony in the desert: the territory so blandly defined is nearly the size of France and includes several other tribal and ethnic groups. Such papers served to establish claims, to recall old friendship, to jog the memory about old times. And some of them were once of potential legal and economic importance: a deed of sale or an agreement about water rights; a declaration of constructive divorce, and so on. They served to date some events, to establish the names of some of the participants, perhaps their ages. They did not do much more than that. Many of the archives I saw were stored in tobacco tins; one man kept his in a biscuit tin, and a shaikh kept his in an old suitcase; but I did not make a systematic survey of private archives.

11. Perhaps it is useful to say that while Zuwaya were generally tolerant of questions about facts, I found it difficult to ask them about the rules or theory of history: for this reason it was difficult to do more than listen to them talk history: it was not possible, as it was with (say) marriage, to ask 'What should a historian do?' and to confront the rules with the practice.

12. A father should give his father's name to his firstborn son, his wife's father's name to his second born, and so on (Peters, 1960).

13. Again, see Peters, 1960. One of the common ways of getting into a genealogical and historical discussion was for someone to say: 'I am called Ibrahim because that was the name of someone who had died in battle', or was, at any rate childless.

14. The exception is those genealogies that Gellner calls Veblenesque, e.g. that trace descent from one of the Prophet Muhammad's sons-in-law (Gellner, 1969:179–200; 261–75).

15. Barthes (1981) lists a number of the games that historians play with time: they can accelerate (by passing over a decade or a century in a page or two); they can slow it down (by dwelling at length on a week or day). They can zig-zag, for example by 'going back' to explain the antecedents of a character newly

introduced to the narrative. And above all they can preface their histories, with a statement in the here-and-now (usually dated and addressed) that the reader will shortly in the future learn new things about the past. Perhaps collapsing time with genealogies might be added – though Barthes is concerned solely with professional historians.

16. Zuwaya did express tensions between fathers and sons: some arose from the use of authority; they expressed others in the formal segregations of fathers and sons implied by the word *tahashsham*: shame or shyness should exclude money, women, and relaxed pleasure from their interaction. But reserve is not the same as contestation.

17. Zuwaya did have contact with the Ottoman government, and were supporters of the Sanusi. They claimed also that in the remote past they had controlled the Berbers of Aujla and the Majabr of Jalu. So it is clearly difficult to maintain that they were consistent and principled refuseniks towards *all* government. In 1979 60 per cent of them were on government payrolls. The ambivalences are discussed in more detail in Davis, 1987.

18. I may say that while I am fairly sure I am right, I am not sure I could specify the characteristics of a good argument against which to assess the validity of what I have done.

19. In any case, Umar al-Mukhtar was the representative and supporter of Idris, then head of the Sanusi Order later to become King. Idris, although clearly ineffectual in many respects, did in fact supply arms and other material to the tribesmen from his exile in Egypt, until the frontier was sealed with barbed wire. And he did eventually become head (King) of an independent Libyan state in 1952. If Cyrenaican tribesmen expressed loyalty to an entity beyond the tribe, it was to him: a religious leader who supplied spiritual as well as rifles, and who eventually led Libya to independence. The main authority on the Order, incidentally, attributes its success to the leaders' policy of respecting tribal autonomy, and to the delicacy with which they usually handled matters involving supratribal authority (Evans-Pritchard, 1949:89).

20. *The Lion of the Desert*, starring Anthony Quinn as Umar al-Mukhtar.

References

Agostini E. de (1922–3) *Le Popolazioni della Cirenaica. Notizie etniche e storiche raccolte dal colonello Enrico de Agostini, con annesse 12 carte*, Bengasi: Tripoli: Governo della Cirenaica, Azienda tipo-litografica della Scuola d'arti e mestieri.

Barthes, R. (1981) 'The discourse of history', in E.S. Shaffer (ed.) *Comparative Criticism. A Year Book*, Cambridge: Cambridge University Press, 3–20.

Bloch, M. (ed.) (1975) *Political Language and Oratory in Traditional Society*, London: Academic Press.

Davis, J. (1982) 'Qaddafi's theory and practice of non-representative government', *Government and Opposition* 17, 61–79.

Davis, J. (1987) *Libyan Politics: Tribe and Revolution. The Zuwaya and their Government*, London: I.B. Tauris.

Evans-Pritchard, E.E. (1940) *The Nuer. A description of the modes of livelihood and political institutions of a Nilotic people*, Oxford: Clarendon Press.

Evans-Pritchard, E.E. (1949) *The Sanusi of Cyrenaica*, Oxford: Clarendon Press.

Gellner, E.A. (1969) *Saints of the Atlas* (Nature of Human Society Series), London: Weidenfeld & Nicholson.

Goody, J.R. and Watt, I. (1968) 'The consequences of literacy', in J.R. Goody (ed.) *Literacy in Traditional Societies*, Cambridge: Cambridge University Press.

John Davis

Graziani, R. (1932) *Cirenaica Liberata*, Milano: Mondadori.
Hassanein Bey, A.M. (1925) *The Lost Oases*, London: Thornton Butterworth.
Lison-Tolosana, C. (1966) *Belmonte de los Caballeros. A sociological study of a Spanish town*, Oxford: Clarendon Press.
Mua'mmr al-Qaddafi, see Qaddafi al-, M.
Parry, J. (1985) 'The Brahmanical tradition and the technology of the intellect', in J. Overing (ed.) *Reason and Morality*, ASA Monographs, 24. London: Tavistock Publications, 200–25.
Peters, E. (1960) 'The proliferation of segments in the lineage of the Bedouin of Cyrenaica', *Journal of the Royal Anthropological Institute* 90, 29–53.
Qaddafi al-, M. (1975–9) *The Green Book. The Third Universal Way*, CCCC: PPPP.

Chapter eight

Israel: Jewish identity and competition over 'tradition'[1]
Robert Paine

More than one 'time', more than one 'place'

Addressing problems of Jewish identity in Israel, it is not out of place to begin with a couple of paradoxes. Here is the first. While widely dispersed throughout the Diaspora, Jews went to elaborate ritual lengths to overcome, symbolically, differences of time and place between them as Jews. 'We were all at Sinai', they said. And whether they lived in Cracow, or Marrakesh, or London, they prayed for rain at times appropriate to the seasons of Palestine. All turned towards Jerusalem to pray, and in synagogues across the globe and across the centuries the salutation would ring out: 'Next year in Jerusalem!' Then, with the Ingathering of the Exiles into the new State of Israel, cultural differences of time and place became salient.

These differences became the basis of discrimination between Jews from Europe and Jews from North Africa and the Middle East (to simplify). On the one hand, there were the 'enlightened' *Ashkenazim* and on the other, the 'primitive' *Mizrahim*. By now the story is familiar enough; and analysed in a score or more of anthropological and sociological studies of which the progenitor was S.N. Eisenstadt's *The Absorption of Immigrants* (1954).[2]

'The culture of Morocco I would not like to have here', said David Ben-Gurion, and Abba Eban had 'great apprehensions' about the Levantization of Israel (Smooha, 1978:88; Eban, 1968:76). It was in this frame of mind that the Ashkenazim took to the task of caring for their 'forlorn brethren' and 'turning this human dust into a cultured nation' (Ben-Gurion, cited in Bernstein and Swirski, 1982:80–1). The important task was nation-building and this did not allow, at that time, for questions about the kind of nation being built. Under Ashkenazi direction, control, and patronage, there was little occasion for ideological debate: the agenda had already been set.

Much has been accomplished:

The process of cultural and social assimilation undergone by Oriental Jews in Israel has been extremely vigorous.

(Smooha, 1986:37)[3]

And:

I, who was born in Iraq and who immigrated to Israel as a lad thirty-five years ago, have far more in common with an academic who just immigrated from the United States than with my father, who immigrated along with myself.

(Amir, 1986:26)

On the other hand, the agenda – or the enforced consensus – is now broken. As Schweid puts it:

The tension which had been relaxed through the effort of rebuilding the national home by postponing problems now became recharged once it was plain that these problems were as real as ever.

(Schweid, 1973:144)[4]

The enforced consensus had been one about 'Israel' – the nation and the state; it was particularly questions about the Jewishness of Israel that had been 'postponed', and there is at the present time a maelstrom of controversy over what Jewishness is or should be. These battlelines are *not* drawn between Ashkenazim and Mizrahim as such, but between secular Jews, Orthodox Jews, and Ultra-Orthodox Jews; and the key to much of the controversy is the matter of redemption.

The centrality of redemption in Jewish culture springs from the fact that in Judaism it is 'an event on the stage of history and within the community' in contrast to Christianity in which redemption is 'an event in the private world of each individual' (Scholem, 1971:1). Buber (1952:viii) is one of many who drew Zionism and redemption closely together: 'Not the improvement of the situation of the Jews is our aim but the redemption of the nation'. And for Schweid (1973:188): 'the essence of redemption is totality of return'.

However, there are those who believe the Jewish *State* is a hindrance to redemption and those who believe its establishment marks the beginning of the redemptive process, and there are others who believe Jewish redemption is wholly a secular matter without an eschatological dimension; and closely entwined with all of these are the opposing ideological positions concerning Israel's continued Occupation of the West Bank.

These differences amount to ideological systems that affect the life styles of their proponents. The life styles themselves cannot be described here; the important point, in the present context, is that the ideological systems are maintained – not incidentally but primarily – through distinctive accounts of time (in the sense of epoch) and of place (as opposed to space). These differences are, in my view, profoundly more significant – more enduring – than those associated, a few decades earlier, with the Ingathering of the Exiles. Then, the differences, having to do with the countries-of-origin of the immigrants, were between traditional ('primitive') and modern (western) ways of life – with modernization (through assimilation) as the prescribed cure for the ills of non-western primitivism. So the problem itself was largely Europocentric in its conception and uncompromisingly (as far as possible) Europocentric in its handling. It has now largely dissolved into issues of relative privilege versus relative deprivation, and the symbols of struggle are those, more or less, of class interests. But the differences concerning the ontology of time and place raise questions like: Is time historical or metahistorical? Is place profane or sacred?[5] And one finds all sides to the controversy even within the population still popularly labelled Ashkenazi.

In short, there are groups who enact their lives as though they are living in different Israels from one another. Each group, each 'Israel', is an attempt to constitute Jewish identity in Israel. Antagonistic versions of that identity become bastions of ideology.[6]

Contributing circumstances to this situation are embedded in the second paradox: the Jews, as a people, are identified by their religion, which is distinctive among the world religions in its territorial focus on *Eretz Yisrael*: the [promised] Land of Israel. Yet the people themselves, clinging to their identity through their religion (see especially Kaufmann, 1974), have been deterritorialized through the millenia. Now that they have restored themselves to the primordial territory (or part of it), the question arises: how are they to behave *there*?

Any answer to this question has to take into account that the people are divided among themselves about the meaning of what has happened. The pragmatic programme of political Zionism associated with Herzl, Weizman, and Ben-Gurion, leading directly to the founding of the State in 1948, provides one account. Simple and simplified. But there is also a transcendental side to Zionism, and the founding of the Old–New State in Eretz Yisrael itself, and not in Uganda or elsewhere, ensured the emergence, sooner or later, of questions and some answers concerning what Martin Buber once referred to as the 'hidden figure' of Zionism 'waiting to be revealed'.

If Israel renounces the mystery, it renounces the heart of reality itself. National forms without the eternal purpose from which they have arisen signify the end of Israel's specific fruitfulness.
If Israel desires less than it is intended to fulfil then it will even fail to achieve the lesser goal.

(Buber, 1952:xxi)

123

After the Six-Day War, Israelis, in greater numbers than ever, took the measure of such thoughts (even as they misconstrued Buber in doing so).

With different ideas of *what* was restored to them nationally (Homeland or Land of Destiny?) and of *how* it happened (by natural or supernatural means?), one thing does certainly follow: Jews in Israel will differ, even radically, among themselves over what is appropriate Jewish behaviour in these circumstances. But in just about all cases, selected parts of 'the past' (an entity that *has* to be interpreted) are an important guide. So in constructing behaviour they reconstruct (or 'continue', many of them would like to say) selected Jewish 'traditions'. This weaving of distinctive accounts of time and place into the different ideological positions looks very much like instances of what Schecher calls 'restored behavior' – restored behaviour in what many of them believe to be a restored situation.

> Restored behavior offers to both individuals and groups the chance to become someone else 'for the time being' [Schecher is here thinking of theatrical groups], or the chance to become what they once were. Or even, and most often, *to rebecome what they never were.*
>
> (Schecher, 1981:3; emphasis added)[7]

The following extracts from my field journals (1983 and 1985) should evoke the struggles over what it means to be Jewish in Israel today. These kinds of statement started me thinking, in a general way, about time and place, identity, and Zionism. From conversations among my middle-class and academic Jewish Israeli friends:

> I came here to be a human being, and Israel has let me be that. This is my country.
> This is not the Israel to which I came and in which I played my part in trying to build.
> If Arik Sharon is a Jew, then I'm quite a different one.
> I feel no nearer to an Ultra-Orthodox Jew in Jerusalem than I would to an Arab in Damascus.
> Earlier values, ones we held to be 'Jewish,' are being challenged.

From interviews with Ultra-Orthodox (*haredim*) rabbis, Orthodox nationalists (*Gush Emunim*) and their Orthodox opponents (Oz veShalom), officials of the World Zionist Organization (WZO), a political scientist, and secular Jewish settlers on the West Bank:

> The Zionists proclaim boundaries, but they do not understand the distinction between where one lives physically and where one lives spiritually: one can reside in Israel and yet at the same time still be in the Diaspora. And one can live in the Diaspora but be in Israel spiritually. (*haredim*)
> We will have nothing to do with the State. It is a sacrilege! (*haredim*)

I was not one of those who danced in the streets of Tel-Aviv on November 29 1947. Why not? Because we had lost the *real* land of Israel. (settler)

What you just called 'Israel proper' [behind the Green Line] is really less 'proper' than Judea and Samaria, it was the area in which the Philistines and Phoenicians lived. (WZO)

I have a dream, like Jacob did – this is not just a right, it's a necessity; I live by my dream and I don't put [territorial] borders around my dream. (settler)

We're not bringing Israel into Hebron: Israel *is* Hebron! We're here until the end of time. (Gush Emunim)

Some of us are saying 'we're here [in Israel] forever'. But that's no certainty. Athens? Rome? Byzantine and Ottoman Empires – what of their 'forevers'? If it is history from which we Jews should learn, then what is our history? It begins with the 'immigrant' Abraham, Abraham born of gentiles; it is a history of 'becoming,' of wandering, exile, and return. A history whose focus is not territorial boundaries but the holiness of the Land. (Oz veShalom)

The Gush Emunim dismiss us as 'traitors,' as 'Hellenists' and as European-oriented: but *their* insistence on boundaries is straight out of European political thought. (Oz veShalom)

. . . but 'geography' has a soul, and if you give back part of it [Judea and Samaria], it is the same as surrendering part of the soul of the Jewish people. (*Gush Emunim*)

The State acts as though the land belongs to 'Jews' and not to its 'inhabitants'. (political scientist)

The job [of building the nation] has not yet been done . . . the State is still in danger. (WZO)

Small in numbers though they may be, these groups are, nevertheless, caretakers of different versions of Jewish values; their active public presence ensures continued concern about the relationship between Judaism and Zionism and between tradition and modernity. In Israel these issues are not marginal, and there is more truth than exaggeration in Schweid's comment that 'every thinking person, be he religious or not' is caught up in them (1973:3).

The allocation of identity – Jewish? Israeli? Zionist? – is sometimes complex indeed, and, as suggested already, raises issues of enduring controversy, even hostility. Consider the *haredim* – the pious ones, the Ultra-Orthodox: they live in Israel (others live abroad) yet do not consider themselves Israelis (pay no taxes, and, of course, do no military service); given to denouncing the present state of Israel as a sacrilege and, in context, decrying 'the Zionists', yet they are themselves Zionists of a kind. It is they, perhaps before anyone else in Israel, who share the anguish of the psalmist from the First Diaspora: 'By the waters of Babylon, there we sat down and wept, when we remembered Zion' (Psalm 137:1; Revised Standard Version). They tell me, 'You must understand that we love Eretz Yisrael, we think about it during most of each day of our lives.'

It's constantly in our minds when we read the Torah. But for the 'Zionists', it is only a finite instrument – a goal they obtained by political means, and for what? A vulgar [profane?] end. We are more 'Zionist' than they are.

And on another occasion the distinguishing mark of their Zionism is stated to me historically: 'We are pre-Herzlian Zionists'.

The name of Theodor Herzl (1860–1904), a secular Viennese Jew, is linked to the successful institutional emergence of political Zionism at the end of the last century and hence to the establishment of the State of Israel half a century later. The new nation–state had to be provided with an appropriate historiography of *Jewish* time and place. Rather than newborn, the nation and its Jewish citizens were reborn.[8] Exilic Jewish historiography with its 'quietist' ideology (Kachan, 1977; Yerushalmi, 1982) was deconstructed and a pre-exilic historiography reconstructed. A key role in the political process fell to David Ben-Gurion. He liked to suggest that:

we who have come to settle in the Jewish state *have taken a leap in time* which makes us closer to David, Uzziah and Joshua bin Nun than to the shtetl in Cracow or the nineteenth-century ideologists of Warsaw.
(cited in Weiner, 1970:241; emphasis added)

He stood forth as a secular prophet of a redemption purged of supernatural and eschatological elements, and, accordingly, as a composer of the time and place ideology of the nation–state.[9] He drew particularly upon King David (Jewish soldier, statesman, and poet)[10] and upon the Bible, which 'should shine with its own light' (cited in Schoneveld, 1976:81) – that is, without the medieval rabbinical 'quibbles and mystical speculations' (cited in Weiner, 1970:241).

But on account of the eschatologic twist that they give to the issue of redemption, the Ultra-Orthodox (even those living in Israel) reject the political claim to redemptive fulfilment of Herzl and his Israeli successors. The Ultra-Orthodox are Zionists who are still waiting, who are still in Exile. The eschatological difficulty for them is that rabbinical Judaism 'did not foresee a middle stage between exile and redemption, the Jewish state [therefore] represents an illegitimate offspring of history' (Katz, 1985:39). Rather, redemption is a timeless vision – it will happen in God's own time; it cannot be 'forced' and efforts to do so only delay its happening. Thus the establishment of 'the Jewish state' meant not 'a re-entry into history but the start of a new and more grievous Exile'; the victorious

Herzlian Zionists 'have dispossessed Israel and call themselves by her name' (Marmorstein, 1952:199).[11]

Thus their view of themselves as Jews is the antithesis of the one that Ben-Gurion publicly urged upon Israelis over the years. In their urban neighbourhoods in Israel, they recreate life, as near as they can, to what it was in the East European ghettos of the nineteenth century; they *do* devote their days to rabbinical 'quibbles and mystical speculations'.[12]

Nor do differences, or opposites, end there. The secular energy of Ben-Gurion's Labour Zionism has also had to face a returning tide of eschatologic energy (1967 is a benchmark) running in the opposite direction to that of the *haredim*. For whereas Ultra-Orthodox messianism is 'uncomplicated by the need for transfiguration into modern nationalism' (Katz, 1982:20), precisely that is the burden of the 'new' Zionism[13] best known to the public through the activities of the Gush Emunim: Bloc of the Faithful.[14] The Six-Day War victory was interpreted eschatologically and the 'correct' political conclusion drawn: namely, Judea and Samaria, as part of the sacred Jewish estate, are not negotiable.

I was told by Gush Emunim leaders: 'We did not initiate the freeing of Eretz Yisrael – it was brought upon us, and afterwards we saw it was an act of God. He wishes us to settle the Land'. And as though in answer to the *haredim*: 'We are not in any sense 'forcing God's hand' but we do consciously seek to serve as the force of God's hand within the redemptive process, and this process has begun'.

The 'Jewishness' of Gush Emunim is nourished, and to some extent generated, through distinctive time and place associations. They draw selectively (as do all Orthodox and Ultra-Orthodox Jews) upon the writings of the medieval rabbinical sages and mystics such as Judah Halevi, Rashi, Maimonides, and Nachmanides, but utterly reject the political and eschatologic quietism of Diaspora Jewry and today's Ultra-Orthodoxy. As did Ben-Gurion, they return to biblical history; but in their case it is to find 'founding father' types of figure whose fight for Jewish national independence was motivated by religious ideology. In particular, Joshua the conqueror of Canaan; and a millenium later, the Maccabees during the Second Temple period and the revered Rabbi Akiva who gave his religious sanction to the revolt of Bar Kochba (at enormous cost of Jewish lives) against the Romans after the Temple was destroyed (Menachem Begin shares much of this historiography (see note 10)). But most of all, it is their bond with the Patriarchs that is important to them. It is a bond that has to be redeemed, rescued from history, and given tangible existence today. First these progenitors and generals of the holy nation are given a 'place' on the ground (notably in Judea and Samaria) and then that place is *settled*.[15]

In sum: by recognizing more than one kind of 'Zionist' we are better able to grasp what is, I suggest, the fundamental point; namely: there is more than one 'time', and more than one 'place' in the space that is Israel, among Jews in Israel today.

Ontological issues

For the remainder of this paper I look at ontological issues raised by this approach, especially in their relation to work by Israeli scholars.

First, the issue of ethnicity and what I gloss as Jewish identity. Israel is a land of immigrants, and the prevalent view in Israel has made immigrants into 'ethnics', and 'ethnicity' one of the problems of nation-building: Jewish immigrants from different lands carried with them into Israel their own cultural and social features from which they had to be weaned so that they could embrace the inclusive model of 'modern' Israeli identity. There was to be convergence. In this process, Moroccans had further to go than, say, Iraqis, and the Hungarians less than the Iraqis, but the Germans and the Poles less than all others for it was they who put in place so many of the cultural and social norms of this reborn Israel.

In this view of identity, the place and time that were to compose the new Israel were not problematized but regarded as political givens: Israel was to be a secular, western democracy and Jewish, even 'messianic'.[16] All at the same time! And all country-of-origin 'ethnic' communities – the key Hebrew word here is *eidah* (pl. *eidot*) – journeyed towards this goal, often under Ashkenazi tutelage. Granted, their journeys would be of different grades of difficulty and so the speeds at which they travelled towards this common Israeli goal would also differ; but just as the goal was predetermined so its achievement was a matter simply of duration – and that would be negligible, even in the 'slower' cases, when weighed against the exilic history of the Jewish people.

This approach to identity, then, is teleological; and social scientists shared it with government. In effect, Eisenstadt's *The Absorption of Immigrants* (1954) set forth government ideology and policy in sociological language and refinement, and at an early stage anthropologists performed not only as ethnographers of this policy but were sometimes actually employed, at the same time, in its management.[17] In the next generation of research on ethnicity in Israel, around the 1960s, rates of progress, and divergences, were recorded: it would be noticed that, for instance, 'political ethnicity' among the *eidot* (in reality, the Afro–Asian populations) had largely become a spent force yet 'cultural ethnicity', as witnessed in pilgrimages and distinct *rites de passage* and other behaviour that only just avoided being labelled folkloric, persisted – even flourished. And so on.[18]

The approach I have taken in this essay is quite another one. First, the methodological reversal: it is the country-of-origin ethnicities of the *eidot* that are treated as givens and the unknown – and so the locus of the whole enquiry – is what this new nation–state of immigrants is to be. The goal itself is at the centre of controversy. This brings to our attention that it is (still today) a matter of 'becoming' and not merely of 'being'. I see the *eidot* not as ethnic groups but as *intra*-ethnic components of a Jewish Israeli identity,[19] and I see the issues of *eidot* properly pertaining to that inclusive level. One of these is the controversy over the relationship between Judaism and Zionism, and about the obligations, if any, that follow from being *Jewish* in this Zionist state. Such considerations lead to another set of issues: 'Who are we in relation to the Gentiles?' (For the Orthodox Jew, I suppose that question is really one of his relationship to God.) And a question of special concern for the majority of Jewish Israelis, including many Orthodox, is the intersubjective 'Who are we to our-selves?' This may mean choosing a Jewish tradition, among several, that they are going to 'rebecome' (Schecher, 1981).

But this does not apply to *eidot* ethnicity. That is negotiable: the most that *eidot* press for is cultural pluralism, no *eidah* wishes to absorb the others, no *eidah* claims exclusive title to Jewishness (not even the Ashkenazi *eidah* these days). But *eidot* identity is also parochial and transitory and to focus on it is to reduce one's vision to exilic identity, which, with equality in Israel, will languish – as Weingrod concedes in his retrospective account of *eidot* ethnicity research (1985:243). In the meantime, different *eidot* are distinguished from each other as much by cultural items of the 'host' cultures of their exile (food, dress, song, even language[20]) as by their own singular Judaic traditions.

Rather, having to choose what to rebecome is both cause and consequence of the situation by which Israeli Jews find themselves at odds among themselves about the very nature of their nation, and hence about their destination. So the teleological approach to identity in Israel misses the mark, today at least. There is no need to compare or contrast *eidot* to understand this, one has only to consider the divisions within the Ashkenazi population. Because of the fundamental nature of the issues dividing them, instead of there being a disposition towards negotiated settlement there is entrenchment. Antagonists do not hear each other. Opponents' ideologies are 'upside-down'.[21] It seems as though differences over metaphysical schemes of time and place are ideologically sought and used as defences-in-depth.[22] And it is here (to repeat myself) that the more serious, interesting, and complex sense of difference among Jewish Israelis is lodged. The challenge this presents to anthropological analysis is an ontological approach to identity.

The historical 'long' view taken of Zionism (by which the anti-Herzlian Ultra-Orthodox are also recognized as Zionists) also separates this essay from the mainstream Israeli position, though in this case I believe I can draw support from Martin Buber and Eliezer Schweid.

I am convinced that it falls to anthropology at least to take a historically and philosophically inclusive point of view here. Accordingly, I see Zionism as a Jewish quest about the meaning and means of redemption. There are considerable differences among Jews — especially today – about both the meaning and the means; so there are different Zionists. However, in common to all in Israel who call themselves Zionists, and who call upon others to join them, is the coupling of redemption with the return, from exile, to the land of Israel – 'the ultimate as well as original homeland of the Jews' (Halpern, 1969:6). The ideological history of Zionism, then, is entwined in the exilic history of the Jewish people. The enforced Jewish Diaspora after the destruction in Jerusalem of the Second Temple, by the Romans in the first century A.D., produced 'Zionists'. So, too, did the destruction of the First Temple and the enforced sojourn of Jewry in Babylon, five hundred years earlier. And long before these events, there was the flight of the Israelites to Egypt and God's prophecy of their eventual return to the Land promised to the descendants of Abraham through Isaac.

I see the energy of Zionism as a lodestone of Jewish identity through the millenia. This being so, one should *expect* dialectically arranged forces at play around Zionism and Judaism and 'being Jewish' today, and also expect them to be embedded in historiography. But this is what is lost when it is said that the story begins with Herzl. Thus Shlomo Avinieri[23] bluntly concludes: 'Zionism, then, is a post-Emancipation phenomenon' (1981:13). But, surely, when Avinieri says *that*, what he is really saying (or should be saying) is that post-Emancipation Zionism is a post-Emancipation phenomenon. The error, as I see it to be, is the settling upon the circumstances of the past century or so, and on one Jewish response (there were several others), in order to define – in a necessarily impoverished way – an ideational force that has endured through the millenia of exilic Judaism. I mean the ideational force of Zionism as redemption – as return from exile. What this 'began-with-Herzl' view of Zionism actually ends up defining is a Jewish response to a revolution within Gentile Europe – the Enlightenment.[24]

Does it matter? It does, because it would prevent us seeing how different Zionisms exist side by side as expressions of different 'times'; and to see this is to begin to appreciate how Herzlian, pre-Herzlian, and 'new' Zionism are used by Jews as forceful and different claims of their identity. Not to see this leads to an unproblematized, unidimensional view of Jewish identity in which it is *this, not that*. The Ultra-Orthodox and the Gush Emunim, are, themselves, both obvious examples of that kind of thinking.

But equally, social scientists who see the birth of Zionism as dating back only to the last quarter of the nineteenth century, are no less 'guilty' of reading history in a way that is suitable to their own identities. For, as Zionists, they are no more exempt than others from grappling with the question: 'And which of the possible historical Others of ourselves shall I adopt and adapt to?' Avinieri is a Hegelian scholar. After noting the

'Hegelianization' of Jewish history that preceded the birth of Herzlian Zionism, he is drawn to conclude; 'Zionism, is, after all, also a revolution against Jewish history' (1981:226). When an observer assumes, in this way, a role among the observed, the risk is that Zionism is defined on the evidence of (as it were) one of its phenotypes, missing the genotype.

Maybe, as a political scientist and one who is writing about Zionism from inside the Jewish and Zionist state, Avinieri has cause to set aside, as lore, the bond that endured through the millenia between Jews and the land of Israel (even though he himself is well aware of the bond (1981:3)). But as an anthropologist and one who is observing and writing from the outside, it is precisely that bond that provides me with the parameter within which to try to understand Zionism.

Finally, Schecher's notion of restored behaviour for understanding ideological life in present-day Israel (p. 124) is worth reviewing briefly. Restored behaviour is *inventive* – I think this is the point to be scored in conclusion. And how else could it be? For context (i.e. the present-day world) has to be 'pulled' into a measure of consonance with the ideological message from a Jewish tradition that is being restored. The 'closed' ghetto life of the Ultra-Orthodox in the heart of a contemporary Jewish world and the symbolic uses to which topophilia are put by the Gush Emunim on the physical margins (Judea and Samaria) of this same Jewish world[25] are both examples of context being 'pulled' (or being put 'in place' – Tuan, 1984). But as complete consonance cannot be achieved, we find the ideological messages becoming distorted and exaggerated: for example, severer self-imposed ritual life than was ever the case in the Diaspora (Ultra-Orthodox); 'idolatry' of the Land (Gush Emunim). Thus elements of actual innovation, together with a heightened self-awareness, enter into the inventiveness of restoring a tradition.

Every effort is made to create and maintain a 'world' in which 'imagination is not subject to conventional constraints' (Aran, 1985:12) and there is 'consciousness of taking part in Jewish destiny' (Schweid, 1973:33) and one may expect 'dramatic alternative definitions of reality' (Aronoff, 1985:66). Yet, looking in from the outside we are returned to the force of Schecher's paradox that much of this activity is a striving 'to rebecome what they never were'. Rhetorically, it is customary for the inventiveness to be couched in a fervent (re)attachment to Jewish messianism – with or without its eschatology. Ben-Gurion, though the champion of secular Zionism, could have been speaking for all ideological parties when he reminded a World Zionist Organization audience that: 'Anyone who does not realize that the Messianic vision of redemption is central to the uniqueness of our people, does not realize the basic truth of Jewish history and the cornerstone of the Jewish faith' (Ben-Gurion, 1959:113). Yet behind this common denominator use of messianism as a Zionist symbol and rallying-cry, there are distinct 'messianic' cultures: secular utopianism for

Ben-Gurion and his Labour Zionism; eschatologic deferral in the case of Ultra-Orthodox, and immanence for the Gush Emunim; moral anguish in the case of Oz veShalom; and for broad ranks of the Israeli population as a whole (including many members of the Gush Emunim), messianism easily lends itself to chauvinism and irredentism. Also, each group is intent on achieving a sense of coevalness (Fabian, 1983) with that period of Jewish history (albeit perhaps read metahistorically) that it finds ideologically compelling. This means that *between groups* there is, necessarily, a rejection of coevalness.[26]

As already suggested, this last outcome is sought – which leads directly to my conclusion: Zionism(s) as the source of the *divisive energy* of Jewish identity in Israel. Because there is competition over tradition and because of the near impossibility of rebecoming, this identity is still in the toils of labour.[27]

Acknowledgement

I wish to thank the Jerusalem Center for Anthropological Research and Dr Edgar Siskin for a contribution to my field expenses in 1983.

Notes

1. For reasons of space, much of the political background as well as the section on topophilia in the original conference paper ('Ethnicity of place and time among Zionists') have been dropped from this essay.
2. For a bibliography consult Weingrod, 1985.
3. Born in Iraq, Smooha is a professor of Sociology at the University of Haifa. His *Pluralism and Conflict* (1978) is a comprehensive reference source for the period of Labour Zionism (1948–77) up to 1975.
4. Professor Schweid was born in Jerusalem and teaches Jewish Philosophy at the Hebrew University; his *Land of Israel* (Eng. trans., 1985) is a key work for, among others, the kind of issues raised in the present essay.
5. See Tal (1986; 1983; 1977), also Benvenisti (1986), and Paine (1983 and n.d.).
6. Throughout I am concerned with Jewish Israelis only. Do I need to remind the reader that *within* the Green Line every sixth Israeli is an Arab (Muslim, Druze, or Christian)?
7. This strikes me as an altogether more anthropologically sensitive concept than Hobsbawm's 'invented tradition' (Hobsbawm and Ranger, 1983).
8. Jacob Katz, doyen of contemporary Jewish historians, writes that it was 'as though the nation was in hibernation or embalmed and they set out to awaken, to revitalize and to re-establish' (1982:9).
9. Along with others, several of whose portraits are in Avinieri, 1981; see also Vital, 1975. Ben-Gurion himself was Prime Minister from 1948–54 and 1956–63; and before the establishment of the State of Israel he had held the key positions of Secretary-General of the General Federation of Labour in Israel (*Histadrut*) and Chairman of the World Zionist Executive.
10. Then when the Likud assumed power in 1977, Menachem Begin was 'the king' and legendary Jewish fighters from immediate post-biblical times, such as the

Maccabees and Bar Kochba, were incorporated into a heroic, defiant Jewish historiography. (See Harkabi, 1983.)

11. Whereas messianism (a favourite word in Ben-Gurion rhetoric) for secular Zionists was no more than a culturally evocative political metaphor, the Jewish faith of the *haredim* rests upon an apocalyptic messianism. On apocalyptic messianism, see Scholem, 1971 and, for a summary, Biale, 1982: Chapter 4.

12. For historical notes on today's Ultra-Orthodox who believe they 'continue' the tradition of yesterday's Orthodox, see Katz, 1985 and Deshen, 1982.

13. Weissbrod (1981; 1985) seems to have coined the term.

14. The Gush Emunim, whose brand of 'Zionist religion' (Aran) strikes powerful chords among the wider Israeli public (Sprinzak, 1981), have also caught the attention of social scientists – for a bibliography see Newman, 1985. However, only a few of these writings are directly concerned with the movement's belief system – see Simon, 1983; Tal, 1983; and (a preliminary paper with a major work following) Aran, 1985.

15. Critical secular reaction aside (e.g. Rubinstein, 1984), fellow Orthodox Zionists – notably two groups: Netivot Shalom and Oz veShalom – have taken Gush Emunim to task on the grounds that they misconstrue the Torah and that their actions as settlers on the West Bank are a travesty of Torah morality.

16. See note 11. For the late Gershom Scholem, the pre-eminent interpreter of messianism in Judaism, secular Zionism was not messianic (for one thing, it is 'within history'). However, he worried about the 'messianic phraseology' of secular Zionism and feared consequences of 'the hubris of the Jews' (Biale, 1982:96–7 and 109–11).

17. For example, Weingrod, 1966; Willner, 1969.

18. Key phrases in the titles of some of the publications of Shlomo Deshen from that time suggest much of the story: *The Predicament of Homecoming* (1974) (with M. Shokeid), 'Breakdown of modernization', *Immigrant Voters*, 'Ethnicity and citizenship', 'Political ethnicity and cultural ethnicity', and 'The business of ethnicity is finished!?' (For full bibliographic entries, see references.)

19. See Lewis (1985) for a particularly insightful essay, constructively sceptical of the *eidot* ethnicity idea.

20. This is part of the Ashkenazi Establishment's concern over Levantization (p. 121).

21. Contributing to the ideological turbulence in Israel today is the belief in (and practice of) the exclusiveness of ideology. An opponent's ideology is held in contumely, it is – much as Williams (1976:128) has written in his 'keywords' note on ideology – founded on 'illusion, false consciousness, unreality, upside-down reality'. By contrast, one's own ideology offers 'absolute ideas [of] the greatest good' (Schweid, 1985:78). Like-minded ideologues discourse together whereas opponents in Israel are, it seems, continually spoken about but seldom spoken to (Knesset debates are something of an exception).

22. I am suggesting that where identity has to be generated (revived, retrieved, restored), people are likely to search for arguments about time and place.

23. A distinguished political scientist of Hebrew University whose *Intellectual Origins* (1981) is a seminal text concerning Herzlian Zionism.

24. As Avinieri himself observes: 'What the Enlightenment and secularization did to the Jews was to change their perception of themselves as well as how they were perceived by the non-Jewish communities' (1981:7). And those Jews who went to Palestine, 'were seeking self-determination, identity, liberation within the terms of post-1789 European culture' (ibid.:13).

25. On topophilia, see Tuan, 1974; and in application to Judea and Samaria, see note 5.
26. The insistence of the Gush Emunim of working with non-religious Jews is, therefore, all the more remarkable and significant.
27. Elsewhere (Paine, 1983) I put forward the idea of 'totemic time', but have left it fallow here, principally because I wanted to make as much as possible of the idea of coexistent times – and to pull in totemic time, as a kind of governing concept, might have hindered this endeavour. But I am now satisfied that totemic time (as I defined it) does have its place in the pluralistic scheme sketched here. (Both the Ultra-Orthodox and Gush Emunim, for instance, think in totemic time to a marked extent, but with difference between them – with the Ultra-Orthodox a passive mood prevails, and with the Gush Emunim a mood of immanence.) I hope to bring things together in another essay.

References

Amir, E. (1986) 'Sephardim and Ashkenazim: a different approach', *The Jerusalem Quarterly* 40.
Aran, G. (1985) 'Redemption as a catastrophe: the gospel of paradox', Paper presented at a colloquium on Religious Radicalism and Politics in the Middle East, at the Hebrew University.
Aronoff, M.J. (1985) 'The institutionalisation and co-optation of a charismatic, messianic, religious–political revitalisation movement', in D. Newman (ed.), *The Impact of Gush Emunim*, London and Sydney: Croom Helm.
Avinieri, S. (1981) *The Making of Modern Zionism. The Intellectual Origins of the Jewish State*, New York: Basic Books.
Ben-Gurion, D. (1959) 'Vision and redemption' (Address to the World Zionist Organization). *Forum* IV:108–24.
Benvenisti, M. (1986) *Conflicts and Contradictions*, New York: Villard Books.
Bernstein, D. and Shlomo, S. (1982) 'The rapid economic development of Israel and the emergence of the ethnic division of labour', *British Journal of Sociology* 33(1).
Biale, D. (1982) *Gershom Scholem. Kabbalah and Counter-History*, 2nd edn, Cambridge, Massachusetts and London: Harvard University Press.
Buber, M. (1952) *On Zion. The History of an Idea*, Edinburgh: T & T Clark.
Deshen, S. (1965) 'A case of breakdown of modernization in an Israeli immigrant community', *Jewish Journal of Sociology* 7:63–91.
Deshen, S. (1970) *Immigrant Voters in Israel: Parties and Congregations in a Local Election Campaign*, Manchester: Manchester University Press.
Deshen, S. (1972a) 'Ethnicity and citizenship in the ritual of an Israeli synagogue', *Southwestern Journal of Anthropology* 28:69–82.
Deshen, S. (1972b) ' "The business of ethnicity is finished!"'? The ethnic factor in a local election campaign', in A. Arian (ed.) *The Elections in Israel – 1969*, Jerusalem: Jerusalem Academic Press, 278–302.
Deshen, S. (1974) 'Political ethnicity and cultural ethnicity in Israel during the 1960s', in A. Cohen (ed.) *Urban Ethnicity*, ASA 12, London: Tavistock, 281–309.
Deshen, S. (1982) 'Israel: searching for identity', in C. Caldarola (ed.), *Religion and Societies: Asia and the Middle East*, The Hague: Mouton.
Deshen, S. and Shokeid, M. (1974) *The Predicament of Homecoming: Cultural*

and Social Life of North African Immigrants in Israel, Ithaca, New York: Cornell University Press.

Eban, A. (1968) *My People: The Story of the Jews*, New York: Behrman House.

Eisenstadt, S.N. (1954) *The Absorption of Immigrants*, London: Routledge and Kegan Paul.

Fabian, J. (1983) *Time and the Other: How Anthropology Makes its Object*, New York: Columbia University Press.

Halpern, B. (1969) *The Idea of the Jewish State*, Cambridge, Mass.: Harvard University Press.

Harkabi, Y. (1983) *The Bar Kochba Syndrome*, New York: Chappaqua.

Hobsbawm, E. and Ranger, T. (eds) (1983) *The Invention of Tradition*, Cambridge: Cambridge University Press.

Kachan, L. (1977) *The Jew and His History*, London: Macmillan.

Katz, J. (1982) 'Situating Zionism in contemporary Jewish history', *Forum* 44:9–23.

Katz, J. (1985) 'Orthodox Jews – from passivity to activism', *Commentary*, 79(6).

Kaufman, Y. (1974) 'On the fate and survival of the Jews', in M.A. Mayer (ed.) *Ideas of Jewish History*, New York: Behrman House.

Lewis, A. (1985) 'Phantom ethnicity: "Oriental Jews" in Israeli society', in A. Weingrod (ed.) *Studies in Israeli Ethnicity: After the Ingathering*, New York: Gordon & Breach.

Marmorstein, E. (1952) 'Religious opposition to nationalism in the Middle East', *International Affairs*, July:344–59.

Newman, D. (ed.) (1985) 'The impact of Gush Emunim', *Politics and Settlement in the West Bank*, London and Sydney: Croom Helm.

Paine, R. (1983) 'Israel and totemic time?', *Royal Anthropological Institute Newsletter (RAIN)*, (59).

Paine, R. (n.d.) 'Jewish topophilia in the Diaspora, in Palestine, and in Israel'.

Rubinstein, A. (1984) *The Zionist Dream Revisited*, New York: Schocken Books.

Schecher, R. (1981) 'Restoration of behavior', *Visual Communication* 7(3):2–45.

Scholem, G. (1971) *The Messianic Idea in Judaism*, New York: Schocken Books.

Schoneveld, J. (1976) *The Bible in Israeli Education*, Amsterdam: Van Gorum.

Schweid, E. (1973) *Israel at the Crossroads*, Philadelphia: The Jewish Publication Society of America.

Schweid, E. (1985) *The Land of Israel, National Home or Land of Destiny*, London and Toronto: Associated University Press.

Simon, U. (1983) 'Religion, morality and politics', in Y. Landau (ed.) *Religious Zionism: Challenges and Choices*, Jerusalem: Oz veShalom.

Smooha, S. (1978) *Israel: Pluralism and Conflict*, London and Henley: Routledge and Kegan Paul.

Smooha, S. (1986) 'Three approaches to the sociology of ethnic relations in Israel', *The Jerusalem Quarterly* 40.

Sprinzak, E. (1981) 'Gush Emunim: The tip of the iceberg', *The Jerusalem Quarterly* 21.

Tal, U. (1977) 'The land and the State of Israel in Israeli religious life', proceedings of the Rabbinical Assembly, 76th Annual Convention, 38:1–40.

Tal, U. (1983) 'Historical and metahistorical self-views in religious Zionism', in Y. Landau (ed.) *Religious Zionism: Challenges and Choices*, Jerusalem: Oz veShalom.

Tal, U. (1986) 'The symbolic and the sacred', Jerusalem: Oz veShalom (English Bulletin, no. 7–8).

Tuan, Y.-F. (1974) *Topophilia. A Study of Environmental Perception, Attitudes, and Values*, New Jersey: Prentice-Hall.

Tuan, Y.-F. (1984) 'In place, out of place', in M. Richardson (ed.) *Geoscience and Man* 24: 'Place: experience and symbol'.

Vital, D. (1975) *The Origins of Zionism*, Oxford: Clarendon Press.

Weiner, H. (1970) *The Wild Goats of Ein Gedi. A Journal of Religious Encounters in the Holy Land*, New York: Atheneum.

Weingrod, A. (1966) *Reluctant Pioneers: Village Development in Israel*, Ithaca: Cornell University Press.

Weingrod, A. (ed.) (1985) *Studies In Israeli Ethnicity: After the Ingathering*, New York: Gordon & Breach.

Weissbrod, L. (1981) 'From Labour Zionism to New Zionism: ideological change in Israel', *Theory and Society* 10:777–808.

Weissbrod, L. (1985) 'Core values and revolutionary change', in D. Newman (ed.) *The Impact of Gush Emunim: Politics and Settlement in the West Bank*, London and Sydney: Croom Helm.

Williams, R. (1976) *Keywords: A Vocabulary of Culture and Society*, New York: Oxford University Press.

Willner, D. (1969) *Nation-Building and Community in Israel*, Princeton: Princeton University Press.

Yerushalmi, Y.H. (1982) *Zakhor. Jewish History and Jewish Memory*, Seattle and London: University of Washington Press.

Chapter nine

German Identity and the Problem of History[1]

Diana Forsythe

Introduction

The problem with which I am concerned is the nature of contemporary German identity and its expression during everyday life. This implies not only such questions as how people understand and use the word German, and what they say and do in the name of Germanness, but also what it means to them to feel – or not to feel – German.

The German case is interesting for a number of reasons. First, in contrast to the minority cultures that anthropologists usually seek out for study (Cole, 1977),[2] German culture is unquestionably a majority tradition. Perhaps in part for this reason, it has received relatively little attention from Anglophone anthropologists (Forsythe, 1984). Second, studying German identity allows us to investigate ethnic-majority status as it is perceived from within. As is well known, ethnic identity tends to be created through a process of opposition (Epstein, 1978:xii). Ethnic minorities typically construct their identity through contrast to some majority tradition. Because the anthropological literature tends to depict majority/minority conflicts from the standpoint of the latter, minority identities often appear as they define themselves – as threatened and vulnerable. Majority identities, on the other hand, appear as they are seen from without, seeming by the logic of the opposition to be strong and secure, if not outright aggressive. Certainly this is how Germanness is perceived in many parts of Europe.

Recent work in Europe has looked critically at the self-construction involved in the creation of minority identities. Chapman (1978; 1980; 1982), Condry (1976), and McDonald (1982; 1986) have all questioned different Celtic groups' presentation of themselves as eternally disappearing in the face of encroaching majority traditions. In this paper I present material on German identity that raises questions about the other side of the opposition. Despite the view from without, the German case demonstrates that majority cultural status does not necessarily confer an ethnic identity that is dominant, or even secure. On the contrary, Germanness as experienced from within has a fragile, ambiguous quality that Germans themselves find highly problematic. In part, this situation reflects the connection between ethnicity and history.

The problem posed by German history

When Germans attempt to define 'Germanness' or to defend it in opposition to people or trends perceived as 'un-German', they tend to cite their own history. Given the nature of that history, however, its use to support assertions of collective German identity is awkward on several levels.

For one thing, Germany's history as a nation is recent. Whereas Celtic nationalists base their claims to collective identity on the distant past (Chapman, 1978; McDonald, 1982; 1986), in Germany when one talks about 'the past' (*die Vergangenheit*) one is often referring to the events of the past one hundred years and primarily those of the past fifty years. This is the period that began with Bismarck's unification of Germany under Prussia in 1871 and took shape with Hitler's rise to power in 1933. Although in German *die Vergangenheit* formally denotes the past in general, the term is frequently used as a euphemism for the Nazi era (1933–45).

People's feelings about being German are bound up with their feelings about their own history as a nation, and this is a touchy, and sometimes painful, topic. Whereas Celtic nationalists seem to view their past (real or imagined) as completely positive (Chapman, 1980:7), for all Germans the past is at least to some extent negative. Even neo-Nazis are at pains to minimize the number of victims murdered in Hitler's concentration camps. The German past is not one that lends itself comfortably to nostalgia, nor is it well-suited to serve as a charter for nationalists' dreams for the future. Since the period of greatest German nationalism (1933–45) is one that many Germans now feel should disappear from consciousness altogether (this task is known as 'overcoming the past' or 'putting it behind us'), it is difficult for most to base a sense of collective identity on that era.

Over the past century, Germans have been exposed to a series of explicit but conflicting national ideologies. Under Bismarck, Wilhelm II, and Hitler, the State attempted to promote German nationalism. After the Second World War, the Allies instituted a programme of 're-education' and 'denazification' designed to destroy German nationalism, substituting an image of 'the good German' as a non-nationalist. As people attempt to clarify their feelings about being German, they confront layer after layer of contradictory images of what they have been told they are and ought to be. In recent years, public interest in coming to terms with this issue has sparked a good deal of discussion in the Federal Republic on various aspects of the so-called German Question (Gaus, 1983; Häussling, Held, Kopelew, and Rölleke, 1985; Weigelt, 1984).

In search of German identity

I began studying German identity by thinking about the research topic as a problem in boundaries. If we assume that the notion of Germanness has meaning to people in relation to the way in which they identify themselves, and that not everyone and everything is thought of as being German, then it makes sense to look at where and how people draw the line. For any given phenomenon, one can examine what is seen as German, what is seen as not-German, and how the boundary between the two is defined and maintained.

Here I will apply this approach on two levels. First, treating boundaries in a physical or territorial sense, I will consider the question 'Where is Germany?' For various historical and political reasons, this is a complicated issue. Second, examining how the notion of Germanness is applied to the classification of people, I will consider the question 'Who is German?' and its corollary, 'Who is not?'

Where is Germany?

The basic inquiry here is, what land is seen by *Bundesbürger* (citizens of the Federal Republic) as German, and where does non-German land begin? If there is land that is in some way anomalous with respect to the dichotomy German/not-German, then where is it and what accounts for its anomalous status?

When Germans are speaking carefully, they tend to refer specifically to the *Bundesrepublik* (the Federal Republic) or the *DDR* (the German Democratic Republic). But during everyday conversation, they are far more likely simply to speak of *Deutschland*. This word is also used frequently in the media and in official documents. What does '*Deutschland*' mean – what is its territorial referent?

In formal political terms, it has no single referent. Rather, there are two states that call themselves German – the *Bundesrepublik* and the *DDR. Deutschland* as a single political entity has not existed since the end of the Second World War. At least, that is the reality on the ground. But the fact is that people use the word *Deutschland* every day and obviously find it meaningful.

In fact, the term is actually used in several different ways. Some people – especially members of the post-war generations – use it as a synonym for *Bundesrepublik Deutschland*. Others – especially older ones – use the term to refer to the territory contained in both Germanies. There is also a third usage, which can be seen in pre-1973 editions of the *Statistisches*

Jahrbuch, a standard source of official statistics on the *Bundesrepublik*. These volumes have a map labelled '*Deutschland*', which – in addition to the *Bundesrepublik* and the *DDR* – includes two territories labelled 'eastern areas of the German *Reich*' (*Ostgebiete des Deutschen Reiches*). These correspond to a large chunk of what is now Poland, plus what used to be called Eastern Prussia (*Ostpreussen*) and is now part of the Soviet Union. In fact, this map depicts the borders of the German *Reich* as of 31 December 1937, and refers to all the territory therein as 'the area of the German state' (*deutsche Staatsgebiet*).[3] Some of my informants – young and old – saw these 1937 boundaries as the true boundaries of *Deutschland* today. They pointed out that there was no peace treaty following the Second World War to allocate territory as the Versailles Agreement did after the First World War. Until such a treaty is agreed, they asserted, the 1937 boundaries remain the legal borders of Germany.[4]

So where is *Deutschland*? Clearly, there are at least three understandings of where its borders lie, and they are quite different. This lack of consensus has been the cause of public debate about the weather map used on the television news. Every night as the announcer says, 'And here is the weather report for Germany', the screen shows clouds and rain superimposed on a map of Central Europe stretching from eastern France to western Russia. At the moment, this map shows no political boundaries. In the past, various maps with boundaries have been used, but no matter how the outlines of *Deutschland* were drawn, some members of the public protested.

When we ask where the boundary lies between German and non-German land, that is between *Inland* (domestic territory) and *Ausland* (foreign territory), it turns out that there is no single boundary upon which all agree. Rather, on the basis of current usage in the Federal Republic we can divide the territory of Central Europe into four categories (Figure 9.1):

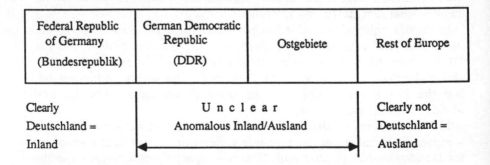

Federal Republic of Germany (Bundesrepublik)	German Democratic Republic (DDR)	Ostgebiete	Rest of Europe
Clearly Deutschland = Inland	U n c l e a r Anomalous Inland/Ausland		Clearly not Deutschland = Ausland

Figure 9.1 Categories of Germanness as they apply to land

1. The Federal Republic is seen by everyone as *Deutschland* and as *Inland*.

2. The German Democratic Republic is clearly *deutsch*, but is not included by everyone as part of *Deutschland*. Asked whether the *DDR* is *Inland*, some people say yes, some say no, and some find it impossible to classify as one or the other. Thus, in terms of the distinction *Deutschland*/not-*Deutschland*, the *DDR* is somewhat anomalous.

3. The two *Ostgebiete* within the 1937 boundaries are also anomalous, but in a somewhat different way from the *DDR*. Historically, Germany has a claim to these areas. They were part of the German state from its founding in 1871 to 1945, and part of Prussia off and on for centuries before that. Some people believe that there is still a legal case for these territories to be considered part of *Deutschland*. Since the end of the war, however, they have been under the control of Poland, Czechoslovakia, and the Soviet Union, and millions of German-speakers have emigrated from them. Although most Germans I have spoken to no longer see the *Ostgebiete* as part of *Deutschland*, my impression is that rather more still see these areas as *deutsch*.

4. The remaining category in Figure 9.1 is the residual one – the rest of Europe, which is clearly *Ausland*. However, while everyone seems to agree that this last category cannot be called *Deutschland*, some informants point out that it does contain areas that they would call *deutsch*. They see Austria and parts of Switzerland as culturally German, largely because their populations are German-speaking.

Clearly, the boundaries of *Deutschland* as a territorial entity are difficult to locate. The geographical ambiguity of *Deutschland* is significant in relation to the question of German identity: if there is no shared definition of what 'Germany' means, then what are people to identify with? Because of the importance of this ambiguity, I will outline some further historical and political reasons why it is so difficult to say just where *Deutschland* is.

First, leaving aside the first German *Reich* formed in the tenth century, *Deutschland* in the form of a unified German state only existed for a short period of time – from 1871 to 1945. Before 1871 there were numerous German states connected in a loose and shifting confederation; from 1949 there were two Germanies, which have never been reunited. If by *Deutschland* we refer to a single unified nation, then *Deutschland* was before 1871 and has been since 1945 only a nation in the mind – a concept, a nationalist dream, but not a material reality.

Second, during the time that a unified German state did exist – during the *Kaiserreich*, the Weimar Republic, and the Third *Reich* – its boundaries fluctuated rapidly. Briefly, the territory claimed as German expanded under Bismarck, contracted following the Treaty of Versailles (1919), expanded under Hitler, and contracted again following the Second World War. At the end of the war, Germany's eastern holdings were divided up between Poland, Austria, the Soviet Union, and Czechoslovakia, while central and western Germany were occupied by the Four Powers. Eventually, the *Bundesrepublik* was created from the British, French, and American zones of occupation, and the *DDR* from the Soviet zone. If the current usage of the term *Deutschland* is rather ambiguous, this ambiguity would seem to mirror fairly accurately the lack of fixity over time of Germany's actual outlines on the ground.

Third, the ambiguity of the term *Deutschland* must be related to the peculiar political status of the *Bundesrepublik* and the *DDR*, both as states in themselves and in relation to each other. After the end of the Second World War, many West Germans hoped that the different zones of occupation would be reunited as a single country. To avoid creating institutions that would prevent reunification, the authors of the West German constitution (*Grundgesetz*) in 1949 treated the division of Germany as temporary. The *Bundesrepublik* was founded as a provisional state: the constitution defines itself as providing for civil order during a transitional phase, until such time as a constitution shall be adopted by the (entire) German people (*Praeambel* and Article 146 as quoted in Hamann and Lenz, 1970:117, 744). Furthermore, the *Grundgesetz* imposes upon the leaders of the Federal Republic the duty of promoting the reunification of Germany, which will automatically mean the dissolution of the constitution and the West German state.

Thus, the *Bundesrepublik* is a provisional state that has existed for nearly forty years, maintaining a rather awkward relationship with a sister state (or zone) that is neither completely a part of itself nor yet altogether foreign. Again, the ambiguity of *Deutschland* as a concept reflects fairly accurately the ambiguity of the political situation on the ground.

For historical and political reasons, then, it simply is not possible to say in any neat sense that this territory is German while that is not. People seem to adopt different definitions of *Deutschland* according to their own age, personal experience, political convictions, and historical knowledge. But it should be emphasized that *none* of the definitions considered here offers a particularly solid referent in terms of which to define oneself. Indeed, it is not easy for contemporary Germans to know just what territorial unit to identify themselves with. This seems to be a particular problem for young people, who have never experienced the unified *Deutschland* to which their parents or grandparents may still refer.

Many informants told me that Germany is a country without a national identity. In this, they contrasted their country with France, whose identity as a nation is felt to be crystal clear.

Who is German?

We turn now to the question 'Who is German'? As before, I will look at how various terms are used in everyday conversation and in the media in order to discern the categories with which *Bundesbürger* classify themselves and others. Once again I will give special attention to categories of people who appear to be anomalous with respect to the dichotomy German/not-German.

In a purely linguistic sense, the categories used by Germans in classifying themselves and others are straightforward: the universe is divided into the theoretically exhaustive and mutually exclusive categories of *Deutsche* (Germans) and *Ausländer* (foreigners). But when one listens to how these words are actually used, it turns out that neither category is quite so straightforward and that certain groups of people do not really belong to either. Although the words *Deutsche* and *Ausländer* are in constant use, the category system Germans actually use to classify people is a good deal more complex than this simple dichotomy implies. A better representation of this system would be a whole series of categories ranged along a continuum of perceived foreignness, with some categories seen as clearly German, some as clearly foreign, and some as ambiguous with respect to this distinction. I will outline some general principles used to place people along this continuum, and then consider the category system itself.

One factor taken into account in deciding whether or not someone is German is language. People whose native language is German have a certain claim to be counted as German. This claim is recognized whether or not they come from an area categorized as definitely or possibly part of *Deutschland*. As this usage implies, at least some Germans think of themselves as part of a language community. However, fluency alone – even having German as a mother tongue – is not enough to ensure that an individual will be categorized as German. On the other hand, there are groups of people who are classified as German but who do not speak the language. As we shall see, other things contribute to the placement of individuals on the continuum.

A second factor, or set of factors, is a mixture compounded of appearance, family background, country of residence, and country of origin. An important concept here is *Deutschstämmigkeit*, being of German stock, which people seem to conceive of in racial or genetic terms. As we have seen, the boundaries of Germany as a political entity have fluctuated considerably through time. In addition, a good deal of migration has occurred in central and eastern Europe through the centuries, so that substantial populations of Germans developed in areas either under occasional German control or outside Germany's historical boundaries altogether. These communities stemmed from migration as long ago as the twelfth century; in some cases German continued to be spoken, and in others it was lost. Hitler concerned himself with these *Volksdeutsche*, settling them on property expropriated from non-Germans. After the war, millions of *Volksdeutsche* fled or were driven out of eastern Europe and the Soviet Union. Many ended up in the *Bundesrepublik*. Millions more have emigrated since the 1940s. They comprise various categories – which, for convenience I will lump as '*Aussiedler*' – and have a legal right to a German passport[5] because of their origins, far back in history as their German roots may lie. So being *deutschstämmig* gives one a certain claim to be considered German, whether or not one actually speaks the language. (In fact, even those *Aussiedler* who do speak German as a mother tongue frequently speak a dialect so altered or of such antiquity as to be labelled unintelligible by modern-day *Bundesbürger*.)

Deutschstämmigkeit is a quality that by definition takes generations to develop. Having been born in Germany alone is not sufficient to make one German if one's parents were not German. The locally born children of *Gastarbeiter* (guest workers) are seen as Turks, Greeks, etc., rather than as Germans – no matter how fluent their command of the language, no matter if they have never set foot outside the *Bundesrepublik*. Legal status does not appear to influence this perception: even the German-born children of immigrants who have become citizens seem to be classified as foreigners.

Thus, a paradoxical situation occurs in which German-born children of German citizens, who speak a dialect indistinguishable from that of their German neighbours, are classified by the latter as foreigners, whereas *Aussiedler* who cannot speak a word of the language are perceived as being far more German. This situation reflects a kind of folk-genetics according to which Germanness is seen as something that can neither be acquired nor lost: you either have it (from ancestors as long ago as the twelfth century) or you do not. In everyday life, this 'genetic analysis' probably turns on appearance: German-born speakers who *look* foreign are sometimes perceived as foreign. Appearance is to some extent a matter of dress and to some extent a matter of perceived racial characteristics such as colour of skin, hair, and eyes. Very dark colouring is seen by many as non-German. In practice, appearance often seems to take precedence over linguistic clues when people are classified as German or non-German. This, plus the association of dark colouring with foreignness, leads to some initial mistakes in classification: whatever their racial theories, Germans are not all blonde and blue-eyed, nor are all foreigners dark.[6]

I have introduced some of the basic criteria used by Germans to distinguish between Germans and non-Germans. These include language use, family background, residence, and appearance. Let us now consider the classification system itself in order to explore some of the complexity hidden beneath the linguistic dichotomy *Deutsche/Ausländer*. I will start with the various subcategories of Germanness (see Figure 9.2).

Informants distinguished between six categories of Germanness, ranging from people who are clearly German and nothing else, to people who have a claim to being considered German but are clearly other things as well in an ethnic sense. I will begin with the category of strongest perceived Germanness.

(a) As seen from the perspective of West German citizens who are *deutschstämmig* and living in the Federal Republic, the most German Germans are probably other people like themselves. Such individuals are presumed to possess various attributes of character that are looked upon as essentially German. For example, they are clean and orderly. They are stable, both in the sense that they know important social rules and are assumed to follow them, and in the sense that they and/or their forebears have been in Germany a long time, as is demonstrated by the fact that they are *deutschstämmig*. They are assumed to be White, and to be Christian – either Lutheran or Roman Catholic, Germany's two main religions. Above all, the most German Germans are familiar and predictable from the standpoint of others like themselves.

(b) The second category represents citizens of the German Democratic Republic who are *deutschstämmig* and living in East Germany. Such individuals are categorized as unquestionably German, but they are German in a slightly different way from *Bundesbürger* (category a). For example, it is often remarked that you can tell a *DDR-bürger* by the way he talks. Along with certain differences in vocabulary and accent are said to go a difference in world view as well as an obvious disparity in experience since the Second World War.

(c) Less German than the first two categories, but still with a clear claim to Germanness in both an emic and a legal sense, are the so-called *Restdeutsche* in eastern European (*Ostblock*) countries. In the years after the Second World War, especially before the construction of the Berlin Wall in 1961, millions of people of this category fled from eastern European countries to West Germany and settled there. In relation to the distinction German/non-German, these migrants occupy an interesting, anomalous, and – for them – uncomfortable position. As long as they remain in their homelands outside the *Bundesrepublik*, *Restdeutsche* appear to be regarded by everyone as German. Because they are seen as German rather than Polish, Russian, etc., they typically suffer discrimination in their country of origin; for the same reason, the West German government goes to trouble and expense to help them get out. When they get to the Federal Republic, however (thus becoming *Aussiedler*), they often have a difficult time. Although these *Aussiedler* have strong claims to Germanness in being *deutschstämmig*, often Ger-

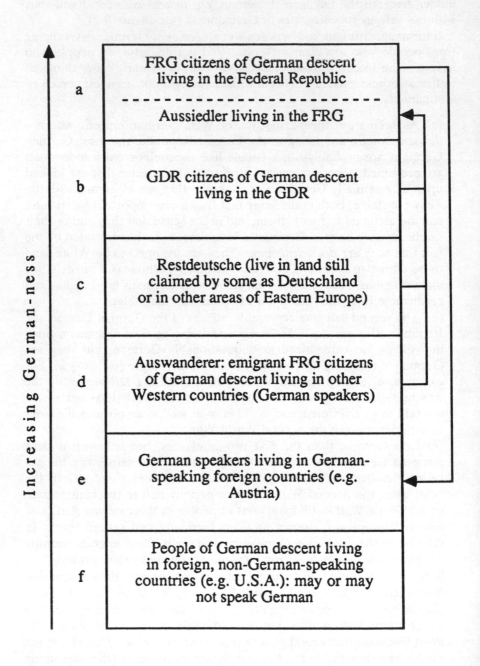

Figure 9.2 Categories of Germanness as they apply to people

man-speaking, and blonde in appearance, in Germany itself they are widely discriminated against as foreigners. Thus, they constitute a category of *Bundesbürger* that is ambiguous – German from the standpoint of their country of origin, foreign from the standpoint of many Germans. They are anomalies – Germans who are not German.

(d) Category d presents us with another anomaly, also as a result of migration. These are the *Auswanderer*, *Bundesbürger* who have chosen to emigrate to other Western countries. As long as they remain in West Germany, potential *Auswanderer* may be unimpeachably German; but having chosen to leave, their status appears to change somewhat. My impression is that some *Bundesbürger* view such emigrants with hostility, regarding them as a kind of traitor. Category d may constitute another variety of Germans who are not German, or something even worse – Germans who have *chosen* not to be German.

(e),(f) Categories e and f represent groups whose Germanness clearly coexists with other national identities as well, but which do not seem to present problems or anomalies from the standpoint of German observers. In category e are people from German-speaking countries that are clearly outside *Deutschland*. The common language is seen as creating a strong affinity. In a cultural sense these people are seen as Germans, but in terms of national identity their loyalty is to a nation other than *Deutschland*. And finally, in category f I have put people who are *deutschstämmig* but living in non-German-speaking countries. These people are the descendents of those in categories a to d, and as such have a kind of folk-genetic claim to being seen as German. This claim is felt to be stronger if they still speak the language.

I have outlined six categories of Germanness. These include two cases in which migration results in a state of ambiguous Germanness – one in which people seen as somewhat less German are suddenly in a position to be seen as more so, and one in which people seen as clearly German appear to reject that status. In both cases, the ambiguity seems to elicit hostility on the part of other Germans. Having defined these categories, let us relate them to the category structure used to order Germans and non-Germans resident within the Federal Republic. This leads us to consider the various subdivisions on the *Ausländer* side of the dichotomy.

Figure 9.3 shows a continuum with increasing Germanness to the left and increasing foreignness to the right. (I attempt here to reproduce conceptions of Germanness and foreignness as seen through German eyes. Thus, it may be that some people categorized here as foreign actually see themselves as German.) The continuum is based on the way the word *Ausländer* is actually used. Strictly speaking, *Ausländer* means foreigner(s), or *nicht-Deutsche*, non-German(s). But in everyday use, the word has been redefined and now has two further restricted meanings. First,

147

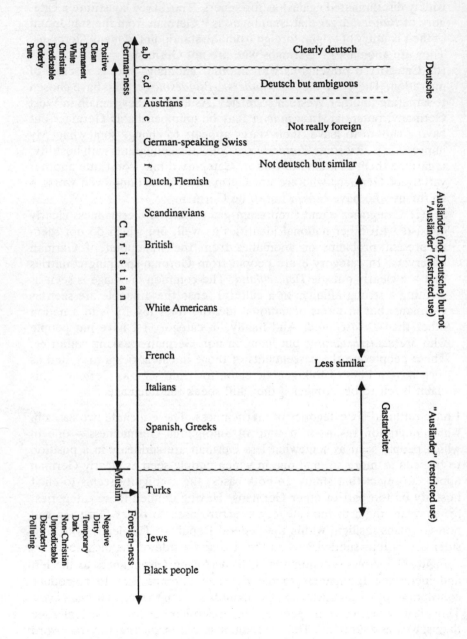

Figure 9.3 The *Deutsche/Ausländer* continuum

the word is often used to mean those foreigners who are seen by Germans as relatively dissimilar to themselves; on the continuum, this means all foreigners to the right of and including Italians. In practice, given the demographic situation in the *Bundesrepublik* at present, this use of *Ausländer* is more or less synonymous with *Gastarbeiter* or *Gastarbeiter* and their families.

Second, the word *Ausländer* is frequently used in an even more restricted sense, to mean Turk. Turks are Germany's largest group of resident foreigners, and are the target of considerable hostility. Among the *Gastarbeiter*, they are the foreigners seen by Germans as most distant from themselves. In the abstract, at least, certain people are seen as being even more foreign, for example, Black people. But while there are few Black people in the *Bundesrepublik* (Black American soldiers are one significant group), there are about 1.5 million Turks, so that the latter probably play a symbolic role for Germans as the incarnation of foreignness in German society.

This redefinition of the word *Ausländer* has two relevant effects for our purposes. First, it produces a certain ambiguity of expression that some Germans at least find useful, since it allows them to appear to be saying one thing whilst actually saying another. Resentment against Turks can be expressed as 'concern about the *Ausländerproblem*' without appearing to be directed at any specific group. A second effect of this widespread redefinition is that certain of Germany's other resident foreigners have become linguistically invisible: in terms of the restricted meaning of the term, North Europeans, British, and White North Americans are not *Ausländer*. Thus, the whole section of the continuum in Figure 9.3 between around e or f (the boundary of Germanness) and the Italians (the beginning of *Ausländer*ness) falls between the categories *Deutsche* and *Ausländer*. In terms of this dichotomy, such foreigners present yet another anomaly – *Ausländer* who are not really *Ausländer*, and yet are not German either.

On one level, of course, people do recognize that other northern Europeans are *Ausländer* according to the literal meaning of the word. But on a number of occasions, Germans reacted with hostility when I applied the word either to myself or to the French, Dutch, English, and Americans as categories. I was told several times that foreigners of this type are not considered *Ausländer*, that they have absolutely no problems in Germany, and that I would be far better advised to concentrate my attentions upon the *Gastarbeiter*. Indeed, I sometimes had the feeling that people thought it ungrateful of me to refer to myself as a foreigner.

As Figure 9.3 is meant to suggest, the boundary between *Deutsche* and *Ausländer* is not straightforward. Germanness tapers off somewhere around categories f or g to the left of the continuum as we move into the category of *Ausländer* who are not *Ausländer*. Of these, those who are seen as most like the Germans are the Dutch and Flemish; the similarity perceived here is both linguistic and cultural. This anomalous category ends with the boundary between French and Italians, where the category of 'true *Ausländer*' begins.

Germans attribute to foreigners certain characteristics opposed to the ones they attribute to themselves. The continuum in Figure 9.3 can be seen as a gradient not only of Germanness, but also of these presumed attributes. Germanness is associated with stability and permanence; foreigners, on the other hand, are seen as – and/or desired to be – temporary. People say about the *Gastarbeiter*, 'They don't intend to stay here, they want to go back again', although 57 per cent of West Germany's resident foreigners have actually been in the country for ten years or more (*Statistisches Jahrbuch*, 1985:69). Germanness is by definition racially White, and is associated with blonde colouring and light skin. Foreignness is dark, and the darker one is, the more foreign one seems to German eyes. Germanness is by definition Christian. Turks are seen as the most foreign of *Gastarbeiter* in part because they are Muslim. Similarly, in the Third *Reich* the religious difference was emphasized in propaganda defining German Jews as non-German. Germanness is associated with reliability and predictability, which by and large are regarded as positive; foreignness, on the other hand, is unfamiliar and unpredictable, which on the whole is negative. And finally, Germanness is seen as clean, whereas foreignness is dirty. This contrast has a number of aspects. For example, it is often said that Turks smell; people complain that they smell of garlic, a food that other *Ausländer* plus the French also have a tendency to eat. Similarly, Germans complain that Turks don't put their garbage in the proper containers, that they refuse to learn how to use western toilets, and so forth.

In short, Germanness is very concerned with order. Germans see themselves as orderly, whereas foreigners are seen as disorderly. Remembering the indefiniteness of the boundary around the category *Deutschland*, one is tempted to speculate that Germans compensate with a particular concern for boundary-drawing in a cultural and social sense. Failing to understand or support German conceptions of order, foreigners are seen as being threatening to it.

I have suggested that people can make claims to Germanness in several ways. These include language usage, *Deutschstämmigkeit*, country of origin, and appearance. Of these, none is by itself both necessary and sufficient to establish a claim to 'genuine Germanness', that is, what I have labelled as categories a and b on Figure 9.2. On the other hand, any one of these factors is sufficient to disqualify one from being seen as 'genuinely German'.

As Tessler notes, 'ethnicity is not immutable' (1981:156). In the present case, one would expect the growing diversity of the West German population to lead to a weakening of some of the internal boundaries within the broad category 'German'. After all, if in the past the *Aussiedler* were often rejected as foreigners, in relation to the more recently arrived *Gastarbeiter* they must appear very German indeed. Germany fulfills two of the conditions cited by Keyes as likely to lead to changing ethnic identity: migration and alteration in the state's boundaries (Keyes, 1981:28). Thus, it may be that Germanness is being redefined.

And finally, in looking at who is German and who is not, we saw that people of different nationalities can be placed along a continuum of perceived Germanness/foreignness, and that their location on this gradient is also associated with the possession of certain attributes seen as characteristic of Germanness vs. foreignness. From the standpoint of Germans, at least, Germanness seems to line up with most positive qualities of cleanliness, stability, Whiteness, Christianity, familiarity, and reliability; in short, with order. Foreignness, on the other hand, is associated with the negative qualities of dirtiness, instability, darkness, non-Christianity, and disorder. But as we saw, the distinction between *Deutsche* and *Ausländer* is not a straightforward one: between these two categories lies a kind of no-man's-land along the continuum in which are placed foreigners who are neither *Ausländer* in the usual restricted sense, nor *Deutsche*. These anomalous foreigners are seen as having characteristics somewhere between Germanness and foreignness, being quite similar to Germans at the Dutch end and quite similar to *Ausländer* at the French end.

What does it mean to be German?

As we have seen, Germany is ephemeral: it offers little in the way of a solid territorial or political entity in terms of which to define oneself. *Deutschland* today exists only as a nation in the mind – but even on that level there is no consensus about what it is or ought to be.

Since *Deutschland* as a concept offers little refuge for those in search of an identity, people may turn instead to the concept of Germanness. But here too there are difficulties. For one thing, as one informant commented, 'Germanness' as a possible identity is *'historisch belastet'* – it is emotionally burdened as a result of the Nazi past. Because Hitler relied so heavily on nationalist propaganda, many people still associate being German with Nazism.

For another thing, several qualities seen as being at the heart of Germanness are themselves rather fragile. As we have seen, Germanness is associated with a whole range of qualities related to order and cleanliness. The list of opposing qualities thought of as German and non-German recalls Mary Douglas' work on purity and danger (1970): the White, tidy aspects of Germanness are seen from within as threatened by the dark disorder of foreignness. As Douglas tells us, dirt is matter out of place;

151

from the standpoint of many Germans, *Ausländer* are *people* out of place whose presence is deeply disturbing. Germans constitute a large majority of the population of the Federal Republic, but the attributes in terms of which they see themselves are by nature vulnerable ones. Cleanliness, Whiteness, stability, order, and purity are bound to be seen as under threat not only from the millions of *Ausländer* who make up the rest of the world, but also – especially – from *Ausländer* within the Federal Republic itself. In short, Germanness is not only different from foreignness, but is also endangered by it.

For a long time I puzzled over why many Germans seemed so worried about the presence of the *Ausländer* in their midst. For some, even the sight of a Turkish family in the streets seems to constitute a violation of public order. This is in striking contrast to the situation I studied in Orkney, where a rural island has been overrun by urban incomers. There the receiving community had a far higher percentage of non-native residents but was very slow to feel threatened by immigration (Forsythe, 1982; 1980). The difference, I think, is in the self-perception of Germans as opposed to Orcadians. Although some Germans complain that the *Ausländer* threaten to swamp them, I suggest that the danger they really fear is not demographic but symbolic. In symbolic terms, these Germans are worried about pollution (Douglas, 1970).

I have suggested that as an identity, Germanness is ephemeral. Thus, it is the very opposite of Frenchness as Germans see it, which is stable and solid, just as the nation itself is seen as having been a stable, centralized entity for two hundred years. To be German, then, is to feel vulnerable and at risk, for one has defined oneself in terms of a nation and/or a set of qualities that can never be regarded as fully secure. If this is how Germans see Germanness, then how do they see themselves in relation to it?

Among my informants, two different attitudes toward being German were discernible. Both have in common the perception of Germanness as fragile, needing support, requiring-to-be-created. Where they differ is in the moral valuation placed upon German identity. These constrasting positions are to some extent associated with different ends of the political spectrum, but are actually only endpoints on a continuum of values: individuals need not adhere to one extreme or the other, and many seem to hold views that are a mixture of both.

One pole sees Germanness as vulnerable but positive: this is the classic right-wing or nationalist view of German identity. From this standpoint, people should be encouraged to feel and be German, and Germanness needs protection from non-German elements that threaten it. Under Hitler, this point of view combined with an explicit ideology of racism to lead to the extermination of millions whose ethnic backgrounds, sexual preferences, or political convictions were viewed as a threat to the purity of the German *Volk*. Today, German nationalism is sometimes expressed as *Ausländerfeindlichkeit* – hostility to foreigners, which in most cases stops short of physical attacks on the victims. A frequently-heard expression of this view of Germanness is the saying; '*Deutschland ist kein Einwanderungsland*' (Germany is not a country of immigration), which these days is clearly a statement of ideal rather than statistical reality. When asked whether they *feel* German, people holding a nationalist view of German identity tend to say yes.

The opposed view reverses the value position, seeing Germanness as negative. People holding this position tend to assert that 'feeling German' should be discouraged. They often equate conscious expressions of German identity with German nationalism, and see the latter as more or less equivalent to National Socialism. This equation places people in a difficult position in defining themselves. First of all, it leads them to attribute the Nazi past to the propagation of a shared German identity. Thus, feelings of Germanness in general are blamed for what was done in the name of a particular image of what is German. Second, it leads them to deny that they are German: in dissociating themselves from the Nazi past, they reject their own German identity as well. Asked whether they feel German, these individuals tend to say no.

When pressed they may describe themselves as German in a political sense, as citizens of the *Bundesrepublik*, and in a linguistic sense, as speakers of German. But they deny that citizenship and linguistic status have anything to do with what they think and feel as individuals. Interestingly, the alternative identity in terms of which such people present themselves is often less rather than more geographically specific. That is, some individuals – especially, it seems, those from Southern Germany – identify themselves in terms of local or regional units (e.g. as *Frankfurter, Schwaben*, etc.). But others declare themselves instead to be Europeans. 'Europeanness' obviously offers an alternative to the unsatisfactory aspects of Germanness. (It is interesting to speculate on the extent to which the *Bundesrepublik*'s strong support for the EEC and its forerunners has derived from the attractiveness of Europeanness in relation to Germanness as a possible identity for non-nationalist Germans.)

This rejection of Germanness in favour of a European identity also provides a possible explanation for a puzzling phenomenon mentioned on p. 149 – the fact that some Germans have reacted with hostility when I referred to Americans or northern Europeans as *Ausländer*. Referring back to Figure 9.3, we recall that foreigners in this category have a marginal status somewhere on the boundary between *Deutsche* and *Ausländer*, as the latter word is normally used. For Germans who affirm their German identity, calling a Scandinavian or Dutch person an *Ausländer* is not disturbing. But to Germans who identify themselves as Europeans, this usage is threatening, since it clearly draws the *Deutsche/Ausländer* boundary at a place where they would prefer not to see it. That is, it deprives them of refuge in the general category 'European' and labels them instead as unequivocally German – the very identity they are trying to reject.

Conclusion

When I first set out to investigate German identity, I thought of it as something solid, possibly even threatening, but unquestionably *there*. To one brought up in an Allied country in the post-war era with its diet of war films and stories, the notion of Germanness did not at first seem problematic. But from within, the image is rather different. As I have tried to suggest, to citizens of the *Bundesrepublik* the concepts of *Deutschland* and *Deutsche* are by no means straightforward. They are difficult, ambiguous categories whose boundaries shift through time and in their application within different social contexts.

My thesis in this paper has been that there is a connection between the elusiveness of *Deutschland* as a geographical and political entity, the ambiguousness of *Deutsche* as a category of people, and the seeming fragility of Germanness as a personal and collective identity in the late-twentieth century. The roots of that connection are to some extent historical. As I have suggested, people react to the tenuousness and the negative associations of 'being German' by seeing themselves in relation to their history in one of two ways – either by consciously affirming their Germanness, 'defending' Germany against non-German people and influences; or by consciously rejecting that history and with it their own Germanness, adopting instead either a local or a European identity and claiming solidarity with non-German people both within and outside of the *Bundesrepublik*.

Notes

1. Fieldwork was conducted in Cologne (1976–9) and Bielefeld (1982–5). An earlier version of this paper was presented to the seminar on 'History, ethnicity and identity: selected cases' at St John's College, University of Oxford. For their helpful comments I am grateful to the late Edwin Ardener and to Michael Hurst, the seminar organisers, and to the seminar participants. I also thank A. Bramwell, G. Baumann, K.-D. Bock, G. Botz, M. Chapman, J.C. Hess, V. Stolke, and A.G. Schutte.
2. At the ASA meeting at which this paper was presented, a member of the audience raised the perennial question of whether anthropology can validly be carried out in western industrial countries. Although anthropological field studies in Europe began sixty years ago (Charlotte Gower (later Chapman) undertook what I believe to have been the first such fieldwork in Sicily in 1928–9 (Chapman, 1971)), some colleagues still seem to find it difficult to accept that our field methods may as legitimately be applied to people rather like ourselves

as to those in, say, Tikopia. For further discussion of this theme, see Cole (1977), Davis (1977), and Forsythe (1984).

3. This map appears in issues of the *Jahrbuch* up to and including 1972. In 1973, the label '*Deutschland*' was taken off the map. In 1974, the map was eliminated, but the *Jahrbuch* continued to provide statistical information 'on the area of the German *Reich*'. Since 1975, both this map and all mention of the *Reich* seem to have disappeared.

4. The 1937 boundaries are more or less those mandated in the Versailles Agreement, before Hitler marched into Austria and the Sudetenland (1938).

5. Formally speaking, there is no separate West German nationality. The document issued by the Federal Republic declares that 'the bearer of this passport is a German' – not a West German.

6. Some of my informants suggested that racial characteristics are simply used as markers for cultural ones, i.e. that people of dark appearance are classified as more foreign not because they are dark, but because their appearance is a clue to cultural differences. Thus, people claim to be classifying on the basis of cultural rather than racial criteria. However, an experiment of my own casts some doubt on this. I marked a series of index cards with different regional and national labels (West German, East German, Pole, Frenchman, Japanese, etc., including White American and Black American), and then asked informants to order the cards to express the relative similarity to themselves of these different identities. Informants tended to place Black American much further away than White American – a suggestion that they were classifying more by race than by culture.

References

Chapman, C.G. (1971) *Milocca: A Sicilian Village*, Cambridge, Mass. and London: Schenker Publishing Company.

Chapman, M. (1978) *The Gaelic Vision in Scottish Culture*, London: Croom Helm.

Chapman, M. (1980) 'Regional identity in the Highlands and Brittany', paper presented to SSRC conference on Anthropological Research in Scotland, Edinburgh, 28–30 March.

Chapman, M. (1982) ' "Semantics" and the "Celt" ', in D. Parkin (ed.) *Semantic Anthropology*, ASA Monograph 22, London: Academic Press.

Cole, J.W. (1977) 'Anthropology comes part-way home: community studies in Europe', *Annual Review of Anthropology* 6.

Condry, E. (1976) 'The impossibility of solving the Highland problem', *Journal of the Anthropological Society of Oxford* XII, (3).

Davis, J. (1977) *People of the Mediterranean*, London, Henley, and Boston: Routledge and Kegan Paul.

Douglas, M. (1970) *Purity and Danger*, Middlesex: Penguin Books.

Epstein, A.L. (1978) *Ethos and Identity. Three Studies in Ethnicity*, London: Tavistock Publications.

Forsythe, D. (1980) 'Urban incomers and rural change: the impact of migrants from the city on life in an Orkney Community', in *Sociologia Ruralis* XX(4).

Forsythe, D. (1982) *Urban–rural Migration, Change and Conflict in an Orkney Island Community*, London: Social Science Research Council, North Sea Oil Panel Occasional Paper no. 14.

Forsythe, D. (1984) 'Deutschland als wenig erforschtes Gebiet: Ein Problem in der Ethnologie Westeuropas', in E.W. Müller, R. König, K.-P. Köpping, and

P. Drechsel (eds) *Ethnologie als Sozialwissenschaft*, special issue no. 26 of the *Kölner Zeitschrift für Soziologie und Socialpsychologie*.

Gaus, G. (1983) *Wo Deutschland Liegt*, Hamburg: Hoffman und Campe.

Häussling, J.M., Held, K., Kopelew, L., and Rölleke, H. (eds) (1985) *Drei Fragen zu Deutschland*, Munich and Hamburg: Albrecht Knaus Verlag.

Hamann, A. and Lenz, H. (1970) *Das Grundgesetz für die Bundesrepublik Deutschland vom 23 Mai 1949. Kommentar*, 3rd edn, Neuwied and Berlin: Luchterhand Verlag.

Keyes, C.F. (1981) 'The dialectics of ethnic change', in C.F. Keyes (ed.) *Ethnic Change*, Seattle and London: University of Washington Press.

McDonald, M. (1982) 'Social aspects of language and education in Brittany, France', D. Phil. thesis, University of Oxford.

McDonald, M. (1986) 'Celtic ethnic kinship and the problem of being English', *Current Anthropology* 27(4).

Statistisches Jahrbuch (ed.) (1952–1985) *Statistisches Jahrbuch für die Bundesrepublik Deutschland*, Wiesbaden.

Tessler, M.A. (1981) 'Ethnic change and nonassimilating minority status: Jews in Tunisia and Morocco and Arabs in Israel', in C.F. Keyes (ed.) *Ethnic Change*, Seattle and London: University of Washington Press.

Weigelt, K. (ed.) (1984) *Heimat und Nation – Zur Geschichte und Identität der Deutschen*, Mainz: v. Hase und Koehler Verlag.

Chapter ten

French Historians and their Cultural Identities[1]
Peter Burke

My brief is to talk about the ethnography of history in France: about the ways in which the past is used in the construction of ethnic identity, and more especially about the place of the professional historians in this production/representation of the past. The period with which I shall be concerned is the last forty years or so, from the Second World War to the present. This happens to be an interesting period in the history of historical writing in France; that of the rise (and some would now say, the fall) of the so-called *Annales* school.[2]

Annales: Economies, Sociétés, Civilisations is the name of a leading historical journal, the mouthpiece of a group of historical revolutionaries who later became the Establishment. It was founded in 1929 by two historians at the University of Strasbourg, Lucien Febvre and Marc Bloch, who were dissatisfied with the kind of history written in their own day. In France, as in other parts of Europe (notably Germany), history had become a profession in the middle of the nineteenth century, supported by the State, and this professionalization was associated with the general acceptance of what might be called the 'Ranke paradigm', according to which historians should concern themselves essentially with the narrative of political events, the life of the State, a narrative based on official documents, emanating from governments and preserved in archives.[3] Bloch and Febvre, on the other hand thought that the historians of their day were preoccupied with politics, not concerned enough with problems (as opposed to periods), and insufficiently open to other disciplines, such as the human geography of Vidal de la Blache and the sociology – or social anthropology – of Durkheim. The identity of the *Annales* group was defined by opposition to the historical establishment. Their new journal, named in homage to Vidal's *Annales de Géographie* (and possibly to Durkheim's *Année Sociologique* as well), provided a forum for a close-knit interdisciplinary group which included the geographer Albert Demangeon, the sociologist Maurice Halbwachs, and the political scientist André Siegfried.

During the Second World War, Marc Bloch played an important part in the Resistance and he was shot in 1944. His older colleague Lucien Febvre, on the other hand, whose move to Paris symbolized the growing intellectual respectability and indeed the intellectual centrality of the *Annales*, survived the war and came to dominate the historical profession in France from his twin power bases at the Collège de France and the Ecole Pratique des Hautes Etudes. He handed over the succession to his favourite son Fernand Braudel (the vocabulary of fictive kinship is appropriate in the case of this close-knit group, almost as close-knit as the Durkheimians).[4] It was Braudel who emphasized the importance of studying *la longue durée*, the long-term, and also of writing *histoire totale* or *histoire globale* (by which he meant not the Pre-Raphaelite attempt to include every detail but the study of a society as a whole). Braudel was absolute monarch in the kingdom of *Annales* from 1956 (if not before) to 1968 (and a kind of grey eminence till his death in 1985, at the age of 83).

The importance of 1968 for the *Annales* is no coincidence, odd as this may sound in this country, where intellectuals generally take themselves less seriously and are certainly taken less seriously by others. But Braudel's response to the events of 1968 was to board the first flight to Paris from Chicago, where he was lecturing, and to change the editorial board of the journal, confiding it to a younger generation less concerned with economic history and more concerned with historical anthropology (*ethnohistoire*, not quite our ethnohistory), the generation whose outstanding representative is Emmanuel Le Roy Ladurie.

More recently, there has been much talk of the decline or, more often, the fragmentation of the *Annales* school (otherwise known as the practitioners of the 'new history'), and there has certainly been a backlash against them.[5] However, they *have* been the dominant group in the French historical profession in the last thirty or forty years, so it makes sense to concentrate on their views and their roles. There is in any case a rough parallel between the position of the *Année* group, sociologists and anthropologists, who only succeeded in entering the French university in the age of Durkheim, and that of the *Annales* group, outsiders in a profession that was already academically established.[6] There were also links between the two groups, as we have seen.

It might be argued that a study of history and identity should concentrate on popular rather than academic history, but in France at least some academic historians do attract the attention of the media, give interviews, appear on television, and so on. Side by side with the specialist monographs on which they made their original reputations, many of them have written books aimed at a wider French public: Le Roy Ladurie's best-selling *Montaillou* (1975) is simply the most spectacular of a cluster of examples.

Concentrating on the *Annales* group also has the advantage that I know many individuals personally and can add to the study of the texts a few observations made in the 'field', which happens in this case to be 54 Boulevard Raspail.[7] From the point of view of the natives of *Annales*, I am an outsider. On the other hand, British social anthropologists will doubtless regard me a member of the tribe of historians whose contribution to an anthropology of history is simply that of a native informant. The best thing to do seems to be to play the part of a cultural broker, a translator from French into English and from the *argot* of historians into the idiom of anthropologists.

What I shall try to do, then, is to describe the sense of identity of the *Annales* group, and the ways in which it informs the history they write; and in the process, to reflect or speculate on the uses of the past and on the relation between past and present in contemporary France. I am deliberately avoiding the term ethnicity, which raises more problems than it solves, and replacing it with the term identity, or better, with the plural, identities, associated not only with language or region but also with religion, class, or profession.

Who, then, are the professional historians, and why do they write? This is certainly no simple matter of French men and women writing about 'their' France. In the first place, this is a group with an acute historiographical and ethnographic (as well as historical and 'ethnic') consciousness. In the second place, most of these historians have chosen to write, not about the nation, but about a region. A striking feature of contemporary French historical writing (compared to British and American historical writing at least), is the importance of the regional monograph.[8] The characteristic product of *Annales* history is the doctoral thesis, which attempts to reconstruct the 'total history' of a region in a particular period, in a manner not unlike an anthropological community study but on a grander scale, a thousand pages or so. Well-known examples from the 1950s to the 1980s include the work of Georges Duby on the Mâconnais, Pierre Goubert on the Beauvaisis, Pierre de St Jacob on Burgundy, Emmanuel Le Roy Ladurie on Languedoc, Maurice Agulhon on Provence, Guy Cabourdin on Lorraine, Jean Nicholas on Savoy, and Alain Croix on Brittany.[9] The tradition goes back before the Second World War to Gaston Roupnel's work on Burgundy and that of Lucien Febvre on Franche-Comté.[10]

Why choose this unit of study? Partly for technical reasons. Given the aspirations of the *Annales* historians to write 'total history' over the 'long term', they have had to limit their ambitions in other ways, since there are limits even to French doctoral theses. The choice of the region also expresses solidarity with the geographers, engaged in similar enterprises, and represents a rejection of the traditional historical concern with the nation–state. There are other reasons too. In some of the aforementioned examples, the authors of the studies chose their region because it really *was* theirs and they identified with it. Febvre, though born in Nancy, regarded himself as a Franche-Comtois by origin and had a country house in the area. Roupnel was a patriotic Burgundian. Agulhon is a Provençal, and Croix a Breton whose work expresses a strong sense of identification with his *pays*. Whether the very existence of these monographs implies a rejection of the idea of France is a difficult question. I doubt whether this was the intention of their authors (apart from the youngest, Croix).

In any case, some regional historians chose their area of research primarily because they knew it was well documented. Goubert had no personal ties to the Beauvaisis. There are also examples of the attraction of opposites: northerners drawn to the south, fascinated by its 'otherness' (I know of no cases of a pull in the opposite direction). Braudel, who came from Lorraine, chose the Mediterranean as his 'field', and began his famous work with the statement that 'J'ai passionément aimé la Méditerranée'. Two of the best-known historians of Languedoc are outsiders; Philip Wolff, a scholar of Alsatian Jewish origin who fled south in the Vichy era, and Emmanuel Le Roy Ladurie, whose family is from Normandy. Vovelle, who comes from Chartres, has become a historian of Provence, while the study of provençal revolts in the sixteenth and seventeenth centuries is the work of another northerner, Pillorget. One is reminded of the many German, British, Scandinavian, or Swiss scholars, from Jacob Burckhardt onwards, who have chosen to specialize in the history of Italy (or indeed of the British, like Richard Cobb, who have chosen France). This cultural drift from the cold north to the sunny south, from beer to wine, introverts to extroverts, etc., hardly needs further explanation. The fact that the images of north and south are obviously stereotyped does not make them any less effective. As a British historian of Italy, I can testify to the immediate and abiding attraction of Venice, Florence, Rome, and even Milan and Naples. In any case, social anthropologists should be the last people to be surprised by this interest in the 'other' (a highly self-conscious interest in the case of some French historians).[11]

There are other kinds of attraction and identification besides the regional. Class, for example, or religion. Elisabeth Labrousse comes of southern Protestant stock, like Pierre Bayle, the subject of her most important book. Janine Garrisson-Estèbe and Philippe Joutard have a similar background and similar research interests.[12] By contrast, regional patriotism and populism have led the anticlerical, atheist Croix to write a sympathetic book about Breton piety. In the case of Emmanuel Le Roy Ladurie, identification has taken a different form. His father was an aristocrat, a landowner, and minister for agriculture during the Vichy regime. Le Roy Ladurie rejected his father and turned to the Communist Party as well as to the south; but he has retained an interest in rural life and even in agriculture.[13]

In short, social identities are multiple rather than single, and in any case, it is not always identification with a subject that inspires the historian's choice. Come to that, what makes anthropologists choose *their* peoples?

There has, however, been a significant change in the last few years, an increasing interest in what might be called 'the problem of France', which is perhaps an expression of concern with the erosion of identity in a world without frontiers, a concern that also takes the form of hostility to Americanization, to 'Franglais', to tourists and immigrants.[14] To complicate matters, the same concerns underlie the revival of regional patriotism, the politicization, and to some degree the fabrication of a sense of regional identity, a consciousness of regional underdevelopment, 'internal colonialism' and so on.[15] Historians have participated in this movement and some of them have not done at all badly out of it, since it is accompanied by increasing concern for the regional past. The 'regionalist revolution' has made Le Roy Ladurie's *Montaillou* a best-seller, like Hélias's *Horse of Pride* and it helps explain the success of a fine series of regional histories published by Privat of Toulouse.[16]

Yet the result of this success is to place the history of 'France' in doubt, and the doubt has been reinforced by the more specific challenge, the gauntlet thrown down by outsiders, Americans or anthropologists. One example of this challenge is the remarkable study by Eugene Weber, *Peasants into Frenchmen*, which discusses the forging of the French national identity in the period 1870–1914 by means of conscription, education (including the teaching of French history), and so on, as if 'Frenchmen' had not previously existed, at any rate outside the towns.[17] Another example is the even more provocatively entitled *L'invention de la France* (1981), the work of two young demographers, Hervé Le Bras and Emmanuel Todd. Todd, incidentally, took his doctorate abroad – in Cambridge. Le Bras and Todd have produced a small atlas of regional variations, with an introductory essay on 'historical anthropology'. They argue that although the diversity of France is usually reduced to a variety of landscapes and cuisines, it goes deeper. It is structural, a matter of family structure in particular. France, unlike other nations, has three types of family structure, not one, and on these depend other variations, from the votes for Mitterrand to the suicide rate. Le Bras and Todd are well acquainted with the work of the *Annales* historians. However, they have used it to draw conclusions that are certainly not explicit in the writings of this group, and, as recent reactions show, are rejected by some of its leading members.

It may be of some ethnographic interest to point to a major contrast between France and Britain in this area. Tom Nairn's *The Breakup of Britain* (1977) has not, so far as I know, set off much of a reaction among historians over here, perhaps because the English, at least, have few doubts about their identity, as a result of living in a country with a long tradition of cultural centralization. On the other hand, the challenge to

'France' is taken more seriously there, presumably because the sense of a French identity is more fragile. Le Bras, Todd, and their allies have so far provoked at least three responses from the *Annales* group. First off the mark, characteristically, was the notoriously prolific Pierre Chaunu, in *La France* (1982). He wrote his essay at the request of a publisher, to answer the question 'Qu'est-ce que la France?' and to give an explicit reply to Le Bras and Todd. Chaunu is a pioneer of quantitative history, a devout Protestant, a nationalist, and a crusader against family limitation.[18] Despite his interest in the Americas in the sixteenth and seventeenth centuries, he is much less involved in historical anthropology than many of his *Annales* colleagues. One of his reactions to the threat posed by anthropology in this instance is personification ('La France est une personne . . . une personnalité collective'), in the manner of Charles de Gaulle, who saw the nation in terms of 'la princesse des contes ou la Madone aux fresques des murs . . . vouée à une destinée éminente et exceptionnelle'.[19] One does not have to be a psychoanalyst to see this reaction as a defence mechanism. Another response on Chaunu's part has been to emphasize 'l'ancienneté, la durée, la constance et la force du sentiment national', going so far as to assert that 'Nous sommes . . . la plus vieille des nations européennes formées'.[20] A third, more thoughtful reaction has been to accept the Le Bras–Todd thesis about diversity and even deep 'fractures' in French culture, but to attempt to relate this diversity to the tradition of political centralization. 'Le paradox d'une telle diversité, c'est l'unité du royaume. Le roi et la République auront donc contribué à faire vivre ensemble harmonieusement ces univers opposés.'[21]

Another reaction to the 'French question' is that of the late Fernand Braudel, who turned at the end of his life to the history of his own country, calling his first volume *L'identité de la France* (1986).[22] It begins with a declaration of the author's passionate love for France (similar in style to the prologue to his *Mediterranean*, quoted on p. 160), coupled with a declaration of his intent to keep his distance; 'je tiens à parler de la France comme s'il s'agissait d'un autre pays'. Accordingly, it treats French identity as a problem, as an ambiguous notion, a question or series of questions rather than as something to be taken for granted.[23] Braudel accepts the fact that, as his master Lucien Febvre put it, 'la France se nomme diversité'. He is aware of the work of Weber, Le Bras, and Todd. In characteristic fashion he studies the problem of French identity over the long term and begins with geography, and the importance for the unification of France of 'la liaison primordiale Rhône-Saône-Seine'.[24] It is too bad that death caught up with him before he reached the planned culture and mentality section of the study.

Chaunu's solution to the problem of France is to emphasize politics; Braudel's, to emphasize geography. A third, collective response to the challenge to France is more cultural or anthropological. It is to study in detail the process by which the French identity (national and republican) has been constructed. This is the task of the contributors to a series of volumes entitled *Les lieux de mémoire* and edited by Pierre Nora, now in the course of publication.[25] The editor, who works for the publishing house of Gallimard as well as at the Ecole des Hautes Etudes, has recruited some of the best-known historians of the *Annales* group, from Maurice Agulhon to Michel Vovelle, to write on what he calls 'notre mémoire nationale' and 'les lieux où elle s'est électivement incarnée'; festivals, monuments, museums, school textbooks, and so on. Thus the first volume includes historical essays on the tricolour, the Marseillaise, and the official celebration (from 1880) of the 14 July.

According to your guidelines, 'This conference is not simply another call for an historical anthropology. It is, rather, a call for an anthropology of history.' The special significance of *Les lieux de mémoire* lies in the manner in which these two projects fuse. Pierre Nora himself contributes an ambivalent essay on memory and history, expressing his nostalgia for as well as conducting an analysis of 'La disparition rapide de notre mémoire nationale', threatened by the acceleration of history and the decline of the peasantry, 'cette collectivité-mémoire par excellence'. His essay is built on a contrast between the spirit and the letter, memory and history. It alternately mystifies and demystifies.[26]

On the one side, in the tradition of the romantic folklorists, intent on saving a few fragments from the destruction of traditional society, we find Nora regretting the rise of an 'irreverent' and critical historiography, to which he prefers memory ('la mémoire, c'est la vie'). He writes as if unaware of the process of 'the invention of tradition' discussed by Eric Hobsbawm and others, or the 'problem of perspective' identified by Raymond Williams (1973), who notes the tendency of writers on rural themes to place the end of the old order in their own childhood, and suggests that they are reworking the myths of Arcadia and the Garden of Eden.[27]

However, Nora does eventually cite the Hobsbawm and Ranger (1983) volume at the end of his own, and the essays he has commissioned are in many ways similar in approach to the studies collected there, even if there is nothing quite as irreverent as Trevor-Roper's attempt to strip the Scots of their kilts. So it is natural to enquire what the editor intended in putting this collection together. In some ways it looks like a reflexive anthropology of the French; but the detachment involved in such an enterprise would surely ally it with the critical historiography that Nora explicitly rejects. The alternative interpretation is that the book is itself intended to be a contribution to national unity, an attempt to recall lost memory, and even, perhaps, a sophisticated response to the challenge to France, which turns the challengers' anthropological weapons against them. Or is the editor trying to do all these things at once, to offer something for everyone?

The dilemma is not of course Nora's alone. His volumes are appearing at a good moment, for in 1989 there will be a grand celebration of the bicentenary of the French Revolution. The French government is spending a good deal of money on the project. The historian in charge of it is Michel Vovelle, one of the contributors to the Nora volume, highly sophisticated, very much concerned with ideology, and interested in *ethnohistoire*. He has been given the opportunity to organize the kind of 'fête révolutionnaire' about which he and his colleagues have written.[28] To what extent will his views shape the celebration? To what extent will the Nora volumes affect perceptions of 1989, or indeed the very 'national memory' they chronicle?

Notes

1. My thanks to Maryon McDonald for encouragement and for criticisms.
2. L. Hunt, 'French history in the last twenty years: the rise and fall of the Annales paradigm', *Journal of Contemporary History* 21 (1986), 209–24.
3. W.R. Keylor, *Academy and Community: the Foundation of the French Historical Profession* (Cambridge, Mass., 1975).
4. Braudel dedicated his famous *Méditerranée* to Febvre as a sign of what he called 'filial affection'.
5. Contrast, J. Le Goff, R. Chartier, and J. Revel (eds), *La nouvelle histoire* (Paris, 1978), with H. Coutau-Begarie, *Le phénomène 'nouvelle histoire': stratégie et idéologie des nouveaux historiens* (Paris, 1983).
6. Cf. T.N. Clark, 'Durkheim and the French university' in *The Establishment of Empirical Sociology*, ed. A. Oberschall (New York, 1972), 152–74.
7. I spent part of 1979 at the Ecole des Hautes Etudes as Directeur d'études associé (not to investigate *Annales*, but to carry out my own research). The following historians are known to me, have worked on France, and in the *Annales* style, whether or not they identify with the group: Maurice Agulhon, the late Philippe Ariès, Yves Bercé, André Burguière, the late Fernand Braudel, Nicole Castan, Yves Castan, Roger Chartier, Philippe Contamine, André Corvisier, Jacques Dupâquier, Jean-Louis Flandrin, François Furet, Philippe Joutard, Dominique Julia, Elisabeth Labrousse, Jacques Le Goff, Emmanuel Le Roy Ladurie, Alain Lottin, Mona Ozouf, Robert Muchembled, René Pillorget, Jacques Revel, Denis Richet, Jean-Claude Schmitt, Michel Vovelle. Despite lack of personal acquaintance I shall also consider Pierre Chaunu, Alain Croix, Georges Duby, Pierre Goubert, Ernest Labrousse, and the late Robert Mandrou.
8. In Britain, A.L. Rowse's *Tudor Cornwall* (1941) has had few successors till relatively recently. The need for regional monographs in American history is argued with passion by Richard Andrews (himself a historian of France) in a special issue of *Review* devoted to an assessment of the *Annales*.
9. G. Duby, *La société aux xie et xiie siècles dans la région mâconnaise* (Paris, 1953); P. Goubert, *Beauvais et le beauvaisis de 1600 à 1730* (Paris, 1960); P. de Saint Jacob, *Les paysans de la Bourgogne du nord au dernier siècle de l'ancien régime* (Paris, 1960); E. Le Roy Ladurie, *Les paysans de Languedoc* (Paris, 1966); M. Agulhon, *La sociabilité méridionale* (Aix, 1966) and *La république au village* (Paris, 1970); G. Cabourdin, *Terre et hommes en Lorraine 1550–1635* (Nancy, 1977); J. Nicholas, *La Savoie au 18e siècle* (Paris, 1978); A. Croix, *La Bretagne au 16e et 17e siècles* (Paris, 1981).

10. L. Febvre, *Philippe II et la Franche-Comté* (Paris, 1911), which, despite its title, is no more concerned with Philip II than Braudel would be in his *Mediterranean*; G. Roupnel, *La ville et la campagne au 17e siècle: étude sur les populations du pays dijonnais* (Paris, 1922).

11. The self-consciousness is particularly explicit in a work by a classicist in the *Annales* group, F. Hartog, *Le miroir d'Hérodote: essai sur la représentation de l'autre* (Paris, 1980).

12. E. Labrousse, *P. Bayle* (2 vols, The Hague 1963–4) and *La révocation de l'édit de Nantes* (Paris, 1985); J. Garrisson-Estèbe, *Tocsin pour un massacre* (Paris, 1968), *Protestants du Midi* (Toulouse, 1981) and *L'édit de Nantes et sa révocation* (Paris, 1985); P. Joutard, *La révolte des Camisards* (Paris, 1977).

13. On his left-wing phase, E. Le Roy Ladurie, *Paris-Montpellier* (Paris, 1982). He does occasionally write about northern France, and it has been suggested (by Denis Richet, in conversation), that the famous essay 'La verdeur du bocage', about a sixteenth-century Norman squire, the sieur de Gouberville, is an allegorical portrait of his father.

14. An all-too-brief discussion in T. Zeldin, *The French* (London, 1983), especially the conclusion, 'What it means to be French'.

15. A clear, lively account by a committed regionalist in R. Lafont, *La révolution régionaliste* (Paris, 1967). Cf. J. Ardagh, *France in the 1980s* (London, 1982), Chapter 3, 'Reform and Renewal in the Regions'.

16. Collection 'Univers de la France', beginning (naturally enough, in Toulouse) with the *Histoire de Languedoc*, edited by Philippe Wolff (1967). The series now runs to some fifty volumes, including documents.

17. E. Weber, *Peasants into Frenchmen: the Modernisation of Rural France* (Stanford, 1976), especially 111–14, 297–8, 330–8; the French translation appeared in 1983 with a more innocuous title, *La fin des terroirs*.

18. His books include *La France ridée* (1979) and *Histoire et foi* (1980).

19. De Gaulle is in fact quoted in P. Chaunu, *La France: histoire de la sensibilité des français à la France* (Paris, 1982), 9–10.

20. Ibid., 371. Chaunu does not make any reference to Eugene Weber's study.

21. Ibid., 39. He does not explain how the strong state was able to emerge.

22. With characteristic ambition he planned a four-volume study, but died in 1985 after writing only two volumes.

23. Braudel, 1986:17.

24. Braudel, 1986:241.

25. Volume I, *La République* (Paris, 1984); II, *La Nation* (3 vols, Paris, 1986). A third volume on the regions, entitled *Les France*, is advertised. Cf. A. Dupront, 'Du sentiment national' in *La France et les français*, ed. M. François (Paris, 1972), 1423–74.

26. The aim of this paper is to write an ethnography, not to engage in polemic. But in order to justify the last comment I must say that I think Nora should replace his simple story of a shift from memory to history over the last few years with a more subtle account of the interaction of oral and written accounts of the past in France over the long term.

27. E. Hobsbawm and T. Ranger, *The Invention of Tradition* (Cambridge, 1983); R. Williams, *The Country and the City* (London, 1973), Chapter 2.

28. Vovelle is the author (among other books) of *Les métamorphoses de la fête en Provence* (Paris, 1976) and *Idéologies et mentalités* (Paris, 1982). Another contributor to the Nora volumes, Mona Ozouf, author of *La fête révolutionnaire* (Paris, 1976), is also involved in the bicentenary celebrations.

References

Agulhon, M. (1966) *La sociabilité méridionale*, Aix: Faculté des Lettres.
Agulhon, M. (1970) *La République au village*, Paris: Plon.
Andrews, R.M. (1978) 'Implications of Annales for U.S. history', *Review* 1:165–80.
Ardagh, J. (1982) *France in the 1980s*, London: Secker and Warburg.
Braudel, F. (1986–7) *L'Identité de la France*, 3 vols, Paris: Arthaud-Flammarion.
Cabourdin, G. (1977) *Terre et hommes en Lorraine 1550–1635*, Nancy: Université de Nancy.
Chaunu, P. (1979) *La France ridée*, Paris.
Chaunu, P. (1980) *Histoire et foi*, Paris.
Chaunu, P. (1982) *La France: histoire de la sensibilité des français à la France*, Paris: Laffont.
Clark, T.N. (1972) 'Durkheim and the French university', in A. Oberschall (ed.) *The Establishment of Empirical Sociology*, New York: Harper, 152–74.
Coutau-Begarie, H. (1983) *Le phénomène 'nouvelle histoire': stratégie et idéologie des nouveaux historiens*, Paris: Economica.
Croix, A. (1981) *La Bretagne aux 16e et 17e siècles*, 2 vols, Paris: Maloine.
Duby, G. (1953) *La société aux xie et xiie siècles dans la région mâconnaise*, Paris: Armand Colin.
Febvre, L. (1911) *Philippe II et la Franche-Comté*, Paris: Champion.
François, M. (ed.) (1972) *La France et les français*, Paris: Pléiade.
Garrisson-Estèbe, J. (1981) *Protestants du Midi*, Toulouse: Privat.
Garrisson-Estèbe, J. (1985) *L'Edit de Nantes et sa révocation*, Paris: Seuil.
Goubert, P. (1960) *Beauvais et le Beauvaisis de 1600 à 1730*, Paris: SEVPEN.
Hartog, F. (1980) *Le miroir d'Hérodote: essai sur la représentation de l'autre*, Paris: Gallimard.
Hélias, P.-J. (1975) *Le Cheval d'Orgeuil*, Paris: Plon.
Hobsbawm, E. and Ranger, T. (eds) (1983) *The Invention of Tradition*, Cambridge: Cambridge University Press.
Hunt, L. (1986) 'French history in the last twenty years: the rise and fall of the *Annales* paradigm', *Journal of Contemporary History* 21:209–24.
Joutard, P. (1977) *La Révolte des Camisards*, Paris: Gallimard.
Keylor, W.R. (1975) *Academy and Community: the Foundation of the French Historical Profession*, Cambridge, Mass.: Harvard University Press.
Labrousse, E. (1963–4) *Pierre Bayle*, 2 vols, The Hague: Mouton.
Labrousse, E. (1985) *La Révocation de l'édit de Nantes*, Paris: Payot/Labor et Fides.
Lafont, R. (1967) *La révolution régionaliste*, Paris.
Le Bras, H. and Todd, E. (1981) *L'Invention de la France*, Paris.
Le Goff, J., Chartier, R., and Revel, J. (eds) (1978) *La nouvelle histoire*, Paris: CEPL.
Le Roy Ladurie, E. (1966) *Les Paysans de Languedoc*, Paris: SEVPEN.
Le Roy Ladurie, E. (1975) *Montaillou village occitan*, Paris: Gallimard.
Le Roy Ladurie, E. (1982) *Paris-Montpellier*, Paris: Gallimard.
Nicolas, J. (1978) *La Savoie au 18e siècle*, Paris: Maloine.
Nora, P. (ed.) (1984) *Les lieux de mémoire, La République*, Paris: Gallimard.
Nora, P. (1986) *La Nation*, 3 vols, Paris: Gallimard.
Ozouf, M. (1976) *La fête révolutionnaire*, Paris: Gallimard.
Roupnel, G. (1922) *La Ville et la campagne au 17e siècle*, Paris: Leroux.
Rowse, A.L. (1941) *Tudor Cornwall*, London: Jonathan Cape.

de Saint Jacob, P. (1960) *Les paysans de Bourgogne du nord au dernier siècle de l'ancien régime*, Paris: Publications d l'Université de Dijon.

Vovelle, M. (1976) *Les Métamorphoses de la fête en Provence*, Paris: Aubier-Flammarion.

Vovelle, M. (1982) *Idéologies et mentalités*, Paris: Maspéro.

Weber, E. (1976) *Peasants into Frenchmen*, Stanford University Press.

Williams, R. (1973) *The Country and the City*, London: Chatto & Windus.

Wolff, P. (ed.) (1967) *Histoire de Languedoc*, Toulouse: Privat.

Zeldin, T. (1983) *The French*, London: Collins.

Chapter eleven

Mormon History, Identity, and Faith Community

Douglas Davies

An anthropology of the body is as necessary as an anthropological interest in history to understand the dynamics of Mormon identity. This chapter explores ways in which history and the physical body are related in Mormon ritual as Latter Day Saints acquire a distinctive sense of identity grounded in accompanying patterns of experience.

Mormons are found not only in their high-density communities in Utah and neighbouring American states but also in small congregations throughout the world. Whether in the subcultural or eclectic congregational mode, Mormons locate the origin of their distinctive identity in the events associated with their founding prophet, Joseph Smith, in the 1820s and 1830s life of New York State. His death, the subsequent persecution of the new church, and the migrations to Utah, where distinctive patterns of life and church organization developed, all contribute to a past deemed divinely significant. Present-day Mormons gain a sense of unity with their founding fathers as genealogical research identifies them, and as living members undergo vicarious ritual incorporating their dead into an ever expanding 'contemporary' community.

A major issue in anthropological analysis of Mormon thought concerns the very concept of history held by various Latter Day Saints. Because this is much debated by Mormons, any anthropological discussion must, of necessity, be conducted at a higher order of discourse. This particular challenge leads to our concluding interpretation of mood as an attribute of embodiment in which current ritual experience is informed by a view of the past to yield a strong contemporary identity or 'testimony'.

Mormons possess such an explicit and self-conscious concern with history that some have seen history as replacing theology within Mormon religion. Paradoxically, yet others have suggested that Latter Day Saints exhibit a form of memorylessness, an inability to outline in detail aspects of the factual past. These issues we will take up in due course but we begin with Mormon sacred scriptures and other authoritative texts, which have profoundly influenced the Mormon worldview by locating it in a purportedly historical context.

According to the *Book of Mormon*, sometime between 600 and 592 B.C. one Nephi recorded the fact that he was about to write, 'a full account of the history of my people' (1 Nephi 9:2). It would document wars and the reign of kings. It would complement another history dealing with religious matters and which outlined a migration of Jews from the Holy Land to Meso-America in the seventh century B.C. Details apart, this and other references suggest a clear concern with history as an account of successive events that furnished a population under divine influence. Indeed the *Book of Mormon* reckons to be the history book of those who migrated on a purpose-built ship to ancient America. The book resembles the Bible in many respects of style even to the extent that its B.C. to A.D. material closely matches the proportion of the Old to New Testament writings in the Bible. Its closing chapter, explicitly dated A.D. 421 marks a silence unbroken until the 1820s when God began a series of revelations to Joseph Smith and inaugurated the Restoration of truth in doctrine and ritual. History became a series of divine dispensations and the body of each believer an actor on the stage of dispensational history as Mormon tradition furnished itself with dates and data for its own retrospective interpretation of the world. In this case it is easy to follow Jack Goody in marking Lévi-Strauss's dictum that 'there is no history without dates', and even more so, his elaboration that there is no history without archives (Goody, 1977:148).

The *Book of Mormon* is profoundly significant to this end in two specific ways. First, because it parallels the biblical account documenting the obedience and disobedience of peoples to God. Describing emigration from the Holy Land to Meso-America about 600 B.C. it plays out on American soil the same theme of prophet and chosen people that underlies the entire Old Testament dynamic of religiosity. But, second, it adds another distinctive element to the biblical material in that the *Book of Mormon* engages in a higher order analysis of history as such. History as a reflection upon events and not merely the documentation of them is what stands out in the *Book of Mormon* (cf. 2.Nephi 4:14, Jacob 1:33). This alertness to historical events, which involves each section of the book being accorded a reckoned date of writing, is continued in other important books generally called Standard Works including the *Doctrine and Covenants*. Covering revelations believed to have been given through Joseph Smith in the 1830s, we find God saying, for example, that, 'it is expedient . . . that my servant John should write and keep a regular history' (47:1. Cf. 69:2,3). Or again that, 'it is the duty of the Lord's clerk . . . to keep a history and a general church record of all things that transpire in Zion' (85:1). The Lord also tells early Mormons that they should 'obtain a knowledge of history' (93:53). This would, it was thought, help advance divine purposes.

This early Mormon commitment to a story that still lay in the future has been matched by the commitment later members have shown to that earliest period. It is now common for people giving talks during religious meetings or when formally bearing their 'testimony' to assert categorically that they know God lives, that Joseph Smith was a prophet of God, and that this Church of Jesus Christ of Latter Day Saints is the true church on the earth today. They add that they know and are grateful for the fact that this church is headed and led by a living prophet who continues the immediacy of access to God and of God to the church. Periodically church members 'sustain' or assert their commitment to their church leaders as proper successors in office to the early-nineteenth-century prophet and apostles.

In so doing, Mormons commit themselves to what is a particular theory of history. Though they would not naturally see it in this way it is just such a theory as is followed by many religious devotees whose traditions interpret the prior life of mankind according to their own theology. Divine dispensations replace more neutral eras. Time in the sense of *chronos* is replaced by time in the sense of *kairos*, mere duration is endowed with a divine intention, and revelation discloses its pattern. In Mormon terms the church now exists in a phase of Restoration of doctrine and ritual. This follows the post-apostolic period when God removed truth from the earth. Moments of apparent religious activity such as the Reformation are interpreted as the outcome of a degree of faith on the part of sincere men but in ages when it did not please God to engage in full-scale revelation. All history becomes the history of the church and as such the history of the Mormon community. In this, Mormons exhibit a more developed scheme of cosmic events than is present in today's mainstream Christianity, yet such was quite common in mid-nineteenth century America, especially in the dispensationist tradition espoused by, for example, Millerites and later groups of Seventh Day Adventists and Jehovah's Witnesses. For ordinary members, a pattern of world and church history serves as one important symbolic framework for understanding doctrine, especially when family genealogical research is integrated within this history in a total process of salvation.

At this point Mormonism becomes problematic as history and theology become confused in moving from the level of uncritical acceptance of the general membership to the deeply questing concerns of historians in the church. Their role is distinctive when Mormonism is compared with other religious traditions for matters of historical validation of religious belief touch questions of truth and also of identity.

History as theology

A leading Mormon historian, R.L. Bushman, concluded his extensive and recent study on the prophet Joseph Smith with the reflection that Mormons have, very largely, found themselves, 'unable to take much interest in formal theology or systematized treatises'. Their interest has been so placed elsewhere that he thinks it true to say that, 'Mormonism was history, not philosophy' (Bushman, 1984:188). This opinion could be supported further by the fact that the Mormon History Association constitutes one of the most influential groups among Mormon intellectuals. Though not a formal church organization, it affords an arena for discussing matters of faith, personal commitment, and trends in church thinking. Similarly, in the 1984 Tanner Lectures on Mormon History, E.S. Gaustad addressed himself to the theme of 'historical theology and theological history: Mormon possibilities', (Gaustad, 1984:99). There, this non-Mormon reminded Mormon historians that they occupied that position in their church which is filled in other traditions by theologians. In fact he thinks that historians constitute *the* professional group in a church that does not possess trained theologians.

While for the remainder of this paper I agree with these points, it should be mentioned that in practice church leaders engage in scriptural and moral comment in ways that foster piety and are not particularly related to historical questions. I have explored this and related issues in my fuller study, *Mormon Spirituality* (Davies, 1987:131ff.). For clarity's sake it is better to say that Mormon pastoral or practical theology lies in the hands of formal priesthood holders who include most adult males active in the church, while formal and more abstract thinking falls into the historians' domain.

One reason for this extreme interest in history lies in the fact that Mormon communal identity is perceived to be grounded in revelations given as recently as the first third of the nineteenth century. These are believed to be verifiable and to validate the religion flowing from them. Questions of religion seem to be questions of history. Historical event is a correlate of faith, or more directly, historical fact is the basis of faith. But, and this is the crux, the miraculous events surrounding the Restoration of doctrine and ritual through Joseph Smith are open to question. Today, as in the time of Joseph Smith, it is a case of trust and intuitive conviction and not of demonstrable certainty. Yet matters of religious doubt still tend to be aligned with matters of historical validation. When religious conviction and identity fall into doubt, it is to history rather than theology that recourse is taken. But the disquieting fact is that critical historical techniques cannot verify what are, in effect, attitudes of faith. In practice the present day believer identifies with the leading figures of the founding period in ways other than those of critical history. At this point psychological factors of identification and association require us to look carefully at the practical distinction between history and myth.

Mormon historians seem to want to maintain canons of interpretation acceptable to the academic community in general whilst not abandoning the church credo concerning Joseph Smith's encounters with God. It is as though they hope that scholarship will yield an analysis implying extraordinariness in Smith's day. Non-scholarly church members view these phenomena just as they view biblical miracles in the ancient past. In functional terms the accounts of divine manifestation and commissioning of the first Mormon leaders serve as myths, as structured patterns of ideas that interpret reality in ways consonant with contemporary religious activity. Here Mormon historians resemble Christian theologians in wishing to invest events with extraordinary significance. The forms of myth and miracle are invaluable for such purposes, but because these concepts seem to throw the notion of verifiability into question they are avoided. The hope of historical proof is an intellectual temptation forever in tension with an overarching commitment to scholarly principles resulting in a degree of faith–history dissonance for many Mormon intellectuals. Further aggravation comes since there is no tradition of theological reflection in Mormonism to dissipate tension by approaching matters of faith in alternative ways. Precisely because Joseph Smith eschewed debate and preferred new revelation, subsequent Saints have not had the facility of and for theological discourse. Comparative theology is also very difficult to accept since the very foundation of the Restored gospel asserts the error of the other systems.

To dwell upon intellectual problems of faith and history any longer would, however, detract from the singular power that has emerged in Mormon culture through an integration of faith and history in forms of practical piety which touch the majority of church members. To these we now turn to explore some of the processes by which Mormon identity becomes established through church ritual, family life, and the framework of popular history.

Identity in kinship and eternity

Extensive European migration to America in the mid- and later-nineteenth century helped form a religious subculture that awaited the return of Christ to America to usher in God's millennial kingdom. No dramatic parousia came. The Saints of the Latter Day thought again and perceived that the great kingdom would emerge slowly throughout the world as church organization spread through missionary endeavour. There was no sense of prophecy failing in this Mormon context. Mormons reflected upon the extensive emigrations and the resulting church and social structure and were satisfied. The church itself was a symbol of divine action; the Mormon community was a sacrament to itself. In this, a complex relation emerged between history, community, identity, and faith.

The historic message preached the necessity to leave wicked Babylon and flee to Zion; these biblical terms were applied to non-Mormon and

Mormon communities and helped converts in reclassifying the world. They gathered but, as already mentioned, the 'miracle' that followed was not the one initially expected. Instead of a revealed Christ there emerged a new community of Saints whose influence was to be far-reaching. Indeed present day membership involves participation in the act of faith of those early Saints whose emigration and settlement form part of later community identity. But those events of migration and settlement were shaped by the biblical models of wilderness wandering and promised land in such a way that it is now practically impossible to differentiate between, for example, demographic factors and psychological motivations of migration. Biblical and mythical dimensions have become part of the historical interpretation of events underlying the identity of today's Saints.

Many Mormon families, especially in America, are able to trace their connection with migrant families so that in one sense, their genealogy takes them into the mythical period of the community's birth. For new converts, too, genealogy remains important. Indeed, few groups have been as occupied with ancestry as the Latter Day Saints, for whom it serves several purposes all of which foster corporate identity and the religious goal of salvation. For more than a century Mormons have diligently and with increasing technological efficiency sought out their family histories around the framework of its kinship network. In a practical sense, though initially this sounds contradictory, families have become increasingly extended even though polygamy was formally abandoned in the 1890s. The kinship network expands as newly discovered ancestors are added to it and have rites performed on their behalf enabling them to benefit religiously in the afterlife. This involves living kin in the ritual and religious lives of dead relations. Such ritual incorporation of dead ancestors into the explicitly Mormon kinship network brings another aspect of the past into the present with the clear motive of making more Mormons for an expanding universe of the saved.

This intersecting of family and salvation brings us to a critical point in our discussion where an analysis of Mormon classification of space and time integrates issues of identity, history, and faith.

Mormons possess two essentially distinct types of ritual space. One is represented in the numerically large number of meeting places, chapels or stake-houses as they are often called. They contain offices, often a community and sports hall, as well as the obvious worship area. The weekly 'sacrament service' or the holy communion is centred here, as are baptisms of new members, testimony meetings, and some daily groups. Such buildings are public and open to non-members. They exist within the dimension of time to serve the purposes of time. In this context the category of time has a specifically Mormon meaning in a binary opposition of time and eternity lying central to the Latter Day Saint conception of reality.

If chapels represent the ritual space devoted to time, it is the temple that serves as the ritual space for eternity. Temples are, geographically, fewer in number than chapels. England, for example, possesses only one whilst many larger towns and most cities can boast a chapel or stakehouse. Temples are not open to the public and are accessible only to selected church members who have been granted a special recommendation of attendance by their local leader, who ensures that candidates support church doctrine and leaders, and live according to prescribed moral principles including the practice of tithing income. In terms of the history of religions this represents the sacred space *par excellence*; it affords a fine example of space and self in relation, as desired by R.L. Moore for anthropological analysis of religion, (Moore, 1984:126). Temple rites of several types are performed. 'Endowments' involve gaining access to increasing levels of knowledge about this life and the future world, and a promise of benefits if basic vows are kept; vows that are themselves solemnly made in the temple. 'Sealings' are associated with temple weddings and with rites by which children are united with their natural parents for eternity. Various vicarious rites including 'baptism for the dead' are performed. In this latter ritual, living actors assume the names of dead kin and are baptized on their behalf to enable the departed to avail themselves of all opportunity to develop as Mormons. Indeed any status that the living may enter through ritual is open to the dead by vicarious ritual.

Rituals make family relations eternal as long as they have been performed in the sacred space of temples. Kinship, thus sacralized, typifies the central process of Mormon identity formation by which mundane factors are located in an eternal frame of reference through rituals of transcendence. Temple ritual transforms time into eternity. In its role of reclassifying reality the temple adds a new value to life. The secret sacredness of temple spirituality motivates future mundane existence. Genealogical work and baptism for the dead mirror this dual perspective of time and eternity. Research on family history takes place 'in time' while vicarious immersion opens the way into eternity for dead kinsfolk who are themselves reclassified through the work done on their behalf. Such mutuality underlies Mormon relations of all sorts making Mormon identity radically corporate. The individual's sense of worth increases as the kin network extends through vicarious ritual.

Identity and ritual affect

Some Mormons speak of a qualitative difference in the experience sensed in the temple compared with that of chapels or elsewhere, and this has particular consequences in their perceived relations with ancestors. When engaged in new genealogical work, some speak of forming increasingly clear images of the dead and of extraordinary occurrences bringing new information to light concerning their lives. They mention these surprising events knowing that others may well see them as mere coincidence, devoid of that spiritual influence perceived by Mormons as contributing to the final vicarious rites that benefit the dead. Attitudes towards the dead can become quite intense and there may even be a sensed awareness of their presence in the ritual. Some Saints talk of their temple work as teaching them that the dead are not far from the living. As with the dead so with God, for the divine presence is often said to be felt in the temple more profoundly than elsewhere.

The temple, then, appears to condense and transform aspects of history, theologizing them in rites that are affectively powerful in fostering the identity of Mormons by assuring them that their work is purposeful. If we assume that the Mormon concept of a 'testimony' is one way of interpreting Mormon identity we may certainly see the temple as a major generator of identity, for Mormons speak of it and its ritual as a most significant means of strengthening their testimony of the truth of their religion. The testimony grows in relation to personalized items of history that have been brought into contemporary experience through genealogical work and vicarious performance of rites. The extended network of kinship, effected by vicarious ritual, combines with the future-directed extended family, guaranteed through temple sealings, to show the power of the temple and of the Melchizedek priestly authority deployed therein in the total scheme of Mormon revelation.

As an institution, then, the temple processes time to yield eternity and as part of that process it invests history with the quality of revelation. This important interpretation of the place of the temple in Mormon piety ought certainly to be remembered when discussing the place of history in Mormon thinking. It is not just the case that Mormons turned all history into dispensations of salvation (such schemes of salvation history are well known in many theologies), the fact that bears more heavily on Mormon identity is that active involvement in temple ritual produces its own rather distinctive form of access to the past (cf. Davies, 1987:53ff.). In a slightly similar way the temple ritual, which adds the sealing of eternity to the natural bonds of time, also makes the domestic family an integrated locus of the present and the eternal future. It is Mormon doctrine that families are the eternal basis of salvation itself. Unlike Protestant theology, this Restoration movement sees individual salvation as inconceivable, a valuable fact in interpreting the concept of the self in Mormonism; men and women are saved in relation to each other and through their family bonds. Indeed, access to Exaltation, which is the highest heavenly state, is available only to married priests holding the Melchizedek priesthood, and to their wives and children. The formal difference between the Melchizedek or higher priesthood and the Aaronic or lower priesthood is itself related

175

to the theme of Mormon identity and history as to our earliest binary opposition between time and eternity.

The Aaronic priesthood is normally held by boys between the age of twelve and nineteen with the Melchizedek priesthood then supplanting it during adulthood. In functional terms the Melchizedek priesthood is what gives a father authority within the family and what makes him the focal nucleus for the eternal family unit. By its power he blesses his children when ill and fosters their development. Structurally, the Melchizedek priesthood in the home mirrors that same priestly power in the eternal world, while the Aaronic priesthood serves the purpose of time. This is especially clearly seen in the ritual that is the focus of Aaronic activity – the Sacrament Service, which takes place, significantly, in the chapel. Unlike all other Christian traditions, which reserve this rite for performance by the most senior of priests or leaders, Mormons have boys in the lower priesthood as officiants. They say the special prayers of blessing and distribute the elements to the people, including the more senior Melchizedek priests also in attendance. So a pattern emerges in the implicit life of faith, with the chapel associated with time and the Aaronic priesthood, while the temple pertains to eternity and the Melchizedek order. Melchizedek priests are important in organizational matters focused on the chapel but the Sacrament Service still displays the symbolic pattern of priesthoods in relation to sacred time and sacred space, of chapel to temple.

Mormons who have received their temple endowment rites enter into a more committed religious life and might be expected to gain a clearer identity as Saints. They are aided in the process of identity maintenance in many ways, two of which are given a historical perspective. First, there is what is called the temple garment. This undergarment should be worn beneath ordinary clothing as a part of everyday life. It is a garment of eternity worn beneath the clothes of time. It perpetuates the sacred amidst the mundane and is a reminder of the other special temple garments worn ritually only in the temple. Just as the temple ritual is secret in the sense of private and personally significant, so is the temple garment worn secretly in the ordinary world. It serves more as a personal boundary marker of identity than as a public sign. The public boundary distinction is to be found in the second item, that which Mormons call the Word of Wisdom, which is a dietary proscription on tea, coffee, and alcohol. The usefulness of such rules has been clear in taking Mormon identity into wider social areas. They have become increasingly important in Britain during the twentieth century when Mormons no longer have the process of emigration available to them as a firm statement of identity and intention. The private temple garment and the public food laws add further historical elements to Mormon identity since the garment is associated with the one made by God for Adam and Eve, while the food rules were revealed to Joseph

Smith. It did not escape Mormon attention that the Jews also had food regulations given to them and this indirectly fostered an identification with Israel that is even more explicit in the distinction Mormons drew between themselves as saints and the rest of the world as gentiles – another basic opposition of categories that has played a vital role in setting Mormon identity within a historical perspective.

Identity and myth

The choice of the distinction between saint and gentile reflects the early Mormon identification with ancient Israel. The Mormons were God's chosen people of the Latter Days, but this simple association becomes increasingly complex when explored in the context of Mormon piety and culture. Indeed to pursue it further is to encounter a problem in distinguishing between historical event and biblically recorded precedent. The extent to which biblical analogues function mythically while being viewed by Mormons as more factual entities is the crucial point. Two examples will pinpoint the problem. The first concerns the office of the Patriarch in the Utah Mormon Church, while the second touches certain mystical figures in another church of the Restoration group that bears a family resemblance to the Utah group.

Alongside the Aaronic and Melchizedek orders of priesthood we have already mentioned, who manage the administrative and hierarchical aspects of church life, there exists a numerically much smaller number of persons serving in the order of Patriarch. Modelled on the Old Testament figure of the Patriarch, who blessed his descendents, the church patriarchs have a similar charge to deal with members individually and personally. Under the guidance of the Holy Spirit the Patriarch tells or foretells aspects of a person's life, including the tribe of Israel to which they belong. Because the tribes of Israel appear as factual entities in the biblical record, which itself is accepted as a historical account, identity is immediately reinforced in a pragmatic way. Once more history is personalized in a context of emotive piety, and at the hands of a figure bearing strong symbolic relation to biblical models.

The relation between the general hierarchy of the church and the office of Patriarch is, in some respects, reminiscent of Needham's elaboration of dual sovereignty in the opposition between jural and mystical categories (Needham, 1980:63ff.). The immediacy of access to the Holy Spirit for others and the lack of power as far as formal church organization is concerned make the Patriarch unlike other office holders in the church. Traditionally, he held office for life and was not called into and out of particular responsibilities as are most priests in the church. His ministry assists the personal thriving of individuals who feel that contact with the Patriarch is not qualitatively unlike some aspects of temple experience.

If the case of patriarchs and piety raises the problem of symbolic persons fostering participation in functional myth, the next and second example will show the dynamics of the issue even more dramatically. It is found in a small Restoration movement called the Church of Jesus Christ at Monongahela in Pennsylvania, which is quite separate from the current Church of Jesus Christ of Latter Day Saints, but traces its origin to the restoration of truth in Joseph Smith, as have several other groups since the 1830s. This church adheres to the doctrine of the Three Nephites. These characters appear in the *Book of Mormon* and are believed to have been granted a boon by God enabling them to live on earth until the final days of divine fulfilment. They continue to do so and may be encountered today by ordinary men and women. The journal of this church, *The Gospel News*, alludes to the belief that some church members have met with them and have derived spiritual benefit from so doing, (Oct. and Dec., 1971). These personages are hundreds of years old, are real people, yet may appear in wonderful ways. They are living links with biblical epochs and in a most literal sense serve to embody tradition. It is not immediately obvious how they may best be classified for they elude the usual ideal types of religious phenomenology. What is obvious is their symbolic function of uniting in themselves the first days of revelation and the present moment of faith in the pious. Their mystical character is an extension of what we have already witnessed in the office of the Patriarch. They foster identity in believers by asserting the unity of the contemporary church with the earliest period of its life. They guarantee authenticity in an embodied manner which, for a prophetic movement, is a vital medium of communication. The Three Nephites function as living mythical figures who may come to figure in the present life of faith in an experiential way. Once more history is not left as an academic discourse but is incorporated into piety. In this, the Monongahela church simply presents a strongly developed example of a principle that is widely present in the Utah movement and is a characteristic attribute of the total Restoration movement. In the other major extant Mormon group, The Reorganized Church of Jesus Christ of Latter Day Saints based at Independence, Missouri, the historical link is strongly represented in its prophet–leader who is still a lineal descendent of Joseph Smith. This person continues to receive revelations from God concerning church matters. He affords the guaranteed link with the founder in the most direct of ways, yet it should be observed that his kinship link is additionally sanctioned by active revelations from God on a regular basis. Here, again, the identity of the ordinary believer is intimately bound up with a personified historical figure.

Identity, embodiment, and self

At the outset I urged that an anthropology of affect was vital in an analysis of Mormon identity. I have described contexts in which the historical dimension is appropriated affectively in Mormon identity formation. In concluding I set this analysis in a more theoretical framework to elucidate some more complex aspects of identity formation than has been possible in simple description (Davies, 1984:137ff.).

It has become increasingly obvious that cultural analysis needs to pay some attention to patterns of experience if it is to present a reasonably balanced account of human life. In anthropological studies of religion this is, I think, especially important. Clifford Geertz's long propounded definition of religion included a stress on mood as engendered by symbols that ought not to be ignored (Geertz, 1966:1ff.). From a more phenomenological perspective, D.M. Levin has pressed the case for 'understanding through embodiment', which the scholar also ignores at his peril (Levin, 1985:211). R.C. Solomon has similarly urged a careful use of empathy as an important anthropological tool (Solomon, 1984:246), while Marcel Mauss's early reflections on the body and psychology have been cited by many to validate a belated anthropological interest in bodily related epistemology (Mauss, 1979:27). Mary Douglas (1970) and Michael Carrithers (1985) are especially noteworthy.

All this counterbalances the traditional anthropological preference for stricter conceptual analysis of social systems. Sperber's attractive analysis of symbolism, despite its criticism of Victor Turner's semanticism, retains a stress on the cognitive. Even his clever interpretation of smell as symbol manages to avoid a discussion of embodiment. Smell is treated non-bodily (1975:115). A good example of an anthropological exploration of the embodied mode of life is Michelle Rosaldo's *Knowledge and Passion*, which analyses very well, 'emotionally oriented images' in the 'creation of mood' (Rosaldo, 1980:27, 32). The emotive power of culturally experienced images is added to the usual anthropological analysis of conceptual classification in a way that brings an additional hermeneutic dimension to the study (cf. Blacking, 1977).

This additional dimension within an 'anthropology of affect' is particularly useful in the analysis of identity (Epstein, 1978:xv). It allows interpretation to go beyond the level reached by the sociological work of, for example, Hans Mol (1976; 1978), and by historians of religion (cf. Hayes, 1986). In this chapter I have sought to show how the Mormon concept of 'testimony' may be seen to represent the analytical notion of identity. We have seen already that a testimony can be gained and strengthened by experiences associated with persons or institutions enshrining the history of the religion. For Mormon *Homo religiosus* there are preferred moods that the tradition perpetuates and fosters in close association with its doctrine. For Mormons the notion of truth is at one level equated with revealed doctrine, but at another it is embedded in specific patterns of experienced emotion. The awareness of being a Mormon depends on more than assenting to specific doctrine, it includes style of speech and expression of emotion during ritual, particular carriage of the body, and forms of bodily activity. Above all it depends upon having had particular experiences that can be shared with others in ways that invite all to accept each as authentic fellow members of the Restoration movement.

At this early stage of mood analysis we lack precise classification. For that reason I have been content to describe contexts and sketch aspects of significant experience in connection with the historical link with identity. I have assumed that mood, like scent, both suffuses and evaporates. But also that, like scent, in its duration it affords the perfect unity of individual and goal of life. Preferred moods demarcate moments of knowing for religious groups, and not merely moments of assenting to dogma. The mood engendered by genealogical research and vicarious ritual is one such and is especially important in relation to history and identity. Genealogical work is at one and the same time a distinctive form of exploratory kinship behaviour and a form of religiosity that integrates history and identity. When extended into the performance of vicarious ritual, it could be described as yielding a bodily felt experience of history. When everyday dress is put aside for temple vesture, and in other rites, the body is anointed with oil and washed ritually; when the body enacts ritual dramas, then the Mormon affectively learns, or perhaps it is better to say with Sperber (1975) concerning symbolism that the individual acquires, a sense of identity. Many Mormon rituals are best viewed as 'accessive' rites, they enable people to gain access to traditionally fostered experience, or to doctrine framed by experience of a selected variety. As rites they are neither simply expressive of dogma nor are they performative. They serve creative ends as doctrinal ideas are intuitively appropriated in a maturing identity. This echoes Turner's argument that, 'we acquire wisdom not by abstract solitary thought but by participation in sociocultural dramas' (Turner, 1985:190). We could go further in agreeing with Turner that drama rather than culture or archive is the best unit of anthropological analysis when the unity of communities is the process under consideration. And in exploring the notion of identity in Mormonism that communal factor is doubly important because Mormon thought avoids the ideal type of the westernized self as an 'autonomous distinctive individual living in society' (Schweder and LeVine, 1984:191). Each self is held responsible for its acts, but even more important is the collective life of families and of the total church community that corporately works together for the salvation of all. Unlike the Protestant-influenced secular notion of the isolated self, Mormons argue that individual salvation is practically a contradiction in terms, and we have already shown how marriage is vital for salvation as one example of that principle.

We could extend Turner's (1985) notion of sociocultural drama to interpret temple rituals as cosmic dramas with the baptism for the dead being a historical drama integrating the dead with the living as well as the living with their past. In many respects Mormon ritual both in the temples and chapels has forged a tradition of *communitas* that has reinforced the *communitas* created by opposition from outsiders and reaches its symbolic perfection in the collective unity of heaven. It is within the liminality of sacred space that Mormon identity develops most strongly. Individualism and factors of mere chronology give way to a sense of the corporate and of the eternal. It is no wonder that Mark Leone discovered what he called 'memorylessness' in his anthropology of Mormonism, but he ought not to have been surprised that people who spend much time on genealogy were unable to speak coherently about the past they had lived through themselves (Leone, 1979:209). Memorylessness in this case expresses a disinterestedness in bare facts and a concern over the faith element in life events.

Mormon interest in history is soteriological not historiographic. It furnishes genealogical tables for the purpose of family redemption through vicarious ritual, and it enables living Mormons to identify with the past in what might best be called a mythical process of appropriation. Identity involves sympathetic association with a theologically schematized past. History, embodied in the founding exemplars of Mormonism, is embodied anew in those gaining a testimony of the truth first enunciated in the primal exemplars.

I would, finally, follow Ioan Lewis's persuasion that faith and scepticism are functions of situations (Lewis, 1986:20). For many ordinary Mormons faith grows in the context of family and temple. For Mormons who are historians, the academic study is an additional context of faith but one of some paradox. For while the religion is avowedly rooted in historical events the faith dimension within it draws its substance beyond the bounds of verification, so the very word 'history' functions differently for historians and non-historians in Mormonism. For the former it has all the limitations that the general academic community has given it, for the latter it is full of all the possibilities engendered by the community of faith. For both, however, the mode of participation in 'history' influences that mood that is an attribute of embodied identity.

References

Blacking, J. (ed.) (1977) *The Anthropology of the Body*, London: Academic Press.
Bushman, R.L. (1984) *Joseph Smith and the Beginnings of Mormonism*, Chicago: University of Illinois Press.

Carrithers, M., Collins, S., and Lukes, S. (eds) (1985) *The Category of the Person*, Cambridge: Cambridge University Press.

Davies, D.J. (1984) *Meaning and Salvation in Religious Studies*, Leiden: Brill.

Davies, D.J. (1987) *Mormon Spirituality: Latter Day Saints in Wales and Zion*, Nottingham: University of Nottingham Series in Theology.

Douglas, M. (1973) *Natural Symbols*, London: Pelican Books.

Epstein, A.L. (1978) *Ethos and Identity*, London: Tavistock Publications.

Gaustad, E.S. (1984) 'Historical theology and theological history: Mormon possibilities', *Journal of Mormon History* 11.

Geertz, C. (1966) 'Religion as a cultural system', in Michael Banton (ed.) *Anthropological Approaches to the Study of Religion*, London: Tavistock Publications.

Goody, J. (1977) *The Domestication of the Savage Mind*, Cambridge: Cambridge University Press.

Hayes, V.C. (ed.) (1986) *Identity Issues and World Religions*, Australia: Australian Association for the Study of Religions.

Leone, M. (1979) *Roots of Modern Mormonism*, London: Harvard University Press.

Levin, D.M. (1985) *The Body's Recollection of Being*, London: Routledge and Kegan Paul.

Lewis, I. (1986) *Religion in Context, Cults and Charisma*, Cambridge: Cambridge University Press.

Mauss, M. (1979) *Sociology and Psychology* (trans. B. Brewster), London: Routledge and Kegan Paul.

Mol, H. (1976) *Identity and the Sacred*, Oxford: Blackwell.

Mol, H. (ed.) (1978) *Identity and Religion*, London: Sage Publications.

Moore, R.L. (1984) 'Space and transformation in human experience', in R.L. Moore and F.E. Reynolds (eds) *Anthropology and the Study of Religion*, Illinois: Center for the Scientific Study of Religion.

Needham, R. (1980) *Reconnaissances*, Toronto: University of Toronto Press.

Rosaldo, M.Z. (1980) *Knowledge and Passion*, Cambridge: Cambridge University Press.

Schweder, R.A. and LeVine, R.A. (eds) (1984) *Culture Theory*, Cambridge: Cambridge University Press.

Shipps, J. (1985) *Mormonism*, Illinois: University of Illinois Press.

Solomon, R.C. (1984) 'Getting angry: the Jamesian theory of emotion in anthropology', in R.A. Schweder and R.A. LeVine (eds) *Culture Theory*, Cambridge: Cambridge University Press.

Sperber, D. (1975) *Rethinking Symbolism*, Cambridge: Cambridge University Press.

Turner, V. (1985) *On the Edge of the Bush*, Tucson, Arizona: University of Arizona Press.

Chapter twelve

'We're Trying to Find our Identity': uses of history among Ulster Protestants[1]

Anthony Buckley

It is old but it is beautiful.
Its colours they are fine.
It was worn at Derry, Aughrim,
Enniskillen and the Boyne.
My father wore it as a youth
As in bygone days of yore.
On the Twelfth of July I long to wear
The Sash my father wore.

(traditional song)

. . . we Ulster people have an identity of our own, separate from the so-called Irish identity that everybody's trying to foist upon us against our will. . . . We just drifted on. We were neither English or Irish or anything, and we lost our own identity, and our own culture, our own folk-heritage. . . . And we've a part to play . . . by showing them their origins.

(Alan Campbell, leader of the Covenant People's Fellowship, UFTM R86–224)

In Ulster there are to be found several specifically 'Protestant' versions of history explicitly related to the present conflict between Catholics and Protestants, nationalists and unionists. One such tradition is associated with the various 'Orange' brotherhoods. Another is a prophetic tradition found chiefly among fundamentalists. Among this group are the 'British Israelites' who claim to be descended from Abraham and Jacob. And there are also people who claim that Ulster Protestants are descended from the Pictish 'Cruthin' who inhabited prehistoric Ireland. All of these groups and individuals (and my list is not exhaustive) are competing to achieve a degree of political or intellectual leadership in specific segments of Ulster Protestant society.

This article will examine something of the breadth of Ulster Protestant attitudes to history. My suggestion is that when this history is directly related to ethnicity it is used in at least three differentiable ways: as a rhetorical commentary that either justifies or condemns; as a 'charter' for action; and as a focus for allegiance. Not all popular history in Ulster is directly intended to uphold the interests of one ethnic group against another (Buckley, 1982; 1983a) and in concrete situations, a supposedly sectarian history can often be used for quite a variety of diverse purposes (Buckley, 1986). Nevertheless, there are to be found in Ulster widely known versions of history identified with specific ethnic groups, and it is these that will be considered here.

When history is used as a political rhetoric, the accounts of the past implicitly (or explicitly) generate 'descriptive models' (Caws, 1974) of the present. Such histories typically uphold the claims of one's own 'side' to power, prestige, and influence in the present while stigmatizing one's opponents. Rhetoric of this kind seems usually to have one of two forms, both depending upon principles of reciprocity. The first consists of a list of the past grievances of the social group awaiting redress. The second makes an assertion of the superiority of one's own group. Here the implication may be that because one's group is superior (in talents, divine favour, culture, etc.), it makes a greater contribution to the general welfare, and it is therefore entitled to greater rewards. Van den Berghe (1981:9ff.) dismisses such ideology as 'deceit'. Sometimes, indeed, there may be dishonesty, and criteria of truth employed by one faction are not always acceptable to another. Often, however, such historical discussion takes place within earshot of rivals or possible allies who demand some degree of plausibility according to the locally universal standards.

History's second major use is as a 'charter' (Malinowski, 1963; Bohannan, 1952). Here, a set of archetypical situations provides rules or guidelines for acting in the present. It is sometimes proper to regard such 'operational models' (Caws, 1974) as having also a rhetorical function for they can 'bridge the gap between the "sacred" rhetorical world of legitimated and unquestioned values and the mundane world of questionable behaviour and problematic experience' (Cohen, 1975:14). Here, however, the history is less of a commentary upon the present, and more of a practical pattern that may be imitated.

In the third of these uses of history, commemorations of historical events in, for example, processions or rituals can provide a focus for ethnic allegiance. They thus form part of the interactive process whereby ethnic boundaries are daily defined and recreated (Barth, 1969). The definition of Ulster's ethnicities is complex, but it includes both descent and religious 'belief'. Of these, the first is the more important (Jenkins, 1986; see also Horowitz, 1985:53ff; Van den Berghe, 1981:19ff) and depends largely upon endogamy. Endogamy effectively defines the two groups in Ulster practically and intellectually. Practically, it restricts important kinship-based activities to one's own 'side' (Donnan and McFarlane, 1986:26). Intellectually, it gives substance to the idea that modern Protestants and

Catholics are lineal descendants of the seventeenth-century 'planters' and 'Gaels'. Definition by 'belief', however, identifies Ulster's ethnic groups with such categories of person as British or continental co-religionists past and present, and indeed with others such as Old Testament figures, with whom there is not necessarily any alleged or real biological kinship.

Versions of history that are explicitly 'Protestant' reflect the interests of the sometimes divergent Protestant factions that propound or might be interested in them. The views examined here reflect one of the more important (but not always clearly defined) disagreements among Ulster Protestants, that between fundamentalists, and those people whom fundamentalists disparage as merely 'religious'. This distinction is reflected (though again not precisely) in the active membership of the two main unionist political parties. The sectional claims of these and other groups, however, are made by propounding justifications for the goals of the Protestant ethnic group considered as a whole.

Irish history: seventeenth century and beyond

The nationalist background

As Ulster Protestant ethnicity is irredeemably linked to Catholic ethnicity, so is loyalist history related to nationalist history. Nationalist history classically portrays an opposition between Britain and Ireland, planter and Gael as one between oppressor and oppressed. Scholarly nationalist histories have appeared throughout this century, whence their ideas have passed into school text books and the general consciousness. Modern historians (e.g. Bowen, 1970; Connell, 1968; Connolly, 1982; Stewart, 1977) still think them important enough to be worth systematic 'revision'.

The central events of this nationalist history (see for example Biggar, 1910; Green, 1908; O'Brian, 1918; O'Hegarty, 1949) arise out of successive invasions of Ireland, the most important of which was by Britain in the sixteenth and seventeenth centuries. These invasions were undertaken with great ferocity (Green, 1908:114), replacing Irish landownership with British. The British removed the rights of tenants (Biggar, 1910:5–6; Green, 1908:118ff). They systematically disrupted Irish industry and trade (Green, 1908:123ff; O'Brian, 1918:383ff). Legal restrictions were imposed upon Catholics. And England is popularly blamed for the 'decline' of the Irish 'culture' found in the Irish language, in ancient texts and in folklore (Foster, 1982; Delargy, 1945:187; Kennedy, 1891; O'Sullivan, 1966). Injustices continued into the nineteenth century. Independence was the solution, but even this was spoiled by the partition of Ireland and by the discriminatory laws and practices of the artificially created 'majority' in the north. The extent of this discrimination is still hotly debated (Hewitt, 1981; 1983; 1985; O'Hearn, 1983; 1985).

Irish nationalist history, therefore, contains a catalogue of grievances whose rhetorical force lies in the reciprocity principle. Since the British (or 'planters') stole the land of their Irish forefathers; since they destroyed Ireland's trade, despoiled its culture, and suppressed its religion, then Irish people have at least the right to claim their land back, to press for the reunification of their island, and to claim fair and equal treatment. In short, Irish history is seen to contain so many injustices perpetrated against native Irishmen by successive generations of British governments and planters, that the nationalists who are their heirs can lay claim to the rhetorical high ground of moral advantage against the putative descendants of their oppressors (see Boyce, 1982:306).

Irish nationalist history has also generated a pantheon of heroes who have withstood this oppression. Among them are O'More, Sarsfield, Grattan, O'Connell, Parnell, Connolly, the Defenders, Ribbonmen, Land Leaguers, and many others. History, therefore, provides Irish nationalism not only with a range of historic ills requiring redress in the present, but also with 'inspiration', i.e. a plethora of legitimate operational models from which to choose actions appropriate to their remedy.

Orange approaches to the seventeenth century

As the seventeenth century is important to nationalists, so also is it to Protestants. Not least this is because the celebration of its events provides them with their most politically charged folk festivals. These are associated with the different Orange brotherhoods (Buckley, 1985–6), although the parades and their significance are widely and popularly known. Most famously, on the Twelfth of July, the Protestant Orange Order celebrates the defeat of the Catholic James II at the hands of William III. On the 13th of July, County Armagh Royal Black Institution, whose members are drawn from the Orange Order, hold a well-attended 'Sham Fight' (Dewar, 1956) in which, with much shotgun fire and mock sword-fighting, James II is similarly 'defeated'. And in August and December, the 'Apprentice Boys of Derry' celebrate the victorious siege of Derry, by marching around the city's walls.

Of all these historical events, this siege has the greatest symbolic significance (Buckley, 1984). It occurred when, in the face of indecision by the city governor, Lundy, Apprentice Boys shut the gates against the advancing James. Lundy escaped by stealth, in consequence of which his huge 16-ft effigy is burned as part of the celebrations each December.

Although it is not central, the rhetorical element in all this cannot be ignored. The siege of Derry can be conceptualized in the Lévi-Straussian (Lévi-Strauss, 1956) manner as a structure of opposites, in which the wicked, uncivilized, tyrannical, and 'rough' people outside the walls confront the good, civilized, freedom-loving, 'religious' people within. In the siege, the 'rough' behaviour of the Apprentice Boys (and by implication that of their successors) is 'mediated' by that fact that it is undertaken in defence of civilization, freedom, religion, and other high ideals (Buckley, 1984; 1987). This 'mediation', however, is better described as a 'justification' (Cohen, 1975:13–14).

The implied rhetoric here is consonant with another idea that I have heard many individuals separately state, viz 'nobody expects that America should be given back to the Indians' (or Australia to the Aborigines). In part, this familiar statement is a plea to let bygones be bygones: 'it all happened a long time ago'. In part, however, it also contains an imperialist rhetoric, that Protestants in Ireland, like White people in America, Australia, and elsewhere in the British Empire, have been the bringers of Christianity and civilization. These views reflect popular Protestant stereotypes that stigmatize Catholics (like other 'natives') as superstitious, untidy, and feckless in comparison with Protestant rationality, tidiness, and hard work (see Donnan and McFarlane, 1986; Harris, 1972:Chapter 8). It is an old argument found, for example in Harrison's *The Scot in Ulster* (1888:33ff, 48) but it is found in modern publications (e.g. UYUC, 1986).

Despite the existence of this implied rhetoric, this is not really to be regarded as the main purpose of these important commemorative processions. For rhetorical purposes, Protestants tend to emphasize more recent history. They therefore argue that since the 1920s Catholics have failed to accept the democratic will of the majority,[2] and have instead subverted the state using even violent means. Thus Protestants, too, have a catalogue of grievances against nationalists, some of them deeply felt, but the list that they nowadays use tends to start in the 1920s.

More important than their implied rhetoric, these celebrations also embody a set of rules or guidelines for action. The events being remembered are the ones that, above all, established a 'Protestant ascendancy' in Ireland. They therefore provide practical models for the reaffirmation of Protestant power. The guidelines are most succinctly contained in such slogans as 'Not an Inch' or 'No Surrender', frequently quoted from political platforms, and identified with the Williamite Wars. They evoke, too, memories of lesser battles, of the Diamond, Glencoe, Machen, and Dolly's Brae, and especially the campaigns of Carson and the Ulster Volunteers, which kept Ulster from the Irish Republic (Dewar, Brown, and Long, c. 1967; McClelland, 1973). These lesser incidents, like the stories of the Williamite Wars themselves, do not seriously attempt to *justify* Protestant claims except by the mildest of implication. They are used, rather, as models for action.

The various processions also contain a strong Durkheimian element (especially Durkheim, 1915). Solidarity is affirmed between bystanders and marchers and their putative ancestors who shared a concern to uphold

Protestant monarchy. This demonstration of cohesion is also intended to show strength and determination against others. In many Orange halls hangs the portrait of William Johnson of Ballykilbeg. Johnson, in 1864, broke a government ban on Orange processions (Dewar, Brown, and Long, c. 1967:141) and his memory is evoked whenever attempts are made to reroute or prohibit processions (as happened, for example in 1985–6). As the gates of Derry were slammed against the wishes of the governor, and as William Johnson defied the government by marching, so, today, Ulster loyalists strive to resist 'Rome Rule' (an echo of Carson's campaign) by resisting compromise by British governments and by other waverers. The processions not only commemorate, but are themselves examples of the defiant strength modelled upon that exhibited in the past.

Biblical history: the chosen few

The Arch Purple and Black Institutions

The Orange Order, the Royal Arch Purple Chapter and the Royal Black Institution are comparable in organizational structure to the different bodies within Freemasonry (Buckley, 1985–6). When a man has been initiated into a lodge of the Orange Order, he may be invited to enter the corresponding chapter of the Royal Arch Purple, whence he may be asked to enter a Black preceptory where he will be initiated into each of eleven degrees. Membership of the Orange Order has long been recruited from a wide cross-section of Protestant men. Until recently, no unionist politician could have become a member of either the Stormont or Imperial Parliaments without being a member. The Black Institution is almost universally regarded as more 'respectable' than the Orange Order, and is drawn from Orangemen of a somewhat higher social status than the average.

The initiation rites of the Arch Purple and Black Institutions consist centrally in the retelling and re-enactment of prescribed Bible stories, and such stories, usually, but not always those used in the rituals, are also painted on the banners carried by Black preceptories on their parades. In a representative sample of banner paintings and other materials relating to Black symbolism and ritual (discussed in much greater detail in Buckley, 1985–6), I discovered that of seventeen different texts employed in these various contexts, fourteen had remarkably similar themes.[3] The dominant framework is of an individual or group in favour with God confronting alien peoples. Some of these 'aliens' are wicked people, as in the story of Noah; some uphold a rival religion, as in the contest of Elijah with the prophets of Baal; others are mainly foreigners. The stories emphasize faithfulness. Someone who is loyal to God is likely to prosper or be rescued from his enemies or from God's wrath. He may gain a victory as did David against the overwhelming strength of Goliath. When a heathen or foreigner changes allegiance and turns to God, as did Rahab or Ruth, that person may also be saved from destruction or become prosperous. But where, as with Ahab, one of God's chosen people turns to foreign gods, he must expect ruin. Thus do the different texts explore variations upon the same theme. This theme is the encounter between heathens or foreigners and God's chosen people. Though it is never stated as a dogma, the metaphorical implication here is that, like Israel and Judah, Ulster Protestants are 'God's Chosen Few'.

It is clear that, like the Williamite Wars, the biblical texts provide a set of practical models useful to those who confront the alien, apostate, or merely wicked. By obvious implications the stories recommend that Protestants should avoid marrying the daughters of their enemies; be loyal to their religion; welcome heathens who turn to the true religion; fight against all the odds; and trust in God.

If, however, these Williamite and biblical histories have similarities one to another, they are not identical. The siege of Derry, for example, is similar to that of Jericho, but its details are quite different. It is not useful to think of Ulster Protestants as somehow 'trapped by their history', for their history provides them with not one 'historical charter', but a whole range of operational models for dealing with their opponents. (Santino, 1983 argues similarly in relation to anccdotes.) The Blackman, in particular, who is already familiar with the history of King William, who has also 'been through', and taken many others 'through' the rites of the Arch Purple and Black Institutions, has acquired from this history much 'food for thought'.

Fundamentalist history

There is a multitude of small Protestant denominations in Ulster whose theology can be classified as 'fundamentalist'. Fundamentalists are also to be found in many 'mainline' churches (Church of Ireland, Presbyterian, Methodist). Commonly, individuals from different denominations gather together for weekday meetings in the 'Mission Halls' found in most towns and villages. Fundamentalists distinguish themselves from both 'modernists' and 'charismatics' who are inclined to be sympathetic to Catholicism. They also differentiate themselves from the merely 'religious', people who typically attend church but who have not been 'saved', who 'think that just by being good they can get to heaven', and who look askance at overeager attempts to interpret the more difficult portions of the Bible.

Politically, the opposition between the two Protestant parties, the Reverend Ian Paisley's Democratic Unionists, and the Official Unionists led by James Molyneaux, reflects that between fundamentalists and the 'merely religious', activists in the DUP tend to be fundamentalists, while, with sometimes significant exceptions, fundamentalists are more rare in the

OUP. Similarly, though there are DUP members in Orange lodges and even in Black preceptories, the DUP leadership and most fundamentalists are somewhat cool towards these institutions. On the other hand, the present Orange Grand Master, the Reverend Martin Smyth is an OUP Member of Parliament, while the Imperial Sovereign Grand Master of the Black Institution is the leader of the OUP, Mr Molyneaux himself. By a paradox, the DUP achieves important electoral strength from working-class people who are well represented in Orange lodges, but who tend to be non-church-going (Wallis *et al.*, 1986).

Whereas in the Black institution, the image of 'God's chosen people' emerges from metaphorical stories that provide merely 'food for thought', for fundamentalists it is more explicitly a doctrine. Its mildest form is found where an individual is said to have been 'chosen' to do God's work. 'Conservative' Presbyterians, Free Presbyterians, and other Calvinists sometimes say they are of the 'elect', but this view blends into the Armini-anism prevalent among fundamentalists who nevertheless say that they act by the 'grace of God'.

These ideas impinge most directly upon both history and ethnicity in millenarian thought. Of this, the most important form in Ulster is a type of 'premillenialism', which asserts that Christians will be taken up (raptured) to meet Jesus in the air before the 'Tribulation', which heralds the one thousand years of Christ's rule. There is much speculation about the events predicted by biblical prophecy. A very common view, for example, is that the ten-horned beast of Revelation 13:1 is identical with the feet of the statue (with ten toes) in Nebuchadnezzar's dream (Daniel 2:31–5), and the fourth beast in Daniel's own vision (Daniel 7). These all refer to the last Roman Empire constituted by the ten kingdoms (as there were in 1981) of the European Economic Community, whose False Prophet is the Pope (see Moloney and Pollak, 1986:402ff; UFTM, R81–164; C81–21). There are many disagreements between funda-mentalists about the precise roles of middle-eastern countries, the Soviet Union, the Common Market, and Rome in the events outlined in Revel-ation. On one matter, however, most fundamentalists agree. For them, the Pope actually *is* the Devil, the Anti-Christ, or the False Prophet as described in scripture.[4]

Such views seriously affect fundamentalist church history. Ministers commonly refer in sermons to those martyrs who died upholding Prote-stantism against Rome. The name of Dr Paisley's church in Belfast, 'Mar-tyrs Memorial', reflects this interest. And modern editions of classic descriptions of Catholic butchery (Foxe, 1563; Tayler, *c.* 1850) are readily available in evangelical bookshops. The steadfastness of these saints is, of course, directly comparable to that of the heroes of the Bible and of Derry, the Boyne, the Diamond, and the Ulster Volunteers. More than this, fundamentalists see themselves as called by God to spread His Word in the face of a Church inimical to God's purposes. Fundamentalists will readily claim that they 'love Catholics' as sinners who need salvation. They nevertheless oppose not only Catholic theology, but also Catholic power, manifested in the IRA, the Irish Government, the Common Market, and also the Soviet Union with all of which the Church of Rome is said to be in league.

British Israelism

British Israelism is found throughout the United Kingdom and elsewhere. In Northern Ireland, BI forms a small but significant strand within fundamentalist debate. Locally prominent political figures are said to be privately sympathetic. A former Orange Grand Master, John Bryans (interviewed UFTM R81-208–9) and the late Reverend Robert Bradford, former Vanguard assemblyman and later OUP Member of Parliament (see UFTM C86-12–16) were vociferous BI supporters. From the 1960s, there existed a paramilitary group called Tara, which upheld BI principles (Moloney and Pollak, 1986:282ff). In the 1950s, BI meetings are said to have filled the spacious Ulster Hall in Belfast. Nowadays, BI is organized as the Covenant Peoples' Fellowship, holding small weekly gatherings in and around Belfast. In churches of all sorts there are individuals who agree with BI ideas, but its main strength is in the Churches of God, pentecostalist congregations whose official teachings include BI. The largest of these in Belfast in the early 1980s had 2,000 people at its Sunday services.

The essence of BI teaching (see, for example, UFTM R84–6; R86–224–6) is that the people of the United Kingdom and hence of the USA and the White Commonwealth are the descendants of ancient Israelites. Following the death of Solomon, the kingdom of Israel was divided. The people of the Northern kingdom, it is said, found their way to northern Europe where, as Angles, Saxons, Jutes, Vikings, and Normans, they reassembled to form the British people. The kingdom of Judah was conquered by the Babylonians, and their history is recounted in the later Bible. Except for some Benjaminites living near Galilee, among them Jesus and eleven of his disciples, the Jews became corrupted by intermarriage. At the time of the Babylonian exile, the prophet Jeremiah, carrying the Ark of the Covenant and the Stone, which had once formed Jacob's pillow at Bethel, travelled with the daughters of Zedekiah, last pre-exilic king of Judah, to County Antrim. One of these daughters, Tamar-Tephi married the Israelitish Irish High King, Eochaidu. The Ark is believed still to rest at Tara where the High Kings of Ireland were once crowned. The Stone, however, was taken to Iona and thence to Scone and it now rests beneath the Coronation Chair in Westminster Abbey. The descent of Elizabeth II is traceable through James I and the Irish

King Fergus the Great, to Eochaidu and Tamar-Tephi, and thence to King David.

Because the British are, in an Old Testament sense, God's chosen people, they have a responsibility to bring Christianity and civilization to the world. The collapse of the British Empire is for them a tragedy, and they support (as do many other Protestants) White rule in South Africa. British Israelites believe that non-White races are capable of civilization and salvation, but that Israelites have the task of helping them get there.

Adherents of BI are aware of the similarity of their doctrine to the symbolism of the Black Institution. But whereas Blackmen can see their *similarity* to certain biblical heroes, British Israelites say they are *descended* from them. The British Isles, according to BI, is the land promised to Abraham and Jacob, but they claim that even foreign lands (America, Australia, Africa) may be occupied, thus benefiting the aboriginal inhabitants.

Apart from providing a generalized justification for British rule in Ireland as elsewhere, this doctrine has a special Irish significance. Even before Jeremiah and Zedekiah, they say, Ireland was inhabited by Israelites. These were, however, driven into Scotland by invading Gaels, who were Phoenicians, half Canaanite, half Israelitish, from Tyre. This admixture of Canaanite blood, I was told, explains the 'instinctive hostility' between southern Ireland and the remainder of the British Isles, and why, for example, Ulster-Scots settlers in America could absorb themselves into the rest of the Israelitish people, while southern Irish people in America have remained a separate ethnic group.

The idea that the Israelites who now live in Scotland were once the inhabitants of Ireland until the Gaels expelled them calls into question much of the rhetoric of Irish nationalism. For it implies that the subsequent invasions of Ireland, and especially those of the seventeenth century by the Scottish and other British were merely a *reconquest* by its former inhabitants. I have heard this argument stated explicitly by British Israelites, but its form is more widely used and has recently been given great prominence.

The Cruthin

The final version of history to be considered here is contained in two books. *The Cruthin* (1974) and *The Identity in Ulster* (1982) written by a Belfast gynaecologist, Ian Adamson. His thesis in outline is neither new nor intellectually disreputable (see O'Rahilly, 1957), but these books are striking because they explicitly relate this ancient history to modern political issues. When he wrote his first book, Adamson lectured to various groups including members of the paramilitary organization, the Ulster Defence Association, who later officially adopted his ideas. The second printing of this book has an introductory preface by Glen Barr, then an officer in the UDA, who became leader of the Ulster Workers Council, which co-ordinated the loyalist general strike that destroyed the 'power-sharing executive' in 1974. Adamson's books have had an appeal elsewhere. In 1986, a pamphlet (UYUC, 1986) was published by the junior wing of the Official Unionist Party, presenting Adamson's views in simplified form, and, indeed, his work is now being more widely popularized (for example, Hall, 1986).

Adamson argues that the earliest inhabitants of Ireland were not the Gaels, but the Cruthin, who were closely related to the Scottish Picts (Adamson, 1974:11). After the Cruthin, came the Fir Bolg (from Britain), other tribes from Gaul, and finally the Gaels. The Gaels established a hegemony everywhere in Ireland except the north-east, where the Fir Bolg tribes of Dalriata and Ulaid formed with the Cruthin an Ulster confederacy. He writes, 'The descendants of the two races are the Ulster Scots' (Adamson, 1974:12). Significantly, he also adds that 'through the kings of the Dalriata are all the kings of Scotland descended, and through this line is descended the present Queen of the British Peoples' (Adamson, 1974:13). By the fifth century, this mainly Cruthinic kingdom of Ulaid (later corrupted to Ulster) was pushed back into Antrim and Down until their defeat at Moira in A.D. 637 resulted in a gradual emigration of the Cruthin into lowland Scotland.

Adamson's attack is on at least three fronts. First, he challenges the naive assumption that all ancient Irish culture is Gaelic. He suggests, for example, that the Book of Darrow and the Book of Kells are Pictish or Scottish–Irish in inspiration (Adamson, 1974:93ff). More damning, he appropriates Cúchulainn, hero of the (Gaelic language) epic *Táin Bó Cuailnge* to the Cruthin. Cúchulainn's statue famously stands in Dublin Central Post Office as a memorial to the nationalist dead of 1916, whose actions precipitated Irish independence. Placed in Adamson's context, however, Cúchulainn clearly personified the struggle of Ulster against the invading Gael. This idea is used with much rhetorical effect in the Young Unionists' pamphlet (UYUC, 1986). Second, Adamson is able to appropriate St Patrick to the Cruthin. 'Patrick makes a clear distinction between the Scotti (Gaels) and the ordinary peoples, the Hibernians (Cruthin and Ulaid)' (Adamson, 1974:42). It is the latter, he says, that Patrick first converted. Thus in a manner comparable to the British Israelites, Adamson argues that the Cruthin are responsible for spreading Christianity. And third Adamson denies 'the claim of the Gael to Ireland'. This is 'by the sword only, and by the sword was it reclaimed in later days by the descendants of those Ancient People . . . of these two Ulster Peoples, the paramount claim belongs to the Cruthin, last of the Picts' (Adamson, 1974:15). Or, as the Young Unionists urge, 'when the Plantation of Ulster got underway, in the seventeenth century, those Scots who came over from the lowlands were in fact members of the Cruthin race returning to the land of their birthright' (UYUC, 1986).

In short, the Cruthin argument addresses directly the rhetorical challenge of Irish nationalist history. It makes the claim that Ulster Protestants, and particularly those who emigrated from Scotland, have at least as much right to live in Ireland as do Irish Catholics. Second, it takes from the nationalist heritage many of its most treasured traits by arguing their Cruthinic rather than Gaelic origins. And finally, the historical lynchpin of Irish nationalism, the Plantation of Ireland, is transformed from a conquest by an oppressive people into a *reconquest* by a people who had formerly been forcefully expelled.

Conclusion

The different forms of history found here appeal to different groups of people in different ways. Many of the biblically orientated theories appeal to a fairly small but significant body of people, the fundamentalists. These people often make claim to represent the essence of Ulster Protestantism, a claim provisionally accepted among the largely non-religious working class, which accepts leadership from the DUP (Wallis *et al.*, 1986). Among fundamentalists, British Israelism has a rather limited appeal. Its advantage is that, if true, it wholly refutes Irish nationalism, giving Ulster Protestants a valuable place both in Ireland and in the cosmic scheme. However, many fundamentalists (and others) have doubts about its historicity – it is, perhaps, just a little too exotic. More important, its claim that the British are chosen by God by virtue of their descent from Jacob seems to question the doctrine of 'justification by faith', the cornerstone of fundamentalist Protestantism itself.

It is appropriate that a secularized and abbreviated version of the BI message, Adamson's *Cruthin* (1974), should be espoused on the one hand by the UDA and, on the other by Official Unionists, both of whom have long been known to be antagonistic to the fundamentalist leadership of the DUP. One form of religious history, that found in the Arch Purple and Black institutions, has an appeal to respectable church-going unionists, especially Official Unionists, who are not, however, fundamentalists. For these people, the implied message that Ulster Protestants are God's chosen people is acceptable as long as it is not stated as a dogma, but is available merely as a set of useful metaphorical images. In a loose kind of way, they can see themselves as defenders of Protestantism or Christianity without being trapped into the rigorous life style and commitments of fundamentalism.

I have suggested, however, that not all of the history directly related to Protestant ethnicity has a rhetorical function: much of it is useful in generating strategems and tactics for action or as an expression and focus for allegiance. In this very generalized survey, I have not attempted to place the uses of history in immediate small-scale, concrete circumstances. My concern has been to explore the themes themselves in the broader context of Northern Ireland politics, and to indicate loosely the uses to which these histories are put.

Ulster Protestant histories reflect a very similar quest to that described by Boyce (1982:193) among Irish nationalists, namely that for a comprehensive concept of identity that transcends the pluralist nature of Irish (or Ulster) society. The rhetorical histories that aspire to justify the claims of Ulster Protestants as a whole and give them a satisfactory identity seem doomed, at least at the moment, to reflect the partisan concerns of specific unionist factions.

Notes

1. This article is based upon fieldwork undertaken for the Ulster Folk and Transport Museum.
   I wish to acknowledge the help of Dr I. Adamson, Mr A. Campbell, and members of the Covenant Peoples' Fellowship, church members in south Antrim and Belfast, and innumerable Orangemen and others who helped me in the course of my fieldwork. I am grateful too for the help of my wife, Mrs L.J. Buckley, and my colleague Dr P.S. Robinson.
2. There are difficulties with the concept of a 'majority' in Ireland. In Northern Ireland, Protestants are a majority; in the island as a whole, Catholics predominate. Legitimacy based on majorities is, therefore, permanently questionable (Poole, 1983).
3. The texts are: 1. Adam and Eve (Genesis:2–3); 2. Noah's Ark (Genesis:6–9); 3. Abraham and Isaac (Genesis:22); 4. Jacob's Dream (Genesis:25–28); 5. Joseph (Genesis:37–50); 6. Moses and the Exodus (Book of Exodus); 7. Rahab and the Battle of Jericho (Joshua:2–6); 8. The Two and-a-half tribes (Joshua:22); 9. Gideon (Judges:6–7); 10. Ruth (The Book of Ruth); 11. David and Goliath (1 Samuel:17–18); 12. The building of the Temple (1 Kings:5–8; 2 Chronicles:2–8); 13. Elijah and the prophets of Baal (1 Kings:16–19); 14. Jehu's purge (2 Kings:10–12); 15. Daniel (Daniel:2–3, 5–6); 16. New Testament references (Matthew:3; John:19–21; Revelation:21); 17. Melchizedek (Exodus:28; Hebrews:7; Genesis:14, 18ff; Revelation:5).
4. UFTM Field Recordings 14:218ff gives a good example of the rationality behind this vision.

References

Adamson, I. (1974) *Cruthin: the Ancient Kindred*, Belfast: Donard.
Adamson, I. (1982) *The Identity of Ulster: the Land, the Language and the People*, Belfast: Pretani Press.
Barth, F. (1969) 'Introduction' to *Ethnic Groups and Boundaries*, London: Allen and Unwin.
Biggar, F.J. (1910) *The Ulster Land War of 1770 (The Hearts of Steel)*, Dublin: Sealy Bryers and Walker.
Bohannan, L. (1952) 'A genealogical charter', *Africa XXII:4*.

Bowen, D. (1970) *Souperism: Myth or Reality?* Cork: Mercier.
Boyce, D.G. (1982) *Nationalism in Ireland*, London: Croom Helm.
Buckley, A.D. (1982) *A Gentle People: a Study of a Peaceful Community in Northern Ireland*, Cultra: Ulster Folk and Transport Museum.
Buckley, A.D. (1983a) 'Neighbourliness; myth and history', *Oral History Journal* 11:44–51.
Buckley, A.D. (1983b) 'Playful rebellion: social control and the framing of experience in an Ulster community', *Man* (NS) 18:383–95.
Buckley, A.D. (1984) 'Walls within walls: religion and rough behaviour in an Ulster community', *Sociology* 18:19–32.
Buckley, A.D. (1985–6) 'The chosen few: biblical texts in the regalia of an Ulster secret society', *Folk Life* 24:5–24.
Buckley, A.D. (1986) 'Collecting Ulster's culture: are there *really* two traditions?' paper presented to British Association, Bristol.
Buckley, A.D. (1987) 'Bad boys and little old ladies: youth and old age in two Ulster villages', *Ethnologia Europaea* XVII:157–63.
Caws, P. (1974) 'Operational, representational and explanatory models', *American Anthropologist* 76:1–10.
Cohen, A.P. (1975) *The Management of Myths: the Politics of Legitimation in a Newfoundland Community*, Manchester: Manchester University Press.
Connell, K.H. (1968) *Irish Peasant Society*, Oxford: Oxford University Press.
Connolly, S.E. (1982) *Priests and People in Pre-famine Ireland 1780–1845*, Dublin: Gill and McMillan.
Delargy, J.H. (1945) *'The Gaelic story-teller: with some notes on Gaelic folk-tales'*, proceedings of the Irish Academy, Oxford: Oxford University Press.
Dewar, M.W. (1956) *The Scarva Story*, Portadown: Portadown News.
Dewar, M.W., Brown, J., and Long, S.E. (*c.* 1967) *Orangeism: a New Historical Appreciation*, Belfast: Grand Orange Lodge of Ireland.
Donnan, H. and McFarlane, G. (1986) 'Social anthropology and the sectarian divide in Northern Ireland', in R. Jenkins, H. Donnan, and G. McFarlane (eds) *The Sectarian Divide in Northern Ireland Today*, London: RAI.
Durkheim, E. (1915) *The Elementary Forms of the Religious Life* (trans. 1968, J.W. Swain), London: Allen and Unwin.
Foster, J.W. (1982) 'Yeats and the folklore of the Irish revival', *Eire*/Ireland XVII:6–18.
Foxe, J. (1563) *The Book of Martyrs*, prepared (1985) by W.G. Berry, Grand Rapids: Baker Books.
Green, A.S. (1908) *The Making of Ireland and its Undoing*, London: Macmillan.
Hall, M. (1986) *Ulster: the Hidden History*, Belfast: Pretani Press.
Harris, R. (1972) *Prejudice and Tolerance in Ulster: a Study of Neighbours and 'Strangers' in a Border Community*, Manchester: Manchester University Press.
Harrison, J. (1888) *The Scott in Ulster: Sketch of the History of the Scottish Population of Ulster*, Edinburgh: Blackwood.
Hewitt, C. (1981) 'Catholic grievances, Catholic nationalism and violence in Northern Ireland during the Civil Rights period: a reconsideration', *British Journal of Sociology* 32:362–80.
Hewitt, C. (1983) 'Discrimination in Northern Ireland: a rejoinder', *British Journal of Sociology* 34:446–51.
Hewitt, C. (1985) 'Catholic grievances and violence in Northern Ireland', *British Journal of Sociology* 36:102–5.
Horowitz, D.L. (1985) *Ethnic Groups in Conflict*, Berkeley: University of California Press.

Jenkins, R. (1986) 'Northern Ireland: in what sense "religions" in conflict?' in R. Jenkins, H. Donnan, and G. McFarlane (eds) *The Sectarian Divide in Northern Ireland Today*, London: RAI.

Kennedy, P. (1891) *Legendary Fictions of the Irish Celts*, Detroit: Singing Tree Press.

Lévi-Strauss, C. (1956) 'The structural study of myth', *Journal of American Folklore* 68:428–44.

Malinowski, B. (1963) 'The foundations of faith and morals', in *Sex, Culture and Myth*, London: Rupert Hart Davis.

Moloney, E. and Pollack, A. (1986) *Paisley*. Dublin: Poolbeg.

McClelland, A. (1973) 'The Battle of Garvagh', *Ulster Folklife* 19:41–9.

O'Brian, G. (1918) *Economic History of Ireland in the 18th Century*, Philadelphia: Porcupine Press (1977).

O'Hearn, D. (1983) 'Catholic grievances, Catholic nationalism: a comment', *British Journal of Sociology* 34:438–45.

O'Hearn, D. (1985) 'Again on discrimination in the North of Ireland: a reply to the rejoinder', *British Journal of Sociology* 36:91–101.

O'Hergarty, P.S. (1949) *A History of Ireland under the Union 1802–1922*, London: Methuen.

O'Rahilly, T.F. (1957) *Early Irish History and Mythology*, Dublin: Institute for Advanced Studies.

O'Sullivan, S. (1966) *Folktales of Ireland*, Chicago: University of Chicago Press.

Poole, M. (1983) 'The demography of violence', in J. Darby (ed.) *Northern Ireland: The Background to the Conflict*, Belfast: Appletree.

Santino, J. (1983) 'Miles of smiles, years of struggle: the negotiation of Black occupational identity through personal experience narrative', *Journal of American Folklore* 96:393–412.

Stewart, A.T.Q. (1977) *The Narrow Ground*, London: Faber.

Tayler, C.B. (*c.* 1850) *Memorials of the English Martyrs*, Toronto: Wittenberg (1984).

UFTM (Ulster Folk and Transport Museum Archives). 'R' and 'C' numbers refer to tape recordings.

UYUC (1986) *CuChulain, the Lost Legend: Ulster, The Lost Culture?* Belfast: Ulster Young Unionist Council.

Van den Berghe, P.L. (1981) *The Ethnic Phenomenon*, New York: Elsevier.

Wallis, R., Bruce, S., and Taylor, D. (1986) ' "No Surrendor!" Paisleyism and the politics of ethnic identity in Northern Ireland', Belfast: Department of Social Studies, Queen's University.

Chapter thirteen

The Cultural Work of Yoruba Ethnogenesis

J. D. Y. Peel

. . . that peace should reign universally, with prosperity and advancement, and that the disjointed units should all be once more welded into one under one head from the Niger to the coast as in the happy days of ABIODUN, so dear to our fathers, that clannish spirit disappear, and above all that Christianity should be the principle religion in the land – paganism and Mohammedanism having had their full trial – should be the wish and prayer of every true son of Yoruba!

With these words the Reverend Samuel Johnson, Pastor of Oyo, brought to an end the main part of his great work, nearly 700 pages long, *The History of the Yoruba, from the Earliest Times to the Beginning of the British Protectorate* (Johnson, 1921:642). Johnson's *History* is not only the indispensable foundation for all historical and anthropological work on the Yoruba. It also has pride of place in a body of work produced by the Christian Yoruba intelligentsia – the creation of an orthography and a literary language, the translation of the Scriptures, local and ethnic histories large and small, written in English or Yoruba, studies of Yoruba traditional religion variously interpretative, polemical, or historical – through which the Yoruba have come to know themselves precisely as such. That we study a people called 'the Yoruba' at all is due largely to them.

To appreciate this achievement for what it is, we have to call into question two contentions common in recent anthropological writing on ethnicity. The first is that ethnicity, though expressed in cultural terms, does not require any cultural *explanation*. Abner Cohen's study of Hausa ethnicity in the Yoruba town of Ibadan (Cohen, 1969), a classic of West African ethnography, argues this forcefully. The second contention, which in a sense is a corollary of the first, is that its explanation need not refer to the past. This may as well take a structuralist as a functionalist form: as Maryon McDonald puts it in a recent study of Breton nationalism, 'the identity of a people is a product of the contemporary structural context in which it exists' (McDonald, 1986:333). Against this 'presentism', I argue the need for a properly cultural and historical explanation of ethnicity. But 'culture' must not be seen as a mere precipitate or bequest of the past. Rather, it is an active reflection on the past, a cultural *work*. And because work supposes a real object, in this case historical experience, an adequate explanation has to be a fully historical one.

It is an irony, then, that Cohen presents his Hausa study as 'social history' (Cohen, 1969:25-7) – though it is so in a significantly limited sense. An account of selected changes in one society, he argues, will provide the anthropologist with a contrast case to the present; and this will enable him 'to isolate variables in a far more satisfactory manner than in the comparison between difficult societies, with different cultural traditions' (Cohen, 1974:20). That is, culture can be excluded because it is held constant. A true sociological functionalist, Cohen argues that 'institutions cannot be sociologically *explained* in terms of past origins or events' (ibid.:21). Concretely, his explanation of why the Ibadan Hausa adopted the Tijaniyya order is in terms of its immediate local conse-quences, as providing 'solutions to some of the problems they faced as a result of the coming of party politics' (Cohen, 1969:152). Cohen is uncon-cerned with questions about why individual Hausa became Tijanis or about the dynamics of Tijaniyya expansion itself.[1] None of this matters, because 'within the contemporary situation ethnicity is essentially a politi-cal phenomenon, as traditional customs are used only as idioms and mechanisms for political alignments' (Cohen, 1974:4; cf. 1969:190). On this view, religious arguments, the historical experience of the Hausa, and their representation of it or ethnohistory, are equally beside the point.

In contrast with Cohen, McDonald takes ethnohistory seriously as a cultural object: 'modern ethnic or minority identity is commonly sought through historicist argument: the present is understood by reference to the past, and the interpretation of the past is made to generate the present' (McDonald, 1986:333). Yet surely it puts a great strain on any concept of *identity* to attach it so firmly to 'the contemporary structural context'. For as its etymology implies (*idem*, 'the same'), the primary thrust of the concept is to assert some degree of continuity despite change, across contexts. As a social psychological notion, it conveys some idea of an internal dynamic to the development of the self, of the constraining or enabling power of past experience (Epstein, 1978:5-6, 44-7).[2] Even the sharpest kind of identity change, such as religious conversion, becomes intelligible only in the light of the continuities and criteria of value, which run through from past to present. To apply the notion of identity at a collective level is precisely to invite attention to the facilitation of common action by shared past experiences. On this view, effective ethnic identity is thus likely to depend on the realities of the past as well as on the demands of 'the contemporary structural context'.

These considerations weigh especially if we see ethnogenesis as arising from a relationship between ethnic intellectuals or 'missionaries' and the less-concerned mass of the ethnic 'constituency'. The sociologists who have focused on the relationship between intellectuals and mass – Smith (1981), for example – show fewer traces of the blocking presentism to which anthropologists are so prone.[3] However compelling the reasons for ethnic mobilization – regionally uneven development, the expansion of nation–states, multi-ethnic urbanization, etc., it still has to be worked at in cultural terms. The resultant ethnohistory or 'historicist argument' has been the standard means of intellectuals or ethnic missionaries to raise their fellows' consciousness. But despite the 'invention of tradition' that it may involve, unless it also makes genuine contact with people's actual experience, that is with a history that happened, it is not likely to be effective. Only in a historical analysis can we see Yoruba ethnicity for what it is: a process or a project, rather than a structure.

Turning now to the Yoruba case, can we agree with Cohen's view that 'ethnicity is . . . basically a political, not a cultural phenomenon' (Cohen, 1969:190)? That it *is* political cannot be in any doubt. The Yoruba, like the Igbo and the Hausa, are one of the 'mega-tribal' groupings particularly characteristic of Nigeria's vast, complex, and regionalized political system. As such it is a modern category entirely, in that the vast bulk of peoples who now know themselves as Yoruba, did not do so in 1900. Originally the word referred to only one Yoruba grouping, the Oyo. Yoruba ethnic identity began to be adopted by other groups (e.g. Ijesha, Egba, Ijebu, Ekiti, Ondo) from the 1920s, as migration, cash-cropping, education, and conversion to the world religions drew more people into a Nigeria-wide sphere of social relations. From the late 1930s, when nationalism really began to get underway, the Yoruba began to shape themselves politically against other 'tribes', especially the Igbo in the political crucible of Lagos. Between 1945 and 1951, the nationalist movement in southern Nigeria fragmented, and national politics assumed the form of a competition between three parties, each associated with one of the 'mega-tribes' that formed the main bloc in one of the three regions. Each party sought to enhance its national strength by gaining support from minority tribes in other regions; but each also had to contend with the propensity of groupings and communities within the mega-tribe in its base region to pursue their more local rivalries (which often had deep historic roots) to the support of rival parties. Thus Ilesha, Ibadan, and several other Yoruba communities supported the Igbo Party (the NCNC) against the Yoruba Party (the Action Group) throughout most of the period 1951–66. Ethnic consciousness, at the level of the mega-tribe, still needed to be worked at. Yet it was, to good effect: by 1979, when civilian politics returned, the Action Group's successor, the UPN, won a much greater share of the Yoruba vote than its predecessor had done. We can sum it up by saying that in Nigeria, administrative units (the regions, and later the 'states') and ethnic groups have helped to shape each other through the medium of politics.[4]

Yet culture was an essential part of this ethnic politics. While it might 'function' to justify a special ethnic interest in terms of a higher or wider value, it was made plausible by its role in the historic formation of the ethnic groups themselves. For the NPC, the Hausa party, it was Islam (Paden, 1986); for the Yoruba parties it was ọlaju or 'enlightenment', a complex of development values rooted in Christianity and western education (Peel, 1978). The iconography of UPN in the 1979 election – its party symbol a lighted torch, its motto 'light over Nigeria' – encapsulated a history as well as an ideology. The policy priority given to education by UPN took to a higher stage the achievements of its Action Group predecessor in the field of primary education in the 1950s. The further we go back, the more we find that Yoruba ethnicity was a cultural project before it was a political instrument. The Action Group (founded 1951) had its origins in a cultural organization, Ẹgbẹ Ọmọ Oduduwa (founded 1945). More importantly, the efficient cause of the extension of Yoruba identity to originally non-Yoruba peoples was education and Christianization through the means of Standard Yoruba, a mission-devised language form. Beyond the Oyo (the 'Yoruba Proper', as Johnson called them), the first Yoruba everywhere were teachers, catechists, and clergymen; the Christian evangelists were, unavoidably, ethnic missionaries too.

The ethnic message that came wrapped in this language of literacy was itself fashioned as a response to a nineteenth-century experience. The sophistication of this message lay in the way it combined an interpretation of the historical experience of Yoruba individuals and communities with a plausible rationale of the particular role of its promoters, the evangelists of Christianity.

The Yoruba, of course, did not present a cultural *tabula rasa* to the missions; the cultural map was not to be redrawn as arbitrarily as the political map of colonial Africa. Beyond the level of their 'town' (*ilu*) and certain named regional groupings, the peoples who would come to call themselves Yoruba might recognize their wider affinity in one of two distinct (but largely overlapping) ways: by similarity of dialect, and by shared customs. These customs included certain principles of political organization, a number of religious cults, and traditions of dynastic descent from a sacred centre, Ile-Ife. However, many of these customs either fell short, sometimes far short, of covering the whole Yoruba-speaking area, or were shared with non-Yoruba too, particularly Dahomey and Benin. Language came first in the definition of this new, wider ethnicity. The Yoruba seem to stand out here, in comparison with their neighbours of the West African forest: the Akan, the Gbe-speakers (including Dahomey and the Ewe)[5] and the Edo-speakers (including Benin). In none of these others did there develop such a close identification of a modern ethnic group with a linguistic community. Superficially, this seems surprising, since the Yoruba were far less united politically in the nineteenth century, when the collapse of Oyo left no stably dominant power among them, such as Asante, Dahomey, or Benin. On a deeper view, however, it appears that this very political vacuum provided the conditions in which a new cultural agency, the Protestant missions, could exploit existing affinities of language and tradition to promote a more explicit regional integration of a cultural kind.

It was in their diaspora, the result of the slave trade, that the Yoruba-speaking peoples first acquired the collective designation of a single name[6] – and particularly in Sierra Leone. Here a linguistically defined category emerged to embrace all the Yoruba-speaking groups. This was 'Aku', derived from the Yoruba mode of greeting, *o* [or *ẹ*] *ku*.[7] So a leading Aku, Isaac Benjamin Pratt (d.1880), is described on his memorial tablet in St George's Cathedral, Freetown, as 'a native of the Ifeh section of the Aku tribe'. The CMS missionary, S.W. Koelle, in his great *Polyglotta Africana* (1854), gave lexical items for twelve dialects of Aku (of which Yoruba was one). He remarked that:

> Aku was not the historical name by which these numerous tribes are united in one nation; but it is retained here because the historical name is not known at present. . . . The missionaries of the country ought to search after the proper national name of the whole Aku country. For the last few years they have very erroneously made use of the name 'Yoruba' in reference to the whole nation. . . .
>
> (Koelle, 1854:5)

How very German and Protestant is this presumption that nations are, first of all, language groups! Koelle says that to use the word Yoruba for the whole nation is like calling Wurtembergers (as he was himself) or Bavarians, Prussians. He was right. Yet, thanks to the CMS, 'Yoruba' it became. Contrary to Koelle's supposition, there was *no* historical or proper national name for Yorubaland; but the CMS adopted the Hausa name of the largest political unit within it, Oyo. The reason why they chose this Hausa name seems to have been that the first eyewitness accounts of Oyo were published in England in 1829–32 by travellers who were oriented towards the kingdoms of the far interior and who used Hausa as their language of communication.[8]

If one wants a precise time and place for the inauguration of the modern Yoruba language, it would be in 1844, when Samuel Ajayi Crowther opened the first Yoruba service in Freetown with a text to declare a historical project: 'Therefore that holy thing which shall be born of thee shall be called the Son of God' (Luke 1:35). The language itself, whose orthography took another thirty years to settle, was thoroughly hybrid:

its morpho-syntax predominantly Oyo/Ibadan, its phonemes markedly of Abeokuta, its lexicon enriched by coinings and the speech of Lagos and Yoruba diaspora (Adetugbo, 1967; Ajayi, 1960). It was most strange to the peoples of the forest who had not known Oyo rule, and so it was indeed largely a *Yoruba* language. Yet it was the Reverend James Johnson, Sierra Leone born of Ijesha/Ijebu descent, who actually had to learn to speak Yoruba when he was transferred from Sierra Leone to Lagos in 1874, who wrote that 'the Bible in the native tongue' was the best thing about the Yoruba Mission.[9] 'This Book must influence the religion, the coming literature, the thought, the language, the phraseology, and the life of the country, if it be rightly and diligently used.' Few missionary prophecies have been so well fulfilled.

The missions that began work in the Yoruba country in the 1840s possessed an advantage that few primary missions elsewhere in Africa had: their personnel already included converts made in Sierra Leone, and in several stations they found a core of nominal or potential Christians among the Saro (as returnees from Sierra Leone were known). The importance of the missions' Saro base, however, lay not so much in the fillip it gave to the growth of local congregations, as in the fact that the Saros' personal experiences of loss and dislocation were quintessential of the upheavals of the country at large. From the 1820s onwards the Yoruba country was in a state of near-continuous violent upheaval. Oyo's collapse produced knock-on effects as refugees flooded to the south and east. The Oyo ex-slaves who predominated in Sierra Leone in the 1820s gave way to Egbas in the 1830s and Ijeshas in the 1840s. The Egbas' new capital at Abeokuta, the rival Oyo successor states Ijaiye and Ibadan, the ancient Ijebu kingdom nearer the coast, were periodically locked in conflict. By the early 1880s virtually the whole of the Yoruba country was at war. In popular social consciousness this was an age of 'confusion', of the 'world being spoiled' (*aiye bajẹ*), of the paramountcy of the 'hot', angry gods like Ogun (god of war), Sopona (god of smallpox), and above all Esu (the intemperate trickster deity, breaker of rules, associated with markets and crossroads), whom the Christians identified as Satan.[10] To this experience the missionaries and especially their Saro-Yoruba personnel brought a social and historical diagnosis that was widely felt to be telling.[11]

The social gospel of the missions was based squarely on an early version of modernization theory, as the Reverend C.A. Gollmer reported in one of his earliest sermons, at Badagry in 1845:

> . . . in times gone past white man's country was like there's [*sic*] is now: worshipping natural phenomena as gods, making idols . . . and missionaries came with the same book as he does. They prayed to that God, and wars ceased and peace was established and so, by and by the country became good . . . To make your country stand the same as

white man's country – this is the reason why we came and why we wish to preach the word of God to you. . . .[12]

But there is the characteristic weakness of modernization theory: how to establish the relevance of the alien model in terms of the particular history of the society where it is to be applied? Some providential history can help a lot. Thus the Reverend H. Townsend, in his 1847 journal from Abeokuta:

> He reviews the collapse of Oyo authority, the desolation of the old Egba towns, and wars involving Ife, Owu and Ijehu. These tribes owed allegiance, he says, to the Yoruba King, but 'now there is no connexion but what arises from speaking a common language'. But 'I doubt not that all that has happened in this country in these afflictions have been from God and are intended, thro' his great mercy, as a means to extend the knowledge of Himself in Africa.' While war was destroying the Egba towns, the missions were being consolidated in Sierra Leone, which became an asylum for the victims of the wars. The people desire to return home. 'A door in the hearts of the people is opened for us. The work is not of man, but of the Lord.'[13]

All this would be equally the view of his Saro colleagues, but their search for meaning and salvation went to deeper levels. For them the essential issue was their personal authenticity as members of a community. It could not be resolved as a matter of being, but only as a matter of becoming. Self-realization, the missionary enterprise, the redefinition of community, and the development of the country were all aspects of one total process.

The Saro evangelists were doubly alienated from their society. Enforced exile had broken many old ties and opened new ones. We should be careful not to exaggerate this: much of the home cultures was kept up in Sierra Leone, and the missionaries in Yorubaland were always complaining of the backsliding of the Saro there. But those who *were* so alienated must have been especially prone to the further alienation that was an inevitable effect of the conscientious adoption of the Christian religion in its Victorian form. The ambivalence of church personnel towards their communities – drawn to them (as home) and repelled by them (as pagan) led them to adopt a two-tier ethnic identification: with their town or 'tribe', entities with a real political existence, and with a concept of Yoruba as a potentially Christian nation, a thing existing only *in posse* but prefigured in the network of Christian congregations using the Yoruba Bible. In the ethnic discourse of the missionaries, the two levels are distinguished, as when 'Ijebbu (another tribe of the Yoruba nation)'[14] is seen as an entity of the same order as Ibadan and the Egba. But the term Yoruba remained to the end of the century and beyond, ambiguous since it referred to one of the existing parts, as well as to the notional whole.

The tensions of local community membership and Christian obligation are well illustrated in the case of Abeokuta, where the missions won their greatest initial successes. Here, the mission had the advantage of a large group of Saro returnees and the patronage of influential chiefs. By 1877 there were 2,295 baptized Anglicans at Abeokuta compared with only 401 at Ibadan.[15] Yet the CMS Superintendent, the Saro James Johnson, was hardly elated by this. In his view, the Abeokuta church had become all too well adjusted to Egba conditions: domestic slave-holding and polygamy, which he abhorred, were rife among its leading members. Johnson considered that the problem was rooted in what he called 'tribal connection': all CMS agents at Abeokuta by the late 1870s were Egba, and so general was the view that no 'stranger . . . should question Egbas in Egbaland', that Yorubans (i.e. Oyos) were known to refuse church appointments there.[16] Johnson even proposed the introduction of a 'superior element . . . from without, from Sierra Leone', to replace compromised church agents; so it is not surprising that he was all but driven from Abeokuta with taunts of 'Ijebu man' ringing in his ears.

Elsewhere it was more common for the Christians, at least until late in the century, to keep a low profile in political and military affairs, to be reckoned (as at Ibadan) 'a quiet people averse to fame and worldly honour'.[17] Particularly the full-time agents (clergy, teachers, catechists, scripture readers) were a dispersed or supralocal status group that saw itself as Yoruba, in the extended sense of the word. Clergy were not usually natives of the towns where they ministered. For a man like the Reverend D. Olubi, for over two decades the Egba pastor of Ibadan's main CMS congregation, the only possible stance was to hold aloof from Egba and Ibadan chauvinism alike. The whole pattern of communication and association of the clergy was pan-Yoruba. There was much intermarriage between clerical families of different towns, and church conferences (usually in Lagos), brought them together from all over the warring up-country.[18] Professionally, they found the blockades and disruptions caused by the wars deeply exasperating. Though many Christian laymen in Lagos were vehement supporters of their communities in the interior, it was a clerical initiative that launched peace discussions in 1882. This was in the name of a Yoruba patriotism hardly yet meaningful outside their circle: 'invoked . . . as patriots and especially as Christians to see that all tribal feelings and jealousies be set aside in the interests of peace to their fatherland' (Johnson, 1921:480). In the negotiations of the 1880s, which eventually led to the resolution of the military stalemate, key mediating roles were played by two Saro clergymen: Charles Phillips on the side of the Ekitiparepo and Samuel Johnson of Ibadan.

The wars were *the* central experience of the Yoruba-speaking peoples in the nineteenth century, and Samuel Johnson, supremely, was their interpreter. Where better to do this from than Ibadan, the 'lion' of the Yoruba country? Samuel Johnson had come to Ibadan from Sierra Leone in 1857 at the age of 11 with his father, a scripture reader. After secondary education at Abeokuta, Johnson became a teacher, at Ibadan, and rose through catechist to priest, at Oyo.[19] A prime objective of Johnson's *History* is to present the wider Yoruba identity promoted by the missions, as the culmination of Oyo history. To make this more plausible, the extent of Old Oyo's regional hegemony is greatly exaggerated. And because the modern concept of a Yoruba nation has such clearly Christian origins (and of course because Johnson was a clergyman) he also needs to place Christianity firmly in the pattern of Yoruba history.

Johnson's *History* falls into two parts. Part I is ethnographic, a survey of the language, customs, and social organization of the Yoruba, including some account of the various non-Oyo groups. Since the Yoruba conventionally express political distinctiveness in terms of distinct stories (*itan*) of origin, Johnson presents legends of origin 'as they are related' here. The ancestor of the Yoruba, Oduduwa, son of Lamurudu (Nimrod), is held to have been driven out of Mecca for having relapsed to paganism and with his idols migrated to Ife. As Robin Law (1984) has shown, this legend is in all its details drawn from Muslim Hausa sources. Indigenous foundation stories by contrast represent the Yoruba, indeed the human race, as descending from heaven to earth at Ife. Its primary purpose is plain, to affiliate the Yoruba to the general stock of humanity, and in this it answers a question that missionaries, steeped in Biblical history, had already posed of the Yoruba. 'From what branch of the Noahic family did they descend?' Nimrod descended through Cush from Ham. That Johnson uses a Muslim Hausa version, like the earlier adoption of the Hausa ethnic name Yoruba, indicates merely the quarter in which it had first become pressing to frame answers to questions about wider group identities and relations. But Johnson does not rest here. He is more than happy to accept that the Yoruba came from the East, but not that they are apostate Muslims. From several details, he argues instead that they probably came from Upper Egypt, and that their ancestors were probably Coptic Christians (Johnson, 1921:3–7). He finds confirming evidence in parallels between several elements of Yoruba mythology and episodes of Scripture, both of the Old and New Testaments. Johnson thus cleverly places Christianity as a precedent in the Yorubas' *own* history; conversion is merely a recovery of what was lost, paganism an unhappy interlude.

Part II, the chronological part, divides Yoruba history into four periods. The first is really a short prehistory, dealing with the 'Mythological Kings and deified heroes' who link Oyo to Ife. That leaves the remaining three as a dialectical triad: (1) Oyo's growth up to Abiodun (d.1789), in whose reign its empire reached its maximum extent; (2) Old Oyo's progressive collapse, under pressure internally and from the Fulani jihad, the dispersion of its people and the eventual establishment of new Oyo towns further south, particularly Ibadan, c.1837; (3) covering the rest of the nineteenth century, entitled 'Arrest of disintegration. Inter-tribal wars. British Protectorate'. It is this last period, to which 376 pages are devoted (well over half the whole), which is the real glory of the work.

It was a bold conception of Johnson's, to present those sixty years of 'inter-tribal wars' leading up to the British Protectorate as a higher-level replay of the ascent of Yoruba (Oyo) power to 'the happy days of ABIODUN'. In his view, there were two positive features of this period: the growth of Ibadan and the Christian missionary enterprise. Though these both meant 'salvation' of a certain kind for the Yoruba, they implied radically opposed values. Ibadan was an intensely militaristic state, many of whose core institutions such as slavery and polygyny, let alone its 'heathenism', were anathema to the missions. The narrative of Johnson's journals, mostly from the 1870s, is continuously threaded round a series of oppositions: war/peace, idolatry/God, Ibadan/the Church, darkness/enlightenment. Yet a major source of the power of Johnson's writing is that he does not try to evade or mute this contradiction but looks for its transcendence in history.

The *History* is more reflective and distanced, more philosophical in the eighteenth-century sense, as well as much more finely worked; in places one can identify passages based on particular sections of the journals.[20] Here Johnson's identification with Ibadan emerges more clearly. It takes two forms. First, his human sympathy and attention is directly engaged by the actions and passions of the leading personalities of a very turbulent community. Second, he finds a providential aspect even to Ibadan's militarism. Though Oyo at its core, it has promoted a wider-than-Oyo sense of Yoruba community:

[After c.1840] the history of the Yorubas centred largely at Ibadan which . . . continued to attract to itself ardent spirits from every tribe and family all over the country, who made it their home, so that while the rest of the country was quiet, Ibadan was making history.

(Johnson, 1921:293)

The appeal to providence is most arresting in a passage describing how the Oyos gained the upper hand over the Ifes, Egbas, and Ijebus among the early settlers of Ibadan. 'Violence, oppression, robbery, man-stealing were the order of the day', writes Johnson unflinchingly:

Yet they were destined by God to play a most important part in the history of the Yorubas, to break the Fulani yoke and save the rest of the country from foreign domination; in short to be a protector as well as a scourge in the land . . .

(ibid.:246)

In thus checking the Fulani Muslims, Ibadan served not only a Yoruba ethnic interest but, by implication, a Christian interest. Fifty pages later, referring to the establishment of the CMS mission at Abeokuta, Johnson openly contrasts Islam and Christianity in relation to Yoruba interest and destiny:

Thus light began to dawn on the Yoruba country from the south, when there was nothing but darkness, idolatry, superstition, blood shedding and slave-hunting all over the rest of the country. There was an old tradition in the country of a prophecy that as ruin and desolation spread from the interior to the coast [a reference to the Fulani jihad] so light and restoration will be from the coast interiorwards.

(ibid.: 296)

What we need to note here is not so much the ancient prophecy fulfilled, but the project declared. The images of light (*imǫlę*) and restoration (*atunṣe*) are an unmistakable anticipation of Yoruba cultural politics as they would be in the twentieth century. The self-image of the UPN, the Yoruba-based party in the 1979 election – its Yoruba name, from its symbol, was *Ęgbę Imǫlę* 'the party of light' – reproduces it exactly. Can it be entirely an accident that there, too, the chief opponent was a northern-based power, the NPN under a Fulani/Hausa leader, Alhaji Shehu Shagari?

Yet despite the ingenuity of this cultural argument, the reality of Ibadan's relations with Christianity and the new pan-Yoruba patriotism urged by the missions was less straightforward. The Ibadan chiefs did not see their opposition to the Fulani Emirate of Ilorin in religious terms. Islam was well established in Ibadan by 1851 and Ibadan was to become a predominantly Muslim community. As for a wider Yoruba sense of identity, Ibadan's influence was felt in two ways. On the one hand, as the largest and most powerful town of the Yoruba country, Ibadan was a major source of cultural homogenization within the region. On the other hand, peace was only possible when Ibadan was decisively stalemated by an alliance of all the other major Yoruba states against her. For all that Johnson was one of the principal peace negotiators, he simply cannot conceal his admiration for Ibadan as a military power: 'Thus stood the Ibadan lion at bay, yet flinching from none, at Ofa [vs. Ilorin], at Kiriji [vs. Ilesha and Ekiti] at Modakeke [vs. Ife] and against the Egbas and the Ijebus at home' (ibid.:478).

Pan-Yoruba solidarity was thus, to an extent, founded *against* Ibadan.

The impact of Johnson's *History* was delayed, since though completed in 1899 it was not published till 1921. The latency of the first two decades of colonial rule did not stop a slow diffusion of the new pan-Yoruba identity. Non-Oyo laymen began routinely to treat the whole region as generically Yoruba, an ethnographic unit.[21] From 1923 there was published in Ibadan *The Yoruba News*, a weekly newspaper that drew support from non-Oyo as well as Oyo towns. Yoruba ethnic identity, especially among non-Oyo peoples, also evolved in critical reaction to Johnson's *History*. Appearing as it did in the 1920s, when today's rivalry of communities for public-development goods began to take shape, it stimulated rival anti-Oyo accounts.[22] None of these was on anything like the scale of Johnson. Such histories of particular towns, as likely in Yoruba as English, most of them produced as pamphlets on smudgy local presses, have continued to be produced – now probably in some dozens. A paradox of this movement in the 1920s is to be especially noted: it was precisely as non-Oyo groups, or rather their educated elements, came to adopt an erstwhile designation of the Oyo, 'Yoruba', that anti-Oyo versions of Yoruba history became essential.

One consequence of this wave of communal and subgroup assertion against Johnson and the Oyo was the elevation of Ife in the definition of Yoruba identity. In one sense there was nothing new about this, since even Johnson accepted Ife as the source of the Oyo dynasty. But where Johnson had striven to represent the Oyo kingdom as the privileged heir of Oduduwa's Ife, the historians of other communities made cases for equal descent of their dynasties from Ife. The historical elevation of Ife may have been made easier by the fact that, from the 1840s to the 1890s, the contemporary Ife had been mostly deserted, its site overshadowed by refugee Oyos at nearby Modakeke and for long periods its king in exile. From the 1880s, in Christian circles, Ife was being spoken of as a spiritual (and so ultimately superior) power, in contrast to the secular power of Oyo, almost *à la* Dumezil. A remarkable document, that seems to express a closely cognate outlook, appeared in the *Nigerian Chronicle* in April 1910, under the pseudonym 'Adesola'. Purporting to be an 'ancient Yoruba religious hymn', it takes the form of an extended divination verse, and was evidently received from a *babalawo* (diviner). It depicts a mythical time when 'the land of Ife' was desolate, and when all the kings of the country came together to find a means to its restoration – which, by finding the spiritual 'healing leaf', they succeed in doing. It is significant equally that nearly all the named kings are from communities in the non-Oyo parts of Yorubaland, to the east and south; and that 'Adesola' should be revealed as yet another clergyman, the Reverend E.T. Johnson.[23]

The Christianity of the main promoters of Yoruba identity was now coming to have a further significance. The two world religions, rapidly expanding by the 1920s, spread regionally in a most uneven way (Peel, 1967). Islam came to predominate to the north and west, in the lands of the old Oyo Empire and in towns flooded with Oyo refugees on its southern fringe (Ibadan, Iwo, Oshogbo, etc.). The east, never under Oyo rule, from north to south, came to be largely Christian. The south to west (Ijebu, Egba, Egbado) was more mixed. The crucial point: Islam, because of its establishment in Oyo as far back as the eighteenth century, spread, after Oyo's collapse, in precisely those areas whence came the Oyo and Egba ex-slaves who were the spearhead of Christianity and 'Yoruba' (*quondam* Oyo) identity. Christianity, however, won its greatest successes in areas where Islam had no head-start, which were, by the same token, the non-Oyo areas where Yoruba identity only penetrated with Christianity.

Yoruba ethnicity now began to reveal a definite 'fault line'. It can readily be set out in structural terms, as a set of paired opposites:

Oyo   : Ife
savannah   : forest
North-western dialects   : South-eastern/central dialects
Yoruba Proper   : 'adopted' Yoruba
Muslims   : Christians
NCNC/NNDP/NPN   : Action Group/UPN

The top three links of the two vertical or syntagmatic chains are most firmly established. Savannah and forest communities did consciously recognize themselves as such,[24] and recognized dialect differences that correlated with it. Then, as the Yoruba-speaking peoples underwent incorporation into a single state, the scheme revealed a potential for the organization of political competition. The links are looser, because only emergent, between the two bottom pairs of the series; dominant world religion and party allegiance. But there is still a definite process by which entirely new categories, as they emerge from the vicissitudes of historical experience, are 'syntagmatically' related to existing ones.

As I have remarked, the world religions spread unevenly in Yorubaland, and that in a way that correlated markedly with the savannah/forest, Oyo/non-Oyo divide. In nearly all communities there are Muslims and Christians; and in predominantly Muslim communities, like Iwo or Ogbomosho, Christians have tended to provide much of the modern political leadership. The accepted view – lately expressed in length in Laitin's *Hegemony and Culture* (1986, esp. Chapter 6) – is that confessional identity has not been politically relevant among the Yoruba. Certainly, in the first period of party politics (1951–66) there was very little Christian/Muslim about the AG/NCNC split. Yet there was a distinctly Christian undertow to the AG's message. It was not just that Christians bulked so large in the party's leadership, but that its programme was so clearly a continuation of the Christian enterprise of Yoruba ethnicity. Consider the symbolism of its most prestigious project – the Western Region's own

University at (of course) Ife: the Olokun head (ancient Ife culture), the open book (godliness and good learning), the blaze of light (ọlaju).

The main exception to all this had to occur at the very centre of the modern Yoruba world, the seat of the AG government of the Western Region, predominantly Muslim Ibadan. In modern politics, the early leadership of Ibadan had come from the small Christian elite, founders of the Ibadan Progressive Union, who naturally gave their support to the Action Group in the early 1950s (Post and Jenkins, 1973). But they were soon eclipsed by a local party called Mabọlajẹ ('Don't spoil the honour (of the town))', led by a Muslim, A. Adelabu, who appealed strongly to the sentiments of indigenous Ibadans as ordinary folk (mẹkunnu) and as Muslims. As their religious appeal was thus linked to class on one side, it was linked to class *and* community on another. The most prominent of the Yoruba immigrants to Ibadan were the Ijebu – many of them very prosperous, especially the many Christians among them, and their interest in acquiring urban land rights brought them into sharp conflict with Ibadan indigenes. Since the leader of the Action Group, Chief Awolowo, was

UPN

Eyi ni ami idibo Ẹgbẹ UPN
(Ẹgbẹ Imọlẹ.)
—Ẹgbẹ Awolọwọ— ti yio han
ni ile idibo ati lori iwe idibo.
UP NIGERIA
UP AWO ! ! !

Figure 13.1
Election poster of UPN (1979). The Yoruba text reads: This is the voting symbol of the UPN Party (Party of Light) – Awolowo's Party – which will appear in the polling stations and on the ballot papers

Arms of the University of Ife (now, Obafemi Awolowo University)

himself an Ijebu Christian, the religious, communal, and political 'codings' of the conflict all coincided nicely.

For pragmatic reasons, Adelabu's Mabolaje allied itself with the 'Igbo' NCNC, as the AG's chief rival throughout the region. Later, Adelabu's thoughts turned to a northern alliance, and he espoused the idea of a separate Central Yoruba State, where Muslims would predominate and provide a wider base for him. Though Adelabu died in 1958, a new anti-AG party, the NNDP, did make this alliance (1964–6). Though NNDP, and its successor in 1979–84, NPN, won *much* less Yoruba support than their NCNC predecessor had done, this support was much more concentrated in the predominantly Muslim, Oyo-Yoruba area, from Ibadan through Ogbomosho up to Ilorin. UPN spoke for the Yoruba, certainly, but especially for Yoruba Christians. The religious factor was especially manifest in Kwara State, mainly Yoruba but part of the old Northern Region: the western area around the Ilorin Emirate was for NPN, while the eastern area (Christian Igbomina and Yagba) was for UPN.

It is fair as far as it goes to speak with Laitin (1986:xi) of the relative 'nonpoliticization of religious differentiation' among the Yoruba. But it is also superficial if we are led to ignore the more discreet, implicit, or potential influences of religion.[25] Here, as elsewhere, the world religions may both create their own interests, or (as is our chief concern here) they may shape or at least encode ethnic interests. So much Cohen clearly saw, in relation to Islam and Ibadan Hausa. But his presentism and his inclination to reduce culture to structure prevented him from giving the historical account that is needed to explain it. Two things give the Yoruba situation its remarkable dynamism. First, at no level is community fixed or monolithic. Second, the spread of the world religions has been such that they are *both* significantly present in most communities *and* also, to a fair degree, regionally concentrated. The impetus of both Muslims and Christians to gloss communal identity in religious terms or to promote their religion as a communal good is thus powerfully restrained by the religious pluralism of their communities.

My account has focused on the role of the Christian missions in promoting Yoruba ethnicity to serve their purposes. They did so by 'expanding' an existing ethnic group (the Oyo), whose own historical destiny has proved to embrace much more of their Islamic rivals. The Yoruba Christian intelligentsia has been remarkably successful, securing them in the pattern of Yoruba history. This historic concern of Yoruba Christians to authenticate themselves as Yoruba stands in sharp contrast to the preoccupation of today's Yoruba Muslims, to authenticate themselves as Muslims (Abubakre, 1980). Culturally, they still look over their shoulders to the Hausa and beyond them to the Middle East. Every *haj* is a small pressure towards an Islamic politics, now more evident, even among the tolerant Yoruba, than ever before. If the story of Yoruba ethnicity has hitherto largely been one of Christian endeavour, the pressing question now may well be how Yoruba Muslims square off their two identities.

A final theoretical comment. I suspect that the way I have approached the topic – as a *story* of Yoruba ethnogenesis – is not quite what the conference organizers may have had in mind. Their call was for 'an ethnography of history: a study of how the past is used, lived, and recounted, in the construction and in the life of categories of ethnic identification and self-identification *in the present*' (my italics). But is this notion of 'the present' as a distinct object of study, and the distinctive focus of anthropology at that, really viable at all? The present has often been treated by anthropologists as a sort of temporal plateau, coterminous with the duration of their fieldwork, inhabited by structures and categories; but it is much more evanescent than that, no sooner come than gone, really no more than the hinge between the past and future. As the other Samuel Johnson put it in *Rasselas* (Johnson, 1976(1759):104), 'the truth is, that no mind is much employed upon the present: recollection and anticipation fill up almost all our moments'. Whether or not this is absolutely true, it does seem to apply rather strongly in the case of those 'peoples who seem to make up the rules as they go along', as Sahlins put it, 'like the Eskimo, the Tswana, Pul Eliya, or the so-called loosely structured societies of New Guinea' (Sahlins, 1985:26–7) or, we might add, the Yoruba. Their truest ethnography may well *be* history. That is why we students of the Yoruba do well to start with the Reverend Samuel Johnson.

Notes

1. On the spread of Tijaniyya among the Hausa generally, see Paden, 1973.
2. The crucial point, drawn from Erikson, is the notion of identity as the condition and product of personal development, of the linking of past, present, and future.
3. Note the quotation from Weber that Smith (1981) uses as a foreword: 'The reason for the Alsatians not feeling themselves as belonging to the German nation has to be sought in their memories'.
4. For a fuller argument about the relations of community, party, and administrative unit see Peel, 1983:221–5.
5. Gbe is strictly a neologism – the word *gbe* means 'language' – but I adopt this name for a group of languages with high mutual intelligibility, following Capo, 1983.
6. In Cuba they were known as Lucumi (Montejo, 1970:26–8). In Brazil they were mostly known by the names of subgroups, but in some areas Nago (the name of a south-western subgroup) was used in a wider, generic sense (Bastide, 1978:193,197,205).
7. On the Aku in Sierra Leone see Fyfe, 1962, Peterson, 1969. As Christian Aku became assimilated to the Christian Creole (Krio) population, the name Aku shifted to its present reference as Freetown Muslims of Yoruba descent (who now speak Krio).
8. For example, H. Clapperton, *Journal of a Second Expedition into the Interior*

of Africa (London, 1829); R. Lander, *Record of Capt. Clapperton's Last Expedition to Africa* (London, 1830); R. and J. Lander, *Journal of an Exploration to Explore the Course and Termination of the Niger* (London, 1832).

9. J. Johnson, Report to CMS Secretary, 30 Jan. 1878, in CA2/056. (This and such subsequent references, are to the CMS Yoruba Mission papers, now in Birmingham University Library.)

10. Many references in CMS Papers, but especially S. Johnson's Journal Extracts for 27 March 1870 and 29 Feb. 1875, CA2/058.

11. The following account is much indebted to Ajayi, 1965; Ayandele, 1966; 1970; Ajayi and Smith, 1964.

12. Gollmer's Journal for Quarter ending 25 June 1845, CA2/M1.

13. Townsend's Journal for Quarter ending 25 Dec. 1847, p. 581, CA2/M1.

14. Gollmer's Journal for 25 June 1845, CA2/M1.

15. J. Johnson's Report, 'From Lagos to Abeokuta', Aug. 1877, CA2/056.

16. J. Johnson to CMS Secretary, 18 Sept. 1879, CA2/056; Ayandele, 1970:124–30.

17. S. Johnson quoting an Ibadan man, Journal extracts for 5 Apr. 1876, CA2/058.

18. Wole Soyinka gives a delightful account of this ambience, albeit from a much later period in his autobiography (1982). He grew up in a church compound in Abeokuta, his mother Egba and his schoolteacher father Ijebu.

19. On Johnson's early life, see Doortmont, 1985. Mr Doortmont, of the Erasmus University, Rotterdam, is working on a doctoral dissertation on Samuel Johnson as a historian.

20. For example, Johnson 1921:28–9, and the remarkable discussion with a diviner who expresses his own cosmological vision recorded in his Journal for 29 Feb. 1875.

21. For example, the six Yoruba laymen who wrote the 'Report on the Yoruba 1910', commissioned by the colonial government. They included Egba and Ijesha as well as Oyo. See Hopkins, 1969.

22. On the Ilesha one, see Peel, 1984:122–4.

23. A Methodist, no relation of Samuel or James Johnson. He is also concerned to argue that the poem shows that ancient Yoruba religion was monotheist. The towns mentioned include Ado, Ire, Ido, Ife, Ilesha, Ara, Ijero, Ondo – only Ketu from the north-western area. The text also appears in an appendix to Farrow, 1926.

24. For example, in the case of Ilesha (a forest community), see Peel, 1983:29.

25. Yet Laitin, too, recognizes 'the growing social relevance of religious differentiation' (Laitin, 1986:126).

References

Abubakre, R.D. (1980) 'The contribution of Yorubas to Arabic literature', unpublished PhD dissertation, University of London.

Adetugbo, A. (1967) 'The Yoruba language in western Nigeria: its major dialect areas', unpublished PhD dissertation, Columbia University.

Ajayi, J.F.A. (1960) 'How Yoruba was reduced to writing', *Odu* 8:49–58.

Ajayi, J.F.A. (1965) *The Christian Missions in Nigeria 1841–91: the Making of an Educated Elite*, London: Longman.

Ajayi, J.F.A., and Smith, R.S. (1964) *Yoruba Warfare in the Nineteenth Century*, Cambridge: Cambridge University Press.

Ayandele, E.A. (1966) *The Missionary Impact on Modern Nigeria 1842–1914*, London: Longman.

Ayandele, E.A. (1970) *Holy Johnson: Pioneer of African Nationalism 1836–1917*, London: Cass.

Bastide, R. (1978) *The African Religions of Brazil*, Baltimore: Johns Hopkins University Press.

Capo, H.C. (1983) 'Le Gbe est une langue unique', *Africa* 53(2):47–57.

Cohen, A. (1969) *Custom and Politics in Urban Africa: a Study of Hausa Migrants in Yoruba Towns*, Manchester: Manchester University Press.

Cohen, A. (1974) *Two-Dimensional Man: an Essay on the Anthropology of Power and Symbolism in Complex Society*, London: Routledge & Kegan Paul.

Doortmont, M. (1985) 'Samuel Johnson and the history of the Yorubas: a study in historiography', unpublished MA dissertation, University of Birmingham.

Epstein, A.L. (1978) *Ethos and Identity: Three Studies in Ethnicity*, London: Tavistock.

Farrow, S.S. (1926) *Faith, Fancies and Fetish, or Yoruba Paganism*, London: SPCK.

Fyfe, C. (1962) *History of Sierra Leone*, Oxford: Oxford University Press.

Hopkins, A.G. (1969) 'A report on the Yoruba, 1910', *J. Hist. Soc. Nigeria* 5:67–100.

Johnson, S. (1976)(1759) *The History of Rasselas, Prince of Abissinia*, Harmondsworth: Penguin Books.

Johnson, S. (1921) *The History of the Yorubas, from the Earliest Times to the Beginning of the British Protectorate*, Lagos: CMS Bookshops.

Koelle, S.W. (1854) *Polyglotta Africana* (revised edn and introduction P.E.H. Hair and D. Dalby), Graz: Akademische Druck, 1963.

Laitin, D.D. (1986) *Hegemony and Culture: Politics and Religious Change among the Yoruba*, Chicago: University of Chicago Press.

Law, R. (1984) 'How truly traditional is our traditional history? The case of Samuel Johnson and the recording of Oyo oral tradition', *History in Africa* 11:195–221.

McDonald, M. (1986) 'Celtic ethnic kinship and the problem of being English', *Current Anthropology* 27(4):333–41.

Montejo, E. (1970) *Autobiography of a Runaway Slave*, Harmondsworth: Penguin.

Paden, J.N. (1973) *Religion and Political Culture in Kano*, Berkeley: University of California Press.

Paden, J.N. (1986) *Sir Ahmadu Bello: a Biography*, London: Hodder & Stoughton.

Peel, J.D.Y. (1967) 'Religious change in Yorubaland', *Africa* 37:292–306.

Peel, J.D.Y. (1978) 'Olaju: a Yoruba concept of development', *Journal of Development Studies* 14:135–65.

Peel, J.D.Y. (1983) *Ijeshas and Nigerians*, Cambridge: Cambridge University Press.

Peel, J.D.Y. (1984) 'Making history: the past in the Ijesha present', *Man* (NS) 19:111–32.

Peterson, J. (1969) *Province of Freedom: a History of Sierra Leone 1787–1870*, London: Faber & Faber.

Post, K.W.J. and Jenkins, G.D. (1973) *The Price of Liberty: Personality and Politics in Colonial Nigeria*, Cambridge: Cambridge University Press.

Sahlins, M. (1985) *Islands of History*, Chicago: University of Chicago Press.

Smith, A.D. (1981) *The Ethnic Revival*, Cambridge: Cambridge University Press.

Soyinka, W. (1982) *Ake: the Years of Childhood*, New York: Random House.

Chapter fourteen

Afrikaner Historiography and the Decline of Apartheid: ethnic self-reconstruction in times of crisis

Gerhard Schutte

Introduction

In this paper Afrikaner historiography will be viewed as a cultural product constructed at a particular time in history under prevailing social circumstances and interests. The existence of a number of Afrikaner historiographies is thus possible. As cultural products I am only interested in those written by Afrikaners on their own ethnic group and its genesis. The paper's focus will be further limited to recent or contemporary reconstructions of the past. The term historiography carries with it a broader connotation than academic convention would normally permit because I wish to include the discussion of 'folk' reconstructions of the past. It is inevitable that excursions into past historiographies will be made in order to illuminate the origin and content of their present counterparts, which, of course, will demonstrate selectivity in their reception and reproduction of past events.

Before proceeding any further, the unavoidable question about what the nature of Afrikaner identity is and which categories of people it embraces needs to be addressed. The answer is not an easy one. Cohen (1974:ix) distinguishes ethnicity and ethnic group. An ethnic group is operationally defined as 'a collectivity of people who (a) share some patterns of normative behaviour and (b) form part of a larger population, interacting with people from other collectivities within the framework of a social system'. The term ethnicity, according to Cohen, is the degree of conformity by members of the collectivity to these shared norms in the course of social interaction.

These definitions take an outsider, objectivist stance in defining the issues at hand. Although the definition of an ethnic group may to a certain extent apply to Afrikaners, the fact that there is such a wide divergence among them with regard to appropriate norms for behaviour requires a more flexible approach. I therefore propose to incorporate relevant aspects of Afrikaner self-definition into an operational concept of Afrikanerness thereby giving expression to the fact that these definitions shape Afrikaner self-concepts and patterns of social interaction.

In view of the fact that no one self-definition of Afrikaner identity exists but that a number of competing ones uncomfortably coexist, the question arises what common denominator of Afrikanerness do they maintain for themselves. Here, the ideology of common descent has great relevance in setting the boundaries of the group. Though controversial in its meaning, common descent from Dutch, French, and German stock is assumed. Room was left for the assimilation of members of other groups such as the Portuguese and English as long as they identified themselves culturally with the Afrikaners through the adoption of their language and mores and, ultimately through intermarriage. Bridging the 'racial' gap remained a most controversial issue.

Another important ethnic marker is identification with a language community. As a form of popular speech, Afrikaans had its origin in the kitchens and fields of eighteenth-century Cape colonists where Dutch, modified by the Malay dialects of slaves, provided the means of communication between master and servant. The language was given respectability in the late nineteenth century by the First Afrikaans Language Movement led by a number of White Cape intellectuals who encouraged people to 'write as they spoke' (Bot and Kritzinger, 1925:ix and xxv f). After the Anglo–Boer War, the Second Afrikaans Language Movement popularized the language within the context of Afrikaner nationalism. Today membership of the language community is a debated issue since there are Afrikaans speakers among all the racially defined population groups.

Afrikaner identity and the relevance of history

In a serious attempt to initiate dialogue on the issue of the interpretation of a crucial moment in Afrikaner history, a joint conference of theologians and historians was called in 1979 by their respective departments at the University of South Africa in Pretoria. F.A. van Jaarsveld, professor of history at the (exclusively White) Afrikaner University of Pretoria, delivered the first paper re-evaluating the significance of the battle of Blood River where the Boers conquered the Zulu. He used terms critical of the conventional Afrikaner nationalist mythology surrounding the event. After about five minutes of reading, a thirty-person contingent of the Afrikaner Weerstandsbeweging (AWB) (Afrikaner Resistance Movement) burst into the hall and poured tar and feathers over the speaker. The leader of the movement grabbed the microphone and read this statement to the bewildered gathering (translated from *Beeld* 29 March 1979):

As young Afrikaners we have reached the end of our tether. Our spiritual heritage and everything we consider holy to the Afrikaner are being trampled underfoot and desecrated by liberalist politicians, 'stray' (Afrikaner) academics and false prophets who hide under the cloak of learning and false religion like Professor Floors van Jaarsveld. In this symposium they defile the holiest of holies of the Afrikaner being. This (their) attitude is blasphemous and annuls the meaning of Afrikaner history.

The leader, Eugène Terre'Blanche, whose name (translated as White Earth) has symbolic significance to his followers, claimed that the Afrikaner knew how to deal with traitors and referred to the Anglo–Boer War hero Danie Theron who once sjambokked an English journalist who belittled Afrikaners.

This incident and its accompanying rhetoric illustrates the different meanings Afrikaner history has for the critical academic historian on the one hand and for the 'folk' historian on the other. Furthermore, it demonstrates the conflict that exists among Afrikaners with regard to their respective self-identifications. The ultra-conservative AWB clings to a timeless and historically fixed self-image that they are prepared to defend aggressively against alternative interpretations. They make a clear distinction between the true brand of young Afrikaners filled with vitality and harbouring the real spirit of Afrikanerness, and the straying members of their group who tend to undermine those valued spiritual and moral qualities. The notion of 'pure' Afrikanerness and the struggle to attain purification fill many pages of Afrikaner historiography on both sides of the liberal/conservative divide. Yet it is strange that the Afrikanerness of all participants in the conflict is staunchly upheld.

In an anthropological paper of this nature a relativist stance will be adopted in order to look at both Afrikaner academic historiography and the more popular versions as essentially cultural products generated within their respective social circumstances. Non-Afrikaner interpretations of Afrikaner history, though most important as corrective perspectives on the past, will not be discussed. These include the products of Black, Liberal, and Marxist scholarship (cf. Van Jaarsveld, 1984:4–7).

However, a number of historical sources written in a neoliberal or class-analytical vein by Afrikaans speakers should be mentioned.[1] They have been published mostly in English; in other words, addressed essentially to an academic community rather than to the broad spectrum of Afrikaners. Since 1984 though, their writings have reached an intellectual stratum of the Afrikaans public through newspapers and through the periodical *Die Suidafrikaan*. The wider public and politically influential Afrikaners take note of these alternative interpretations of history more by way of repressive tolerance than by incorporating these insights into 'Wirkungsgeschichte' or 'effective history' that would influence party politics or the structure of school syllabuses. Their potential for a redefinition or change of ethnic boundaries is a mildly corrective one though only abstractly so. The authors belong to a category of Cape Afrikaans intellectuals considered by mainstream Afrikaners and even by their own peers to be far out to the left of the spectrum.

Folk historiography and ethnic consciousness

Among all the controversy surrounding Apartheid and the Afrikaner today, it is most amazing that no up-to-date ethnography about this White 'tribe' exists. Many academic interpretations of the dominant discourse among leading Afrikaners can be traced[2] but very little had been written on the everyday lives and experiences of ordinary Afrikaners, especially of those living in towns.[3] Knowledge about their appropriation of the past is therefore largely lacking. Van Jaarsveld argues that the Afrikaner's tended to lose interest in their history after the Republic of South Africa was founded in 1961. To them the future became more important than the past (Van Jaarsveld, 1984:26,31). This may have been the case in the 1960s but political developments in the last decade, the emergence of right-wing Afrikaner politics, and the international community's view that the Afrikaners were expatriate settlers have prompted many sections of the Afrikaans population to re-examine the justification of their historical presence in the country. It is almost needless to elaborate on the fact that those reconstructions of the past that had been handed down through generations of school textbooks suddenly receive new topicality. The right-wingers are quick to manipulate this situation by increasing their influence in school boards. The more enlightened and intellectual Afrikaners attempt the formulation of alternative accounts that take cognisance of new developments in Africa.

What, then, is the content of this popular folk history? For source material I had to rely on numerous conversations, remarks, sermons, public speeches, narratives of the older members of my extended family, newspaper reports, and letters to the editors of Afrikaans newspapers. School textbooks provide a most important source of popularized history. J.M. Du Preez (1983) examines what he calls 'master symbols' in some fifty-three South African high-school textbooks. Fourteen history textbooks were subjected to thematic analyses.[4] Other textbooks covered such disciplines as Afrikaans and English literature, geography and social studies. The author then lists some twelve master symbols of an axiomatic nature that recur in the books. These are:

(a) Legitimate authority is not questioned.
(b) Whites are superior; Blacks are inferior.
(c) The Afrikaner has a special relationship with God.
(d) South Africa rightfully belongs to the Afrikaner.

(e) South Africa is an agricultural country; the Afrikaners are a farmer nation (*boerevolk*).
(f) South Africa is an afflictcd country.
(g) South Africa and the Afrikaner are isolated.
(h) The Afrikaner is militarily ingenious and strong.
(i) The Afrikaner is threatened.
(j) World opinion of South Africa is important (sic).
(k) South Africa is the leader in Africa.
(l) The Afrikaner has a God-given task in Africa.

(Du Preez, 1983:71)

Let us take these findings as a lead-in to the sketch of the contemporary folk view of the past. Most of these propositions have entered into Afrikaner self-consciousness by way of an ethnic reconstruction of history, repeated at school, in the media, and in popular discourse fuelled by sermons and political rhetoric.

Permeating the consciousness of religiously inclined Afrikaners, vastly the majority, is the idea that history is not accidental. Apart from the deeply held Calvinist-inspired belief in the ultimate authority of the Bible (*Sola Scriptura*), history is also believed to be a source of God's revelation to a specific people demonstrating His omnipotence and foresight. History is therefore no profane matter but it is filled with the divine plan of collective salvation. The individual finds salvation in the group God has called unto Him. It is as member of this group that the individual shares a common salvation and call. You are thus called as an Afrikaner to perform your life's work within the context of your group. God is the ultimate authority in heaven and on the earth. He instituted worldly authority and left His divine stamp on the 'natural' bearers of authority and wielders of power, namely the fathers and, to a lesser extent, the mothers, the older generation in general, but in particular on the political authorities and their executives. The xenotic[5] use of kinship terms in everyday language is of interest here. Afrikaans speakers would address members of the older generation as *oom* and *tante* (uncle, aunt). They in turn could demand respect and obedience from younger people. Although these practices have faded in middle-class town settings today, they are still widely prevalent in rural areas.

Depicting the past relativistically as folk history is at variance with the indigenous rendering of it. In this case the past is appropriated as sacrosanct. Historical actors are seen as heroes and are venerated in superhuman representations in literature, marble and bronze. The sacred tradition possesses authority and a standardization that allows for a narrow margin of interpretation or correction. It cannot be revised in any extensive way and should such revisions be undertaken by academics, they are seen as blasphemous.

The myth of Afrikaner ethnogenesis and group cohesion is traced back to the times of the first Dutch settlers in the seventeenth century. It was not until some 150 years ago that the Dutch speakers began acting in a corporate way. With the Great Trek in the mid-nineteenth century, they collectively became known as *Voortrekkers* (first pioneers). They called themselves *Boere* (farmers) although a certain Bibault was reported to have used the term 'Africaander' as far back as 1707 (Franken, 1953). In the pre-Trek era the notion of a people (*volk*) barely existed. There were small incidents of resistance to bad government but those that bore an anti-British sentiment received greater emphasis in historical accounts. The frontier experience in the eastern Cape of being wedged between the expanding southern Nguni and the British colonial force extending its domination, created among *Oosgrensboere* (farmers of the eastern border) a sense of solidarity in the early decades of the nineteenth century. They spoke the same language and embraced a form of religiosity modelled on that of the Old Testament patriarchs, whose semi-nomadic existence was quite similar to their own. It is during this period that the analogy with Israel as a people probably received its contours. The Boers considered their advance to the east and north Cape as justified. The British were the oppressors who prevented them in their task of opening up the country and subjecting the Blacks. Instead, the British delivered the Boers unto the barbaric forces of the heathen. The abolition of slavery was a further blow, since its practice was not seen as clashing with the precepts of the Bible.

The scene was thus set for the Boers defining themselves as the oppressed within the context of British colonialism. One of their leaders, P. Retief, summarized the nature of their oppression in a manifesto of 1837, which became one of the first documents that clearly defined the social boundary between the moral 'we'-group, the Boers, and the forces that surrounded them: the British, who acted in cahoots with the false prophets of Christianity, the missionaries, and with the heathens, the Blacks. The British were held to have attained unjustly their position of power and the Blacks were seen as inferior and pre-Christian, destined to be servants forever. How strong at that time the notion was that the Blacks were the children of Ham, I do not know. In his manifesto, Retief expressed the view that the Voortrekkers 'should adopt such regulations as will maintain the proper relationship between master and servant'.[6]

The constitutions of the Boer republics founded in the mid-nineteenth century contained clauses that explicitly excluded *Gelijkstelling* (equality). The same policy was adhered to by the various Afrikaans churches of which one, the Hervormde Kerk, even today upholds its Article 3 that excludes Black membership. A *Masters and Servants Act* remained in force well into the second half of this century.

During and after the Great Trek, Blacks were viewed as outcast, inferior, and dangerous to the Afrikaner. The xenophobia that haunts so much of Afrikaner history produced the notion of *Swart Gevaar* (Black danger): a danger that receives new contours in the context of contemporary Black emancipation.

The setting of ethnic boundaries by the Afrikaner cannot be properly understood without reference to the belief in their collective call by God to open up and tame the interior of the continent. Although disputed by academic historians, it is generally accepted by Afrikaners that the Voortrekkers entered into a Covenant with God before the Battle of Blood River. This Covenant established the Afrikaner as an elect people with an undisputed and exclusive right to the land as long as they remained obedient to God and followed His laws. Since the analogy with Israel is an explicit one, the injunction to maintain racial purity followed. Liaisons with Blacks were inconceivable and marriages to the English were also deemed to be some form of self-excommunication from the Afrikaner fold unless the stranger-incomer demonstrably identified her/himself with Afrikaner symbols and values.

The Voortrekkers and Afrikaners thus see themselves as landholders. Under the Calvinist-formulated precept of *Sola Gratia* they assumed they held the land by the grace of God. Their ownership was not deemed to be final but they believed they held the land as if it was granted by God as a trial, with the promise that, should they fulfil their calling, they would encounter prosperity and abundance and, ultimately, inherit the land for generations to come. To praise themselves for their achievements was therefore wrong because whatever they had was due to the grace of God. This humility is quite deceptive and never took account of Black perceptions of the situation. Furthermore, God subjected the Afrikaners to many ordeals using the Blacks and the British in the process. They therefore had to suffer great hardship before they could call their land their own. Hardship was but one of the tests of Afrikaner faith. Contemporary Afrikaners hold that the period between the beginning of the Great Trek and the establishment of the Boer Republics was a period of moral purification through suffering. This purification was deemed to be an act of God establishing the Afrikaners as a special and elect people whose destiny was predetermined. Suffering was therefore a source of strength rather than a debilitating moment in history.

The Anglo–Boer War inaugurated a second important phase in Afrikaner history. The old themes of purification through suffering reappear. The British were seen to be sent as a scourge. Their colonial expansionist tendencies were understood to be part of a larger plan that fitted the Afrikaner ethnocentric eschatology. God had a purpose with the humiliation of his people, namely to purify and sanctify them more than ever before. God's standards were set very high for His elect. The materialism and selfishness of the mineral- and money-grabbing British were contrasted with the righteous suffering of the Afrikaners, who were the designated holders of the land. Among all this suffering and humiliation the Afrikaners believed in the divine promise of justice through the restitution of their land.

The *South Africa Act* of 1909 and the subsequent unification of the country entrenched political rights for Whites. The old Boer generals, who adopted a conciliatory stance towards the English in the early decades of this century in taking on leading positions in the Union Government, fell into disfavour and were ultimately outvoted in the 1948 election, which put the (Afrikaner) National Party into power. This party established and consolidated Afrikaner political power and 'assured' internal peace through a policy of separation and unequal treatment whereby the Black masses were removed from the day-to-day experience of the Whites except where they were needed to minister to the needs of the powerful.

After the establishment of the Republic of South Africa in 1961, historical justifications for Afrikaner exclusivism in the political domain were less pronouncedly sought. The rumblings of African Nationalism during the following decade and the traumatic shootings at Sharpeville in the wake of passbook protests engendered fear and fostered a spirit of solidarity among Whites. The relationship between Afrikaans and English speakers remained uneasy. Afrikaners never felt comfortable with the more tolerant and liberal racial attitudes of the English. In the 1960s the Afrikaners' sense of insecurity further increased through their fear of communism. They started drawing boundaries between loyal and liberal Afrikaners. Their sense of insecurity was greatly enhanced with the Soweto Revolt of 1976 and the urban unrest of the 1980s. In the last two decades the National Party drew greater support from English speakers and so became even more popular. Its image of an exclusively Afrikaner party changed as a result of this but also because it suffered two breakaways by right-wing groupings through the formation of the *Herstigte Nasionale Party* (Re-established National Party) in 1969 and the founding of the *Konserwatiewe Party* (Conservative Party) in 1983. Though more diverse in their political organization now, Afrikaner solidarity with regard to group survival was stronger than ever before.

Today the old fear of a *Swart Gevaar* achieves new significance. Those elements of past history that highlight the precariousness of Afrikaner existence and their isolation, their having to 'go it alone' as a people whose birthright is endangered receive renewed emphasis. The liberal, multiracialism of the Progressive Federal Party (PFP) is viewed with distrust. Liberal politicians tried to play down the differences between English and Afrikaans supporters. They were only partly successful, however. At the beginning of 1987 a prominent member of the PFP with an Afrikaans name resigned, alleging that he felt discriminated against because of his Afrikanerness. This event was immediately taken up by an Afrikaans newspaper as evidence of *boerehaat* (hate of Afrikaners/Boers). This attitude reveals a suspicion towards liberal-minded English-speakers, who were not quite to be trusted and a realization that Afrikaners were, in the end, alone. On the other hand, though, one also encounters a range of pragmatic attitudes among them that would allow for a degree of social experimentation with other groups, including socializing with Coloureds and Asians.

It should be noted that the folk view of history so imbued with religious symbolism and legitimations and so strongly present in the Afrikaner self-image would be hard to modify. Ethnic boundaries receive a new salience and tend to harden under political pressure, especially on the right wing of the political spectrum where history is most strongly manipulated. The deeply embedded xenophobia of the *uitlander* (expatriate) who 'expropriated' the Afrikaner before the Great Trek and during the Anglo–Boer War is easily conjured up, and even nowadays, identified with the indigenous Black population whom Nationalist politicians tried so hard to strip of their citizenship.

Afrikaner academic historiography and the setting of ethnic boundaries

As early as the First Language Movement, S.J. du Toit, and other pioneers of Afrikaans published *Die Geskiedenis vans ons Land in die Taal vans ons Volk* (The history of our country in the language of our people Du Toit, *et al.*, 1877). Later historians made the point that English-language histories distorted the image of the Afrikaner and they persisted in not only setting the record straight but also in enhancing the reputation of Afrikaner heroes, especially among schoolchildren. It is remarkable how this need was felt both among Cape Afrikaners and those of the two Boer republics. A positive image of the Afrikaner was derived from the Voortrekker and the Republican Boer. Prior to the Anglo–Boer War, these anti cultural-imperialist symbols were shared by Afrikaners of the north and the south. After the war though, Afrikaners were increasingly seen as inhabitants of the Transvaal and Orange Free State. Cape Afrikaners were accorded the image of a tolerant, easygoing, urban, and bourgeois population, prone to suffering from 'English-sickness', i.e. liberalism. Since the Cape Colony was not involved in the war, its population escaped the suffering it brought with it. The British Anglicization policy that followed affected the Transvaalers and Free Staters more, and it was in this context that the Afrikaner historiography of the first years of this century was produced. Afrikaner historians felt the need to restore a feeling of self to the Afrikaner and consciously engaged in constructing myths of origin. They maintained that a thorough knowledge of one's people's history was a prerequisite for a sense of identity. Afrikanercentric historiography has persisted until the present (see the list of 'master symbols' cited on p. 219–20). It was sometimes explicitly cast in a functional mould of exhorting the readers, especially the youth, to pursue national-istic ideals – even at the expense of truth: G. van N. Viljoen, Rector of the Rand Afrikaans University in Johannesburg and later Minister of Education wrote as late as 1971:

[A people (*volk*)] has the need for myths to help support their ethnic existence. Even in those cases where their content is incongruent with the objective external historical or contemporary reality, it may yet mirror certain internal values and ideals that bind the community toge-ther through their acceptance of and faith in it. [Myth] . . . has an inspiring value in a people's life. It has the value of creating ideals, positing norms and integrating the people. . . . To debunk or to demy-thologise such a conviction can have a debilitating and destructive effect on a people.[7]

(Viljoen, 1978)

This Afrikanercentric view of history revealed yet another dimension as the struggle towards national political hegemony began. In addition to the necessity of overcoming the English sentiment in the country, the ubiqui-tous presence of the vast Black population was defined as a problem. All White interest groups seem to have agreed on the principle of territorial segregation after Unification. It was not until the 1930s that apartheid was seen as the solution. P. van Biljon published his PhD thesis of 1937, *Grensbakens tussen Blank en Swart in Suid-Afrika*[8] (Boundary Markers between Black and White in South Africa) in 1947, after it found wide acclaim among Afrikaans audiences. He argued that apartheid typified the Afrikaner's national race policy at best. To Afrikaner Nationalists, apartheid was not the same as the pragmatic segregation practised before 1948. Apartheid constitutes the final solution to the 'racial question' (Van Jaarsveld, 1979:9).

However, before 1960 the complete segregation of White and Black was only seen as an ideal by Afrikaner pragmatists. Around the 1960s though, historians such as G.D. Scholtz (*Die Gevaar uit die Ooste* – The Oriental Threat) (1957) and H.J.J.M. van der Merwe (*Segregeer of Sterf* – Segregate or Perish) (1961) insisted that total territorial segregation was necessary unless Afrikaners wished the downfall and disappearance of the Whites in the country. Any halfhearted approach to segregation would be detrimental to Afrikaner and, therefore, to White survival.

The criteria used to define the boundaries between Black, Briton, and Afrikaner varied through time. On a primary level, predating the Great Trek, religion was the great divider between Christian and heathen. Some-where along the line, pariah/labourer status was added as a differentiating factor. Blacks were now seen as both heathen and destined to hard labour.[9] The picture became more complex when the British arrived. As noted, their liberal and egalitarian ideas were completely foreign to Afrikaners who were opposed to the *gelijkstelling* (equality) such attitudes were seen to harbour. The notion of a radical segregation was motivated by the fear of miscegenation that would inevitably destroy Afrikaner distinctness and identity. Scholtz (1957:200) saw the incorporation of Black labour into the national economy as the thin end of the wedge of integration. His clarion call for White-labour self-sufficiency sounded strangely anachronistic in view of the existing economic interdependence of White and Black. Nevertheless, at the end of the 1960s, the views of these historians also heralded the decline of the pragmatic attitude to strict segregation among politicians.

Let us therefore follow another strain in historical philosophy that contributed to extremer forms of segregationism. Between the world wars, many Afrikaans intellectuals studied on the European continent, especially in Holland. Without going into too much detail, one of the Dutch intellectual strains Afrikaner thinking found great affinity for was the reinterpretation of Calvinism by the theologian–statesman Abraham Kuyper. Kuyper maintained that organic social groups existed within the wider framework of society and that their existence could be theologically justified. This justification of the parallel existence of social and cultural groups within a wider society was just what Afrikaner educationists wanted for legitimating a separate educational system for Afrikaans children. Combining these thoughts with the nineteenth-century European tendency to romanticize language communities and given a lingering anti-British imperialism, the stage was set for the implementation of a Christian–National education policy. But more than that, these thoughts theologically underpinned the existence and creation of separate social, cultural, and political structures within the wider geographic configuration of South Africa. In 1947, a sociologist and two theologians published *Regverdige Rasse-apartheid* (Just Racial Apartheid) (Cronjé *et al.*, 1947) in which these points were underscored.

Although Afrikaner intellectual life was strongly influenced by National Socialism before and after World War Two, it was the theological justification of social and cultural parallelism that provided the moral escape hatch for the Verwoerdian notion of 'separate development'. Suddenly the monolithic category of 'Black' was looked at in a differentiated way. Black people were still a separate category but this overall racial categorization was now underplayed in favour of cultural diversity expressed in the assumed existence of discrete ethnic units. School history books followed this trend and taught children about the different 'Bantu' peoples. Ethnicity also became an important theme in the disciplines of political science and ethnology at Afrikaans universities. Graduates with the appropriate emphases in their degrees found ample employment opportunities in civil service departments concerned with the administration of Black affairs.

In the 1950s and 1960s, anthropology, but more specifically ethnology (*Volkekunde*) was co-opted by government agencies to document the 'histories' of the politically discovered ethnic units in order to assist the rulers in determining their territorial boundaries. These boundaries were adjusted within the framework of the 13.7 per cent of the country's area set aside for Blacks in 1936.

South Africa's Afrikaner politicians further attempted to 'scientify' their policies by adopting the model and concept of a plural society. The pluralist perspective provided politicians and historians with a scientific and neutral perspective. The otherwise 'enlightened' Afrikaner historian, F.A. van Jaarsveld writes:

> The recognition of ethnicity that by no means has become extinct in the present world does not necessarily amount to racism because South African society consists of historically identifiable communities. Together they will form a plural South African nation. This is different to a multiracial unitary state or to ethnic integration. Preservation of identity and group autonomy is the purpose of democratic pluralism.
>
> (van Jaarsveld, 1979:22)

The pluralist perspective and the emphasis on ethnic pluralism in the international social-scientific discourse of the 1970s added scientific respectability to the politics of inequality in South Africa.

Among establishment historians with their wide readership and constituency among Afrikaner politicians, teachers, and ministers of religion, one encounters a fairly consistent line of reasoning: the Afrikaner is in jeopardy. As a people they are endangered by tremendous forces. Yet, they have survived amongst these tremendous odds. The way in which they survived was for many, first and foremost, through the will of God but also through their divinely sanctioned separateness, which helped them retain their distinctness, racial purity, and moral standing. When industrialization and commercial farming made strict separation of Black and White impossible, caste-like barriers were erected. In recent decades, however, the radical separatist idea has been modified in favour of a pluralist notion in which discrete ethnic groups received recognition. Even the more liberal Afrikaans establishment historians would not go beyond this conceptualization, since the utmost preoccupation with the preservation of the *volk* as an ethnic group obsesses the mind of even very enlightened Afrikaners. The self-preservation of the Afrikaners is, of course, not a purely ethnic matter in South Africa, since Whites in general feel that their fate is tied to that of the Afrikaners.

Afrikaner ethnicity and the future of South Africa

Drawing on a view of history that maintains on both the folk and academic levels the importance of ethnic separateness, it is hard to envisage how Afrikaners will adapt to a future Black-majority-ruled South Africa. I estimate that about a third of Afrikaans speakers support right-wing parties. These parties propose a socio-political model that would ensure the preservation of ethnic identity by territorial separation – thus, a return to the ideal of physical apartheid, where Whites with the Afrikaners as their core would politically dominate. Right-wing parties vary with regard to the extent to which they would allow Black labourers without civil rights into their territory. To them, ethnicity is a total identity embracing the cultural, political, economic, territorial, and even religious domains. This model of the Afrikaner is one that dogmatically maintains separateness or apartheid as a necessary condition for ethnic survival.

A second view would maintain that strong ethnic solidarity among Afrikaners was a condition for the survival of all ethnic groups in the country. The Whites with the Afrikaner as the solidarized core must remain in control in order to prevent competition for power among other ethnic groups. Such competition, it is believed, would lead to massive internecine conflicts among groups, for no one Black ethnic group would subject itself to the political domination of another. This view of a potential future scenario is justified with ample reference to South African 'Black' history and to events in other independent African states. Afrikaner political solidarity is thus seen as the saving grace for the country by holding back the unbridled forces of Black power-grabbing. (The *swart gevaar* attitude reappears here in a contemporary guise.) This perspective is prevalent among a great number of National Party supporters. It reflects the pragmatic attitude to separateness and apartheid as means of ensuring the survival of all ethnic groups in the country. Simultaneously, Afrikaner identity, power, and interests are consolidated in this position.

The third perspective recognizes the inevitability of the participation of the total South African population in the political process. Supporters maintain that group rights rather than individual rights ought to be constitutionally enshrined and that power should be shared among these groups. Such power sharing would guarantee the continued existence of various groupings. How these groups would be constituted is not always clearly stated. However, it is quite clear that Whites would form such a group and their rights ought to be protected. As far as the Afrikaners are concerned, this would guarantee their continued existence as a separate group without being overwhelmed or displaced by any others. Although this position is adhered to by more enlightened supporters of the National Party, and by some Afrikaners to the right of the Progressive Federal Party (PFP) (until May, 1987 the official opposition in parliament), it lies remarkably close to its political right-wing counterpart. The first position sketched previously adheres to a dogmatic separatism that aims at its territorial expression. It thus accepts Afrikaner political-minority status within the total geographic configuration of the country. The 'liberal' counterpart to this version accepts the ethnic and political-minority status of the Afrikaner within common geopolitical borders. Afrikaners in this category adopt a less partisan view of their past that allows for fairness in historical interpretation and a critical attitude to their forebears.

Finally, there are some Afrikaans intellectuals who maintain that Black-majority rule is inevitable. To them, political power is no longer a guarantee for Afrikaner survival. The Afrikaner ethnicity of the future would be a cultural and social one. The ethnic boundary would not be racially fixed but would be based on the identification with the language and culture. As an ethnic entity, the Afrikaners will survive in a multiparty democratic state because they will use their votes judiciously by allying themselves with those political forces willing to guarantee their continued existence. These intellectuals note that Afrikaners have been realists throughout their history and have never committed suicide by taking on vastly superior forces. They rather tended to maximize their opportunities rationally and resourcefully exploited to their own advantage the new system that was imposed on them after the Anglo–Boer War. The Afrikaners nowadays, it is maintained, have reached historical 'maturity' and are prepared to rewrite their history in a conciliatory fashion, realizing that they were not the elect few who conquered the interior of the country on a divine mandate, but that they were caught up in a world-historical phase of imperialist expansion.

Very few Afrikaners hold this intellectualist view, which differs in most important respects from the others because it breaks with the ascriptive construction of ethnicity and introduces the notion of individual choice and identification as the basis for Afrikanerness.

Notes

1. See Giliomee and Elphick (eds), 1979 and especially Giliomee and Du Toit, 1983.
2. See, for example, Moodie, 1975; Adam, 1971; and Wilkinson and Strydom, 1978; and most recently Adam and Moodley, 1986.
3. Du Toit, 1974, Russel and Russel, 1979, and Crapanzano, 1985 all deal with rural Afrikaners or with special cases of rural isolation.
4. The author attempts to apply a specific form of content analysis to the material. Thematic analysis was chosen rather than lexical or semantic analysis and involves the classification of explicit and implicit themes as they occur.
5. 'Xenotic use' here means addressing strangers in kinship terms.
6. Quoted in Scholtz, 1961.
7. Translated from Afrikaans from Viljoen, 1978:71. The quote comes from a speech made in 1971.

Gerhard Schutte

8. Quoted in Stals, 1974. This is an inaugural lecture held at the Randse Afrikaanse Universiteit. The addendum contains a very complete bibliography on
   the historiography of Black–White relations in South Africa.
9. Oral evidence from older Afrikaners indicates that the term *kamsketels* was
   used for many generations to describe Blacks. It literally means that they were
   the kettles of Ham, the biblical figure – black kettles. The Afrikaner generation
   of the post-Anglo–Boer-War period sometimes saw Blacks as damned beings;
   damned to toil and labour; people whose condition was unalterable in principle
   but who could experience some relief from that state by associating themselves
   with Whites as labourers. They were privileged to have Whites in their midst
   since it is they who brought civilization and Christian decency. Blacks, though,
   were trapped in their barbarism and heathenism and would never equal the
   Whites. These Whites maintained *eenmaal 'n kaffer, altyd 'n kaffer* (once a
   kaffir, always a kaffir). (Original meaning of kaffir: infidel.)

References

Adam, H. (1971) *Modernizing Racial Domination*, Berkeley: University of Califor-
nia Press.
Adam, H. and Moodley, K. (1986) *South Africa Without Apartheid: Dismantling
Racial Domination*, Berkeley: University of California Press.
Bot, A.K. and Kritzinger, M.S.B. (eds) (1925) *Letterkundige Leesboek*, Pretoria:
J.L. van Schaik.
Cohen, A. (ed.) (1974) 'Introduction' in *Urban Ethnicity*, ASA monograph series
12, London: Tavistock.
Crapanzano, V. (1985) *Waiting, the Whites of South Africa*, New York: Random
House.
Cronjé, G., Nicol, W., and Groenewald, E.P. (1947) *Regverdige Rasse-apartheid.
'n Diepdringende Beligting van ons Blank-nieblank Verhoudinge teen die Agter-
grondsituasie van Kontak, Integrasie en/of Segregasie van die Kleurgroepe*, Stel-
lenbosch: Christelike Uitgewers Maatskappy.
Du Preez, J.M. (1983) *Africana Afrikaner. Master Symbols in South African School
Textbooks*, Alberton: Librarius.
Du Toit, B.M. (1974) *People of the Valley*, Cape Town: Balkema.
Du Toit, S.J., Hoogenhout, C.P., and Malherbe, G.J. (1877) *Die Geskiedenis
van ons Land in die Taal van ons Volk*, Cape Town: Genootskap van Regte
Afrikaners.
Franken, J.L.M. (1953) *Taalhistoriese Bydraes*, Cape Town: Balkema.
Giliomee, H. and du Toit, A. (1983) *Afrikaner Political Thought: Analysis and
Documents, vol. 1, 1780–1850*, Cape Town: David Philip.
Giliomee, H. and Elphick, R. (eds) (1979) *The Shaping of South African Society
1652–1920*, London: Longmans.
Moodie, T.D. (1975) *The Rise of Afrikanerdom*, Berkeley: University of California
Press.
Russel, M. and Russel, M. (1979) *Afrikaners of the Kalahari*, Cambridge: Cam-
bridge University Press.
Scholtz, G.D. (1957) *Die Gevaar uit die Ooste*, Johannesburg: Voorwaarts.
Scholtz, G.D. (1961) 'The origins and essence of the race pattern in South Africa',
SABRA fact paper.
Stals, E.L.P. (1974) *Die Verhouding tussen Blankes en Nie-blankes in die Suid-
Afrikaanse Geskiedskrywing*, Johannesburg, Rand: Afrikaans University (Publi-
cation series A64).

Van Biljon, P. (1947) *Grensbakens tussen Blank en Swart in Suid-Afrika. 'n Historiese ontwikkeling van Grensbeleid en Grondtoekenning aan die Naturel in Suid-Afrika*, Cape Town: Juta.

Van der Merwe, H.J.J.M. (1961) *Segregeer of Sterf*, Johannesburg: Afrikaanse Pers Boekhandel.

Van Jaarsveld, F.A. (1979) *Die Evolusie van Apartheid*, Cape Town: Tafelberg.

Van Jaarsveld, F.A. (1984) *Omstrede Afrikaanse verlede. Geskiedenis, Ideologie en die Historiese Skuldvraagstuk*, Johannesburg: Lex Patria.

Viljoen, G. van N. (1978) *Ideaal en Werklikheid*, Cape Town: Tafelberg.

Wilkinson, I. and Strydom, H. (1978) *The Super-Afrikaners, inside the Broederbond*, Johannesburg: Jonathan Ball.

Chapter fifteen

Ethnic Identities and Social Categories in Iran and Afghanistan
Richard Tapper

The populations of Iran and Afghanistan are heterogeneous according to relatively objective criteria: language, religion or sect, local or tribal affiliation, productive activity, wealth, and so on. The size and distribution of groups classified according to such criteria can be and have been depicted in official and scholarly tables and maps. But what these criteria, and groups based on them, mean for people so classified, is not so easily established.

This paper examines the basis for the construction of 'ethnic' identities and social categories in these two countries, considering both official and popular discourses, as well as the influence of historiography, human geography, and ethnography. Whereas official and academic categories are simple and clear-cut, being used for administrative and comparative purposes, the identities and categories of popular discourse, having to cope with everyday, face-to-face political and social realities, are complex and essentially flexible and ambiguous. These themes are illustrated and explored through the cases of the Shahsevan of Iran and the Durrani of Afghanistan.[1]

Academic discourse on ethnicity

In 1969, F. Barth and A. Cohen, both familiar with the Middle East, published books that inspired a generation of anthropological research on ethnicity. They were slow to affect research on the Middle East, however, where social and political scientists, as well as ethnographers, continued until recently, with few exceptions, to accept Coon's classic 'mosaic' model (1958) of a 'diversity of peoples and cultures', with its implicit assumption that ethnic groups were biological units of fixed membership. A major research aim in Middle Eastern ethnography was historical and geographic in nature: to establish the 'real' identity of ethnic groups by mapping their territorial distribution, tracing their origins and movements in time, and listing their 'fundamental characteristics'.

Ethnographers, historians, and political scientists play a crucial and largely unrecognized role as creators and manipulators of identities (cf. Ovesen, 1983). Our supposedly objective findings and analyses are used by policy makers to create order, both classificatory and political. Those of us working in the Middle East who, following conventional practice, sought out and 'appropriated' for study some exotic tribal, nomadic, or minority group, justified our choice by asserting both the representativeness of our particular study for that group, and the cultural uniqueness of the group. This enabled generalists to summarize the group: so many people, occupying such a territory, practising such a way of life. Our findings are conveniently summarized in maps and tables showing numbers, distribution, and fundamental traits of different named groups.

Ten years ago, criticisms of this kind of exercise began to penetrate writings on Iran and Afghanistan. Jon Anderson (1978), Pierre Centlivres (for example, 1979; 1980) and others working on Afghanistan, showed how the complexities of ethnic and other groupings in that country were completely glossed over by the mosaic-type approach, and how identities were essentially changing, flexible, multiple, and negotiable.

Official categories of society

Official categorizations of the population have differed significantly as between the two countries. In Iran economic, political, and class characteristics have been stressed, while in Afghanistan, cultural criteria (kinship/ descent, language, religion) have been more prominent. In part these differences relate to contrasts in physical and cultural geography, which should first be outlined.

The dominant physical feature of Afghanistan is its mountainous backbone, inhabited by several religious, linguistic, and tribal minorities, such as Imami and Isma'ili Shi'ites and the formerly pagan peoples of Nuristan. The Sunni majority, including the politically dominant Pashtuns/Pakhtuns and the Uzbek and Tajik minorities, inhabit towns and villages in the surrounding steppes, plateaux, and hills. All the major groups straddle the national frontiers, with fellow-members in Iran, Pakistan, and the Soviet Union: even the 'land-locked' Hazaras, as Shi'ites, often look to co-religionists in Iran.

The centre of Iran, on the other hand, is a vast plateau surrounded by mountain ranges and steppes, the main areas of settlement being in or on the fringes of the plateau, where the urban, peasant, and tribal populations belong to the majority Shi'ite sect or to the non-Muslim minorities. The remoter mountains and steppes are chiefly occupied by linguistic minorities, often tribally organized and of the Sunni sect, and mostly, again, straddling the frontiers.

Persian is the language most understood in both countries, though the major tribal groups and the ruling dynasties (before the Pahlavis in Iran, and up to 1978 in Afghanistan) were not originally Persian-speaking. Most cities have long been centres of Persian language and civilization, which has often proved stronger in the long run than invading tribal cultures. Iran, however, has always been more a city-oriented society, Afghanistan more a confederation of tribal groups. The dominant cleavage in Iranian society until recently was between Turk (militarily dominant but 'uncouth' tribes, usually nomads) and Tat or Tajik (subordinated but 'civilized' townspeople and peasants). This is to some extent parallelled in Afghanistan by a cleavage, not between tribe and non-tribe, nor between nomad and settled, but between Pashtun (Afghans) and the rest, whether urban, peasant, or tribal.

In Afghanistan, the official conception is of a 'homeland' (*watan, heywād*) or 'country' (*mamlakat*) populated by a 'nation' (*mellat, wolus*) divided into 'peoples' (*qaum, tāyfa*), by which is usually implied a distinct linguistic and religious identity, often region of origin or residence, though not occupation or class. The main *qaum* are tribally subdivided, but discussion of 'tribes' (*qabila*, also *qaum, tāyfa*), as traditional support or opposition to the ruling elite, tends to denote Pashtun tribal divisions; the Ministry of Tribes and Nationalities deals mainly with the groups of the Pakistan frontier – Pashtun and Baluch.

The official conception in Iran is of a 'homeland' (*vatan, meyhan*) or 'country' (*keshvar*) inhabited by a 'people' (*mellat, mardom, qoum*). Divisions of the people are less clearly distinguished. Until recently, the only groups referred to as *agaliyat* (minority) were the non-Muslims (Christians, Jews, Zoroastrians), who have played a more significant role than in Afghanistan. Other terms used for variously defined groups are *tabaqeh* ('class' in a broad sense), *goruh* (group), *jamā'at* (community). *Tabaqeh* in particular has an established usage among urban populations, while the population at large is classified by the use of suffixes like *-neshin* (-dweller), as in *shahrneshin* (city-dweller), *chādor-neshin* (tent-dweller), and many others; or *-zabān* (-speaker), as in *tork-zabān* (Turkish-speaker). The terms *qoum* or *tāyfeh* may be used of major linguistic or tribal groups, but far less frequently than their equivalents in Afghanistan. A major category of the population is *ilāt va 'ashāyer* (the tribes), which often appears to subsume non-tribal linguistic and regional minorities. *Ilāt* (see Lambton, 1971) has long been used both in indigenous court chronicles and by European historians, usually with the connotations that tribes have chiefs, are organized on a basis of descent, and are pastoral nomads. This official construction of 'tribes' has influenced perceptions of such groups not only by non-tribal outsiders (including academics) but the tribespeople themselves.

During the twentieth century, rulers of both countries have been concerned with the 'national integration' of their heterogeneous populations, hoping, as in other newer nations, that economic and political development would bring the withering of cultural, regional, and tribal distinctions. Governments pursued discriminatory policies against linguistic and cultural minorities, for example, allowing teaching and publication only in official languages. The Pahlavis attempted to Persify the population of Iran; the later Durrani rulers, particularly Daud, tried to Pashtunize Afghanistan. Minority religious groups also suffered intermittent oppression. The most vigorous policies were those of Reza Shah in Iran: perceiving the nomad tribes as a major political threat, he acted particularly harshly against them, disarming them, imprisoning their chiefs, and later forcibly settling them. Such policies have sometimes backfired, inspiring previously non-existent or dormant separatist movements, or leading to the emergence of opposition based on other criteria such as class.

In recent decades, new trends have emerged. Abandoning cruder policies of national integration, governments have openly recognized cultural pluralism. This now has the effect, if not the aim, of allowing a degree of 'retribalization' among the national minorities, while partially defusing the threat to government and local elites posed by the emergence of sectarian or class-based opposition. In Iran by the 1970s, after decades of oppression and neglect of tribal and regional minorities, their threat to the state was officially held to have disappeared, and their cultures were 'discovered' as respectable objects of academic and touristic interest. However, growth of opposition to the regime, though largely urban, found strong echoes among some linguistic and tribal minorities, especially Sunni groups straddling the frontiers. Whatever the political colour of the various movements, they demonstrated increasing resentment of political discrimination at both local and national levels and of the imposition of outsiders in positions of authority, and articulated aspirations for some regional autonomy and the right to cultural self-expression. Under Khomeyni, this process has apparently continued, though Higgins (1984) argues that discrimination is now directed more at religious than linguistic minorities.

In Afghanistan too, during the 1970s there was a brief recognition of the rights of minorities such as Uzbeks and Baluches to cultural self-expression, for example via radio time. Since 1978, governments have further promoted a Soviet-style 'nationalities policy', designed apparently both to undermine unity of opposition to the regime and to prepare the way for eventual assimilation of non-Pashtun groups in the north with the nationalities of Soviet Central Asia. The nature of the regimes and their policies has, however, fostered the religious solidarity of the linguistically and tribally varied resistance groups.

Popular discourses on identity

Popular discourses are distinct from, but both influenced by and influencing official discourses. Here, we must make a further distinction, between terms that denote bases of identity and those labels and names that constitute identities.

Afghan popular discourse uses three main terms for bases of identity: *qaum*, *watan*, and *mazhab*. The first two have meanings ranging far beyond their use in official discourse; all three are ambiguous, or rather polysemic, but to varying degrees.

Most definitive is *mazhab* (sect), whose main ambiguity is a question of scope or level: for example Muslim → Shi'ite → Isma'ili. Canfield (1984) suggests that *mazhab* is the prior basis of identity, but it is part of regular discourse only in certain regions and contexts of confrontation between Sunnis and Shi'ites and between Imami and Isma'ili Shi'ites. Elsewhere, competing political and economic interests divide Sunni groups, which are also distinguished by language, culture, or tribe, and each side may accuse the other of 'irreligiosity', while one is often politically allied with the local Shi'ites (Tapper, 1984a,b). Perhaps *din* (religion) is even more fundamental, not only in external confrontations with non-Muslims but as a basis for the evaluation of the conduct of fellow-Muslims.

Watan (homeland) is ambiguous both as to place (village, valley, district, province, region, nation) and time (place of origin, or of residence). Identity based on *watan* is very strong for most people – even nomads identify themselves with their *watan* (usually winter quarters) and the varied population there, as against fellow-tribespeople or nomads from other regions.

Qaum, finally, is perhaps the term most widely used among Afghans (and researchers) for social groups and identity. Its use in Afghan contexts has recently been discussed in detail by various writers.[2] It implies common origins and basic cultural unity and identity. The most used markers of *qaum*-membership are stereotypes of language, dress, food customs, comportment, and somatology. Among its connotations are 'ethnic group' and 'tribe', but it can be both broader and narrower than these: not merely 'nation' but also descent group at all levels, and linguistic, sectarian, regional, or occupational group. Perhaps most often it implies linguistic and/or tribal identity. It is a highly ambiguous and flexible concept, allowing scope for strategic manipulations of identity, as we shall see.

There are no common terms that cover all categories of occupation or class as bases for identity, but various categories of occupation and status are regularly ranked hierarchically. In some urban contexts, especially where there is a form of guild organization, trades, crafts, and other occupations may be the major basis of identity, overriding if not implying others. Otherwise, at least until the 1970s, objective class positions (based on occupation or relation to the means of production) did not command loyalties stronger than those to *qaum*, *watan*, or *mazhab*.

In Iran, *mazhab* and *din* are as fundamental to identity as in Afghanistan, but again they are potentially the stuff of discourse only in the limited areas of contact. Non-Muslim minorities (including Baha'i and Ahl-e Haqq as well as Christians, Jews, and Zoroastrians) are mainly Persian-speakers, resident in towns and cities, where they often concentrate in particular economic activities, and are subject to consequent prejudice. Between Sunni and Shi'ite, on the other hand, relations are complicated by the fact that the main Sunni groups (Baluch, Turkmen, Kurds, Arabs, and others) are also geographically peripheral, tribal, and (unlike the Shi'ite minority in Afghanistan) linguistic minorities.

Among the Shi'ite majority in Iran, bases of distinction and identity appear to be implicit in the names and labels used. *Vatan* and *qoum* have rather narrower usage than in Afghanistan: *vatan* and *mellat* are more current for the country and people of Iran, while *qoum* may be used for a major linguistic group, but more often in a strict family/descent group sense. In an interaction between strangers, language, region, town, or urban quarter of origin and/or residence, as well as way of life, occupation, and class, can normally be ascertained from manner of speaking, appearance, and answers to the standard question, *ahl-e kojā-i?* (Where are you from?) Character stereotypes abound for each such name or label, and both bases of identity and classification and actual identities (names and labels) tend to be used dichotomously, marking we/they distinctions.[3]

Actual names and labels, furthermore, tend to be highly ambiguous and flexible in meaning, though this ambiguity takes a different form in each country. First, we should recall the factor that is essential to, if not determinative of this ambiguity. Given the history of spontaneous and forced population movements into and around the area, none of the main tribal or linguistic groups are racially or historically homogeneous. Genealogies and pedigrees are often well known to be inventions. Some tribal groups have no shared genealogy, but rather refer to a historical (mythical) event by which they were formed. Yet other groups do not even pretend to common origins or any such basic 'ethnic' assumption, though maintaining an ethnic identity of cultural–political separateness. Anyone with close knowledge of the culture, social organization, legends, and recorded history of any of the supposedly homogeneous groups in these countries will know that its origins are in fact heterogeneous and that any notions of common descent are mythical.

Most groups do have genealogies or stories of common origins, but these represent not a pure line of descent from the origin or founders of the group but a disputed and changing ideological charter for present-day social and cultural relations among members of the group and a basis for claims as against other groups. Shared and distinctive language, religion, customs, are the product, not of generations of isolation from others, but of processes of assimilation, negotiation, accommodation, and social construction, in a context of power relations with the state and with competing groups. Essential to these proccsscs is thc ambiguity of the names and labels concerned.

In Afghanistan the greatest ambiguity is between different *qaum*-names, that is labels with primarily language or descent-reference.[4] *Qaum*-names that are also language names are the most ambiguous in usage. One of the best known is 'Pashtun', used by most Pashtuns thcmsclvcs and by foreign writers as the standard label for all Pashto-speakers, but rarely so used by members of other groups, who call Pashtuns 'Afghan', as do some Pashtuns themselves. For most Pashtuns, however, the defining criteria are not language or religion, which one can change, but recognized descent from the ancestor of all Pashtuns and the practice of endogamy. 'Uzbek', generally denoting speakers of Uzbeki, is also a label used loosely by some Pashtuns in the north for all non-Pashtuns. 'Tajik' (in most of the country) is a residual category of Persian-speakers who are not tribally organized and are mostly Sunni Muslims. 'Parsiwan' (lit. Persian-speaker) is an identity ascribed in different contexts to a variety of categories of people, few of whom use it of themselves. In the north-central region, for example, Turkic-speakers refer loosely to all non-Turkic-speakers, including Pashtuns, as 'Parsiwan'; Pashtuns use the term similarly for all non-Pashto-speakers, including Turkic-speakers; Durrani Pashtuns use it more precisely for non-Durrani Pashto-speakers who like themselves came originally from the south-west.[5]

Others (Baluch, Moghol, Arab) call themselves by names indicating languages they no longer speak. Baluches in Saripul, for example, culturally and linguistically resemble the neighbouring Durrani Pashtuns, by whom they are classed as Parsiwan; while Baluches to the northeast are Tajik in all but name (Centlivres, 1979:27–8). Most major *qaum*-names, such as Pashtun or Baluch, include the widest conceivable variations in language, culture, and political affiliations (cf. Barth, 1969).

In Iran the ambiguities are rather different. Far more frequently than in Afghanistan, names of tribal and linguistic groups are also the names of regions. Most inhabitants of Azarbayjan, Baluchistan, Kurdistan, Luristan, Arabistan (Khuzistan), speak the languages to which those names also refer. Residents of Bakhtiari, Mamasani, Boir Ahmad, Qaradagh, and other regions commonly belong to the tribal groups bearing the same names. Some names (Kurd, Lur, Shahsevan, Arab, Baluch), officially denoting linguistic or tribal identity, locally connote 'tented nomads'. Other apparent linguistic labels in practice connote political allegiance: in Fars, for example, the Qashqa'i, many of whom speak Luri, are 'Turks', while their neighbours and historical rivals, the Khamseh, who are mostly Turkish or Persian-speakers, are 'Arabs'.

Cultural identities, whether ethnic or otherwise, make sense only in social contexts, and they are essentially negotiable and subject to strategic manipulations. Individuals claim status, present themselves, in different ways in different contexts. How they do so depends particularly on power relations, government policies, and local hierarchies. Numerous cases of permanent changes of ethnic identity by groups or individuals have been reported; for example, in Azarbayjan, from Turk to Kurd and vice versa, and from Shahsevan to Tat and vice versa; or from Pashtun to Baluch in western Pakistan (Barth, 1969) but vice versa in northern Afghanistan. Other minority groups (Moghol, Arab) adapt culturally to a variety of different neighbours without losing their identity. In many areas it is common for an individual to claim a variety of identities that would be mutually exclusive in other contexts. In other cases, individuals claim a particular identity and insist on its exclusivity: it goes without saying that those who insist loudest on ethnic purity are likely to be those with either a skeleton in the cupboard or a wolf at the door!

Many of these themes are illustrated in the following contrasting accounts of historical consciousness and ethnic identity among the Shahsevan of north-western Iran and the Durrani of northern Afghanistan.

Shahsevan

Shahsevan is the name of a collection of tribal groups – Turkish-speaking Shi'ites – brought together some time between the sixteenth and eighteenth centuries in eastern Azarbayjan. By the twentieth century, they had acquired three rather different versions of their origins.

The conventional version identifies the Shahsevan as a heterogeneous group formed by Shah 'Abbas the Great in around 1600 into a special tribe of his personal followers (hence the name Shahsevan, 'who love the Shah'). There is no historical evidence to support this story, which is based on a misreading of chronicle sources by Malcolm (1815); it was none the less adopted by later historians and has been assimilated into Iranian and, through modern education, current Shahsevan mythology. Another version comprises a variety of traditions, recorded from Shahsevan leaders mainly in the nineteenth century, about the immigration of Shahsevan ancestors to Iran from Anatolia; these traditions, which are historically plausible, stress descent-based class differences among the tribal groups and a centralized hierarchy of authority among their leaders. This version has given way in the present century to both the first version and a third, commonly articulated among ordinary tribespeople and in modern writings on them, to the effect that the Shahsevan are '32 tribes', all of equal status, and never centralized under a paramount chief.

These different versions of Shahsevan origins have been reflected in varying constructions of their identity and their more recent history, by themselves and by observers of their political behaviour (Tapper, n.d.a). Whatever their actual origins or their present construction of them, one element in Shahsevan identity remains consistent with all versions: their name has always prompted a conccrn, particularly among observers of their political behaviour, with the question of the legitimacy of Iran's rulers, especially in terms of the special semi-divine character of the Safavid Shahs that their successors tried to perpetuate. There are three main elements in Shahsevan self-identification: religious (Muslim), political (tribespeople), and economic (pastoral nomad); during the present century their relative importance in Shahsevan constructions of their identity and recent history has shifted, reflecting changing relations with the state and with non-Shahsevan neighbours.

Before 1923 eastern Azarbayjan was dominated by tribal chiefs and Shahsevan political action was ideologically committed to the Shah and Islam as against the Russians, their despised and hated enemies just across the frontier. Shahsevan identity depended on membership of a recognized tribe (*tayfa*), which came not through descent but through allegiance to the chief. Most Shahsevan tribespeople were tented pastoral nomads, but many also had villages and practised agriculture. The contrasting category, 'Tat', signified peasant, eking out a living as a crop-sharing tenant or labourer on the land of some absentee landowner and continually vulnerable to tribal raids and exactions. Shahsevan who abandoned their camps or villages became Tat. A Tat could become Shahsevan by joining a chief's retinue of servants, but more permanent membership of a tribe was impossible without access to tribal pastures or farmlands, already the object of severe competition among the tribespeople themselves. Thus Tats, propertyless and oppressed, formed a residual category, while any Shahsevan, through his place in the tribal organization, could claim association with the dominant forces in the region. Symbolic elements in tribal unity and chiefship were stressed, and Shahsevan identity was associated more clearly with particular names, dress, and behaviour than with pastures, flocks, and tents.

Recently, however, these latter elements have become more prominent. After 1923, the Government suppressed chiefs and tribes, and the Shahsevan lost their political dominance. Settled authority prevailed, agricultural pursuits and village forms of organization were officially favoured. Among pastoral nomads, economic security came less from allegiance to tribal groups and deposed chiefs than from ownership or occupation of pastures and possession of tents. Tat villagers took their flocks to pastures bought or rented in tribal areas, and many claimed membership of one or other Shahsevan tribe; others even created new tribal groups by adding the Turkish suffix -*lu* to their village name. Although long-established nomads were slow to recognize such claims, mere adoption of their way of life was now often enough for acceptance among the Shahsevan.

By the 1960s the 'ethnic' opposition between Shahsevan and Tat, which continued to form the theme of much local folk literature, depended less on political than economic criteria: it was synonymous less with *äshayer* (pastoral tribesmen) versus *rayät* (agricultural peasants) than with *obali* (camp-dweller) versus *kätli* (villager) or *köchärä* (nomad) versus *oturagh* (settled). But the opposition now connoted a whole complex of cultural differences; pastures, migrations, and tents had become symbols of central importance to Shahsevan identity.

The earlier elements in Shahsevan identity were still recalled, however. Older people at times related glorious battles against the Russians, depicting themselves as patriotic defenders of Islam and the Shah, in conformity with their name. At other times, they recalled the former character of the Shahsevan as a powerful and vigorous tribal minority which, posing an age-old threat to the stability of government, was eventually pacified and (temporarily) sedentarized under the Pahlavi regime. And at times they stressed their present peaceful nature as tent-dwelling pastoralists subject directly to the provincial administration.

Shahsevan social categories have always been relatively clear-cut, whether in relation to the tribal structure or to major economic and social classifications. *Oba* means a camp of any size or composition, but has no connotations wider than co-residence. There is little ambiguity about *il* (the confederacy), *tayfa* (tribe), *tirä* (tribal section), or the terms translated earlier as nomad and settled. A tribe is a territorially defined political group of between fifty and several hundred families; very few tribes are also descent groups, but most have a separate chiefly dynasty. Sections too are well-defined political groups, averaging about thirty families led by a recognized elder, but they are usually also descent groups (*göbäk*), and communities (*jamahat*) – terms used interchangeably with *tirä*, but without significant ambiguity. There are no strict marriage rules relating to either tribe or section, or even the Shahsevan as an ethnic group; though in practice the tribe is largely endogamous, and marriages are controlled by section elders.

The emphasis in Shahsevan identity has shifted, from tribalism to nomadism. The constant factor in Shahsevan identity seems to be the name itself, and its associated ideology.[6]

Durrani

The Durrani Pashtuns of Afghanistan have a strong sense of cultural identity and superiority, based on a unified genealogy establishing descent from one of Muhammad's first converts and tribal ties with the rulers of the State. There is a more-or-less fixed configuration of major tribes and tribal divisions, perpetuated by written Durrani and local histories and held to have a permanent reality overriding temporary political groups.

The configuration is by no means agreed on in detail, however, and indeed at every level of the genealogy there are irregularities. A major section of the Ishaqzai tribe has its own tradition of Sayyid origins on the paternal side; other Ishaqzai subtribes are considered by some to be of non-Pashtun origins, while the subtribe I studied was of quite heterogeneous origins and composition. The ideal of segmentary order is an indigenous fiction that covers a fluid reality, shifting with the movements, dispersals, and regroupings of communities throughout the area. Order for Durrani is constantly recreated through a combination of marriage practices and economic and political expediency. Thus, when two Durrani groups come to live near each other, and there is doubt about the identity of one, the other will acknowledge them, if expediency dictates, by an exchange marriage. That is, Durrani marriage authenticates male claims to identity; language and religious affiliations on their own are regarded as unreliable indicators.

Much political and economic activity is devoted to the establishment and reinforcement of claims through proper marriages. Such manipulations of history through 'must-have-been' logic are possible only by means of an extensive vocabulary of ambiguous identities and social categories.

Although all Durrani regard the south-west of Afghanistan, particularly Kandahar, as their original *watan*, Durrani communities are now scattered throughout most of the country, in towns and cities, villages and nomad camps. The distinction between nomad and settled is rarely of any social or cultural relevance. Communities are typically localized 'subtribes' of 100 to 150 families, farmers or nomads. Family heads claim descent from a common recognized ancestor without necessarily being closely related to each other. Few individuals know their own pedigrees further than two or three generations back, and descent ideology is formally relevant to Durrani only at the level of the ethnic group, where it defines their equality and determines marriage choice and political allegiance.

Durrani use a variety of terms interchangeably for groups of various kinds and at various levels – a lack of precision that may perplex the ethnographer but has many advantages for the actors. Different terms may refer to the same, or more or less the same, group of people. However, these terms are not necessarily used synonymously. Most often they connote nuances of social structure and/or organization, but because their referents may be the same grouping on the ground, the terms are polysemic. For this reason, ethnographers who find patrilineality an adequate explanatory device, with its elegant simplicity, naturally find their view confirmed.

Actual social groups are constituted according to a combination of principles, the three most important of which are patrilineality, affinity, and neighbourhood. Phrases using *aulād* (offspring), *-zai* (offspring), or *plār* (father), specifically refer to descendants of a particular ancestor:

from children of a living man, to all Durrani, to all human beings, the children of Adam. Thus a tribe or subtribe are the people of one *plār*, the *aulād* of the ancestor whose name the group bears with the suffix *-zai*. Three other terms, however, also with descent connotations, refer to social groups at different levels. Thus tribes and their divisions may be termed *tāyfa* (clan, tribe, family), a word also used for recognized divisions of any larger category of animate creatures such as insects or jinns. More often *qaum* is used for human groupings of all kinds, while *wolus* (people, nation, tribe) implies the political nature of social groups at a variety of levels: *wolusi* is any concerted action taken by such a group. One of the main social groups designated by these three terms is the subtribe.

As the gloss on the meaning of *wolus* shows, though it may refer to a group organized at least in part on the basis of descent, it actually denotes other aspects of group identity and behaviour. In this respect, *wolus* differs in a very basic way from *aulād* or *plār*, whose meaning derives explicitly from the principle of patriliny. In the same way, though *tāyfa* and *qaum* have descent connotations, they denote other principles. Thus, *tāyfa* contains a historicity, and used of a social group it emphasizes a particular location in time and space; in other words, it suggests a certain territoriality and implies external relations with other *tāyfa*. *Qaum*, by contrast, refers to a social group in terms of the mutual support of group members and the desirability of intermarriage between them. This latter preference is a key aspect of social grouping, and one that needs further consideration.

Common descent establishes the equality of all Durrani and their superiority to others. The use of *qaum* adds a further important dimension: since a *qaum* is ideally endogamous, the term defines all Durrani as equally eligible as affines. Thus a man may use *qaum* to refer to any descent group to which he belongs, and as long as he marries a Durrani he may claim that he has married within his *qaum*. In effect, conformity with the ideal of endogamy (which is often expressed independently of its association with *qaum*) does not require distinctions to be made between fellow Durrani. The usage of *qaum* itself allows the ideal to be achieved quite easily without any bounded marriage isolates being formed among Durrani.

A further ambiguity of *qaum* assimilates relations of affinity to those of agnation. Through marriage, people of different groups (*aulād* or *tāyfa*) may 'become *qaum*' while retaining their separate membership of different named tribal divisions. Where marriage is deliberately used to unite separate kin groups for reasons of political expediency, the ambiguities created by the juxtaposition of *qaum* with its near synonyms *aulād*, *tāyfa*, and *wolus* are of considerable importance. Agnation and affinity of themselves impose few specific rights and obligations to economic and political support, but such support (*qaumi*) and common action (*wolusi*) are automatically consequent upon common residence and allegiance to particular local leaders.

Clearly, the way *aulād*, *tāyfa*, *qaum*, and *wolus* combine to express all levels of social grouping among Durrani creates and supports the ideal of the unity of the ethnic group as a whole and the equality of all its members. Given the multiplicity of referents for these terms it is not surprising that Durrani insist that within the ethnic group there is complete freedom of marriage choice and that named subdivisions (tribe, subtribe) are simply irrelevant for the purposes of marriage.

Durrani ethnicity, in other words, involves an identity of common descent with the rulers of the state, and the constant recreation of a fixed 'history' at the local level through a rule of endogamy and the manipulation of ambiguous social categories. By contrast, Shahsevan identity amounts more to an ideological commitment than a statement of substance; their history appears as external and indeterminate; while their social categories at the local level are relatively unambiguous.

Notes

1. This paper draws on fieldwork in Iran (between 1963 and 1966) and in Afghanistan (between 1968 and 1972), support for which is acknowledged fully elsewhere.
    The paper is one of a series discussing aspects of ethnicity and history in the Middle East, with special reference to the Shahsevan and the Durrani. Interested readers can refer to (or await) the following: R. Tapper (1988) elaborates many of the more general points within the context of the history of academic discourse on ethnicity in the Middle East, while R. Tapper (1983 and n.d.b) examines how historians and anthropologists approach the 'problem of tribe' in the region. R. Tapper (n.d.a) discusses at greater length the different versions of Shahsevan origins, and how these reflect varying constructions of their identity and reconstructions of their history, while R. Tapper (n.d.c) is a comprehensive ethnohistory of the Shahsevan. R. Tapper (1984a) compares Shahsevan and Durrani religiosity in relation to ethnicity and history; N. Tapper (1980) compares Shahsevan and Durrani gender relations in relation to ethnic boundaries. R. Tapper (1984b) discusses a general shift from ethnic to class identities in northern Afghanistan; N. and R. Tapper (1982) gives more specific examples of the essential ambiguity of Durrani social categories, particularly with reference to marriage. For further studies of ethnicity and history in Iran and Afghanistan, see Digard (1988).
2. Centlivres (1979:35–6 and 1980:33–4); Anderson (1983); Beattie (1982); and cf. Geertz, Geertz, and Rosen (1979) on the similar term *nisba* in Morocco.
3. For example, in Afghanistan *qaumi/rasmi* (the tribal or popular as opposed to the official way of doing things), or *qaum/gund* (tribal versus factional politics). Musulman is opposed to Kafir, Shi'ite to Sunni, Imami to Isma'ili. In different contexts Kabuli is opposed to Turkistani, Kandahari, Herati, etc.; Afghan (Pashtun) to Tajik, Uzbek, Hazara, Parsiwan. Nomads and settled are opposed in terms such as *māldār* (stockowner) to *mulkdār* (landowner). In the north, if not elsewhere, local political cleavages are expressed by tacking the suffix *-iya* to the major *qaum* names (e.g. Afghaniya/Uzbekiya). In Iran common

dichotomies are Turk/Tajik, *mālik/rāyat* (landlord/peasant), *rustā'i/shahri* (rural/urban), *ilāt/dehāt* (tribal/village), *'ashāyer/rāyat* (tribal/peasant), *bādi/khāki* (nomad/settled), *sāhib/kārgar* (boss/worker).

4. Among *mazhab* names, only Shi'ite is subject to any ambiguity: common discourse among Sunnis tends to use the label Shi'ite interchangeably with the *qaum*-name Hazara, even though many Shi'ites would not accept this identity. Most *qaum*-names connote only very broad categories of *watan* or occupation, to specify which, a composite identity must be named, for example Kandahari Pashtun, Panjsheri Tajik, Arab *māldār*.

5. For several other meanings elsewhere in the country, see Centlivres (1980:33–4). It is reported that several hundred thousand 'Parsiwans' live near Herat, but it is unclear to me whose label this is.

6. A few years after the fall of the Shah, the Shahsevan were renamed Ilsevan (friends of the confederacy/people); I do not know who chose this new identity or why, and can only guess its significance.

References

Anderson, J.W. (1978) 'Introduction and Overview', in J.W. Anderson and R. Strand (eds) *Ethnic Processes and Intergroup Relations in Contemporary Afghanistan*, occasional paper no. 15, New York: Afghanistan Council.

Anderson, J.W. (1983) '*Khan* and *Khel*: dialectics of Pakhtun tribalism', in R. Tapper (ed.) *The Conflict of Tribe and State in Iran and Afghanistan*, London: Croom Helm.

Barth, F. (1969) 'Pathan identity and its maintenance', in F. Barth (ed.) *Ethnic Groups and Boundaries*, London: Allen and Unwin.

Beattie, H. (1982) 'Kinship and ethnicity in the Nahrin area of Northern Afghanistan', *Afghan Studies* 3, 4:39–51.

Canfield, R.L. (1984) 'Islamic coalitions in Bamyan: a problem in translating Afghan political culture', in M.N. Shahrani and R.L. Canfield (eds) *Revolutions and Rebellions in Afghanistan*, Berkeley: Institute of International Studies.

Centlivres, P. (1979) 'Groupes ethniques: de l'hétérogénéité d'un concept aux ambiguités de la représentation. L'exemple Afghan', in E. Ehlers (ed.) *Beiträge zur Kulturgeographie des Islamischen Orients*, Marburg/Lahn: Geogr. Inst. der Univ. Marburg.

Centlivres, P. (1980) 'Identité et image de l'autre dans l'anthropologie populaire en Afghanistan', *Revue Européenne des Sciences Sociales et Cahiers Vilifredo Pareto* 13 (53):29–41.

Cohen, A. (1969) *Custom and Politics in Urban Africa*, London: Routledge.

Coon, C. (1958) *Caravan: the Story of the Middle East* (revised edn), New York: Harper and Row.

Digard, J.-P. (ed.) (1988) *Identité et Expérience Ethnique en Iran et en Afghanistan*, Paris: Editions du CNRS.

Geertz, C., Geertz, H., and Rosen, L. (1979) *Meaning and Order in Moroccan Society*, Cambridge: Cambridge University Press.

Higgins, P.J. (1984) 'Minority-state relations in contemporary Iran', *Iranian Studies* 17(1):37–71.

Lambton, A.K.S. (1971) Ilāt. *Encyclopedia of Islam* (2nd edn) 4.

Malcolm, Sir J. (1815) *The History of Persia*, London.

Ovesen, J. (1983) 'The construction of ethnic identities: the Nuristani and Pashai of eastern Afghanistan', in A. Jacobson-Widding (ed.) *Identity: Personal and Socio-Cultural*, Uppsala Studies in Cultural Anthropology, 5.

Tapper, N. (1980) 'Matrons and mistresses: women and boundaries in two Middle-Eastern tribal societies', *European Journal of Sociology* 21:58–78.

Tapper, N. and Tapper, R. (1982) 'Marriage preferences and ethnic relations among Durrani Pashtuns of Afghan Turkestan', *Folk* 24:157–77.

Tapper, R. (1979) *Pasture and Politics*, London: Academic Press.

Tapper, R. (1983) 'Introduction' in R. Tapper (ed.) *The Conflict of Tribe and State in Iran and Afghanistan*, London: Croom Helm.

Tapper, R. (1984a) 'Holier than thou: Islam in three tribal societies', in A.S. Ahmed and D.M. Hart (eds) *Islam in Tribal Societies*, London: Routledge.

Tapper, R. (1984b) 'Ethnicity and class: dimensions of inter-group conflict in north-central Afghanistan', in M.N. Shahrani and R.L. Canfield (eds) *Revolutions and Rebellions in Afghanistan*, Berkeley: Institute of International Studies.

Tapper, R. (1988) 'Ethnicity, order and meaning in the anthropology of Iran and Afghanistan', in J.-P. Digard (ed.) *Identité et Expérience Ethnique en Iran et en Afghanistan*, Paris: Editions du CNRS.

Tapper, R. (n.d.a) 'History and identity among the Shahsevan', paper presented at Middle East Studies Association Conference, Baltimore, November 1987.

Tapper, R. (n.d.b) 'Your tribe or mine? Historians and anthropologists on the problem of tribe in the Middle East', paper presented at Conference on Tribe and State Formation in the Middle East, Harvard, November 1987.

Tapper, R. (n.d.c) *The King's Friends: A History of the Shahsevan of Iran*, in preparation.

Chapter sixteen

Catalan National Identity: the dialectics of past and present

Josep Llobera

Theoretical introduction

National ideologies are often said to reflect the French cliché, 'Plus ça change, plus ça reste la même chose'. In this paper I shall maintain that if we want to understand nationalism we should reverse the cliché to obtain 'Plus ça reste la même chose, plus ça change'. In this sense national ideologies are a dialectical precipitate of the old and the new. Though they project an image of continuity, they are pierced by discontinuities; though they conjure up the idea of an immutable ideological core and an adaptable periphery, in fact both core and periphery are constantly redefined.

The history of nationalism in western Europe offers a good number of examples in which the nation is conceived as a quasi-eternal, motionless reality. The idea of *la France éternelle* is not only a metaphor of romantic French historiography, it also has been a first-class ideological weapon of all republican regimes in France. The echoes of such an idea reverberate even in Braudel's (1985–6) posthumous work on French identity.

Why this pretence of continuity? A psychologist might say that the explanation must reside in some sort of irrational fear that peoples have of the historical void. It is true that in its origins and fundamentals national identity is an attempt to preserve the 'ways of our foreparents', but reality is constantly changing and the effect of nationalist ideologies is that we tend to perceive the same image where there are in fact different realities. Even modernizing or future-oriented nationalisms must pay lip service to this idea of continuity. Expressed in positive terms, nationalism emphasizes the need for roots, the need for tradition in the life of any community; it evokes 'the possession in common of a rich heritage of memories' (Renan, 1947:903). The organic analogy is here an inevitable point of reference. And yet the organic conception of the nation is hardly an adequate theoretical tool to handle the complexities of the would-be modern nation–state. The reason is that for the ideologists of the nation–state the cultural definition of the nation (Herder) is always subordinated

247

to political objectives or implicitly abandoned because of recalcitrant internal national heterogeneity.

The sociological myth of the nation–state, that is the belief that because the nation–state happens to be the paramount ideology of the modern state it must correspond to a sociological reality, is a serious epistemological obstacle for the explanation of nationalism. For how can we account for the survival of ethnonational identities in harsh political environments, particularly in cases where the modern state engages all its bureaucratic machinery in policies of cultural, if not physical, genocide? It is my contention that contemporary ethnonationalist ideologies, if they have managed to establish themselves on a sound cultural and political basis, are extremely resilient and can endure, at times in a hibernated form, all sorts of repressive policies.

In the long run, the history of western Europe is the history of the qualified failure of the so called nation–state. The celebration of the national state, however, continues unabated both by social scientists and politicians. The question to ask is how much of a success story was state-generated nationalism in western Europe? There is, of course, no easy answer to the question. The fact of the matter is that the *nation*–state is far from being hegemonical; in other words, most western European states are, to a varying degree of consciousness, multinational. In fact, the history of Europe after 1789 shows that ethnonations are not anomalous entities or mere vestiges from the past, but rather dynamic configurations with a life of their own. Whether they form an independent state or not is often the result of a variety of factors including the international conjuncture. In any case, there is every good reason to see ethnonations as one of the typical paths to modernity, though this point may be in opposition to all those authors (Wallerstein, 1974; Tilly, 1975; Gellner, 1983; Giddens, 1985) who see European history in terms of the rise and practical monopoly of the nation–state in modern times. What is the case is that old national identities die hard, even if in practice they have to survive in revamped form.

Now historical nationalities or ethnonations are not self-propelling entities; they may, of course, survive for a long time as cultural and linguistic fossils, but the question is surely under which conditions can they have a new lease of life? A variety of theories have been put forward in the past few years to account for the persistence or revival of ethnonationalism. In some cases they are only revamped theories from the past.

There are at least four different ways of conceiving the nation, from which derive four major explanatory frameworks: essentialism, economism, culturalism, and eclecticism (Llobera, 1987).

The essentialist conception, originating in Herder and Romanticism in general, assumes that nations are natural, organic, quasi-eternal entities created by God in time immemorial. Each nation is characterized by the existence of a peculiar language, a culture, and a specific contribution to make to the design that divinity has installed for mankind. The idea that every nation has been chosen by God to perform a specific role in history can easily be secularized, and hence the appearance of ideas such as 'manifest destiny' and 'common historical destiny'. Furthermore, the essentialist vision of the nation emphasizes the ideational and emotive aspects of *communitas*, but tends to exclude economic, social, and political dimensions, and fails to perceive the intrinsic historicity of the nation. Today this particular conception of the nation is limited, at least in its extreme form, to naive or radical advocates of nationalism.

An extremely popular form of explanation has been economism. It comes under different guises and it is favoured both by Marxists and non-Marxists alike. In the final analysis, however, the common denominator of classical Marxism, internal colonialism, world-systems theory, and some modernization theories is the assumption that underneath the idea of nation lie economic interests. Now the fact that by its own ambiguity the nationalist discourse can be used to justify, hide, or combat economic inequality or exploitation, as well as political power and cultural supremacy, is not a sufficient reason to reduce nationalism to the ideology of a class, and in doing so deny the specificity of the national phenomena.

Culturalism seems to stand as the polar opposite of economism. In fact, both are variants of a conception of society that assumes that the part can explain the whole. By focusing on culture as the key to nationalism, an array of historians and sociologists of modernity have undoubtedly located a crucial factor in the development of nationalism in the last two centuries: the need for some sort of cultural identity and adaptation at a time of rapid social and economic change, with its concomitant effects of alienation and anomie. Whether the nation also satisfies the psychological need for belonging or whether it embodies a sacred character borrowed from religion is a matter for discussion. In any case, culturalism envisages nationalism as a ready-made response to the requirements of modernization. By ignoring the long-term genesis of nationalism and its multifarious phenomenal appearances, culturalism privileges just one particular moment, no matter how important, of its existence.

Eclectic explanatory frameworks are the result of the disenchantment with unidimensional, factor theories of nationalism. They follow, on the whole, the palaeofunctionalist argument that a social precipitate originates as the result of a combination of interacting elements. The candidates for such combinations, as well as the specific weight attributed to each of them, will vary from author to author, but we can be certain of encountering geographic, economic, cultural, religious, historical, and linguistic factors. Eclectic approaches are as unobjectionable as they are uninteresting. The idea that society consists of interrelated parts was a revolutionary invention, but it belongs in the annals of the contributions made by the *philosophes* of the Enlightenment to the social sciences. Today the minimum programme of functionalism is a pure sociological truism, and it should not be metamorphosed into a theoretical framework.

The point of view adopted in this paper, that of the concrete totality, keeps clear of both economism and culturalism, while at the same time transcending eclectic empiricism by conceiving of society 'as a structural, evolving, self-forming whole' (Kosik, 1976:18). The social totality is not constituted by facts, rather the latter can only be comprehended from the standpoint of the whole. History is the result of a complex dialectical process in which no *a priori* primacy is given to any factor. However, once ideas and institutions have appeared in history they acquire a life of their own and under certain conditions, to be empirically investigated, have a perdurable effect on society. Structural history cannot explain all that happened and why it happened. Many areas of social life, particularly in the sphere of nationalism, are the result of historical events that are difficult to predict (wars, invasions, annexations, etc.) and may always remain impervious to our enquiries.

Catalonia: an historical case-study

The history of Catalonia provides an excellent laboratory for the study of the vicissitudes of the national question in the nineteenth and twentieth centuries. In its modern form, Catalan national identity was recreated in the second half of the nineteenth century (Llobera, 1983). The development and consolidation of such an identity was made possible by the existence of the following conditions:

1. *A strong ethno-national potential.* The standard raw materials on which national identity is built were definitely present in Catalonia. To start with, there is the existence of a long-lasting and original medieval Catalan polity with a clearly differentiated political autonomy within the Crown of Aragon (Bisson, 1986). When the dynastic union of crowns of Castile and Aragon was effected in the second half of the fifteenth century, the sovereignty of the Catalan parliament (*Corts*) was preserved (Reglà, 1973). The Catalan revolts of 1640 and 1701 against the monarchy reflected, no matter how ambiguously, a reaction against the real or potential loss of autonomy (Elliot, 1963). Second, there is the differential fact of a written and literary language in existence since the Middle Ages (Nadal and Prats, 1982). Although after the end of the fifteenth century, Catalan declined as a language of culture, and after 1714 suffered state persecution, by the nineteenth century it was still the language spoken by the majority of the population (Carbonell, 1979). Third, there is the existence of a common body of ideas, beliefs, practices, norms, etc. that may be referred to as culture in the widest sense of the term (Vicens-Vives, 1954). Fourth, a certain sense of

historical identity had been preserved (Garcia-Cárcel, 1985). However, all these elements are no doubt problematic in that they are not clear-cut objective factors, but rather ideological constructs and hence malleable and open to manipulation.

2. *The appeal of the model of romantic nationalism.* The development of romantic historiography in different parts of Europe in the early nineteenth century had a profound effect on Catalonia. While the Napoleonic invasions had generated feelings of both Catalan and Spanish patriotism (Vilar, 1973; Fontana *et al.*, 1980), by the 1840s romantic historians started to glorify the Catalan past. There followed between 1833 and 1866 an intellectual attempt to revitalize Catalan culture and language known as *Renaixença* (Pi de Cabanyes, 1979).

3. *A thriving bourgeois civil society.* Catalonia was the first area within the Spanish state to experience the Industrial Revolution. While the rest of the country exhibited a preindustrial social structure characterized by the existence of a traditional, landowning oligarchy and a subjected peasantry, in Catalonia a modern capitalist system developed with the appearance of two major antagonistic classes: the bourgeoisie and the proletariat (Vicens-Vives and Llorens, 1958; Izard, 1978). These developments were far from sudden: there had been a dynamic bourgeois civil society for a good part of the eighteenth century (Vilar, 1961). The existence of such a more-or-less enlightened bourgeoisie was the precondition for the intellectual take-off of Catalan cultural nationalism in the nineteenth century (Moreu-Rey, 1966; Lluch, 1973). This is not to deny the existence of a popular though diffuse consciousness of Catalan identity during the same period, which manifested itself first through Carlism and then through Republican Federalism (Camps i Giró, 1978; Termes, 1976).

4. *A weak and inefficient Spanish state.* This expression has to be understood in relative terms. The centralizing and uniformist tendencies of the Spanish state in the nineteenth and twentieth centuries were as pronounced as they were elsewhere. The model adopted by Spanish politicians often mirrored the Jacobin French state (Linz, 1973). Two caveats, however, should be entered. First, the Spanish state had neither the financial nor administrative machinery to enforce the cultural and linguistic uniformization of the country as the French did between 1870 and 1914 (Weber, 1979). Second, from the moment in which Catalan nationalism became a political force at the turn of the century, an additional and formidable obstacle to uniformization was erected (Rossinyol, 1974).

5. *A strong Catalan 'national' Church.* In the modern period the Catholic Church in Catalonia has exhibited a firm commitment to defend the Catalan language and culture against the impositions and encroachments of the Spanish state. In this sense, it has often been, because of

its relative autonomy from the state, the only collective entity that could articulate and propagate Catalan identity to vast masses of the population. There is a clear historical continuity in this attitude of both the hierarchy and the rank and file of the parish priests that justifies the expression Catalan 'national' Church (Bonet, 1984).

The special way in which these five factors were combined explains how between 1886 and 1906 the Catalan people gave themselves a nationalist ideology (Solé-Tura, 1974; Riquer, 1977) and later managed to obtain through political struggle a representation of their interests in the Spanish parliament (Gonzalez-Casanova, 1974). This process culminated in the concession of limited autonomy in 1913 (*Mancomunitat*) (Camps i Arboix, 1963) and the establishment of a form of self-government (*Generalitat*) during the Second Republic in the 1930s (Gerpe, 1977). The nationalist movement in Catalonia was never the monopoly of a single class, though its leadership might have been at certain moments in time. In any case, by the 1930s it was a popular-based movement led by a centre-left party (Sallés, 1986; Poblet, 1975).

The Spanish Civil War (1936–9) was fought on both sides not only as a class war, but also as war in which there were different conceptions of the nation and of the state at stake. The Republicans were defending a moderately autonomic vision of the Spanish State, the Francoists a highly centralized and uniform one on the fascist model (Ramirez, 1978). Not surprisingly, both Basques and Catalans sided firmly with the Republican faction, even if their political philosophy was much more radically federalist or independentist than the Republican consensus allowed for. It should be made absolutely clear that the centralist vision of the State was not a monopoly of the extreme Spanish right, but was typical of the whole political spectrum (Gerpe, 1977). The main difference was, of course, that while the democratic parties were prepared to compromise and accept part of the demands of autonomy from Catalans and Basques, the fascists were not.

With Franco's victory there began a systematic cultural genocide of the Catalan nation. Except for the upper echelons of the bourgeoisie, which performed a *volte face* after July 1936 and decided to support Franco by sacrificing their Catalan identity at the altar of their class interests, the Catalan population had been steadfastly Republican and had backed the autonomous government (*Generalitat*) (Cruells, 1975). Francoist repression was hence conceived from the very start as a surgical operation aimed at extirpating the cancer of Catalan nationalism; there was an organized attempt to wipe out all the symptoms of the political disease referred to as 'separatism'. This expression was understood, not only in the strictly political dimension of self-government, but was also a rather blanket term including the spoken or written use of the language in most spheres of life, the display of symbols of Catalan identity (flags, monuments, music, etc.), the existence of Catalan civic institutions (of professional, literary, cultural, recreational, etc. character), and so on (Benet, 1973). It should also be made absolutely clear that the Francoist state, modelled as it was on the fascist models, was no longer a weak and inefficient state in that it used all its modern machinery (education, the media, etc.) to consciously generate a Spanish national ideology. For the first time in the modern period there was a serious attempt of the Spanish state at nation-building (Arbós and Puigsec, 1980).

The history of the forty years of Francoism in Catalonia is first and foremost the history of the survival of a diffused and contracted Catalan identity and then, in the 1950s, of the progressive consolidation of such identity, fundamentally at the cultural and linguistic levels, but also with a political dimension. After 1959, the political element became more apparent only to explode after Franco's death. To many observers of Catalan political reality, including many social scientists, the sudden nationalist effervescence of the late 1970s came as a complete surprise in so far as they had wrongly assumed that nationalism, at least in Catalonia, was a crepuscular ideology. It is the more surprising that anthropologists, who should know better than to focus on surface structures, also believed that Catalan identity was disappearing and that it was not a political force to be reckoned with. A case in point of early dismissal of Catalan nationalism was, of course, Hansen's *Rural Catalonia under Franco*, which was published in 1977 at the time when more than a million Catalans were demonstrating for political autonomy in the streets of Barcelona. *Sic transit gloria mundi.* Hansen's (1977) book is just one of many examples of the dangers of generalizing about an (ethno)nation on the basis of traditional fieldwork and poorly digested history. Furthermore, it illustrates the incapacity of modernization theories to account for the survival of ethnonationalism.

The attitude of the majority of the Catalan population towards cultural genocide was that of passive resistance. Research on this topic is fraught with ideological and methodological problems and not surprisingly is rather rare. In the early period, public manifestations of Catalan identity were limited and ambiguous. In the private sphere of the family things were different, and it was here that Catalan was spoken and a certain amount of cultural identity was preserved. In any case, the task of upholding, continuing, and transmitting Catalan national identity, particularly at the height of the repression (1939–59) was the work of a small but devoted intelligentsia who had survived the common fate of the vanquished (execution, exile, prison, ostracism) and who, against all odds, went against the current of history (Colomer, 1984; Fabre *et al.*, 1978). This attitude is best exemplified in a lyric composition written in 1965 by

Salvador Espriu (1975:113), one of the leading Catalan poets of the post-war period, and which became a popular song of the late 1960s and 1970s:

But we have lived to save the words for you,
To return to you the name of everything,
That you may travel along the straight road
That leads to the mastery of the earth.

Now ye say: 'We shall be faithful and true
For ever more to our people's service'

The long period of fascist repression generated a predictable defence mechanism among the custodians of Catalan identity: an essentialist vision of the nation, i.e. the idea that in the final resort the Catalan nation, if not altogether eternal and immutable, was a multisecular reality based on quasi-biological, environmental, and psychological facts. Even the most scholarly of philosophico-historical works of the period (and in terms of influence one would have to mention J. Ferrater-Mora's *Les Formes de la vida catalana* (1944) (1955), J. Vicens-Vives' *Noticia de Catalunya* (1954), and J. Fuster's (1962) *Nosaltres els valencians*) did not escape an essentialist tint, though as S. Giner (1980) has remarked these three books constitute serious attempts to tackle in a structural way the history of Catalonia.

Catalonia: an excursus on essentialism

Nationalist ideologies may well partly be responses to the processes of industrialization and modernization, but they also encapsulate the traditional values of the society. Catalonia is no exception. As I have mentioned on p. 251, nineteenth-century *Catalanism* incorporated, from its very inception, a belief in an idealized, romanticized past. This vision did not only refer to military or literary glories, but also assumed the existence, in some unidentified but foregone time, of an idyllic, conflict-free peasant society (Llobera, 1983). This conservative ideology, often referred to as *pairalisme*, was usually allied with a Catholic conception of the history of Catalonia (Ramisa, 1985) and with the belief that the political wisdom of the Catalans resides in compromise (*pactisme*) (Sobrequés, 1982).

It is arguable how important this traditional component was, but nationalisms against the state – and Catalonia is a typical example – are particularly vulnerable to essentialist conceptions of the nation. In fact, because of their precariousness these nationalisms need to mythologize the past in order to take off as viable ideologies. It is true that at a later stage, as the evidence from Catalonia between 1900 and 1936 confirms (Gali, 1978), they become more involved in forward-looking communal projects in which people can participate in a rational-instrumental way, though the integrative aspects of the mythologico-ritual are also preserved. The force of nationalism as a symbolic system lies in the fact that it mediates the past with the future, while providing an affective dimension for the present.

Modernity, in its post-French revolutionary mood, equates state with nation, and nation with the participation of the people (whichever way this participation is defined) in the state. What we have here is, of course, a political nationalism in which the identification is with the state, though a special kind of state since the demise of the absolute, personalized monarchy. On the other hand, fascism represents the apogee of state nationalism. The existence of cultural nationalism complicates the picture by focusing on the so called natural factors of *convivència* (living together), and allows us to see the state in terms of artificiality, uniformity and compulsion. The following table of opposites could be suggested:

Nation	State
Culture	Politics
Variety	Uniformity
Freedom	Compulsion
Organic	Artificial
Romantic	Rational
Religious	Secular
Individualism	Collectivism
(individualizing collectivity)	(collectivizing individuality)
Affective	Instrumental

The process of industrialization that took place in Catalonia in the nineteenth century was accompanied by major social changes along patterns similar to those that were happening in other industrializing western European countries (Vicens-Vives and Llorens, 1958). Barcelona, from being a city-emporium with its ups and downs since the Middle Ages, suddenly became the most important industrial centre of Spain. At first, modernization affected only the Catalan hinterland: the late nineteenth century and early twentieth century saw a massive migration from countryside to town, especially in the direction of Barcelona, which soon became a megalopolis. By the 1930s, migration from other parts of Spain was already visible, though only to become numerically significant during Franco's era. Latest figures suggest that 60 per cent of the people living in Catalonia are of non-Catalan origin: the result of different waves of migrations from different regions of Spain, but particularly from the south (Andalusia) (Termes, 1984). While prior to the war a significant percentage of the migrant population was assimilated culturally and linguistically, this was not the case with the large influx of people during the Franco period (Candel, 1964). It was not only a question of numbers, but of the existence of a political regime that not only did not acknowledge Catalan national identity, but until its very end stifled its multifarious manifestations. Not surprisingly the majority of the immigrants did not learn the language and culture of Catalonia, nor did they develop a Catalan national consciousness (Vallverdu, 1980; Strubell, 1981; Esteva, 1984).

The presence in Catalonia of a large, newly arrived working-class population, which was culturally and linguistically non-Catalan, was potentially conflictive. At the bottom of the system of social stratification, the immigrants were the carriers of the official language of the state and hence were perceived as linguistic oppressors. But dictatorships blur differences; and in any case the magnitude of the problem was not realized until the 1970s, at the height of nationalist fervour. It was at this time that the two-communities theory began to appear, albeit reluctantly and indirectly, in the language of the politicians. Some intellectuals voiced the right of the immigrant community to defend their language, culture, and identity of origin now potentially threatened by Catalan essentialism (De Miguel, 1980). What had happened was that the two communities had not only lived apart for a long time, but under Franco had had no chance to articulate and express their ideological positions. In fact, the underground political parties had reached a sort of implicit ideological truce concerning the national question: they all acknowledged, at least in principle, the right of Catalonia to self-government (Colomer *et al.*, 1976). It is a reflection of the isolationism of the Catalan ideologists during Franco's period, that they decided to stick to an essentialist vision of Catalonia in which the immigrant population was not considered an important variable. In their idealist conception it was assumed that the immigrants would be miraculously assimilated (Pujol, 1976).

Another idea that was partly the consequence of the intense Catalan essentialism of Franco's era was a pan-catalanism of sorts. Having focused on a traditional definition of the nation (common language, common culture, common past), it followed that, territorially, the area that fitted the definition, and which we could designate as Catalan Countries (*Països Catalans*) was larger than the area in which a modern Catalan national consciousness had developed. The starting point of the notion of Catalan Countries was of course the idealized medieval Kingdom of Aragon in which Catalonia *sensu stricto* played the leading economic, political, military, and cultural role. The Kingdom of Aragon, as described on p. 250, was created by the dynastic union of Catalonia and Aragon in the mid-thirteenth century. Conceived as a confederation in which its constituent parts preserved their identity and autonomy, it expanded southwards and eastwards. Some of the conquered territories (the Balearic Islands) were colonized by Catalans, others (like Valencia) jointly by Catalans and Aragonese. Within the Crown of Aragon the different territories had their own self-governing institutions that were preserved with the union of the crowns of Castile and Aragon in the second half of the fifteenth century (Bisson, 1986).

The slow emergence of the Spanish state no doubt had negative effects on the Catalan identity of the different territories (Castilian becoming the only prestige language in Spain). Furthermore, a portion of the north-east of Catalonia was forcefully incorporated into the French state by the mid-seventeenth century. But it was not until the beginning of the eighteenth century that the autonomic institutions were scrapped and that a policy of linguistic Castilianization was implanted (Ferrer, 1985). By the late-nineteenth century, when Catalan nationalism developed, all the territories which in the Middle Ages could have been defined as 'Catalan' had taken different economic, social, and political paths, even if they still preserved a certain linguistic and cultural unity. Though the ideologists of Catalanism maintained the fiction of a Greater Catalonia, in practice the notion was never on the political agenda. The Francoist period contributed only to exacerbate the differences and even rivalries between the different areas of the supposed Catalan Countries (Balcells, 1980). Rightly or wrongly, the Principality (*Principat*) of Catalonia was often seen as exerting a kind of cultural domination that was at times presented as oppressive by certain sectors in the Balearic Islands and Valencia.

The period between 1969 and 1976 is noticeable for a remarkable flourishing of free ideological discussions on Catalan nationalism. Free because the arguments were basically unencumbered by the consideration of *realpolitik*, which was characteristic of the post-1977 political positioning. In this period there developed the idea of a utopian Greater Catalonia in which cultural and linguistic diversity was minimized if not altogether ignored. This was the work of a relatively small group of intellectuals, writers, professionals, and politicians belonging to all shades of the political spectrum of Catalonia, but with some participation also from the other Catalan-speaking areas (Cahner *et al.*, 1977).

The party politics of the late 1970s and 1980s shattered the utopian vision of a Greater Catalonia, particularly after the Spanish Constitution, while accepting the right of the nationalities and regions of Spain to autonomy, consecrated what was already a *fait accompli*: the separate existence as political entities of Catalonia, Valencia, and the Balearic Islands (Solé-Tura, 1985). More importantly, it also confronted many politicians with the bitter reality of a Catalonia that was splitting into two different communities: the division was along linguistic and cultural lines, but coincided roughly with class and status lines. The nationalist coalition occupies the centre of the political semicircle and attracts mainly the Catalan-speaking middle and lower-middle classes (Marcet, 1984; Lorés, 1985). Although their Catalanism is moderate, they are often perceived by Castilian-speakers as extreme. The fact that the parties of the left, while representing on the whole the non-Catalan-speaking working-class constituencies, are in fact controlled by leaders and cadres who in the main belong to the Catalan-speaking intelligentsia and hence endorse Catalanism in its basics, explains why the politics of confrontation between the two communities has been kept, for the time being, to a minimum (Lorés, 1985).

Conclusion: the eternal recurrence?

In Catalonia the time of illusions is now over. For the time being, the great effervescence of nationalism, which flourished in the aftermath of Franco's death, is a thing of the past. It is obvious that the two communities are there to stay and that they exhibit real differences. What is at stake is whether they can live together: in other words, whether a common project of the future is feasible. It will no doubt require concessions on both sides, particularly at the linguistic level. Language is a key marker of Catalan identity, but Catalan is far from being the language of the majority of the population of Catalonia. Until recently, most sociolinguistic studies on the future of Catalan as both a popular language and a language of high culture were pessimistic in tone (Argent et al., 1981). But the history of Catalan language shows that these Cassandra-like predictions have been disproved by the sheer determination of an often small but extremely committed and active group of people who fought against the 'current of history' and managed to change its direction. Whether those heroics are still possible in a mass-media society dominated by alien cultures is another matter.

The present linguistic policies of the autonomous government (General-itat) aim at creating, in the course of a generation, a perfectly bilingual population, though insisting, in accordance with the Statute of Autonomy, that in fact Catalan is the 'natural' (propi) language of Catalonia, while Castilian is the official language of the Spanish state. Because class confrontations can easily manifest themselves as ethnic confrontations, Catalan society will have to make provisions for a system of economic rewards and mobility that is seen to operate freely and equitably by the Spanish-speaking working classes. At a time of economic crisis this is not always easy to implement.

But the viability of Catalonia as a nation will depend, in the final instance, on the ability to develop a cultural and political identity that, while appearing to preserve the essence of the past, will allow the possibility of a common future for all those who live in Catalonia. In this context, we have seen in the past few years a number of attempts at redefining Catalan culture with the aim of forging a weapon with which to face the challenge of the post-modern era (Castellet, 1983; Vilar et al., 1983; Gifreu et al., 1987). A cultural model should provide not only a way of mediating in the contradictions of Catalan society sensu stricto, but also a means of relating to the Catalan Countries, the Spanish state, the EEC, and to the world at large. It is plain that an exclusively inward-looking culture will not be viable, while an exclusively outward-looking culture could mean a total loss of the traditional identity.

Cultures have, indeed, a life of their own, independent of individual human wills. Cultural models propounded by an otiose intelligentsia from its intellectual ivory tower may be construed as mere *flatus vocis*, but organic intellectuals may be rooted in the life of the community and hence they may be in a better position to articulate projects that respond to the cultural requirements needed for the survival of a given society. In any case, the living forces of the community will decide which particular project (or combination of projects) is to become cultural reality. Paraphrasing Marx, we could say that although history sets constraints on human behaviour, conscious human beings make their own history.

References

Arbós, X. and Puigsec, A. (1980) *Franco i l'espanyolisme*, Barcelona: Curial.

Argente, J.A. (1981) 'Stateless nation, tongueless people?', *The Bulletin of Scottish Politics* 2:162–81.

Balcells, A. (ed.) (1980) *Història dels Països Catalans*, 3 vols, Barcelona: Edhasa.

Benet, J. (1973) *Catalunya sota el règim franquista*, Paris: Edicions Catalanes de Paris.

Bisson, T.N. (1986) *The Medieval Crown of Aragon*, Oxford: Clarendon Press.

Bonet, J. (1984) *L'església catalana, de l'illustració a la Renaixença*, Montserrat: Publicacions de l'Abadia de Montserrat.

Braudel, F. (1985–6) *L'identité de la France*, 3 vols, Paris: Arthaud-Flammarion.

Cahner, M. *et al.* (1977) *Debat sobre els Països Catalans*, Barcelona: Curial.

Camps i Arboix, J. (1963) *La Mancomunitat de Catalunya*, Barcelona: Bruguera.

Camps i Giró, J. (1978) *La Gueera dels Matiners i el catalanisme politic (1846–49)*, Barcelona: Curial.

Candel, F. (1964) *Els altres Catalans*, Barcelona: Edicions 62.

Carbonell, J. (1977) 'Elements d'història social i politica de la llengua catalana', *Treballs de sociolingüistica* 2:87–102.

Castellet, J.M. (1983) *Per un debat sobre la cultura catalana*, Barcelona: Edicions 62.

Colomer, J. *et al.* (1976) *Els grups politics a Catalunya*, 2 vols, Barcelona: L'Avenç.

Colomer, J. (1984) *Espanyolisme i catalanisme*, Barcelona: L'Avenç.

Cruells, M. (1975) *La societat catalana durant la guerra civil*, Barcelona: Edhasa.

De Miguel, A. (1980) *Los intelectuales bonitos*, Barcelona: Planeta.

Elliot, J.H. (1963) *The Revolt of the Catalans*, Cambridge: Cambridge University Press.

Espriu, S. (1975) *The Lord of the Shadow*, Oxford: The Dolphin Book.

Esteva, C. (1984) *Estado, etnicidad y biculturalismo*, Barcelona: Ediciones Península.

Fabre, J. *et al.* (1978) *Vint anys de resistència catalana*, Barcelona: Edicions de la Magrana.

Ferrater-Mora, J. (1944, 1955) *Les formes de vida catalana*, Barcelona: Editorial Selecta.

Ferrer, F. (1985) *La persecució politica de la llengua catalana*, Barcelona: Edicions 62.

Fontana, J. *et al.* (1980) *La invasió napoleònica*, Bellaterra: Publicacions de la UAB.

Fuster, J. (1962) *Nosaltres el valencians*, Barcelona: Edicions 62.

Gali, A. (1978) *Història de les institucions i del moviment cultural de Catalunya*, vols I–III, Barcelona: Fundació A. Galí.

Garcia-Cárcel, R. (1985) *Historia de Catalunya, Siglos XVI–XVII*, 2 vols, Barcelona: Ariel.

Gellner, E. (1983) *Nations and Nationalism*, Oxford: Blackwell.

Gerpe, M. (1977) *L'Estatut d'Autonomia de Catalunya i l'estat integral*, Barcelona: Edicions 62.

Giddens, A. (1985) *The Nation–state and Violence*, Cambridge: Polity Press.

Gifreu, J. *et al.* (1987) *Segones reflexions critiques sobre la cultura catalana*, Barcelona: Department de Cultura de la Generalitat.

Giner, S. (1980) *The Social Structure of Catalonia*, Sheffield: The Anglo–Catalan Society Occasional Publications.

Gonzalez-Casanova, J.A. (1974) *Federalismo y autonomia*, Barcelona: Grijalbo.

Hansen, E.C. (1977) *Rural Catalonia under Franco*, Cambridge: Cambridge University Press.

Izard, M. (1978) *El segle XIX. Burgesos i proletaris*, Barcelona: Dopesa.

Kosik, K. (1976) *Dialectics of the Concrete*, Dordrecht: Reidel.

Linz, J. (1973) 'Early state-building and late peripheral nationalisms against the state', in S.N. Eisendstadt and S. Rokkan (eds) *Building States and Nations*, Beverly Hills: Sage, vol. 2:32–116.

Llobera, J.R. (1983) 'The idea of *Volksgeist* in the formation of Catalan nationalist ideology', *Ethnic and Racial Studies* 6:332–50.

Llobera, J.R. (1987) 'Nationalism: some methodological issues', *JASO* XVIII(1):13–25.

Lluch, E. (1973) *El pensament económic a Catalunya (1760–1840)*, Barcelona: Edicions 62.

Lorés, J. (1985) *La transició a Catalunya (1977–1984)*, Barcelona: Editorial Empúries.

Marcet, J. (1984) *Convergència Democràtica de Catalunya*, Barcelona: Edicions 62.

Moreu-Rey, E. (1966) *El pensament illustrat a Catalunya*, Barcelona: Edicions 62.

Nadal, J.M. and Prats, M. (1982) *Història de la llengua catalana*, 3 vols, Barcelona: Edicions 62.

Pi de Cabanyes, O. (1979) *La Renaixença*, Barcelona: Dopesa.

Poblet, J.M. (1975) *Historia de l'ERC (1931–1939)*, Barcelona: Editorial Pòrtic.

Pujol, J. (1976) *L'immigració, problema i esperança de Catalunya*, Barcelona: Nova Terra.

Ramirez, M. (1978) *España 1939–1975. Régimen político e ideologia*, Barcelona: Guadarrama.

Ramisa, M. (1985) *Els origens del catalanisme conservador*, Vic: Eumo.

Reglà, J. (1973) *Introducció a la història de la Corona d' Aragó*, Palma de Mallorca: Editorial Moll.

Renan, E. (1947) *Oeuvres complètes*, vol. I, Paris: Calman Levy. (Original 1882.)

Riquer, B. de (1977) *Lliga Regionalista*, Barcelona: Edicions 62.

Rossinyol, J. (1974) *Le problème national catalan*, Paris: Mouton.

Sallés, A. (1986) *Quan Catalunya era d'esquerra*, Barcelona: Edicions 62.

Solé-Tura, J. (1974) *Catalanismo y revolución burguesa*, Madrid: Cuadernos para el Diálogo.
Solé-Tura, J. (1985) *Nacionalidades y nacionalismos en España*, Madrid: Alianza Editorial.
Sobrequés, J. (1982) *El pactisme a Catalunya*, Barcelona: Edicions 62.
Strubell, M. (1981) *Llengua i població a Catalunya*, Barcelona: La Magrana.
Termes, J. (1976) *Federalismo, anarcosindicalismo y catalanismo*, Barcelona: Anagrama.
Termes, J. (1984) *La immigració a Catalunya*, Barcelona: Editorial Empúries.
Tilly, C. (ed.) (1975) *The Formation of National States in Western Europe*, Princeton: Princeton University Press.
Vallverdu, F. (1980) *Aproximació critica a la sociolingüistica catalana*, Barcelona: Edicions 62.
Vicens-Vives, J. (1954) *Noticia de Catalunya*, Barcelona: Destino.
Vicens-Vives, J. and Llorens, M. (1958) *Industrials i politics (Segle XIX)*, Barcelona: Teide.
Vilar, P. (1961) *La Catalogne dans l'Espagne moderne*, 3 vols, Paris: Sevpen.
Vilar, P. (1973) *Assaigs sobre la Catalunya del segle XVIII*, Barcelona: Curial.
Vilar, P. *et al.* (1983) *Reflexions sobre la cultura catalana*, Barcelona: Departament de Cultura de la Generalitat.
Wallerstein, I. (1974) *The Modern World System I*, New York: Academic Press.
Weber, E. (1979) *Peasants into Frenchmen*, London: Chatto & Windus.

Name Index

Abubakre, R. D. 212
Adamson, Ian 192–4
Adelabu, A. 211–12
Adetugbo, A. 203
Aeschylus 12
Agulhon, Maurice 159–60
Ajayi, J. F. A. 203
Akiva, Rabbi 127
Amir, E. 122
Anderson, A. O. 32
Anderson, Jon 233
Anderson, M. O. 32
Aran, G. 131
Arbós, X. 253
Ardener, Edwin vii, 2–3, 5–9, 17–18, 22–32, 74
Argente, J. A. 258
Aristotle 12
Aronoff, M. J. 131
Attila the Hun 28
Austin, M. M. 73
Autenrieth, G. 13
Avinieri, Shlomo 130–1
Awolowo, Chief 211–12

Balcells, A. 257
Balsdon, J. P. 13
Barr, Glen 193
Barth, F. 17, 184, 232, 238, 239
Barthes, Roland 107, 108, 118–19n
Bartlett, F. 26
Bayle, Pierre 160
Bēdi Kūbu 57–8, 60–1, 63
Bellenden, John 32
Ben-Gurion, David 121, 123, 126–7, 131–2
Benet, J. 253
Bernstein, D. 121

Bidou, Patrice 69n
Biggar, F. J. 185
Bisson, T. N. 250, 257
Blacking, J. 179
Bloch, Marc 157
Bloch, Maurice 38, 116
Boece, Hector 32
Bohannan, L. 184
Bonet, J. 252
Boon, J. 54
Bot, A. K. 217
Bowen, D. 185
Boyce, D. G. 186, 195
Bradford, Robert 191
Braudel, Fernand 158, 160, 162, 247
Brown, J. 187–8
Browning, P. 74
Bryans, John 191
Buber, Martin 122–3, 129
Buckley, Anthony vii, 183–95
Burckhardt, Jacob 160
Burke, Peter vii, 157–65
Bushman, R. L. 170–1

Cabourdin, Guy 159
Cahner, M. 257
Campbell, Alan 183
Campbell, J. K. 71–2, 78
Camps i Arboix, J. 252
Camps i Giró, J. 251
Candel, F. 255
Canfield, R. L. 236
Carbonell, J. 250
Carrithers, Michael 179
Castellet, J. M. 258
Caws, P. 184
Centlivres, Pierre 233, 238
Chadwick, H. M. 7, 32

Chapman, Malcolm vii, 1–20, 137–8
Chaunu, Pierre 162
Clogg, R. 74, 78–83
Cobb, Richard 160
Cohen, A. P. 184, 187
Cohen, Abner 1, 198–200, 212, 216, 232
Cole, J. W. 137
Collard, Anna vii, 10, 89–102
Colomer, J. 253, 256
Condry, E. 137
Connell, K. H. 185
Connolly, S. E. 185
Cook, Captain James 45
Coon, C. 232
Croix, Alain 159–60
Cronjé, G. 226
Crowther, Samuel Ajayi 202
Cruells, M. 252
Cunliffe, R. 13

Dakin, D. 74, 79–80, 83
da Matta, Roberto 68n, 69n
Darwin, Charles 3, 22
Davies, Douglas vii, 9, 168–81
Davis, John vii, 7, 104–19
Delargy, J. H. 185
Demangeon, Albert 157
De Miguel, A. 256
Deng, Francis Mading 41
Dewar, M. W. 186–8
Donnan, H. 184, 187
Douglas, Mary 24, 151–2, 179
Dronke, U. 32
Duby, Georges 159
Du Preez, J. M. 219–20
Durkheim, Emile 3, 43, 157, 187
Du Toit, B. M. 224

Eban, Abba 121
Eisenstadt, S. N. 121, 128
Elcock, W. D. 13
Eliot, T. S. 6
Elizabeth I, Queen of England 24–5
Elliot, J. H. 250
Epstein, A. L. 17, 137, 179, 199
Espriu, Salvador 254
Esteva, C. 256
Evans-Pritchard, E. E. 4, 22, 41, 108
Eyde, David 50–1

Fabian, J. 132
Fabre, J. 253

Fallmerayer 82, 85
Fardon, Richard 8
Febvre, Lucien 157–8, 159, 162
Ferrater-Mora, J. 254
Ferrer, F. 257
Firth, Raymond vii, 9, 37–40, 48–52
Fletcher, R. 85
Fontana, J. 251
Forsythe, Diana vii, 18–19, 137–55
Fortes, M. 34
Foster, J. W. 185
Foucault, Michel 43
Foxe, J. 190
Franken, J. L. M. 221
Fulop, M. 61–2, 65
Fuster, J. 254

Gali, A. 254
Garcia-Cárcel, R. 251
Garrisson-Estèbe, Janine 160
Gaulle, Charles de 162
Gaus, G. 139
Gaustad, E. S. 171
Geertz, Clifford 179
Gellner, E. 18, 248
Gerpe, M. 252
Giddens, A. 248
Gifreu, J. 258
Gilhodes, C. 40
Giner, S. 254
Glazer, N. 15
Gluckman, M. 34
Gollmer, Revd C. A. 203–4
Gonzalez-Casanova, J. A. 252
Goody, J. 169
Goody, J. R. 108
Gosse, Edmund 22
Gosse, Philip 22
Goubert, Pierre 159–60
Graziani, R. 107
Green, A. S. 185

Halbwachs, Maurice 157
Hall, M. 193
Halpern, B. 130
Hamad Hasan al-Harash 108
Hamann, A. 142
Hansen, E. C. 253
Harris, R. 187
Harrison, J. 187
Hassanein Bey, A. M. 107
Hastrup, K. 4, 23
Häussling, J. M. 139

Hay, Will 26
Hayes, V. C. 179
Held, K. 139
Hélias, P.-J. 161
Henry VIII, King of England 24–5
Herder, J. G. von 247, 248
Herodotus 12, 73
Herzfeld, Michael 84–5, 86n
Herzl, Theodor 123, 126, 130
Hewitt, C. 185
Higgins, P. J. 235
Hobsbawm, Eric 163
Hogbin, H. Ian 40, 41
Homer 12
Horowitz, D. L. 184
Hose, C. 34
Hugh-Jones, Stephen vii, 9, 45, 53–69
Hughes, Everett C. and H. 16
Hutton, J. H. 36, 41

Ipsilandis, Prince Alexander 82–3
Izard, M. 251

Jackson, A. 2, 10, 18
Jenkins, G. D. 211
Jenkins, R. 184
Jesus Christ 24
John, the Baptist 24
Johnson, Revd E. T. 209
Johnson, Revd James 203, 205
Johnson, Revd Samuel 198, 205–9
Johnson, Samuel 213
Johnson, William 188
Joutard, Philippe 160
Just, Roger vii, 8, 11–14, 16, 71–87

Kachan, L. 126
Katz, Jacob 126–7
Kaufman, Y. 123
Kazantzakis, Nikos 82
Keesing, Roger 34
Kennedy, P. 185
Keyes, C. F. 151
Kingsley, Charles 27
Koelle, S. W. 202
Kolettis, John 79–80
Kolokotronis 83
Kopelew, L. 139
Kosik, K. 250
Kritzinger, M. S. B. 217
Kuyper, Abraham 226
Kyriakides, S. P. 84

la Blache, Vidal de 157
Labrousse, Elizabeth 160
Laitin, D. D. 210
Lambton, A. K. S. 234
Law, Robin 206
Leach, Edmund vii, 9, 17, 23–6, 34–46,
    48–9, 52n
Le Bras, Hervé 161–2
Lenz, H. 142
Leone, Mark 181
Lévi-Strauss, Claude 3, 17, 22–4, 35,
    44, 53–4, 69n, 169, 186
Levin, D. M. 179
LeVine, R. A. 180
Lewis, I. M. 1, 4
Lewis, Ioan 181
Liddell, H. G. 13
Linz, J. 251
Lison-Tolosana, C. 104–6, 112, 116
Llewellyn Smith, M. 81
Llobera, Josep vii, 6, 19, 247–59
Llorens, M. 251, 255
Lluch, E. 251
Long, S. E. 187–8
Lorés, J. 257–8

Macbeth 30–1
McClelland, A. 187
McDonald, Maryon vii, 1–20, 137–8,
    198–9
McDougall, W. 34
Macfarlane, A. 4
McFarlane, G. 184, 187
Mackridge, P. 79
McLeod, Malcolm 42
Malcolm, Sir J. 239
Malinowski, Bronislaw 3, 36, 40–1, 184
Marcet, J. 257
Marmorstein, E. 127
Mauss, Marcel 179
Mills, J. P. 41
Mol, H. 179
Moloney, E. 190–1
Molyneaux, James 189–90
Moore, R. L. 174
Moreu-Rey, E. 251
Mowatt, D. 32
Moynihan, D. P. 15
Müller, Max 24

Nadal, J. M. 250
Nairn, Tom 161
Needham, R. 177

Nicolas, Jean 159
Nora, Pierre 163–4

O'Brian, G. 185
O'Hearn, D. 185
O'Hegarty, P. S. 185
Olubi, Revd D. 205
O'Rahilly, T. F. 192
O'Sullivan, S. 185
Overing, J. 2
Ovesen, J. 233

Paden, J. N. 201
Paine, Robert vii, 121–34
Paisley, Revd Ian 189
Paolozzi, Eduardo 42
Parkin, D. 2
Parry, J. 108
Patrick, St 193
Peel, J. D. Y. vii, 5–6, 198–214
Peters, E. 106
Phillips, Revd Charles 205
Piaget, Jean 24
Pi de Cabanyes, O. 251
Pillorget 160
Pindar 12
Poblet, J. M. 252
Pollack, A. 190–1
Post, K. W. J. 211
Prats, M. 250
Pratt, Isaac Benjamin 202
Puigsec, A. 253
Pujol, J. 256

Qaddafi al-, Mua'mmr 112, 115

Radcliffe-Brown, A. R. 3, 34, 44
Ramirez, M. 252
Ramisa, M. 254
Ranger, T. 163
Rankin, H. D. 13
Reglà, J. 250
Renan, E. 247
Retief, P. 221
Riquer, B. de 252
Rivers, W. H. R. 36
Rölleke, H. 139
Rosaldo, Michelle 179
Rossinyol, J. 251
Roupnel, Gaston 159–60

Sahlins, Marshall 2, 45, 213

St Clair, W. 83
Saint Jacob, Pierre de 159
Sallés, A. 252
Santino, J. 189
Saussure, F. de 3
Schecher, R. 124, 129, 131
Schermerhorn, R. 16
Scholem, Gershom 122
Scholtz, G. D. 225–6
Schutte, Gerhard vii, 8, 10, 216–30
Schweder, R. A. 180
Schweid, Eliezer 122, 125, 129, 131
Scott, R. 13
Shakespeare, William 30
Sherrard, P. 78
Siegfried, André 157
Smith, A. 18
Smith, A. D. 200
Smith, Joseph 168–72, 178
Smooha, S. 121–2
Sobrequés, J. 254
Solé-Tura, J. 252, 257
Solomon, R. C. 179
Sophocles 12
Southall, A. 17
Spencer, Herbert 3
Sperber, D. 26, 179–80
Spillius, J. 52n
Sprague de Camp, L. 29
Steqart, A. T. Q. 185
Strubell, M. 256
Swirski, S. 121

Tapper, Richard viii, 9–10, 232–45
Tayler, C. B. 190
Termes, J. 251, 255
Terre' Blanche, Eugène 218
Tessler, M. A. 150
Theron, Danie 218
Thompson, E. P. 10, 91
Thompson, P. 8
Tilly, C. 248
Todd, Emmanuel 161–2
Tonkin, Elizabeth viii, 1–20
Townsend, Revd H. 204
Tsatsos, Constantine 86–7n
Tuan, Y.-F. 131
Turner, Victor 179–81

Umar al-Mukhtar 114

Vallverdu, F. 256
Van Biljon, P. 225

Van den Berghe, P. L. 184
Van der Merwe, H. J. J. M. 225
Van Jaarsfeld, F. A. 217–19, 225, 227
Vasiliou, P. 95
Vicens-Vives, J. 250–1, 254–5
Vidal-Naquet, P. 73
Vilar, P. 251, 258
Viljoen, G. van N. 225
Vovelle, Michel 160, 164

Wallerstein, I. 248
Wallis, R. 190, 194
Wallman, S. 14

Wārībi 57–64, 66–7
Watt, I. 108
Weber, Eugene 161, 251
Weigelt, K. 139
Weiner, H. 126
Weingrod, A. 129
Weizman, Chaim 123
Williams, Raymond 163
Wolf, Eric 53
Wolff, Philip 160

Yeba 63–4
Yerushalmi, Y. H. 126

Subject Index

Aborigines, Australian 34
Afghanistan 233–44; Durrani Pashtuns 238, 241–4; language 233–4; nationalism 234–5; official categorizations 233–5; popular discourses on identity 236–7, 238–9
Afrikaners 216–29; academic historiography 224–7; ethnicity, future 228–9; folk historiography 219–24; identity 217–19; language 217; myth 224–5; politics 223–4, 226–9; religion 217, 220, 222
Agios Vissarios 89–102
Amazonia 44, 53–69; and Christianity 65–7; history 56; *Wārībi* myth 54–68
American Indians 35, 44
Annales school 157–64
anthropology, and history 1–9, 22–3; *see also* ethnography
apartheid 223, 225–7; *see also* Arikaners
Arch Purple Institution, Ulster 188–9, 192, 194
Ashkenazim 121, 123
Association of Social Anthropologists of Britain and the Commonwealth (ASA) 1–2, 4, 8, 19
Astounding Magazine 29, 32
Ausländer 143, 147–51, 152

Balkan Wars 80–1
Barasana Indians 54–69
barbaros 12–13
Belmonte de los Caballeros 104–6, 110, 112, 116
Bible 23–4; and Afrikaners 220; and British Israelism 183, 191–2; and Israel 124–5, 127; and Mormons 169;

and Ulster Protestants 183, 188–92, 195n
Black Institution, Ulster 188–9, 192, 194
Boer War 217, 221–2
bricolage 6, 29
British Israelism 183, 191–2, 194
Byzantine Empire 73–4, 78

Catalonia 250–9; essentialism 254–8; history 250–4; immigration 255–6; language 256, 258; as object of study 19; politics 253, 257–8; religion 251–2; theory 247–50
categorization 5
change 35, 44, 53–4, 247–8
Christianity: and Afrikaners 217, 220–2; and ethnography 37, 39, 40–1, 49; and *ethnos* 12–14; Greece 74, 78, 81–2; Ulster 183–95; and *Wārībi* myth 65–7; Yoruba 198, 201–13; *see also* Bible
classification 5; of peoples 17
'cold' *vs.* 'hot' societies 35, 44, 53–4
colonialism 39–44; *see also* missionaries
conflict 8, 137
construction of history 22–32; memory of events 24–5, 26–7; and myth 25; Northern Tales 27–31; simultaneities 27; and social anthropology 22–3; and structuralism 23–6; 'vestiges of creation' 22, 27
continuity, and change 35, 44, 53–4, 247–8
creation 22, 27
Cruthin 183, 192–4
culturalism 249

culture 43, 76, 198–9

debricolage 6, 29
deconstruction 5, 29
density, historical 27
diffusionism 36
Dinka 41
Durrani Pashtuns 238, 241–4

eclecticism 249–50
Eddas 28, 32
essentialism 248–9; Catalonia 254–8
ethnic 14–15
ethnic groups 14–16, 216
ethnicity 2, 11–17, 232–3, 247–50; and conflict 137; definition 216; establishment of 75–6; etymology 11–13; Germany 139–51; Greece 71–87; Iran and Afghanistan 232–44; Israel 128–32; and politics 200–1; process or structure 8–9; uses of history 183–5; Yoruba 198–213; *see also* history
ethnography: as fiction 9, 11, 34, 44, 48–51; tribal 34–46
ethnology 14
ethnos 11–13; Greece 71–87
evolution 3, 22, 36
exhibitions, anthropological 42
experience 91

fiction, ethnography as 9, 11, 34, 44, 48–51
films 42
France 157–65; diversity 161–2; identity 142, 247; identity construction 163–4; regions 159–61
functionalism 36–7, 43

Gaels 193
genos 12
gentile 13, 14
Germany 137–55; and *Ausländer* 143, 147–51, 152; categories of Germanness 145–50; culture 137; history 138–9; identity 139–51; land 139–42; meaning 151–4; myth 28–9, 30; nation 138–40; Nazism 138, 151, 152–3; as object of study 19; people 143–51
Greece: Byzantine Empire 73–4, 78; Christianity 74, 78, 81–2; Civil War 93–4, 97–100; classical 82–5; *ethnos* 12–13, 71–87; history 73–4, 92–102; identity 71, 99; *kratos* 72–3, 75, 77, 79, 81; and Macedonia 71, 80–1; Megali Idea 79–81; Ottoman Empire 74, 78–80, 95–7; social memory 89–102; and Turkey 81–2; War of Independence 73, 79; World War II 92–3
groups: ethnic 14–16, 216; majority and minority 18–19, 137
Gush Emunim 124–5, 127, 132

Hausa 198–9
Hawaii 45
historicity 8
historiography 2; nations 7–8
history: Afrikaners 216–29; Catalonia 250–4; construction of 22–32; ethnic uses of 183–5; and ethnicity 2, 11–17; fact and fiction 9–11; France 157–64; Germany 138–9; Greece 71–87, 89–102; Israel 121–8; Libya 106–19; Mormons 169–72, 181; object of study 17–20; and social anthropology 1–9; social relations of production of 104–19; Ulster 183–95; Yoruba 198–213
'hot' *vs.* 'cold' societies 35, 44, 53–4

Icelandic Free State 23
identity 16–18, 199
Iran 233–41; language 233–4; nationalism 234–5; official categorizations 233–5; popular discourses on identity 237–9; Shahsevan 239–41
Ireland *see* Ulster
Islam: Germany 149–50; and Greece 81–2; Iran and Afghanistan 233, 237; Yoruba 206, 208, 210–12
Israel 121–34: ethnicity 128–32; immigrants 121, 123, 128–9; Jewish identity 124–7; and Mormons 177; nation-building 121–2, 126; redemption 122, 126–7; time and place 121–8; Zionism 122–5, 129–32
Israelism, British 183, 191–2, 194

Jews, Israel (*q.v.*) 121–34

Kachins 39–40, 41

Kalabari 42
kinship: Mormons 172–4; Zuwaya
    107–12
kratos 72–3, 75, 77, 79, 81

language 76, 143; Afghanistan 233–4;
    Afrikaners 217; Catalonia 256, 258;
    Germany 143; Iran 233–4; Yoruba
    201–3
Latter Day Saints *see* Mormons
Libya 106–19; nation 112–16; and
    Qaddafi 112–13, 115; Zuwaya
    107–12

Macedonia 71, 80–1
Malaita 40, 41
Megali Idea 79–81
memory 6–7, 24–5, 26–7; Greece
    89–102; Mormons 173, 181; social
    90–1
Middle East *see* Afghanistan; Iran
    missionaries 37, 39, 40–1, 49; and
    Yoruba 198, 201–9, 212–13
Mormons 168–81; embodiment and
    self 179–81; history 169–72, 181;
    kinship 172–4; myth 177–8, 181;
    ritual 174–7, 181; space 173–4
Museum of Mankind 42
myth: Afrikaners 224–5; Amazonian
    Indians 54–68; and construction of
    history 25, 35, 45; Mormons 177–8,
    181; Northern Tales 27–31

nation-state 247–50, 255
nations 72–3; historiography 7–8; study
    of 18
Nazism 138, 151, 152–3
Nibelungenlied 28, 30, 32
Nigeria, Yoruba (*q.v.*) 198–213
Northern Tales 27–31
Nuer 41

Orange Order, Ulster 186–7
Orkney 152
Ottoman Empire 13–14, 74, 78–80,
    95–7
Oz veShalom 124–5, 132

Pashtuns 238
'people' 34
politics 200–1; Afrikaners 223–4,
    226–9; Catalonia 253, 257–8; Libya
    112–15; Yoruba 200–1, 211–12

present, and past 5–6

race 14–15, 16, 43, 76–7
records, historical 37
religion: Afrikaners 217, 220, 222;
    Catalonia 251–2; Germany 145;
    Greece 74, 78, 81–2; Iran and
    Afghanistan 233, 237; Israel
    122–31; Mormons 168–81; Ulster
    183–95; Yoruba 198, 201–13

Sarakatsani 71–2
Scotland 30–1, 32, 192, 193
Shahsevan, Iran 239—41
simultaneities, of action and definition
    9, 27
social anthropology, and history 1–9,
    22–3
social memory 90–1; Greece 89–102
societies: 'hot' and 'cold' 35, 44, 53–4;
    traditional 34–5, 44, 48–9
South Africa *see* Afrikaners
Spain *see* Catalonia
structuralism 3–4, 23–6

Tallensi 34
Tariana Indians 58
Tikopia 37–40, 49–51, 52n
traditional societies 34–5, 44, 48–9
tribal ethnography 34–46; and
    colonialism 39–44; continuity and
    change 35, 44; evolution and
    diffusion 36; functionalism 36–7, 43;
    Kachins 39–40, 41; myth 35, 45;
    records 37; Tikopia 37–40, 49–51, 52n
tribe 14–15, 34
Trobriand Islanders 41
truth 10
Tukano 62, 65
Turkey 81–2, 149–50

Ulster 183–95; Arch Purple and Black
    Institutions 188–9, 192, 194; British
    Israelism 183, 191–2, 194; and
    Catholics 185–6, 187, 190–1;
    Cruthin 183, 192–4; ethnic uses of
    history 183–5; fundamentalism
    189–91; nationalist history 185–6,
    194; Orange Order 186–7
United Kingdom ethnography 161

Vaupés Indians 54–69
Volsungasaga 28, 32

Wārībi myth 54–68
White people, contact with: Hawaii 45;
  missionaries (*q.v.*) 37, 39–41, 49;
  and *Warıbı* myth 57–68

Yoruba 198–213; ethnicity 198–213;

Islam 206, 208, 210–12; language
201–3; and missionaries 198, 201–9,
212–13; politics 200–1, 211–12

Zionism 122 5, 129–32
Zuwaya 107–12